DRAGONLANCE®
SHADOW OF THE DRAGON QUEEN™

CREDITS

Project Lead: F. Wesley Schneider
Art Director: Kate Irwin
Writers: Justice Arman, Brian Cortijo, Kelly Digges, Dan Dillon, Ari Levitch, Renee Knipe, Ben Petrisor, Mario Ortegon, Erin Roberts, James L. Sutter
Rules Developer: Jeremy Crawford
Editors: Sydney Adams, Judy Bauer, Janica Carter, Laura Hirsbrunner, Adrian Ng, Jason Tondro
Senior Graphic Designer: Trish Yochum
Graphic Designer: Matt Cole
Cover Illustrators: Cynthia Sheppard, Chase Stone
Cartographers: Francesca Baerald, Mike Schley
Interior Illustrators: Mark Behm, Olivier Bernard, Zoltan Boros, Bruce Brenneise, Ekaterina Burmak, Dawn Carlos, Jedd Chevrier, CoupleOfKooks, Daarken, Kent Davis, Nikki Dawes, Olga Drebas, Caroline Gariba, Evyn Fong, Alexandre Honoré, Ralph Horsley, Sam Keiser, Julian Kok, Katerina Ladon, Linda Lithen, Andrew Mar, Robson Michel, Scott Murphy, David Auden Nash, Jessica Nguyen, Irina Nordsol, Chris Rahn, Caio E Santos, David Sladek, Crystal Sully, Svetlin Velinov, Magali Villeneuve, Lauren Walsh, Shawn Wood, Zuzanna Wužyk, Kieran Yanner
Concept Art Directors: Richard Whitters, Shawn Wood
Concept Artists: Alix Branwyn, Tyler Jacobson, Chris Rahn, Magali Villeneuve, Shawn Wood
Project Engineer: Cynda Callaway
Imaging Technicians: Daniel Corona, Kevin Yee
Prepress Specialist: Jefferson Dunlap

D&D Studio

Executive Producer: Ray Winninger
Director of Studio Operations: Kyle Brink
Game Architects: Jeremy Crawford, Christopher Perkins
Design Manager: Steve Scott
Design Department: Justice Arman, Judy Bauer, Eytan Bernstein, Janica Carter, Makenzie De Armas, Dan Dillon, Amanda Hamon, Adrian Ng, Ben Petrisor, F. Wesley Schneider, Jason Tondro, James Wyatt
Art Department: Matt Cole, Trystan Falcone, Bree Heiss, Kate Irwin, Bob Jordan, Emi Tanji, Trish Yochum
Senior Producers: Lisa Ohanian, Dan Tovar
Producers: Bill Benham, Robert Hawkey, Lea Heleotis, Andy Smith
Director of Product Management: Liz Schuh
Product Managers: Natalie Egan, Chris Lindsay, Hilary Ross, Chris Tulach

Special thanks to the original Dragonlance creative team and adventure designers, including Mike Breault, Michael Dobson, Larry Elmore, Anne Gray, Michael Gray, Jeff Grubb, Bruce Heard, Laura Hickman, Tracy Hickman, Harold Johnson, Roger Moore, Bruce Nesmith, Douglas Niles, Elizabeth Riedel, Lisa Smedman, Carl Smith, Garry Spiegle, Margaret Weis, Michael Williams, Janet Vialls, Peter Vialls, and many more!

Additional thanks to the hundreds of playtesters whose efforts made this a better book!

ON THE COVER

Dragons, draconians, and other servants of the Dragon Queen prepare for their invasion of Kalaman in this painting by Cynthia Sheppard.

ON THE ALT-COVER

The grim visage of the death knight Lord Soth, Knight of the Black Rose, glares from of a tangle of charred thorns in this cover by Chase Stone.

620D0992000001 EN
ISBN: 978-0-7869-6834-3
First Printing: December 2022

9 8 7 6 5 4 3 2 1

 CE UK CA

Disclaimer: The Dragon Armies cannot ensure that owners of this book will not have their lives repurposed in the service of the Dragon Queen's glorious will. Promises to the contrary should be considered best-case scenarios, not statements of certainty. Thank you for supporting the Dragon Armies and a cataclysmically bright future for all of Krynn.

Tell us what you think of *Dragonlance: Shadow of the Dragon Queen*. Take our survey here!

Printed in the USA. ©2022 Wizards of the Coast LLC, PO Box 707, Renton, WA 98057-0707, USA. Manufactured by: Hasbro SA, Rue Emile-Boéchat 31, 2800 Delémont, CH. Represented by: Hasbro, De Entree 240, 1101 EE Amsterdam, NL. Hasbro UK Ltd., P.O. Box 43 Newport, NP19 4YH, UK.

CONTENTS

To the Council of Maelgoth:

War is coming—that truth I can no longer deny. Here in Solamnia's eastern reaches, rumors swirl of human-led armies on the march, their ranks swelled by hobgoblins, minotaurs, ogres, and mysterious hooded mercenaries, all seeking a share of the spoils. Our allies in Nordmaar have fallen silent, and desperate travelers say the people of Khur have joined the enemy en masse. Whispers also speak of winged doom, wild reports of riders on dragonnels—and I dare imagine worse.

I don't yet understand the shape of our enemy. Their motivations, their origins, and their very nature remain opaque. What is clear is that we face a threat unlike any since the Cataclysm. And when it comes, it will come for Kalaman.

Good lieges, I pray you make overtures toward healing the old wounds between our order and the Beacon of the East. If we knights are to meet this threat, we need the sharp eyes and strong shields of Kalaman as allies.

To aid your efforts, I have compiled my notes on the Kalaman region's history, neighbors, and lore. I hope this knowledge proves useful in meeting the threat before us.

Live with honor,
Becklin Uth Viharin,
Knight of the Crown

WAR COMES TO KRYNN

THE WORLD HAS ENDED, AND IT'S ENDING AGAIN. Three hundred years ago, the Cataclysm brought ruin to the world of Krynn. In a single day, an age of wonders came to an end. Countless innocents died, the face of the world was re-shaped, and the gods themselves faded into legend. Through ages of struggle, the peoples of Krynn survived, but the world isn't what it was. Those nations that remain linger in the shadows of their ancestors' wonders. Only slowly have they begun to push back centuries of darkness and rediscover how the world has changed.

Then came the Dragon Armies, legions of soldiers devoted to the wicked god Takhisis the Dragon Queen, and the world faces ruin once more. The War of the Lance has begun, and in a conflict between gods and dragons, a wounded world hangs in the balance.

USING THIS BOOK

This book presents a glimpse of the world of Krynn through the lens of a specific conflict. Rather than providing an overview of the entire world, the book focuses on the region surrounding the city of Kalaman in the nation of Solamnia as the War of the Lance first reaches its borders. Details of the world and the perils facing Kalaman are presented through this introduction, supplemented by reports from Solamnic scholars and soldiers. Beyond this, the book is divided into the sections below.

Chapter 1 explores how to create characters prepared to take part in the War of the Lance. It details the peoples of Krynn, such as kender, along with feats, backgrounds, and a subclass to immerse characters in the world.

Chapter 2 provides an overview of this book's adventure and how to start playing. It also contains a series of short encounters to immerse characters in the world's mysteries.

Chapters 3 to 7 present an adventure detailing the Dragon Armies' invasion of Solamnia and their pursuit of a terrifying magical weapon.

Beyond these chapters, appendices support the adventure with equipment, magic items, stat blocks, and other resources. A poster map of the continent of Ansalon is included with this book, depicting the regions mentioned throughout and those beyond.

DAVID AUDEN NASH

Scholars and soldiers across Solamnia spread warnings of sinister forces rising beyond their nation's borders.

History of Krynn

While every world's history is vast and fractured, with missing pieces and forgotten perspectives, Krynn's tale has been shattered by the global catastrophe called the Cataclysm. The world of Krynn was forged and destroyed, yet—broken and scarred—it continued on. Most of its people, seeking merely to survive in their slowly healing lands, care little for eons past. But the sages who piece together fragments of the past focus on three periods: before the Cataclysm, the Cataclysm itself, and the dire age since.

Before the Cataclysm

Krynn's earliest centuries have passed into mythohistory. The story begins in the Age of Starbirth when the gods forged the world from primordial chaos. This period's records are mere legends and scriptures, and few credit their details as fact.

Next came the Age of Dreams, a time when heroes battled the forces of evil. Many modern cultures and institutions saw their origins in this era, including the Knights of Solamnia, the Mages of High Sorcery, and the dwarven kingdom of Thorbardin. Ironically, these cultures often dismiss one another's foundational stories as baseless myths while fiercely insisting on the veracity of their own.

During a terrible conflict known as the Third Dragon War, the knight Huma Dragonbane was granted the first of the fabled *dragonlances*. He used it to defeat the evil god Takhisis the Dragon Queen and end the war, forcing the god and her dragons to leave Krynn. The good dragons of Krynn soon departed as well, leaving the world to mortals and the remaining gods.

During the thousand years before the Cataclysm, known as the Age of Might, several human nations flourished, conquering vast swaths of the continent of Ansalon in the name of good. But the triumph of the Age of Might sowed the seeds of its downfall.

Over the centuries, the city of Istar in eastern Ansalon grew into a continent-spanning empire, thanks in part to a military alliance with the Knights of Solamnia. Istar came to be ruled by a series of kingpriests who declared Istar the center of the world and themselves the holy messengers of the gods of good. Under their leadership, Istar declared war on actions, peoples, and even thoughts the kingpriests considered evil. Increasingly rigid and theocratic, Istar reached its apex of power just before its apocalyptic fall. The last kingpriest undertook ever more audacious magical feats, culminating in a ritual to attain godhood and rule Krynn forever in the name of good. At last, the gods acted, united in their condemnation of Istar.

The Cataclysm! It looms larger than any other event in the history of our world, forever dividing time into before and after. Even our calendar reflects this, marking our last four chaotic centuries in years After Cataclysm (AC), while the millennia before, stretching back into shrouded myth, are Pre-Cataclysm (PC).

Many records of the time before the Cataclysm are lost to us. Those that do survive are often perplexing, referencing nations and cultures that no longer exist and geography that has changed beyond recognition.

Still, it is possible to piece these scattered sources together. At the request of the good knights of Maelgoth, here are my notes, compiling a rough introduction to the histories recorded here at the Great Library of Palanthas.

Nikkas of Palanthas, Assistant to the Librarian

THE CATACLYSM

As a last effort to avoid mass destruction, the gods sent the Thirteen Warnings, a series of signs meant to deter the kingpriest. Trees wept blood, fires raged unnaturally, and cyclones struck the gleaming Temple of the Kingpriest. The gods also warned a few chosen mortals, reasoning that if any of them reached Istar and prevented the ritual, the world might not be beyond redemption. But the messengers failed—the kingpriest and his followers dismissed the warnings as the work of evil and continued on their path. As the hour of the kingpriest's ritual to attain godhood arrived, the gods whisked away their most devout followers and unleashed punishment on all who remained.

A mountain of fire fell from the sky, destroying Istar. The Blood Sea—a new ocean that split eastern Ansalon—consumed the empire. Coastlines shifted all over the world, sundering nations, drowning whole regions, and stranding ports miles from the sea. Though some lands escaped the worst of the destruction, none were spared divine wrath.

The gods and their blessings then faded from the world, and in time, even their names were all but forgotten.

AFTER THE CATACLYSM

The Cataclysm ushered in a period of chaos. During the next three centuries, known as the Time of Darkness, cultures and ecologies were radically altered, causing famine, plague, and mass migrations. The Knights of Solamnia, the champions who might've kept Ansalon united, were distrusted as former allies of Istar and persecuted across the continent, even in Solamnia.

The elven nations shut their borders. The dwarves of Thorbardin withdrew to their deep tunnels, refusing entrance to refugees from the surface. Many societies turned on one another or fell to disease and war. Nations of hobgoblins and ogres spread, capitalizing on humanity's decline and claiming whole regions. Much that survived the Cataclysm was lost in darkness.

At length, the worst effects of the disaster waned. Though many elves and mountain dwarves remained reclusive, other cultures tentatively rebuilt. Explorers ventured forth to map the drastically altered continent. Societies reestablished bonds of trade that united and diversified them.

As the civilizations of Krynn rebuilt, and new societies arose, the world learned to live with a jarring truth: the gods were truly gone. Religion on Krynn was altered forever. True clerics, who once worked miracles on behalf of their gods, had vanished. While some people remained devout, many others turned to false religions in search of answers and comfort. Some of these new faiths were founded by charlatans, others by zealots. Some claimed the names of the gods, others dismissed them entirely. In this radically changed world bereft of immortal insight, truth became subject to conjecture, even among Krynn's most dedicated scholars.

THE DRAGON QUEEN'S RETURN

Even as Ansalon healed, a new threat grew. The Dragon Queen Takhisis—known as Tiamat on other worlds—was banished from Krynn over a thousand years ago. Since then, she had waited patiently, plotting her return. Unbeknownst to the other gods, she planted a piece of the kingpriest's ruined temple at Neraka—hidden in the volcanic Taman Busuk region. There it grew into a baleful shadow of Istar's greatest edifice. Though this allowed the Dragon Queen to influence the world through a portal opened there, a fragment of the temple's foundation stone was missing, preventing her from fully returning to the world. She called on the evil dragons who served her, long withdrawn from the world, and began once more to plot the conquest of Krynn.

Chromatic dragons, acting on their god's orders, stole the eggs of good metallic dragons. The metallic dragons reluctantly pledged to not interfere in the coming war in exchange for the promised safety of their abducted broods.

But the Dragon Queen's servants secretly broke their promises. Takhisis taught her followers to corrupt the stolen eggs into monstrous warriors known as draconians, gambling that draconian armies will conquer Ansalon by the time the metallic dragons learn of this betrayal.

Unrivaled by gods or dragons, the Dragon Queen unleashes her forces upon a shattered world. In their god's name, these Dragon Armies begin their conquest of Krynn.

THE DRAGON ARMIES

The Dragon Queen's forces are organized into five Dragon Armies. Draconians fill the ranks of each, though the armies' numbers also include humans, goblins, hobgoblins, ogres, and others who seek wealth and a return to pre-Cataclysm glories. Each Dragon Army is supported by chromatic dragons and their smaller kin, such as dragonnels and wyverns. These winged terrors provide a staggering advantage not seen on battlefields for over a thousand years.

DRAGONLANCE: WARRIORS OF KRYNN

During this book's adventures, heroes have the opportunity to influence clashes between mighty armies. If you have the *Dragonlance: Warriors of Krynn* game, you can play out certain dramatic battles using that game (though it isn't required). If you use that game, this book's adventure will point you to sidebars like this one that detail when to use the board game and which mass-combat scenarios affect the adventure. Not every one of that game's scenarios appear in this book. *Dragonlance: Warriors of Krynn* also provides details on how to play D&D characters in its scenarios, as well as other heroes players can play in them.

The Dragon Queen has elevated her five most cunning and devout followers to the rank of dragon highlord, each commanding one of her armies. The highlords all report to Takhisis's champion, Duulket Ariakas, but there is no shortage of treachery between—and within—the Dragon Armies. The Dragon Queen encourages these conflicts, trusting them to bring the most ruthless and capable leaders to prominence.

The Red Dragon Army—the first, largest, and most powerful of Takhisis's forces—is commanded by the fanatical Dragon Highlord Verminaard, but he has temporarily given control of many of its troops to his acolyte, Dragon Highmaster Kansaldi Fire-Eyes, tasking her with spearheading a daring attack on Solamnia. Meanwhile, Verminaard's force follows whispers from the Dragon Queen into the southern lands of Abanasinia.

The ambitious Highlord Kitiara Uth Matar commands the Blue Dragon Army. Second in power among the Dragon Queen's forces, the Blue Dragon Army prepares to join the Red Dragon Army's multipronged invasion of Solamnia. The Green Dragon Army recently came under the command of Salah-Khan, a Khur leader who united the region's nomads under Dragon Army rule. The half-ogre Lucien of Takar commands the Black Dragon Army, whose focused force supports the other armies and occupies the lands they conquer, including Nordmaar and Goodlund. Finally, the small White Dragon Army is led by Highlord Feal-Thas, a Silvanesti elf and black-robed member of the Mages of High Sorcery.

THE WAR OF THE LANCE

As the Dragon Armies emerged from Neraka, they set into motion the events that will come to be known as the War of the Lance. Major events in the war are presented here. Each date occurs in the era after the Cataclysm (AC).

NORDMAAR FALLS

348 AC

The first true military test of the Dragon Armies was the Red and Green Dragon Armies' successful invasion of the unprepared realm of Nordmaar. This victory convinced many neutral bands of hobgoblins and ogres in the Taman Busuk region to align with the Dragon Armies, though many holdouts remain.

KHUR JOINS

Early 349 AC

The Green Dragon Army was dispatched to the steppes of Khur to subdue the tribes there. Rather than fight a protracted campaign, Ariakas allowed the cunning Khur leader Salah-Khan to defeat the Green Dragon Army's original highlord in

battle, then offered to make Salah-Khan highlord in his place. In exchange for control over Khur and the surrounding lands, Salah-Khan accepted and pledged his people to Takhisis, adding to the Dragon Armies' ranks. Few can say whether he did so to further his own ambitions or to spare Khur a long, bloody conflict, but many Khur view Salah-Khan as a traitor to his people and fiercely resist the Green Dragon Army's occupation.

BALIFOR AND GOODLUND ABSORBED

Mid 349 AC

Without substantial military resistance, Balifor and the Goodlund Peninsula fell to the Black and White Dragon Armies. Though the land's residents are largely resigned to the Black Dragon Army's ongoing occupation, the kender of Kendermore lead the region's resistance, waging a guerrilla war against the occupiers.

SILVANESTI CAMPAIGN

Late 349 AC through 350 AC

The Red and Blue Dragon Armies attacked the elven nation of Silvanesti. The elves mounted a stiff resistance, and the siege stretched on in a brutal campaign.

After a year of fighting, the Silvanesti elves evacuated from their ancestral home and sailed for Southern Ergoth. The elves' leader, Speaker of the Stars Lorac, attempted to use an *orb of dragonkind* to protect his homeland but succeeded only in transforming it into a land of nightmares, useless to both sides.

DRAGON ARMIES REGROUP

351 AC

With virtually all of eastern Ansalon under their control, the Dragon Armies have spent much of the last year regrouping and consolidating their power. The Blue and Red Dragon Armies have returned to the Taman Busuk region, tasked with preparing to invade Solamnia. The White Dragon Army has ventured south to conquer Icereach, where its white dragons can fight effectively in its frozen lands. The Green and Black Dragon Armies focus on their occupied lands abroad.

In Neraka, zealots and black-robed mages devise magical plans to empower Dragon Army forces. One such plot, involving the ruins of an Istarian city, captures the imagination of Dragon Highlord Verminaard. He tasks his devotee, Kansaldi Fire-Eyes, with claiming a devastating new weapon for the Dragon Armies.

One week. One week since these creatures swept down on us in numbers too vast to count. It feels like a decade. Everything is upside down.

They're everywhere. We've avoided the bulk of their forces, but their patrols scour the countryside for resistance to subdue and goods to plunder. We've heard rumors that these monsters are called "draconians."

Even in death, these reptilian warriors cause misery, exploding in gouts of acid or plumes of gas. Be careful.

Even if we survive the invaders, we don't have enough to eat, and little planting is being done in the surrounding lands with armies on the march. How do we live through a year with no harvest?

I don't know how long we'll hold out or who'll read this. I hope only these words serve as a warning to someone.

Ollen Nahled, Commander at
Wheelwatch Outpost

OLIVIER BERNARD

LIFE ON ANSALON

While Krynn holds many lands and cultures, the War of the Lance and adventures surrounding that conflict unfold on the continent of Ansalon. Here are a few details regarding everyday life there.

LANGUAGES

Across Ansalon, language is an expression of upbringing and exposure. Before the Cataclysm, Common served as a language of commerce under the empires of Ergoth, Solamnia, and Istar. After the Cataclysm, migrating refugees communicated using Common, and today it's spoken in every corner of the continent. Nevertheless, the local languages of most lands still flourish, and Common is used primarily in markets and in dealings with travelers.

With the DM's approval, players can exchange a language granted by their characters' race for a different language from the Standard Languages of Ansalon table or the Rare Languages of Ansalon table.

STANDARD LANGUAGES OF ANSALON

Language	Main Speakers	Script
Common	Trade language of Ansalon	Common
Abanasinian	Abanasinia	Common
Dwarvish	Abanasinia, Kayolin, Thoradin, Thorbardin	Dwarvish
Elvish	Qualinesti, Silvanesti, Southern Ergoth	Elvish
Ergot	Northern Ergoth	Common
Gnomish	Sancrist	Common
Kenderspeak	Goodlund, Hylo	Common
Kharolian	Plains of Dust, Tarsis	Common
Khur	Khur	Istarian
Nordmaarian	Nordmaar	Istarian
Solamnic	Sancrist, Solamnia	Common

RARE LANGUAGES OF ANSALON

Language	Main Speakers	Script
Draconic	Dragons	Draconic
Goblin	Taman Busuk	Dwarvish
Istarian	Ancient Istarians	Istarian
Kothian	Minotaurs	Kothian
Nerakese	Neraka	Istarian
Ogre	Blode, Kern	Ogre
Primordial	Elementals	Primordial
Sylvan	Fey creatures	Sylvan

TRAVELERS APPROACH THE TOWN OF GATEWAY, A COMMUNITY SHELTERED AMID THE ROOTS OF A TOPPLED VALLENWOOD TREE.

Calendar

The lands around Kalaman use the Solamnic calendar, which has twelve months, each containing four weeks. Weeks have seven days, and days have twenty-four hours.

Solamnic Months

Month	Name	Month	Name
January	Newkolt	July	Fierswelt
February	Deepkolt	August	Paleswelt
March	Brookgreen	September	Reapember
April	Yurthgreen	October	Gildember
May	Fleurgreen	November	Darkember
June	Holmswelt	December	Frostkolt

Solamnic Days

Day	Name	Day	Name
Sunday	Linaras	Thursday	Misham
Monday	Palast	Friday	Bakukal
Tuesday	Magetag	Saturday	Bracha
Wednesday	Kirinor		

Currency

Since the Cataclysm, the harsh realities of daily survival leave little room for impracticality. For years after the devastation, steel's value skyrocketed until it was valued as highly as gold, thanks to the difficulty of forging steel and its obvious practical applications. Similarly, bronze was valued on par with silver. While the value of steel and bronze has diminished to pre-Cataclysm standards, trade coins of bronze and steel remain in use across Ansalon.

Currency of Ansalon

Coin	cp	bp/sp	gp/stl	pp
Copper (cp)	1	1/10	1/100	1/1,000
Bronze (bp) or Silver (sp)	10	1	1/10	1/100
Gold (gp) or Steel (stl)	100	10	1	1/10
Platinum (pp)	1,000	100	10	1

SCOTT MURPHY

Rumors of War

Factual reports of war in eastern Ansalon and the Dragon Queen's return are slow to spread. Many of Ansalon's communities are isolated, and the Dragon Armies work to suppress information of their conquests. As a result, most people in Solamnia and west of the mountainous Taman Busuk region aren't aware of the Dragon Armies' threat beyond vague rumors.

Roll or choose a result from the Wartime Rumors table whenever characters hear a rumor regarding the Dragon Armies or strange happenings in eastern Ansalon. Each rumor notes how truthful it is, but even inaccurate rumors hold a grain of truth. At the start of the adventure, characters have each heard one of these rumors.

Wartime Rumors

d10	Rumor
1	Warlords from Taman Busuk have united an army of mercenaries and warlike groups. (True)
2	Some claim to hear the whispers of the old gods and believe their miracles are returning to the world. (True)
3	The kender homeland of Kendermore suffered some disaster. Kender are traveling far, seeking help but also getting into trouble. (True)
4	Armies in the east are recruiting anyone who will fight for them, promising wealth and glory not seen since before the Cataclysm. (True)
5	A deadly band of mercenaries has trained flying, dragon-like creatures called dragonnels to serve them. (Inaccurate; the Dragon Armies widely employ these creatures.)
6	The nation of Khur has been united under a powerful warlord who seeks to conquer the world. (Inaccurate; Khur has been conquered by the Dragon Armies.)
7	A great fleet of elven ships was sighted heading west. The elves are retreating to their secret homeland. (Inaccurate; the Silvanesti elves have fled their homeland for Southern Ergoth.)
8	Travelers report sightings of cloaked lizardfolk raiders. No one knows where they've come from or what they want. (Inaccurate; such rumors misidentify draconians.)
9	Members of the Mages of High Sorcery spread lies of dangers in the East to keep people isolated, scared, and under their secret control. (False)
10	Fools claim to have seen dragons in the East, but these are only wyverns and illusions. (Inaccurate; people do claim to have seen dragons, but these are rare sightings of actual dragons.)

Kalaman Region

Situated in the province of Nightlund in Solamnia's eastern reaches, Kalaman is one of the nation's most vital gateways to the outside world. The city, known as the Beacon of the East, rises along a deepwater port near the mouth of the Vingaard River, Solamnia's greatest trade artery. Blessed with the bounty of the river, the benefits of trade, and the fertile soil of the Solamnic plains, the Kalaman region flourished even after the Cataclysm.

City of Kalaman

Kalaman began as a sleepy fishing village on the coast of the Turbidus Ocean. It might have remained so if not for the arrival of an Istarian trading mission centuries before the Cataclysm. Seeing the potential of a deep harbor so close to the mouth of a great river, the Empire of Istar invested heavily in the town, transforming it into a thriving trade hub. Solamnia soon found Istar's stranglehold on the booming port intolerable, and after a climactic battle on the plains west of the city, Istar ceded control of Kalaman.

Today, long after the fall of Istar and the trials of the Cataclysm, Kalaman remains a thriving port city surrounded by tall Istarian-built walls that have never been breached. In its busy harbor, vessels from all over Ansalon go about their business under the light of the city's two grand beacons, pre-Cataclysm marvels that have survived for generations. At the center of the city, the ancient Castle Kalaman rises intimidatingly on a sheer hill. The castle's architectural marvels include defenses yet to be recreated in the modern age. The city of Kalaman is further detailed in Chapter 4.

OLGA DREBAS

People of Kalaman

The city of Kalaman is notably cosmopolitan, while most people in surrounding communities make their livelihood through fishing and farming. Many of the region's inhabitants are Solamnic humans, while others descend from the city's Istarian founders. Traders from all over Ansalon settle in Kalaman through preference or necessity. As a result, some humans hail or have ancestors from Abanasinia, Nordmaar, Ergoth, Estwilde, and farther-flung lands. Kender, hill dwarves, and gnomes are common in the region, while some elves, mountain dwarves, and other people also make their home in the city. Anyone is welcome in Kalaman if they come peaceably with goods to trade.

Surrounding Regions

To the west of the Kalaman region lies Hinterlund. Even farther west lie the Plains of Solamnia, from where crops and crafted goods make their way to Kalaman for trade. Even in parts of Solamnia closer to the port of Palanthas, it's often cheaper and easier to move goods down the river to Kalaman.

North of Kalaman, the grasslands characteristic of Solamnia give way to the broken steppes and labyrinthine canyons known as the Northern Wastes. Deadly beasts, treacherous cliffs, and unpredictable flooding make the wastes a dangerous land where it's said nothing survives for long.

East of Kalaman, the lands of Estwilde hold inhospitable terrain and peoples who have been unfriendly to Solamnia since the days of Istar. Across the bay in northern Estwilde lie the swamps of Qwalmish. To the south and east of Kalaman are the rolling steppes of Qlettaar, which in turn give way to the forbidding peaks of the Taman Busuk region beyond Estwilde.

Nightlund

For generations, the Soths of Dargaard Keep—a family of Knights of Solamnia—ruled the Solamnic province once known as Knightlund. Before the Cataclysm, the gods of good forewarned Knightlund's leader, Lord Loren Soth, about the coming destruction and offered him a chance to stop it, but he failed to accomplish this task. Since then, the province has had a cursed reputation. People have come to know the land as Nightlund and ascribe the region's frequent storms to the old gods' disfavor.

Lord Soth and his defiance of the gods is detailed in chapter 4.

Religion and the Gods

The gods of Krynn are said to have abandoned the world, and in the great cities of Ansalon, temples and centers of faith are few. Nevertheless, small miracles occur across the world. Druids and hidden communities offer prayers in the old ways and employ mysterious magic. Long-lived peoples remember the worship of the gods and see their shapes in nature and the constellations above. Ancient, forgotten sanctuaries hold wonders beyond imagination, and divine whispers reach those with the minds and hearts to listen. The gods haven't wholly abandoned Krynn, and as threats grow, mortals turn to them once more—sometimes after a remarkable encounter with a messenger of the gods.

The gods of Krynn loosely align with one another along the principles of good, neutrality, and evil. While such alliances can be tenuous, the gods often work together to enact their shared will across the world or to oppose unions of their foes. The Deities of Krynn table and the following pages summarize the gods most active in the world. Among Krynn's diverse lands and peoples, gods take various names, genders, and forms. Those presented in the following sections are the representations best known in Solamnia.

It's easy to blame the gods for the Cataclysm. They sent the Thirteen Warnings and the burning mountain that followed. They sank Istar beneath the waves, shattered the continent, and withdrew from the world. They chose to cause the immense suffering of the disaster and the centuries since.

But let us suppose that the gods of good love this world and want us to flourish. That the gods of neutrality strive to steward and uphold the agency of mortals. That even the gods of evil, selfish as they are, seek power and influence, not destruction for its own sake. Why, then, would they punish us with the Cataclysm and leave us in a godless world?

I fear we've forgotten more than we remember. Worship of the true gods is ever waning, and false religions rise in their place. I pray every day that we've learned our lesson—that the gods will return, and that I may cede this chair to one who hears their voices and bears their true blessings.

Time alone will tell.

Rosamund Heward, Knight of the Crown
Acting High Clerist

DEITIES OF KRYNN

Gods of Good	Alignment	Province	Common Symbol
Paladine	LG	Good dragons, guardians, rulers	Silver triangle
Branchala	NG	Music	Bard's harp
Habbakuk	NG	Animal life, natural balance	Blue bird
Kiri-Jolith	LG	Honor, war	Bison's horns
Majere	LG	Mediation, order	Copper spider
Mishakal	LG	Healing	Blue infinity sign
Solinari	LG	Good magic	White circle or sphere

Gods of Neutrality	Alignment	Province	Symbol
Gilean	N	Knowledge	Open book
Chislev	N	Nature	Feather
Lunitari	N	Neutral magic	Red circle or sphere
Reorx	N	Craft	Forging hammer
Shinare	N	Trade, wealth	Griffon's wing
Sirrion	N	Change, fire	Multicolored fire
Zivilyn	N	Wisdom	Great green or gold tree

Gods of Evil	Alignment	Province	Symbol
Takhisis	LE	Evil dragons, hatred, night	Spiral of five dragon claws
Chemosh	LE	Undead	Yellow skull
Hiddukel	CE	Greed, lies	Broken merchant's scales
Morgion	NE	Disease, secrecy	Hood with two red eyes
Nuitari	LE	Evil magic	Black circle or sphere
Sargonnas	LE	Fire, vengeance	Stylized red condor
Zeboim	CE	Seas, storms	Turtle shell

SYMBOL
OF HABBAKUK

GODS OF GOOD

The gods of good provide healing and comfort to the mortals of Krynn. Although they oppose the evil gods' attempts to rule the world, their goal isn't the eradication of evil or its gods. Rather, their highest pursuit is preserving mortal choice, despite the sorrowful knowledge that mortals sometimes choose ruinous paths.

PALADINE

Paladine is known as the Father of Good, the Master of Law, the Platinum Dragon, and—on other worlds of the multiverse—Bahamut. He leads the gods of good and watches over the world with an eye toward order, justice, and mercy. He teaches that wise and just laws are the basis of a functioning society, and his clerics often aid in crafting and upholding such laws. Paladine sometimes appears on Krynn in the guise of Fizban, a befuddled old human mage in faded robes.

BRANCHALA

Called the Bard King, Branchala is the god of music, poetry, and the inner beauty of all living things. Many elves and kender worship him above all other gods. Both groups revere him as a champion of life and laughter, bringing solace and joy to those who listen.

HABBAKUK

Habbakuk, known as the Fisher King, oversees animal life, the sea, and the balance of nature. Many sailors, farmers, and hunters revere him. His holy sites are often marked with the image of a blue bird or a phoenix wreathed in blue flames.

KIRI-JOLITH

Kiri-Jolith is the god of righteous war. He blesses all who fight in the name of good and scorns those who delight in slaughter and lust for battle. He is particularly revered by the Knights of the Sword, an order of the Knights of Solamnia that seeks to root out evil wherever it dwells.

SYMBOL
OF MAJERE

SYMBOL
OF MISHAKAL

SYMBOL
OF KIRI-JOLITH

SYMBOL
OF SOLINARI

MAJERE

Austere and aloof, Majere is the god of meditation and discipline. Monks, his most devoted followers, honor him by leading lives of quiet contemplation in remote monasteries. Many orphans are raised in the monasteries of Majere; some become monks themselves, while those who leave the monastic life often take the surname Majere out of respect.

MISHAKAL

God of compassion, healing, and love, Mishakal is widely worshiped by healers and community guardians. Throughout history, she has reached out to chosen heroes to soothe others' suffering. Her faithful offer healing and solace to all—even enemies.

SOLINARI

Solinari, the god of good magic, is patron of the Mages of High Sorcery's Order of the White Robes and other benevolent mages. His power manifests through the white moon of Krynn, the brightest of its three moons. Along with his cousins Lunitari and Nuitari, he watches Krynn from the heavens and encourages magic that aids, heals, and protects.

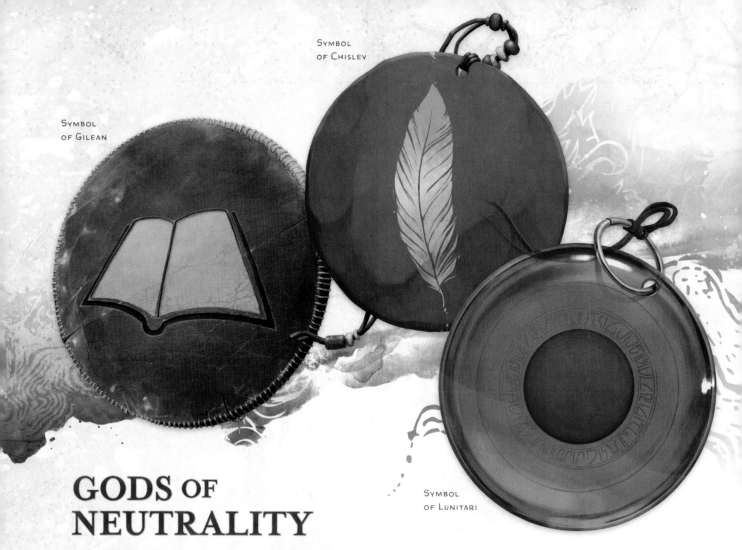

GODS OF NEUTRALITY

The neutral gods of Krynn vary widely in their motivations and methods. Some are passive and distant, dedicated to recording the actions of mortals or upholding the balance between societies and nature. Others take a more active hand, injecting elements of chaos and innovation into mortal life. Unlike the gods of good and evil, the neutral gods have little interest in the struggle over mortal destinies.

GILEAN

The god of knowledge and nominal leader of the neutral gods, Gilean embodies the ideal of neutrality. He stands back and observes, recording all that unfolds. Gilean is keeper of the *Tobril*, a book said to contain all the knowledge of the gods, though portions are sealed to all but Gilean. Some people believe the scribe Astinus of Palanthas to be Gilean in human form.

CHISLEV

Chislev is the god of nature on its own terms, governing the rhythms of life that unfold heedless of mortal action. Though enigmatic and shy, they are fiercely protective of their domain, regarding all plants and animals as their children. Chislev's followers are often hermits, druids, and others who revere nature without asking anything in return.

LUNITARI

Lunitari, the god of neutral magic and illusions, is patron of the Mages of High Sorcery's Order of the Red Robes and other neutral mages. With her cousins Solinari and Nuitari, she watches over the people of Krynn from the heavens, conveying her power through the red moon that shares her name. She appears as a trickster figure in mythology, using her mastery of illusions to fool gods and heroes alike.

REORX

Reorx is the god of creation, inspiration, and artisanship, credited with creating the gnomes, dwarves, kender, and even Krynn itself. He invents new things that alter the world and spur its people to action.

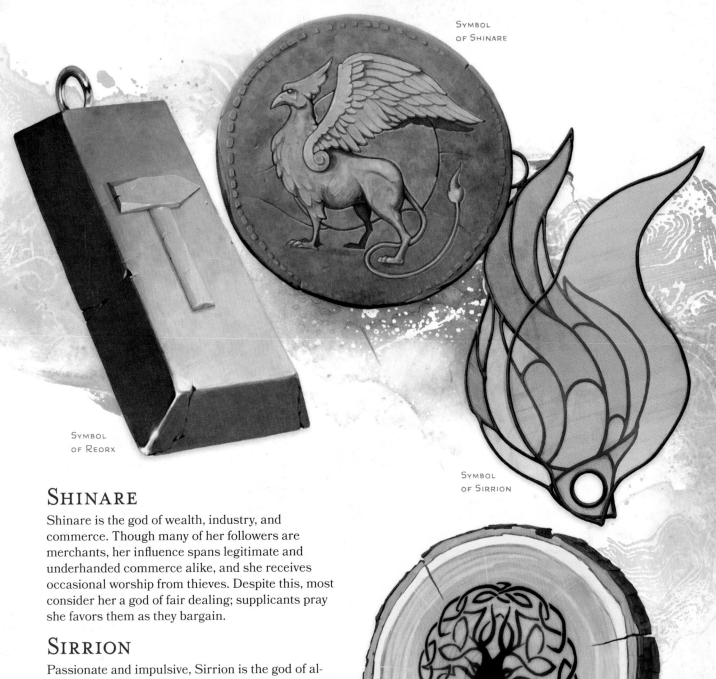

Symbol
of Shinare

Symbol
of Reorx

Symbol
of Sirrion

Symbol
of Zivilyn

Shinare

Shinare is the god of wealth, industry, and commerce. Though many of her followers are merchants, her influence spans legitimate and underhanded commerce alike, and she receives occasional worship from thieves. Despite this, most consider her a god of fair dealing; supplicants pray she favors them as they bargain.

Sirrion

Passionate and impulsive, Sirrion is the god of alchemy, transformation, serendipitous creation, and flames. He embodies momentary excitement, flaring quickly into fiery passion and smoldering long afterward. Sirrion's followers embrace extremes of emotion as forms of divine expression.

Zivilyn

Where Gilean embodies knowledge, Zivilyn exemplifies the calm wisdom necessary to wield knowledge in the world. He's said to exist in all times and places, possessing the collected wisdom of every plane of existence. Zivilyn often attracts the worship of eccentrics, philosophers, and sages.

SYMBOL OF TAKHISIS

SYMBOL OF CHEMOSH

SYMBOL OF HIDDUKEL

GODS OF EVIL

The evil gods of Krynn embody power, vengeance, and other ideals that elevate self above community. They wish to rule the mortal world, believing only they are worthy of such dominion. They rely on temptation and subjugation to secure the service of lesser creatures. In every age, some mortals are willing to sell their souls for power, and the gods of evil are eager to oblige.

TAKHISIS

Takhisis, leader of Krynn's evil gods, is known as the Dragon Queen, the Queen of Darkness, and—on other worlds—Tiamat. She is the god of power, pride, and control, as well as the queen of chromatic dragons. She tempts mortals to her service with offers of dominance over others. Barred from Krynn since before the Cataclysm, she found her chance to return in the centuries that followed. She sometimes appears as a powerful human warrior with gleaming armor and long black hair, but her true form is a five-headed dragon.

CHEMOSH

Chemosh is the god of undeath and false redemption, tempting his followers with the promise of immortality. Those who heed him find that while they may live forever, their bodies still decay and putrefy. Followers of Chemosh embrace his baleful reputation, dressing in white skull masks and black robes.

HIDDUKEL

Hiddukel is the god of greed and treachery. He holds domain over all ill-gotten wealth in the world, and criminals and unscrupulous traders worship him in secret. While Hiddukel gladly accepts their worship, his true goal is the acquisition not of riches, but of souls.

MORGION

Solitary and secretive, Morgion is the god of disease and decay. He doesn't consult or act in accord with the other gods, preferring to brood in his otherworldly fortress, the Bronze Tower, and pursue his own schemes. His worshipers follow his example, meeting in the dark and maintaining secrecy in all things.

SYMBOL
OF MORGION

SYMBOL
OF NUITARI

SYMBOL
OF SARGONNAS

NUITARI

Nuitari, the god of evil magic and darkness, is patron of the Mages of High Sorcery's Order of the Black Robes and other wicked mages. He encourages selfish and destructive magic. His power flows through the black moon that shares his name, which is visible only due to the stars it blocks in the sky.

SARGONNAS

Sargonnas is the unpredictable god of flame, vengeance, and wrath. Though he's a consort to Takhisis, he schemes against her as often as he fights on her behalf. He is worshiped by those who seek retribution. His true form is that of a monstrous minotaur, and many minotaurs revere him under the name Sargas.

ZEBOIM

Zeboim is the god of the ocean in its destructive aspect, including storms and dangerous sea creatures. She is a mercurial god, and even her followers aren't safe from her frequent bouts of rage. Most sailors pray to Habbakuk to keep Zeboim at bay, but some make offerings to Zeboim to allay her wrath.

SYMBOL
OF ZEBOIM

Adventuring defenders of Solamnia bring down a red dragon servant of the Dragon Queen.

CHARACTER CREATION

S THE DRAGON QUEEN'S FORCES MARCH across Krynn, heroic souls rise to defy her. Forged in the crucible of war, these remarkable few are all that stand between the peace-loving peoples of Krynn and an age of oppression.

This chapter presents player-facing details of peoples and groups in Krynn, as well as character options supplementing the rules in the *Player's Handbook*. Herein, you'll find the following sections:

Peoples of Krynn. Learn about the peoples of Krynn and how they might inspire your next character.

Race Option. Play as a kender, a character race known for bravery and curiosity.

Organizations. Discover two of Krynn's most influential groups, the honorable Knights of Solamnia and the mystical Mages of High Sorcery.

Backgrounds. Learn how war shapes your character, and choose from two new backgrounds: the Knight of Solamnia and Mage of High Sorcery.

Feats. Draw on the power of magic, honor, or the gods with this selection of feats.

Subclass Option. Tie your magic to Krynn's three mystical moons with the Lunar Sorcery sorcerer subclass.

PEOPLES OF KRYNN

The Dragon Armies threaten all the peoples of Krynn. This section presents information about the inhabitants of the continent of Ansalon and contextualizes the races from the *Player's Handbook* within the world of Krynn. The locations referenced in this section appear on the poster map included with this book.

DWARVES

While known for their great subterranean nations, dwarves have long traded and traveled among the peoples of Krynn's surface. The Cataclysm devastated many dwarven lands and destroyed some of their greatest underground kingdoms. Others, like the nation of Kayolin, were isolated from their allies as the New Sea flooded the land. And some, like the great dwarven realm of Thorbardin, turned inward and have yet to rejoin the world.

THORBARDIN AND THE DWARFGATE WAR

The kingdom of Thorbardin has endured beneath the Kharolis Mountains of southwest Ansalon for thousands of years, but the centuries since the Cataclysm have created new divisions within it.

The dwarves of Thorbardin divide themselves into ancient clans. Many generations before the Cataclysm, dwarves who dwelled on the surface established the Neidar clan, known for working the land and trading with other surface folk. In the wake of the Cataclysm, with food scarce and the future uncertain, the High King of Thorbardin sealed the gates of the kingdom to all outsiders, including the Neidar. Betrayed and hungry, these surface dwarves allied with other desperate refugees and unsuccessfully attempted to take Thorbardin by force. The conflict that came to be called the Dwarfgate War caused deep enmity between the dwarven communities of the surface and those that live below.

MOUNTAIN DWARVES

Led by the aristocratic Hylar clan, mountain dwarves are the unquestioned rulers of Thorbardin. Many great fighters, engineers, and artisans call these magnificent halls home. Proud and reserved, most Thorbardin clans want nothing to do with outsiders—dwarves or otherwise. However, some

DWARF ADVENTURER FROM THE NATION OF THORBARDIN

dwarves grow tired of life within their ancient tunnels and wonder about rejoining the world above.

As a mountain dwarf, you might come from a dwarven nation like Kayolin or Thorbardin. You could be part of an expedition of traders or explorers, sent by your people to live on the surface for years before reporting back. Or you might have ventured forth on your own, eager to see what the wider world holds.

HILL DWARVES

The dwarves barred from Thorbardin experienced the years following the Cataclysm on the surface. Now known as hill dwarves, they lived among the lands and peoples of the surface for centuries. Few still call themselves by their old name, the Neidar, preferring to forget their ties to their mountain dwarf cousins.

Some hill dwarves live as traveling traders, while others make their homes among the communities of Ansalon's other peoples. Still other groups eke out lives in ruins or harsh lands as reclusive survivalists.

As a hill dwarf, you might come from lands near the great mountain dwarf nations or from a diverse town far away. Or perhaps you come from everywhere, having been raised in a traveling community that's seen most corners of Ansalon.

ELVES

Several distinct elven cultures inhabit Ansalon, including the Qualinesti and Silvanesti high elves, the Kagonesti wood elves, and the Dargonesti and Dimernesti sea elves.

Over two thousand years ago, the Kinslayer War divided the high elves of Ansalon into two groups, Silvanesti in the east and Qualinesti in the west. Through the intervening millennia, neither group has sought reconciliation. In the even more distant past, both high elf nations separated from their Kagonesti kin, while the waves themselves isolate Dargonesti and Dimernesti from their surface-dwelling cousins.

As the elves of Ansalon largely keep to themselves, half-elves are few and are rarely seen outside the elven nations.

SILVANESTI HIGH ELVES

Silvanesti, the original elven kingdom, lies in southern Ansalon. For untold generations, the aloof Silvanesti elves lived in a stratified society closed to outsiders. They don't hate their cousins in Qualinesti, but they consider their ways misguided.

In recent years, war has come to Silvanesti. When the Dragon Armies besieged the realm, the leader Lorac Caladon, Speaker of the Stars, ordered his people to evacuate. Lorac then attempted to defend the kingdom with an *orb of dragonkind*—but the

artifact's magic unexpectedly warped Silvanesti into a nightmarish land. The surviving elves of Silvanesti now find themselves a people without a homeland. Most journeyed together across the sea to Southern Ergoth, seeking refuge with the Kagonesti, while others refused to give up Silvanesti and sought to reclaim their ancestral home.

As a Silvanesti high elf, you know what few in Ansalon do: the home of the elves has fallen. During the Dragon Armies' invasion of Silvanesti, you might have been separated from your people or even taken captive before escaping the Dragon Armies in unfamiliar lands. You could have fled Silvanesti with your people but now seek a way to restore your homeland. Or perhaps you've spent your life exploring the world, cultivating relationships with people other than your kin.

QUALINESTI HIGH ELVES

Long ago, a group of high elves left Silvanesti, desiring a more egalitarian society. They traveled far to the west and founded a new forested homeland called Qualinesti. Less hierarchical than their progenitors and more willing to deal with outsiders, Qualinesti elves even enjoyed good relations with the dwarves of Thorbardin. Since the Cataclysm, however, they've withdrawn from the world, and few outsiders dare approach their well-guarded borders.

As a Qualinesti high elf, you might have been raised in seclusion in the forests of Qualinesti. You could have been sent forth to learn the state of the wider world or to pursue rumors of Silvanesti's fate. Or perhaps your family left Qualinesti long ago, and you have connections with folk from other lands.

KAGONESTI WOOD ELVES

Kagonesti are the descendants of elves who never settled in the forest cities of Silvanesti, instead living a nomadic way of life and seeking harmony with nature. Most of these wood elves live in small tribes in the forests of Southern Ergoth. Although few outsiders intrude on the Kagonesti's ancient forested lands, thousands of Silvanesti refugees have begun seeking their aid. While the Kagonesti welcome their cousins and seek to support them, they refuse to be overwhelmed by the Silvanesti's numbers and distinct ways.

As a Kagonesti wood elf, you likely spent a great deal of your life in the forest and know much about the natural world. You might have left years ago to explore the world, or perhaps you've just begun your travels, seeking to prevent the threats that befell the Silvanesti from reaching your people's home.

PEOPLE FROM BEYOND

Peoples who aren't native to the world still might find their way to Krynn. It's possible to find individual members—or even small enclaves—of folk like dragonborn, halflings, tieflings, or any other race in Ansalon. Perhaps such individuals stepped through a portal and found themselves on Krynn, or traded with one of Krynn's great empires before the Cataclysm. Use such possibilities to play characters of any race you please in your adventures across Krynn.

SEA ELVES

Two groups of sea elves inhabit the oceans surrounding Ansalon. Dargonesti, also known as deep elves, call the vast oceans home. Their cousins, Dimernesti, are often called shoal elves. Although Dimernesti live closer to land, they have deep bonds with the sea and all life within. Both groups of sea elves are rarely seen by the peoples of Ansalon and keep to their own aquatic communities. Though sea elves are exceptionally rare, you can create sea elf characters using *Mordenkainen Presents: Monsters of the Multiverse*.

GNOMES

The tinker gnomes of Mount Nevermind are the best-known gnome community on Krynn. Despite living in a world steeped in magical forces, many of these rock gnomes indulge in specialized scientific pursuits and create complicated inventions.

Mount Nevermind—a hollow, dormant volcano on the island of Sancrist—is a hub of wonders and catastrophes. Here, energetic gnome inventors endlessly create and test stupendous devices—and learn from equally stupendous failures.

Forest gnomes are less populous in Ansalon. Their few communities lie deep in the forests of Sancrist and Kendermore, where they embrace harmony with nature over the pursuit of invention.

As a gnome, you might be a tinker pursuing some niche scientific endeavor, coaxed from Mount Nevermind to conduct research or to seek inspiration beyond the mountain. Alternatively, you might be a forest gnome, exploring the wonders of the world or seeking to heal the lands of the Cataclysm's scars.

HUMANS

Humans are ubiquitous on Ansalon. They ruled the continent's largest empires before the Cataclysm, then were scattered during the devastation that followed. Many humans never resettled after the Cataclysm, joining itinerant and nomadic cultures. Human cities are few and usually small, developed around natural structures that sheltered communities following the Cataclysm.

As a human, you might hail from any corner of Krynn. Below are just a few of the distinct human nations of Ansalon. You might be a member of any of these societies, or you can choose another home to define as you please.

ABANASINIA

Several peaceful communities dot the Abanasinia region, including Solace, a village built among the branches of towering Vallenwood trees. In recent years, the theocratic Seekers have risen to power in the region. This power-hungry religion controls the city of Haven and surrounding settlements in the name of vague, fickle deities who condemn the use of magic.

The broad plains of the northern Abanasinian peninsula are home to nomadic humans known as Plainsfolk. Divided into several tribes with territories across the region, Plainsfolk are skilled warriors, traders, and collectors of stories that predate the Cataclysm.

NORTHERN AND SOUTHERN ERGOTH

The Cataclysm split the land of Ergoth in two, dividing the remnants of the human empire that once ruled there. On Northern Ergoth, scattered communities claim to be inheritors of the fallen Empire of Ergoth and dwell among the remnants of its cities and fortresses. These Ergothians enjoy a

A TINKER GNOME FROM MOUNT NEVERMIND
FINE-TUNES HIS LATEST INVENTION.

prosperous peace with the kender enclave of Hylo and the goblins of the arid southern lands, with whom they share their island. Fewer humans make their home on Southern Ergoth, living primarily along the coast and avoiding dangerous groups of ogres and giants.

SOLAMNIA

Once a mighty empire, Solamnia has fallen from the glory it knew. Though Solamnia remains one of the largest and most prosperous nations on the continent, its provinces are self-concerned and prone to squabbling. The land's once-legendary defenders, the Knights of Solamnia, are much diminished in numbers. Nevertheless, the knights still stand as defenders of the innocent and paragons of honor.

TARSIS

After the Cataclysm, the verdant plains of southern Ansalon wasted away, becoming the Plains of Dust. Coastlines shifted, and the city of Tarsis found itself a seaport without a sea. In the dry harbor, decrepit remnants of the city's famed ships list on waves of sand. The rest of the city clings to life as a trade hub for small communities and itinerant bands across the plains. Those who dwell here have adapted their ancestors' seafaring ways to their current arid environment, becoming hunters, scavengers, and traders.

OTHER LANDS

Other parts of Ansalon are home to distinctive tribes of nomads and small, diverse settlements.

Estwilde. The fiercely independent human tribes of Estwilde travel the steppes of Qlettaar from the Turbidus Ocean to New Sea. These nomads brook no trespassing on their lands, whether by Solamnics or hobgoblin raiders from the east.

Goodlund. While Goodlund is predominantly inhabited by kender, scattered human tribes wander the Dairly Plains and coasts bordering the Blood Sea of Istar. Many inhabit ancient Istarian ruins, occasionally forced to grapple with half-understood technology and magic from the ancient past.

Icereach. The humans of Icereach live in the frozen south, where they compete with groups of thanoi (walrus-folk) for hunting grounds.

Khur. The nomadic human tribes of Khur inhabit a harsh, rocky land. These groups have been forcibly united under the local leader Salah-Khan, who allied his people with the Dragon Armies. A robust resistance, centered at the trade hub of Khuri-Khan, opposes the invaders.

Nordmaar. Most humans of Nordmaar live either in rugged coastal communities to the north or among the nomadic tribes of the south. Both proud groups have strong ties with the people of Solamnia.

LINDA LITHEN

KENDER ADVENTURERS FOLLOW THEIR
CURIOSITY TO THEIR NEXT ADVENTURE.

RACE OPTION

The kender is a race option for player characters in Dragonlance and other D&D settings.

CREATING YOUR CHARACTER

If you create a kender character, follow these additional rules during character creation.

ABILITY SCORE INCREASES

When determining your character's ability scores, increase one of those scores by 2 and increase a different score by 1, or increase three different scores by 1. Follow this rule regardless of the method you use to determine the scores, such as rolling or point buy.

The "Quick Build" section for your character's class offers suggestions on which scores to increase. You're free to follow those suggestions or to ignore them. Whichever scores you decide to increase, none of the scores can be raised above 20.

LANGUAGES

Your character can speak, read, and write Common and one other language that you and your DM agree is appropriate for the character. The *Player's Handbook* offers a list of widespread languages to choose from. The DM is free to add or remove languages from that list for a particular campaign.

CREATURE TYPE

Every creature in D&D, including every player character, has a special tag in the rules that identifies the type of creature they are. Most player characters, including kender, are of the Humanoid type. Creature types don't have rules themselves, but some rules in the game affect creatures of certain types in different ways. For example, the text of the *cure wounds* spell specifies that the spell doesn't work on a creature that has the Construct type.

LIFE SPAN

The typical life span of a player character in the D&D multiverse is about a century, assuming the character doesn't meet a violent end on an adventure.

HEIGHT AND WEIGHT

Player characters, regardless of race, typically fall into the same ranges of height and weight that humans have in our world. If you'd like to determine your character's height or weight randomly, consult the Random Height and Weight table in the *Player's Handbook*, and choose the row in the table that best represents the build you imagine for your character.

KENDER

During the mythical origins of Krynn, Reorx, god of craft, indulged in an age of unfettered creation. Many peoples sprang from his divine forge, but not all among them remained as the god created them. Altered by unbridled magic, a group of gnomes were transformed and given almost supernatural curiosity and fearlessness. These were the first kender.

Originating on the world of Krynn, kender are diminutive Humanoids who look like humans with pointed ears and diverse appearances. Kender have a supernatural curiosity that drives them to adventure. Due to this inquisitiveness, many kender find themselves falling through portals to other planes and worlds.

Kender sometimes amass impressive collections of curiosities. Some might collect mundane knickknacks or relics from magical sites, while others might become professional thieves.

KENDER TRAITS

As a kender, you have the following racial traits.

Creature Type. You are a Humanoid.

Size. You are Small.

Speed. Your walking speed is 30 feet.

Fearless. You have advantage on saving throws you make to avoid or end the frightened condition on yourself. When you fail a saving throw to avoid or end the frightened condition on yourself, you can choose to succeed instead. Once you succeed on a saving throw in this way, you can't do so again until you finish a long rest.

Kender Aptitude. Thanks to the mystical origin of your people, you gain proficiency with one of the following skills of your choice: Insight, Investigation, Sleight of Hand, Stealth, or Survival.

Taunt. You have an extraordinary ability to fluster creatures. As a bonus action, you can unleash a string of provoking words at a creature within 60 feet of yourself that can hear and understand you. The target must succeed on a Wisdom saving throw, or it has disadvantage on attack rolls against targets other than you until the start of your next turn. The DC equals 8 + your proficiency bonus + your Intelligence, Wisdom, or Charisma modifier (choose when you select this race).

You can use this bonus action a number of times equal to your proficiency bonus, and you regain all expended uses when you finish a long rest.

ORGANIZATIONS

In eras past, when Krynn faced times of exceptional darkness, champions stepped forth from the ranks of the virtuous Knights of Solamnia and the mystical Mages of High Sorcery. These two organizations are detailed here.

KNIGHTS OF SOLAMNIA

Many celebrated heroes have risen from the Knights of Solamnia, the most storied knighthood on Ansalon. The knighthood began over a thousand years ago, during the reign of the Ergothian Empire in western Ansalon. Vinas Solamnus, head of the Ergothian imperial guard, was sent to eastern Ergoth to put down a massive rebellion. However, Solamnus learned of the rebels' grievances and, won over to their cause, he and the rebels marched on the Ergothian capital of Daltigoth. The capital fell, and Vinas Solamnus was crowned king of a new independent nation on the eastern plains, called Solamnia in his honor.

King Solamnus sought above all to rule this new society justly. On the Isle of Sancrist, at a black granite stone in a secluded glade, he prayed to the gods for guidance. Three of the gods of good appeared to him: Paladine, god of justice and order; Kiri-Jolith, god of just warfare; and Habbakuk, god of nature, loyalty, and the elements. The three gods inspired three orders of knights that would guard the realm together as the Knights of Solamnia.

TARNISHED PRIDE

Before the Cataclysm, Solamnia was a beacon of peace and prosperity. The knights established great cities and castles across the Plains of Solamnia, including Solanthus, Castle Brightblade, and Dargaard Keep. They ruled in accordance with the ideals of Vinas Solamnus, and they forged an alliance with Istar that spread those ideals across the world. The people of Solamnia attributed their prosperity to the wise and just rulership of the knights.

In the wake of the Cataclysm, faith in the knighthood soured to suspicion. Rumors spread that the knighthood had possessed the power to avert the Cataclysm and either failed to or chose not to—perhaps to dispense with Istar and solidify the knights' power.

Most knights still tried to defend the realm as their duty demanded, but they found themselves beset on all sides, dying to protect people who rejected and persecuted them. Most fled to Sancrist Isle in the west or retreated to the protection of their strongholds and keeps, while others disguised themselves to continue their work.

EMBLEM OF THE ORDER OF THE CROWN

EMBLEM OF THE ORDER OF THE ROSE

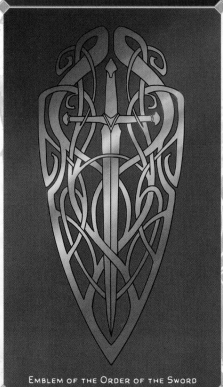

EMBLEM OF THE ORDER OF THE SWORD

Their power waning, the knights today are locked in a bitter internal feud: Is it better to maintain their strict codes even in the face of obsolescence, secure in the knowledge they were true to themselves? Or should they embrace a changing world and fight to defend it, even if the knights must change with it?

THE OATH AND THE MEASURE

The Knights of Solamnia follow a chivalric code with two parts: the Oath and the Measure, both inspired by the writings of Vinas Solamnus. The Oath is simple and aspirational—a star to navigate by—while the Measure lays out specific rules for the organization and conduct of the knighthood.

The Oath. The Oath of the Knights of Solamnia has been the same since Vinas Solamnus founded the knighthood: "Est Sularus oth Mithas," or "My Honor Is My Life." This principle—to sacrifice all for the sake of honor—guides the actions of every knight, at least in theory.

The Measure. In contrast to the Oath, the Measure is a staggeringly complicated, excruciatingly specific guide to knightly life. Originally put forth by Vinas Solamnus as an organizational scheme and code of conduct for the knightly orders, the Measure grew over the years to encompass thirty-seven volumes, covering everything from courtly etiquette to the proper saddling of mounts. According to the Measure, the knights no longer have sufficient numbers to elect a new Grand Master, the highest office in the knighthood, leaving them without an authority who could overrule or update the Measure.

Despite this, a growing minority of knights push for a reform of the Measure, believing that it's unwieldy and outdated and that it no longer serves the ideals laid down by their founder.

KNIGHTLY ORDERS

Each Solamnic knight belongs to one of three orders. Each order, led by a High Knight elected from among its number, has its own hierarchy and rules for admission.

Knights of the Crown. Most knights begin their journey as squires in the Knights of the Crown, who honor the god Habbakuk as their patron. The order emphasizes ideals of loyalty and obedience that serve as a bedrock whether a knight chooses to remain within the order or move beyond it. Knights of the Crown are expected to aid any knight who requires assistance and any kingdom on the List of Loyalty, the official roll of the Knights' allies.

Knights of the Sword. Dedicated to heroic honor, courage, and reverence for the true gods, this order upholds the virtues of Kiri-Jolith, the god of just war. Members dedicate themselves to courageous sacrifice, pledging to defend the defenseless without regard for the knights' personal suffering. Knights who join this order often undertake a heroic quest to prove their worth.

Knights of the Rose. Guided by the god Paladine, the Knights of the Rose exemplify honor tempered by wisdom and justice. Before joining their ranks, most knights rise within the Knights of the Sword after serving with the Knights of the Crown. Those who prove both their loyalty and courage are fit to join this order, which upholds the knighthood's highest ideals.

MAGES OF HIGH SORCERY

Many magic-users on Krynn are members of an ancient organization known as the Mages of High Sorcery. Predominantly composed of wizards—with a lesser number of sorcerers, warlocks, and other spellcasters—members are divided into three orders. Each order dedicates itself to virtues extolled by a god of magic and honors the moon its deity is associated with. The three orders cooperate as part of a single organization, overseen by a council of experienced members known as the Conclave.

Equally devoted to the study of magic and united in defending their knowledge and traditions, the three orders differ in their fundamental reasons for using magic.

ORDER OF THE WHITE ROBES

Dedicated to the good god Solinari, the White Robes accept the solemn responsibility of using magic only to make the world a better place. The path they walk is a narrow one, and almost daily, a mage of the White Robes faces the agonizing decision of whether to intervene in the affairs of others for the greater good.

ORDER OF THE RED ROBES

Inspired by the neutral god Lunitari, the Red Robes help others when it suits them and use their gifts for their own enrichment as they desire. Mages of the Red Robes are expected to wield their power responsibly, represent their order faithfully, and uphold the balance between good and evil in their own actions and the world at large.

ORDER OF THE BLACK ROBES

Often reviled and feared in equal measure, the Black Robes follow the example of the evil god Nuitari, the black moon of Krynn. A mage of the Black Robes is expected to first further their own ambitions, then pursue the goals of their order, and then support the continued well-being of the Conclave.

TOWERS OF HIGH SORCERY

Thousands of years ago, the Mages of High Sorcery cooperated to build five Towers of High Sorcery, centers of learning to advance the craft of magic and the interests of the orders. Three of the towers were destroyed during the Cataclysm, and a fourth—the once unsurpassed Tower of Palanthas—lies cursed and empty. The only tower remaining in operation, the Tower of Wayreth, now serves as headquarters of the Mages of High Sorcery and repository of their greatest secrets.

THE TEST OF HIGH SORCERY

An apprentice mage who seeks to join one of the three orders must first pass a trial known as the Test of High Sorcery. Every mage's test is different, tailored to both the order they wish to join and their own personal challenges and aspirations. Nonetheless, a few elements are always present.

Lethal Failure. The primary purpose of the test is to weed out those who would misuse magic. Every test is designed so failure means death. There is no judge, no score, and no chance of surviving a failed test.

Magical Acumen. A mage must wield magic with competence, creativity, and control. Every test requires a mage to use the most advanced magic they've learned—and, sometimes, to push beyond it.

Test of Character. The mages of the Conclave need to know the apprentice will honor the laws of their order, no matter the circumstance. To this end, the test confronts an apprentice with bitter moral and emotional choices as well as magical challenges.

Illusion and Reality. Friends, enemies, and loved ones might appear in the test, along with all manner of hazards and puzzles. The applicant has no way of knowing which challenges are illusory and which are real. In some cases, the test has lasting consequences for an applicant's life beyond the order.

RENEGADE MAGES

If a spellcaster leaves or is thrown out of the Mages of High Sorcery, or they fail the Test of High Sorcery and survive, the organization's leaders forbid them from continuing to practice magic. Mages who practice magic in defiance of the Conclave are deemed renegades. Members of the robed orders are duty-bound to report and oppose such renegades. Some order members hunt renegades, seeking to punish or slay those who've defied the Mages of High Sorcery.

BACKGROUNDS

When you make a character for a Dragonlance campaign, choose one of the backgrounds in this section or select a background from the *Player's Handbook* or another source.

This section presents two new backgrounds for characters from the world of Krynn: the Knight of Solamnia and the Mage of High Sorcery.

BONUS FEATS

Whatever background you choose for a character in a Dragonlance campaign, you gain bonus feats, as detailed below. Characters involved in the War of the Lance or other conflicts on Krynn are changed by the dramatic experiences they face.

1ST-LEVEL BONUS FEAT

If you select the Knight of Solamnia or the Mage of High Sorcery background, you gain the feat specified in that background. If the background you choose doesn't provide a feat, you gain a bonus feat of your choice from the following list (a parenthesis tells you where to find the feat):

- Skilled (*Player's Handbook*)
- Tough (*Player's Handbook*)

4TH-LEVEL BONUS FEAT

At 4th level, you gain another bonus feat of your choice from either the 1st-level list above or the following list (a parenthesis tells you where to find the feat):

- Adept of the Black Robes (this chapter)
- Adept of the Red Robes (this chapter)
- Adept of the White Robes (this chapter)
- Alert (*Player's Handbook*)
- Divinely Favored (this chapter)
- Knight of the Crown (this chapter)
- Knight of the Rose (this chapter)
- Knight of the Sword (this chapter)
- Mobile (*Player's Handbook*)
- Sentinel (*Player's Handbook*)
- War Caster (*Player's Handbook*)

You gain this bonus feat at 4th level regardless of your background—even if you have the Knight of Solamnia or Mage of High Sorcery background. You must meet all prerequisites if the feat you choose has any.

KNIGHT OF SOLAMNIA

Prerequisite: Dragonlance Campaign

You have trained to be a valorous warrior known as a Knight of Solamnia. Strict rules guide your every action, and you work to uphold them as you strive to defend the weak and oppose evil. Your honor is as important to you as your life.

Skill Proficiencies: Athletics, Survival
Languages: Two of your choice
Equipment: An insignia of rank, a deck of cards, a set of common clothes, and a pouch containing 10 gp

FEATURE: SQUIRE OF SOLAMNIA

You gain the Squire of Solamnia feat (presented later in this chapter).

In addition, the Knights of Solamnia provide you free, modest lodging and food at any of their fortresses or encampments.

BUILDING A KNIGHT OF SOLAMNIA CHARACTER

Any class that has martial prowess can be a good fit in the Knights of Solamnia. Fighters and paladins make up the bulk of the knighthood's forces. Clerics (often with the War domain) can also be found among the knights' ranks.

For a more unusual take on a Knight of Solamnia character, consider playing a bard of the College of Valor (or the College of Swords from *Xanathar's Guide to Everything*) or a barbarian devoted to the ideals of the nature god Habbakuk (perhaps adopting the Path of the Zealot from *Xanathar's Guide to Everything*).

A KNIGHT OF SOLAMNIA
OF THE ORDER OF THE SWORD

EKATERINA BURMAK

Knight of Solamnia Trinkets. When you make your character, roll once on the Knight of Solamnia Trinkets table instead of on the Trinkets table in the *Player's Handbook* for your starting trinket.

KNIGHT OF SOLAMNIA TRINKETS

d6	Trinket
1	A flat silver disk you record your heroics upon
2	A piece of a fallen knight's armor
3	A pendant featuring a crown, a rose, or a sword
4	The pommel of your mentor's sword
5	A meaningful favor from someone you defended—perhaps a handkerchief or glove
6	A locket with a sketch of a silver dragon inside

MAGE OF HIGH SORCERY

Prerequisite: Dragonlance Campaign

Your talent for magic came to the attention of the Mages of High Sorcery, an organization of spellcasters that studies magic and prevents its misuse. You've trained among the Mages, but whether you'll face the dangerous test required to become a full member of the group remains to be determined. Your passion for studying magic has likely already predisposed you toward one of the organization's three orders: the benevolent Order of the White Robes, the balance-pursuing Order of the Red Robes, or the ruthless Order of the Black Robes.

In the world of Krynn, many refer to the Mages of High Sorcery as the Wizards of High Sorcery. The organization accepts more than wizards, though, with sorcerers, warlocks, and other spellcasters included among their ranks.

Skill Proficiencies: Arcana, History
Languages: Two of your choice
Equipment: A bottle of colored ink, an ink pen, a set of common clothes, and a pouch containing 10 gp

FEATURE: INITIATE OF HIGH SORCERY
You gain the Initiate of High Sorcery feat (presented later in this chapter).

In addition, the Mages of High Sorcery provide you with free, modest lodging and food indefinitely at any occupied Tower of High Sorcery and for one night at the home of an organization member.

BUILDING A MAGE OF HIGH SORCERY CHARACTER
Mages of High Sorcery are typically sorcerers, warlocks, or wizards and might have any subclass. Spellcasters who gain their magic through devotion are less likely to be welcomed among the traditionalist mages. Nevertheless, the Mages of High Sorcery are shrewd, and they rarely let unique opportunities or individuals pass them by. Even members of martial classes who train in magic might find a rare place among the group's three orders.

Mage of High Sorcery Trinkets. When you make your character, roll once on the Mage of High Sorcery Trinkets table instead of on the Trinkets table in the *Player's Handbook* for your starting trinket.

MAGE OF HIGH SORCERY TRINKETS

d6	Trinket
1	An unopened letter from your first teacher
2	A broken wand made of black, red, or white wood
3	A scroll bearing an incomprehensible formula
4	A purposeless device covered in colored stones that can fold into various enigmatic shapes
5	A pouch or spellbook emblazoned with the triple moon symbol of the Mages of High Sorcery
6	A lens through which you can see Krynn's invisible black moon, Nuitari

FEATS

This section introduces feats related to the Knights of Solamnia and the Mages of High Sorcery, along with a general feat available to characters seeking a special divine connection. These feats are available to you whenever you normally choose a feat, and they follow the feat rules in the *Player's Handbook*.

ADEPT OF THE BLACK ROBES

Prerequisite: 4th Level, Initiate of High Sorcery (Nuitari) Feat

You chose the moon Nuitari to influence your magic, and your ambition and loyalty to the Order of the Black Robes have been recognized, granting you these benefits:

Ambitious Magic. You learn one 2nd-level spell of your choice. The 2nd-level spell must be from the enchantment or necromancy school of magic. You can cast this feat's 2nd-level spell without a spell slot, and you must finish a long rest before you can cast it in this way again. You can also cast this spell using spell slots you have of the appropriate level. The spell's spellcasting ability is the one chosen when you gained the Initiate of High Sorcery feat.

Life Channel. You can channel your life force into the power of your magic. When a creature you can see within 60 feet of you fails a saving throw against a spell that deals damage that you cast, you can expend a number of Hit Dice equal to the level of the spell. Roll the expended Hit Dice and add them together. The damage that the creature takes increases by an amount equal to that total.

ADEPT OF THE RED ROBES

Prerequisite: 4th Level, Initiate of High Sorcery (Lunitari) Feat

You chose the moon Lunitari to influence your magic, and your dedication to maintaining the balance between all things has been recognized by the Order of the Red Robes, granting you these benefits:

Insightful Magic. You learn one 2nd-level spell of your choice. The 2nd-level spell must be from the illusion or transmutation school of magic. You can cast this feat's 2nd-level spell without a spell slot, and you must finish a long rest before you can cast it in this way again. You can also cast this spell using spell slots you have of the appropriate level. The spell's spellcasting ability is the one chosen when you gained the Initiate of High Sorcery feat.

Magical Balance. When you make an attack roll or an ability check and roll a 9 or lower on the d20, you can balance fate and treat the roll as a 10. You can balance fate in this way a number of times equal to your proficiency bonus, and you regain all expended uses when you finish a long rest.

ADEPT OF THE WHITE ROBES

Prerequisite: 4th Level, Initiate of High Sorcery (Solinari) Feat

You chose the moon Solinari to influence your magic, and your oath to use magic to make the world a better place has been recognized by the Order of the White Robes, granting you these benefits:

Protective Magic. You learn one 2nd-level spell of your choice. The 2nd-level spell must be from the abjuration or divination school of magic. You can cast this feat's 2nd-level spell without a spell slot, and you must finish a long rest before you can cast it in this way again. You can also cast this spell using spell slots you have of the appropriate level. The spell's spellcasting ability is the one chosen when you gained the Initiate of High Sorcery feat.

Protective Ward. When you or a creature you can see within 30 feet of you takes damage, you can use your reaction to expend a spell slot and weave protective magic around the target. Roll a number of d6s equal to the level of the spell slot expended and reduce the damage the target takes by the total rolled on those dice + your spellcasting ability modifier.

DIVINELY FAVORED

Prerequisite: 4th Level, Dragonlance Campaign

A god chose you to carry a spark of their power.

You learn one cantrip of your choice from the cleric spell list and one 1st-level spell based on the alignment of your character, as specified in the Alignment Spells table below. You also learn the *augury* spell.

ALIGNMENT SPELLS

Alignment	1st-Level Spell
Evil	Choose one 1st-level warlock spell
Good	Choose one 1st-level cleric spell
Neutral	Choose one 1st-level druid spell

You can cast the chosen 1st-level spell and the *augury* spell without a spell slot, and you must finish a long rest before you can cast either of these spells in this way again. You can also cast these spells using spell slots you have of the appropriate level.

Your spellcasting ability for this feat's spells is Intelligence, Wisdom, or Charisma (choose when you select this feat).

In addition, you can use a holy symbol as a spellcasting focus for any spell you cast that uses the spellcasting ability you choose when you select this feat.

INITIATE OF HIGH SORCERY

Prerequisite: Dragonlance Campaign, Sorcerer or Wizard Class or Mage of High Sorcery Background

You've received training from magic-users affiliated with the Mages of High Sorcery.

Choose one of the three moons of Krynn to influence your magic: the black moon, Nuitari; the red moon, Lunitari; or the white moon, Solinari. You learn one cantrip of your choice from the wizard spell list and two 1st-level spells based on the moon you choose, as specified in the Lunar Spells table.

LUNAR SPELLS

Moon	1st-Level Spell
Nuitari	Choose two from *dissonant whispers*, *false life*, *hex*, and *ray of sickness*
Lunitari	Choose two from *color spray*, *disguise self*, *feather fall*, and *longstrider*
Solinari	Choose two from *comprehend languages*, *detect evil and good*, *protection from evil and good*, and *shield*

You can cast each of the chosen 1st-level spells without a spell slot, and you must finish a long rest before you can cast them in this way again. You can also cast the spells using any spell slots you have.

Your spellcasting ability for this feat's spells is Intelligence, Wisdom, or Charisma (choose when you select this feat).

KNIGHT OF THE CROWN

Prerequisite: 4th Level, Squire of Solamnia Feat

You are a Knight of Solamnia aligned with the Order of the Crown, a group that extols the virtues of cooperation, loyalty, and obedience. You excel in group combat and gain these benefits:

MAGES OF HIGH SORCERY OF THE ORDERS
OF THE BLACK, RED, AND WHITE ROBES

Ability Score Increase. Increase your Strength, Dexterity, or Constitution score by 1, to a maximum of 20.

Commanding Rally. As a bonus action, you can command one ally within 30 feet of yourself to attack. If that ally can see or hear you, they can immediately make one weapon attack as a reaction. If the attack hits, the ally can roll a d8 and add the number rolled as a bonus to the attack's damage roll. You can use this bonus action a number of times equal to your proficiency bonus, and you regain all expended uses when you finish a long rest.

KNIGHT OF THE ROSE

Prerequisite: 4th Level, Squire of Solamnia Feat

You are a Knight of Solamnia aligned with the Order of the Rose, a group known for leadership, justice, and wisdom. Your resolve grants you these benefits:

Ability Score Increase. Increase your Constitution, Wisdom, or Charisma score by 1, to a maximum of 20.

Bolstering Rally. As a bonus action, you can encourage one creature you can see within 30 feet of yourself (you can choose yourself). If the target can see or hear you, the target gains temporary hit points equal to 1d8 + your proficiency bonus + the ability modifier of the ability score increased

by this feat. You can use this bonus action a number of times equal to your proficiency bonus, and you regain all expended uses when you finish a long rest.

KNIGHT OF THE SWORD

Prerequisite: 4th Level, Squire of Solamnia Feat

You are a Knight of Solamnia aligned with the Order of the Sword, a group devoted to heroism and courage. Bravery steels your spirit, granting you these benefits:

Ability Score Increase. Increase your Intelligence, Wisdom, or Charisma score by 1, to a maximum of 20.

Demoralizing Strike. Once per turn, when you hit a creature with a weapon attack roll, you can attempt to frighten that target. The target must make a Wisdom saving throw (DC equals 8 + your proficiency bonus + the ability modifier of the score increased by this feat). On a failed save, the target is frightened of you until the end of your next turn. On a successful save, the target has disadvantage on the next attack roll it makes before the end of its next turn. You can use this benefit a number of times equal to your proficiency bonus, and you regain all expended uses when you finish a long rest.

LINDA LITHEN

Membership in Knightly Orders

Knights of Solamnia are only ever members of one of their organization's orders. In the course of their training, most knights begin as members of the Knights of the Crown and then move on to join other orders. Whether a character follows this path or another, they retain what they learned as a member of an order even if they join another. Characters can change what knightly order they're a part of, but they always have access to any Knight of Solamnia feats they've acquired.

Squire of Solamnia

Prerequisite: Dragonlance Campaign, Fighter or Paladin Class or Knight of Solamnia Background

Your training in the ways of the Knights of Solamnia grants you these benefits:

Mount Up. Mounting or dismounting costs you only 5 feet of movement.

Precise Strike. Once per turn, when you make a weapon attack roll against a creature, you can cause the attack roll to have advantage. If the attack hits, you roll a d8 and add the number rolled as a bonus to the attack's damage roll. You can use this benefit a number of times equal to your proficiency bonus, but a use is expended only if the attack hits. You regain all expended uses when you finish a long rest.

Sorcerer Subclass

A sorcerer has the Sorcerous Origin feature, which offers you the choice of a subclass. The following option is available when making that choice: Lunar Sorcery.

Lunar Sorcery

On many worlds, the moon is a revered celestial body with magical properties. On Krynn, the gods of magic are associated with the world's three moons. On the world of Toril, the god Selûne uses the light of the moon to battle darkness. On Eberron, scholars of the Draconic Prophecy decipher ancient secrets from the waxing and waning of that world's twelve moons.

You or someone from your lineage has been exposed to the concentrated magic of the moon (or moons) of your world, imbuing you with lunar magic. Perhaps your ancestor was involved in a druidic ritual involving an eclipse, or maybe a mystical fragment of a moon crashed near you. However you came to have your magic, your connection to the moon is obvious when you cast sorcerer spells—perhaps making your pupils glow with the color of a moon from your world, causing spectral manifestations of lunar phases to orbit you, or some other effect.

Lunar Embodiment

1st-Level Lunar Sorcery Feature

You learn additional spells when you reach certain levels in this class, as shown on the Lunar Spells table. Each of these spells counts as a sorcerer spell for you, but it doesn't count against the number of sorcerer spells you know.

Lunar Spells

Sorcerer Level	Full Moon Spell	New Moon Spell	Crescent Moon Spell
1st	*shield*	*ray of sickness*	*color spray*
3rd	*lesser restoration*	*blindness/deafness*	*alter self*
5th	*dispel magic*	*vampiric touch*	*phantom steed*
7th	*death ward*	*confusion*	*hallucinatory terrain*
9th	*Rary's telepathic bond*	*hold monster*	*mislead*

Whenever you finish a long rest, you can choose what lunar phase manifests its power through your magic: Full Moon, New Moon, or Crescent Moon. While in the chosen phase, you can cast one 1st-level spell of the associated phase in the Lunar Spells table once without expending a spell slot. Once you cast a spell in this way, you can't do so again until you finish a long rest.

Moon Fire

1st-Level Lunar Sorcery Feature

You can call down the radiant light of the moon on command. You learn the *sacred flame* spell, which doesn't count against the number of sorcerer cantrips you know. When you cast the spell, you can target one creature as normal or target two creatures within range that are within 5 feet of each other.

Lunar Boons

6th-Level Lunar Sorcery Feature

The current phase of your Lunar Embodiment can affect your Metamagic feature. Each Lunar Embodiment phase is associated with certain schools of magic, as shown here:

Full Moon. Abjuration and divination spells
New Moon. Evocation and necromancy spells
Crescent Moon. Divination and transmutation spells

Whenever you use Metamagic on a spell of a school of magic associated with your current Lunar Embodiment phase, you can reduce the sorcery points spent by 1 (minimum 0). You can reduce the sorcery points spent for your Metamagic a number of times equal to your proficiency bonus, and you regain all expended uses when you finish a long rest.

WAXING AND WANING

6th-Level Lunar Sorcery Feature

You gain greater control over the phases of your lunar magic. As a bonus action, you can spend 1 sorcery point to change your current Lunar Embodiment phase to a different one.

You can now cast one 1st-level spell from each lunar phase of the Lunar Spells table once without expending a spell slot, provided your current phase is the same as the lunar phase spell. Once you cast a lunar phase spell in this way, you can't do so again until you finish a long rest.

LUNAR EMPOWERMENT

14th-Level Lunar Sorcery Feature

The power of a lunar phase saturates your being. While you are in a Lunar Embodiment phase, you also gain the following benefit associated with that phase:

Full Moon. You can use a bonus action to shed bright light in a 10-foot radius and dim light for an additional 10 feet or to douse the light. In addition, you and creatures of your choice have advantage on Intelligence (Investigation) and Wisdom (Perception) checks while within the bright light you shed.

New Moon. You have advantage on Dexterity (Stealth) checks. In addition, while you are entirely in darkness, attack rolls have disadvantage against you.

Crescent Moon. You have resistance to necrotic and radiant damage.

LUNAR PHENOMENON

18th-Level Lunar Sorcery Feature

As a bonus action, you can tap into a special power of your current Lunar Embodiment phase. Alternatively, as part of the bonus action you take to change your lunar phase using the Waxing and Waning feature, you can immediately use the power of the lunar phase you are entering:

Full Moon. You radiate moonlight for a moment. Each creature of your choice within 30 feet of you must succeed on a Constitution saving throw against your spell save DC or be blinded until the end of its next turn. In addition, one creature of your choice in that area regains 3d8 hit points.

New Moon. You momentarily emanate gloom. Each creature of your choice within 30 feet of you must succeed on a Dexterity saving throw against your spell save DC or take 3d10 necrotic damage and have its speed reduced to 0 until the end of its next turn. In addition, you become invisible until the end of your next turn, or until immediately after you make an attack roll or cast a spell.

Crescent Moon. You can magically teleport to an unoccupied space you can see within 60 feet of yourself. You can bring along one willing creature you can see within 5 feet of yourself. That creature teleports to an unoccupied space of your choice that you can see within 5 feet of your destination space. In addition, you and that creature gain resistance to all damage until the start of your next turn.

Once you use one of these bonus action benefits, you can't use that benefit again until you finish a long rest, unless you spend 5 sorcery points to use it again.

A HUMAN SORCERER DRAWS ON THE MAGIC OF KRYNN'S MOONS.

NIKKI DAWES

DRAGON HIGHMASTER KANSALDI
FIRE-EYES LEADS THE RED DRAGON
ARMY TO WAR AGAINST SOLAMNIA.

CHAPTER 2

PRELUDE TO WAR

T HE DRAGON QUEEN'S CONQUEST OF ANSALON has begun. The eastern half of the continent has already fallen, and the Red Dragon Army has tested its forces against isolated and fractious lands. The Dragon Army now turns its attention to the west—to the land of Solamnia, a nation known as the home of knights and heroes. Now, the true war begins.

Dragonlance: Shadow of the Dragon Queen tells the tale of the Dragon Army's first strike into Solamnia and thrusts a group of heroes into the path of a world-altering war. This chapter provides an overview of the adventure presented in the chapters to come, as well as details on how to further involve the characters in the plot.

OVERVIEW

Dragonlance: Shadow of the Dragon Queen is a DUNGEONS & DRAGONS adventure optimized for four to six player characters. The characters are the heroes of the story; this book describes the villains the heroes must overcome and the locations they must explore to bring the adventure to its conclusion.

This book also presents the continent of Ansalon on the planet of Krynn, home of the Dragonlance campaign setting. The introduction and chapter 1 cover broad details of the world but focus on the lands surrounding the city of Kalaman in the nation of Solamnia—the setting of the adventure presented in this book. Prominent details about the setting are covered in these sections, but the wider world is left for you to detail as you please.

Running the Adventure

To run the adventure, you need the fifth edition core rulebooks (*Player's Handbook*, *Dungeon Master's Guide*, and *Monster Manual*).

> Text that appears in a box like this is meant to be read aloud or paraphrased for the players when their characters first arrive at a location or under a specific circumstance as described in the text.

When a creature's name appears in **bold** type, that's a visual cue pointing you to its stat block as a way of saying, "Hey, DM, you better get this creature's stat block ready. You're going to need it." The *Monster Manual* contains stat blocks for most of the creatures encountered in this adventure. The rest can be found in appendix B.

Spells and equipment mentioned in the adventure are described in the *Player's Handbook* unless the text points you to appendix A. Magic items are described in the *Dungeon Master's Guide* unless the text directs you to an item's description in appendix A.

Using the Maps

This book contains a number of interior maps and a foldout poster map.

Interior Maps

Maps that appear in this book are largely for the DM's eyes only. As the characters explore locations on a given map, you can redraw portions of the map on graph paper, a wet-erase mat, or another surface to help your players visualize locations that might have unusual shapes or features. Your maps don't need to be exact replicas of the originals, and you can alter their features as you see fit. Omit details that aren't readily visible (such as secret doors and other hidden features) until the characters can detect and interact with them. Appendix E provides two maps for player use. Reproduce these maps and share them with your players as you see fit.

Poster Map

The poster map is meant to be shared with the players. It depicts the continent of Ansalon on the world of Krynn. While this adventure takes place on only one small part of this map, the lands depicted here are referenced throughout this book. Players can use this map to gain context for the adventure and to determine what lands are important to their characters.

Adventure Flow

The adventure flowchart visualizes the narrative flow of the adventure. As the DM, keep in mind the narrative goals described below as the adventure progresses. Before you begin, make sure the players are comfortable with playing in a campaign focused on war, as detailed in the "Playing War" section later in this chapter.

Chapter 2: Preludes

This chapter provides introductory elements to develop the bonds between characters and set them on the path to the community where the adventure begins. The rest of the chapter provides prelude encounters that establish important details about the world of Krynn.

Chapter 3: When Home Burns

The characters come to the village of Vogler to attend the funeral of a friend and to participate in the Kingfisher Festival, a local tradition. During the festival, a reenactment of a legendary battle goes awry when treacherous mercenaries attack. This ambush foreshadows a greater attack by the Dragon Army. The characters must help the people of Vogler escape the village before the Red Dragon Army overwhelms them.

Encourage the characters to forge connections to each other and to the earnestly hospitable people of Vogler. Many of the people the characters meet here will be their allies throughout the adventure, and the characters should have developed a relationship with the community by the time the Dragon Army attacks.

Chapter 4: Shadow of War

The characters and the people of Vogler flee to the city of Kalaman. There, the characters are conscripted to fight alongside Kalaman's troops against the Dragon Army menace. The characters and their allies defend against Dragon Army threats, culminating in a surprise attack on Kalaman by the death knight Lord Soth.

In this chapter, the characters must ally with Kalaman's military against the Dragon Army. The characters' experience in Vogler should give them personal stakes in this conflict. The characters' relationship with Kalaman's military is flexible, whether they're members of the army, special adventuring agents, or something less formal. The characters should view Kalaman and its military leadership as allies.

Chapter 5: The Northern Wastes

The characters' encounter with Lord Soth revealed the Dragon Army desires more than just conquest in the Kalaman region. In the Northern Wastes, the forces of the Dragon Queen seek a ruin called the City of Lost Names. The characters and a detachment of Kalaman's troops venture into the Northern Wastes to find the lost city and prevent whatever wickedness the Dragon Army plots.

In this chapter, the characters and their allies from Kalaman's military explore the dangerous Northern Wastes and discover the region isn't as empty as the people of Kalaman say. This part of the adventure is largely free form, and how it progresses is up to you and the players.

Chapter 6: City of Lost Names

Upon finding the City of Lost Names, the characters must infiltrate the ruin as it teems with enemy forces. There, the characters learn the Dragon Army seeks to make the ancient, magical ruin fly as it did in the distant past. The characters must find the source of the ancient city's magic and prevent Dragon Army commanders from taking control.

This chapter presents a vast ruin the characters can explore as they please while dodging the occupying Dragon Army forces. Here, the Dragon Army's plan in the Northern Wastes comes into view: to reactivate the City of Lost Names as a magical flying war machine. Use defeated Dragon Army forces and captured intelligence to direct the characters toward the Dragon Army's leaders and, potentially, the restoration of a *dragonlance* (see appendix A). Also use these forces to deter the characters from visiting the Bastion of Takhisis, which takes center stage in the next part of the adventure.

Chapter 7: Siege of Kalaman

The City of Lost Names shatters into dozens of flying pieces. One of these carries an ancient temple of the evil gods into the sky. This flying citadel and the rest of the Dragon Army converge on Kalaman. The characters must aid in the city's defense, then infiltrate the flying citadel and bring it down.

This chapter pits the characters and their allies against the full might of the Dragon Army. The lead-up to the Dragon Army's attack is a great time for allies to return and support the characters. Ultimately, the characters have the opportunity to infiltrate the Dragon Army's flying citadel and destroy it. This daring operation will bring the characters face-to-face with the infamous Lord Soth and the Dragon Army commander Highmaster Kansaldi Fire-Eyes (detailed later in this chapter).

Adventure Flowchart

Chapter 2: Prelude to War

For 1st-level Characters
Before arriving in Vogler, the characters encounter strange magic, a divine vision, or something worse.

Chapter 3: When Home Burns

For 2nd- to 3rd-level Characters
The characters visit the village of Vogler and protect its people from invasion.

Chapter 4: Shadow of War

For 4th- to 5th-level Characters
Allying with the forces of Kalaman, the characters face off against the Dragon Army.

Chapter 5: The Northern Wastes

For 6th- to 7th-level Characters
The characters follow agents of the Dragon Army into a deadly wasteland in search of a magical ruin.

Chapter 6: City of Lost Names

For 8th- to 9th-level Characters
Dragon Army commanders seek to reawaken the City of Lost Names as a flying war machine. The characters must navigate the occupied ruin and try to prevent this.

Chapter 7: Siege of Kalaman

For 10th-level Characters or Higher
Armed with a flying citadel, the Dragon Army besieges Kalaman. The characters must protect the city and destroy the deadly magical weapon.

AFTER CENTURIES OF SECRECY, THE FOLLOWERS OF THE DRAGON QUEEN EMERGE PREPARED FOR WAR.

THE DRAGON QUEEN'S THREAT

Throughout this adventure, most of the characters' foes are servants of Takhisis the Dragon Queen, an evil god who seeks to conquer Krynn. Her agents are many, but her organized forces are known as the Dragon Armies. This book's introduction provides additional details on Takhisis and the Dragon Armies. As the adventure unfolds, the characters find themselves opposed by several of the Dragon Queen's agents. The characters' goal in this adventure isn't to lay low the entirety of the Dragon Armies or to stop the threat of the Dragon Queen herself. Rather, their deeds will oppose the Red Dragon Army's forces seeking to conquer the Kalaman region.

DRACONIANS

As early as the preludes later in this chapter, the characters will face the Dragon Army's secret weapon: draconians. These dragon-like monstrosities are unnatural creatures born of the Dragon Queen's foul magic. All draconians are fanatically devoted to Takhisis and want nothing more than her conquest of the world. They are utterly loyal to the Dragon Army and those who speak in their god's name. In the course of the adventure, present draconians as magical, monstrous, fanatical, and unknowable. They aren't creatures with their own goals and ambitions. Rather, they are magical manifestations of the Dragon Queen's thirst for conquest, and they wreak her will with lethal efficacy.

The various draconians of Krynn are detailed in appendix B.

KANSALDI FIRE-EYES

Dragon Highmaster Kansaldi Fire-Eyes leads a massive contingent of the Red Dragon Army. Following orders from her master, Dragon Highlord Verminaard, Kansaldi seeks to conquer Kalaman in the Dragon Queen's name. To aid in this mission, Kansaldi has ordered the black-robed wizard Lohezet to follow his research to a ruin in the Northern Wastes, where he believes a great weapon lies in wait. An array of lesser commanders supports Kansaldi's operations, including her trusted adviser, Belephaion (detailed in chapter 6), and the dragonnel-riding ace known as Red Ruin (see appendix B). The Dragon Queen has ordered the death knight Lord Soth to cooperate with Kansaldi. While

CRYSTAL SULLY

Kansaldi respects the knight's lethal efficacy, she largely leaves him to his own dreadful devices.

Kansaldi is the ultimate villain of this adventure and confronts the characters at the climax of chapter 7. Throughout the adventure, use apprehended Dragon Army soldiers and captured intelligence to reveal details about Kansaldi, primarily her fanatical devotion to the Dragon Queen, the fear and respect she commands from her troops, her tactical prowess, and her signature crimson eye.

More details on Kansaldi appear in appendix B.

LORD SOTH

As the Dragon Queen turns her ambitions toward Solamnia, she summons forth one of its foulest villains: the infamous death knight Lord Soth. This villain has allied himself with the Dragon Queen to retake his ancestral land of Nightlund and take vengeance against the hated Knights of Solamnia. However, he isn't a member of the Dragon Army or a commander of its troops. Soth and his Undead knights keep their own council and have their own agendas. The only person whose lead Soth follows is Kansaldi Fire-Eyes, and that is only because she speaks on behalf of the Dragon Queen herself.

While Lord Soth is well known in tales of the Dragonlance setting, this adventure doesn't assume the characters, or most of Kalaman's people, know the death knight's legend or expect him to be at work in the world. The characters can learn relevant details about Lord Soth throughout the adventure. Even as the characters reach their highest levels, Lord Soth likely remains too great a threat for them to defeat. Rather than presenting him as a foe to be challenged in combat, portray Soth as a terrifying example of the villains in the Dragon Queen's service—a lurking threat to be avoided. By the adventure's end, the characters will have opportunities to undermine Soth's plans and remove him from the Dragon Army's service—at least for a time.

Lord Soth's stat block appears in appendix B, and his history is summarized in chapter 4.

CHARACTER CONNECTIONS

Players should use chapter 1 to create characters connected to Krynn and, if possible, to one another. They should also each have a connection to a mutual friend named Ispin Greenshield. Ispin has recently passed away, and the characters are invited to his funeral in Vogler.

ISPIN GREENSHIELD

Before retiring to the village of Vogler, Ispin Greenshield traveled across Ansalon as a teacher, trader, and adventurer. Along the way, he forged friendships with each of the characters. Each character knows the following information about him:

- Ispin was a good-natured human adventurer from Solamnia.
- Ispin took his name from a distinctive green shield he found early in his adventuring career. He claimed the shield was magical, but it had no obvious magical properties.
- The bighearted Ispin loved telling tall tales of his travels to anyone who would listen.
- Ispin used to adventure with a human Knight of Solamnia named Becklin and a hill dwarf warrior named Cudgel. These two featured in many of Ispin's stories of fighting sea monsters and goblin raiders.
- Ispin retired from traveling years ago, becoming a permanent resident of a little-known village in Solamnia called Vogler.

The Meeting Ispin Greenshield table suggests a few ways characters might have come to know and likely respect Ispin. Players can elaborate on these connections however they'd like. Characters can use their relationship with Ispin to reinforce how they know one another.

MEETING ISPIN GREENSHIELD

d6	Experience
1	Ispin was a close friend of one of your parents. You've known him since you were a child.
2	You and Ispin defended a community from a notorious band of goblin raiders.
3	Ispin tracked you down to return something precious that a thief stole.
4	Ispin visited your homeland, bringing with him goods and stories from far-off lands. He taught you much about the world.
5	Ispin spent a season with your family and taught you swordplay, sailing, a language, or another skill.
6	You and Ispin once competed for the same person's affections, only to discover each other's friendship.

INVITATION TO A FUNERAL

Ispin Greenshield wished to have his life celebrated in a simple way, with friends from the lands he traveled joining for festivities and sharing stories. Upon Ispin's death, his friend Becklin Uth Viharin, a Solamnic knight stationed in Vogler, sought to fulfill Ispin's wish and sent each of the characters a copy of the letter presented as handout 2.1.

Each character has agreed to attend Ispin's funeral and has set off on the road to Vogler. The extent of this undertaking might vary for each character. Characters who travel by sea disembark at the port of Kalaman (detailed in chapter 4) and then travel by road to Vogler. The characters' travels are largely uneventful until the final leg of their journey (see the "Preludes" section). Chapter 3 gives characters who have not been traveling together the opportunity to reunite and share details of their journeys.

PRONUNCIATION GUIDE

The Pronunciations table highlights notable people, deities, and locations, along with how to pronounce their names. The "Introduced" column notes where in the book you can find their introduction or more details about them.

PRELUDES

This section presents three short encounters for 1st-level characters, each highlighting a unique aspect of the Dragonlance setting. These encounters focus on the following events:

"Broken Silence" heralds the gods' return and provides participating characters with a better understanding of their relationship to the gods.
"Eye in the Sky" sets participating characters on the path to becoming members of the Mages of High Sorcery (see chapter 1).
"Scales of War" reveals the mysterious draconians.

Before starting the adventure in chapter 3, review the encounters here and choose one or more to run that are relevant to characters in your group. The Prelude Overview table notes what types of characters are likely to be interested in which encounters.

PRELUDE OVERVIEW

Encounter	Focal Characters
"Broken Silence"	Clerics, druids, paladins, and other characters with god-given powers
"Eye in the Sky"	Sorcerers, warlocks, wizards, or others seeking membership in the Mages of High Sorcery
"Scales of War"	Any character

> ### WARRIORS OF KRYNN INTRODUCTION
>
> If you are using the *Dragonlance: Warriors of Krynn* board game alongside this adventure, consider playing scenario 0 in that game after completing the "Preludes" section and before proceeding with chapter 3. This scenario has no ties to the overarching adventure, but it will familiarize the players with the game before it becomes relevant in chapter 3.

RUNNING PRELUDES

The encounters in this section take place after characters have received their invitations to Ispin Greenshield's funeral. Before heading to Vogler or on their way to the village, each character should participate in a prelude encounter.

After you've determined which preludes to run, choose which characters will participate in which. Then consider how to best run each prelude you're using:

Focus on Specific Characters. Run the prelude with a spotlight on the focus characters. Consider running it with a single player or a small group of players before the adventure begins. The "Broken Silence" and "Eye in the Sky" preludes lend themselves to this.

Dear friend,

I am Becklin Uth Viharin. I've heard much about you from our mutual friend, Ispin Greenshield. It grieves me to share the news that our dear friend Ispin passed away peacefully here at his home in Vogler. May fortune and the old gods protect his soul.

Ispin's friends are holding a memorial for him in the manner he always wanted. It will take place here in Vogler on the eve of the Kingfisher Festival. I write to ask you to do Ispin one last honor and attend. Should you come, accommodations will be available at the Brass Crab.

Though the circumstances are sad, I am eager to meet you and, through our memories, to revel in the life our great friend.

Becklin Uth Viharin
Knight of the Crown

HANDOUT 2.1

PRONUNCIATIONS

Name	Pronunciation	Description	Introduced
Akhviri	AK-veer-ee	Black dragon serving the Red Dragon Army	Chapter 5
Alstare Bellis	AL-stair BELL-is	Human vampire servant of Chemosh	Chapter 7
Bakaris Uth Estide	bah-kah-RIS ooth es-TIDE	Insufferable human Solamnic noble	Chapter 4
Becklin Uth Viharin	BEK-lin ooth ve-HAR-in	Human Knight of Solamnia stationed in Vogler	Chapter 3
Belephaion	be-LEF-ee-an	Blue dragon servant of Takhisis	Chapter 6
Caradoc	kare-AH-dock	Spectral seneschal of Lord Soth	Chapter 4
Cithcillion	SITH-sil-lee-on	Elven spirit of a Silvanesti ambassador	Chapter 7
Clystran	kly-STRAN	Human explorer from Heart's Hollow	Chapter 5
Dalamar	DHAL-ah-mar	Elf mage researching the Northern Wastes	Chapter 5
Darrett Highwater	DARE-et HIGH-wah-ter	Human Knight of Solamnia in training	Chapter 3
Demelin	dem-ME-lin	Elf high mage of the city of Onyari	Chapter 6
Duskwalker	DUSK-wahl-ker	Treant guardian of the City of Lost Names	Chapter 6
Draydan	DRAY-den	Aurak draconian commander	Chapter 7
Elthar	el-THAR	Human owner of the Fishbowl in Vogler	Chapter 3
Gragonis	gra-GON-iss	Half-ogre mercenary commander	Chapter 3
Grasha Migan	GRASH-ah ME-ghan	Dwarf matron of a reclusive clan	Chapter 5
Ishvern	ish-VERN	Sea elf leader of a group of Dimernesti elves	Chapter 5
Ispin Greenshield	ISS-pin GREEN-shield	Deceased storytelling human adventurer	Chapter 3
Istar	ISS-tar	Land destroyed during the Cataclysm	Chapter 6
Jeyev Veldrews	jay-EV VELL-drews	Human mercenary scout commander	Chapter 3
Kalaman	KAL-ah-man	Walled trade city in eastern Solamnia	Chapter 4
Kansaldi Fire-Eyes	kan-SAWL-dee FIE-ur-eyes	Human commander of the Red Dragon Army forces	Chapter 2
Karavarix	kare-AH-vare-ix	Murdered gold dragon	Chapter 4
Leedara	lee-DAR-ah	Mysterious elven performer	Chapter 3
Lohezet	low-ZHET	Black-robed human mage serving the Dragon Army	Chapter 6
Loren Soth	LORE-an SAWTH	Infamous death knight	Chapter 2
Lorry Wanwillow	LOR-ee WAN-will-oh	Kender vampire	Chapter 7
Nestra Vendri	nez-TRA ven-DREE	Human leader of Kalaman's military	Chapter 4
Nezrah	NEZ-rah	Leader of Heart's Hollow, disguised bronze dragon	Chapter 5
Onyari	AWN-yar-ee	Istarian name for the City of Lost Names	Chapter 6
Paladine	PAL-ah-dine	God of rulers and guardians, Bahamut	Introduction
Ridomir Ironsmile	rid-OH-mere EYR-on-smile	Dwarf captain of the Ironclad Regiment mercenaries	Chapter 3
Solamnia	so-LAM-nee-ah	Ancient land of knights and heroes	Chapter 3
Takhisis	ta-KEE-sis	God of night and hatred, Tiamat the Dragon Queen	Introduction
Tatina Rookledust	ta-TEE-na ROO-kel-dust	Reclusive gnome inventor	Chapter 4
Than	THAWN	Gnome inventor from Vogler	Chapter 3
Vingaard	VIN-gard	Mighty Solamnic river	Chapter 3
Virruza	vee-RUE-zah	Obsessed bozak draconian at the Sunward Fortress	Chapter 5
Vogler	VOG-ler	Quaint fishing village	Chapter 3
Wakenreth	wah-ken-RETH	Ruined elven monument	Chapter 5
Wersten Kern	WER-sten KERN	Undead standard bearer of Lord Soth	Chapter 7
Wyhan	WHY-an	Human black-robed Mage of High Sorcery	Chapter 4
Yalme	YALL-me	Human keeper of the Brass Crab in Vogler	Chapter 3
Yearkal	YEAR-kal	Sea elf servant of Habbakuk	Chapter 5
Zanas Sarlamir	ZHAN-as sar-LAH-meer	Deceased human Knight of Solamnia	Chapter 4
Zhelsuel	ZHEL-soo-el	Elf leader of a group of Silvanesti mages	Chapter 5

Focus on the Group. Run the prelude for a group of characters. These characters meet during their travels and participate in the encounter together. The "Scales of War" prelude lends itself to this.

Throughout these preludes, mentions of "characters" refer to those characters who are the focus of the prelude. Characters can participate in preludes that don't focus on them; they just won't gain a divine connection as a result of participating in the "Broken Silence" prelude or a relationship to the Mages of High Sorcery in the "Eye in the Sky" prelude if they don't want to join that organization.

Once you've run any preludes you deem appropriate for your group, all characters advance to level 2. After this, proceed with chapter 3.

BROKEN SILENCE

For hundreds of years, the world of Krynn has been bereft of those who call upon the favor of the gods. Legends say deities turned away from the world after the Cataclysm, and the prayers of the few who remember them have been met with silence ever since. But that silence is now being broken. A chosen few hear the call of the gods and awaken to their power. This prelude suits characters who hear that calling and respond to it.

RUNNING THIS PRELUDE

Characters in this prelude can come from any background. Perhaps they're discovering the gods for the first time, or they might be steadfast followers. Characters who draw their magic from gods won't have access to spells or magical class features until the end of the encounter, as this prelude details a meeting with their deity. Characters with no special interest in serving a deity might participate in the "Scales of War" prelude instead.

The prelude unfolds in a surreal, dreamlike situation where characters can follow a divine calling to learn about their deity's goals and become one of their chosen. You may alter any of this prelude's elements to better match individual gods' virtues and identities.

Before you begin, make sure any players involved have chosen gods for their characters. Krynn's deities and their provinces are listed in this book's introduction.

VISIONS OF DIVINITY

This prelude focuses on characters who have been experiencing a recurring vision that comes to them in times of great turmoil or doubt. This vision might be a recent occurrence or something they've been experiencing for a long time, possibly since childhood.

The read-aloud text below describes such a vision. You can add details that correspond to each character's deity. For example, a character who worships Sirrion might find the surrounding forest aflame, while a character called by Paladine might notice the fallen soldier's eyes turning into pools of silver.

Read or paraphrase the following text to describe the vision the characters have been having:

> You stand at the center of a forest clearing. Clashing steel echoes from the thicket beyond. As you look around, you realize piles of bodies cover the ground. One of the fallen clutches something against their chest. You're not sure what it is, but you feel the urge to reach for it. Before you can, the object glows and then flashes with intense light.

The characters wake after having the vision and find nothing out of the ordinary. They realize the object in the vision was an amulet. The amulet bears a design they might not recognize, but is the symbol of the god the character's player chose during character creation. The echoes of battle don't mean anything in particular to the characters but feel like a bad omen.

LOST AND FOUND

Prior to the vision, the characters were traveling to Vogler and had stopped to camp or rest near a forested path. After experiencing the vision, the characters wake to find their camp sacked and some of their belongings missing. The characters are the only creatures in the camp; no one else who might have been traveling with them is in sight.

A character who examines the surroundings finds a trail of food, cloth, and discarded trinkets that leads into the brush. A few hundred feet away, the characters find their belongings discarded in the middle of the forest. Nothing is missing or damaged. There is no sign of what brought the characters' possessions here.

Mysterious Symbol and Temple

Among their belongings, the characters find an item that closely matches the amulet from their visions. As in the vision, the characters might feel inexplicably drawn to the item. If the characters have different gods, they each find a holy symbol for their chosen deity. As soon as a character touches the amulet, a pulse of divine energy ripples from them, causing the amulet to vanish from their hands. The pulse flattens the surrounding vegetation, creating an unnatural clearing similar to the one in the characters' visions. The cleared plants also reveal overgrown ruins nearby:

> A crumbling stone structure lies among the undergrowth. Its roof is pierced by the trunk of an immense tree, but its walls are mostly intact. A large, empty doorframe leads inside.

Characters who don't approach the ruin feel supernaturally drawn toward the place, as if a familiar voice were calling their name. As characters approach the door, they hear faint voices inside.

Read the following text when the characters enter the ruin:

> The tree visible from outside breaks through the ruin's marble floor and stretches through the collapsed ceiling. Around it, broken statues line the remaining walls, standing in crumbling alcoves.

The statues were once larger-than-life depictions of several of Krynn's deities, but most of them are ruined. A character who succeeds on a DC 12 Intelligence (Religion) check can identify as many of the statues as you deem appropriate. The character instantly recognizes the statue of the god whose symbol they just found.

Divine Manifestation

Soon after the characters enter the room, a faint glow begins emanating from the statue of the god whose symbol they just discovered. The glow coalesces around the ruined statue, creating a spectral semblance of what the statue looked like in the past. Depending on its nature, the holy symbol might also appear somewhere on or near the statue, perhaps held or worn by it. If the characters have different gods, this happens to multiple statues.

Once a character approaches the statue of their deity, they hear that deity's voice in their thoughts. The deity invites the character to take the holy symbol and become their herald in the world. Use the

Kiri-Jolith, God of War, is one of many deities seeking followers to carry their faith back to Krynn.

details on Krynn's deities from the introduction to roleplay the deity. The deity wants the character to carry their power and divine message into the world now—when Krynn needs it most. The god won't elaborate on why they chose the character or why they're revealing themself now. This brief conversation allows characters to learn as much as you deem necessary about their gods, and it ends with the characters gaining access to any god-granted spells and divine class features.

Conclusion

As soon as the characters exit and leave sight of the temple, the structure vanishes.

The characters find no trace of any disturbance in their camp. If they were traveling with anyone else, their companions are waiting for them when they return. Any fellow travelers didn't notice the characters leaving the camp and have no recollection of anything strange happening.

Any attempt to return to the ruined temple fails, as if it was never there.

Eye in the Sky

The Mages of High Sorcery harness the magical power of the three moons of Krynn: Solinari the White, Lunitari the Red, and Nuitari the Black. Those blessed by the moons might show talent for magic and, with proper training, become apprentice mages. But to be accepted into one of the robed orders, a mage must officially join the Mages of High Sorcery and be subjected to the Test of High Sorcery, wherein their dedication to the magical arts is challenged. Failing the test can be deadly, but those who dare to seek magical power without passing the test are branded renegades and enemies of the Mages of High Sorcery.

Running This Prelude

The prelude focuses on characters who are apprentice spellcasters aspiring to take the Test of High Sorcery. Characters of any background are welcome, but the focal characters must be able to cast spells. Spellcasting characters with no interest in joining the Mages of High Sorcery might participate in the "Scales of War" prelude instead.

Night of the Eye

Every year and a half, the moons of Krynn align in an event known as the Night of the Eye. This prelude unfolds during one of these fateful nights, shortly before the characters head to Vogler.

Placing the Prelude

The prelude happens at the Barb, a centuries-old spire where promising apprentice mages go to test their magic. The Barb is located anywhere in the world that befits your story. It was built before the Cataclysm by the Mages of High Sorcery, but its intended purpose is lost to time. Many extradimensional spaces within it remain active, though they're accessible only during the Night of the Eye.

Trial of the Barb

The prelude begins with the characters nearing the Barb:

> Tonight is an important night. Ahead rises the Barb: a jagged, half-ruined spire of gray stone. Many who aspire to join the Mages of High Sorcery have come here to prove their magical proficiency. The Barb is usually nothing more than a ruin, its construction predating the Cataclysm. But tonight, on the Night of the Eye, when Krynn's three moons align, the ruin is alive with magic once more. Soft light shines from the archway leading into the structure.

A Spellbook Emblazoned with the Symbol of the Mages of High Sorcery

The characters know that they're here to participate in a test and that if they succeed, they'll learn the next steps to joining the Mages of High Sorcery. They also know any of the information from this prelude's introduction.

When the characters enter the Barb, read the following description to set the scene:

> The arch opens into a large atrium lit with flaming sconces and adorned by grand tapestries depicting Krynn's three moons. Doors circle the room. The light of the moons cascades through broad windows high above. At the center of the room stands a serene-looking woman with long, gray hair and red robes. She nods as you enter.

The red-robed mage is named Rovina, and she serves as the Barb's caretaker. She welcomes the characters to the atrium. She explains that the Barb is a place of ancient power where, during the Night of the Eye, magic flares to life to test would-be mages. Rovina also answers any questions the characters have about the Mages of High Sorcery (as detailed in chapter 1).

Characters who examine the tapestries recognize each of the three moons and their relation to the three orders of the Mages of High Sorcery.

A character who succeeds on a DC 10 Wisdom (Perception) check realizes that while the doors in the room should lead outside, no other entrances into the Barb were visible from the exterior.

Rules of the Trial

Rovina leads the characters to a door and shares the following information:

- To pass the night's test, the characters must face the trial in one of the tower's rooms, which are accessible only for the night.
- The trial requires magical talent but carries none of the dangers of the Test of High Sorcery. It provides a foundation for the real test.
- The goal is to complete the challenge presented in the room, implying different apprentices will face different challenges.
- The characters have until the Night of the Eye ends, at which point the rooms vanish, expelling everyone inside.

The Trial Begins

Once the characters are ready, Rovina opens a door, revealing a portal filled with swirling amber light. She directs anyone intending to face the trial to enter the portal together. If a single character is going through this prelude and you think they'd appreciate assistance, Rovina can also admit another visiting apprentice (an **acolyte**) to aid the character.

Hall of Sight

As characters pass through the door, read the following text:

> The door opens into a wide rotunda with black stone floors and walls carved with elaborate runes. The interior is empty save for a single pedestal at the room's center. Atop the pedestal, an ornate key balances on its tip.
>
> Behind you, the door you entered through vanishes. On the opposite side of the room, an identical, closed door appears.

The room is 100 feet in diameter, with a door on the wall opposite the characters and the pedestal at the center. The door is locked and can be opened only by the key at the center of the rotunda or by casting the *knock* spell on the door.

Invisible Maze. If the characters move more than 5 feet toward the pedestal, they run into an invisible wall. The wall extends to the ceiling and is part of an invisible, shifting maze that the characters must traverse to reach the key at the center. The maze is 90 feet in diameter, leaving a 5-foot gap between it and the rotunda's walls.

A character who casts *detect magic* sees the walls of the maze glow with auras of illusion and transmutation magic. Other spells that reveal invisibility, such as *faerie fire* or *see invisibility*, also reveal the walls. Characters who can see the walls can easily navigate to the maze's center. Characters who can't see the walls can still complete the test, but doing so takes an hour and requires a successful DC 14 Intelligence (Investigation) check. Characters can attempt this check again after an additional hour of effort.

Wall Carvings. The carvings on the wall around the rotunda are magical runes. A character who examines the carvings learns their meaning by succeeding on a DC 14 Intelligence (Arcana) check or by spending an hour studying them. The runes are an arcane cipher for the *knock* spell. Reading the spell from the wall allows a character to cast the spell as if they were casting it from a *spell scroll* of *knock*, except the spell on the wall isn't consumed. The characters can use this spell to open the door and complete the test.

Golden Key. Touching the key at the center causes the walls of the maze to vanish. The key can then be used to open the locked door. The key vanishes once it is used.

After completing the Trial of the Barb, an adventurer receives this scroll and instructions to take it to Wyhan in Kalaman.

CAIO E SANTOS

Conclusion

Upon completing the trial and passing through the door, the characters emerge into the atrium of the Barb. Rovina congratulates them on passing the challenge and deems their apprenticeship complete. They are now ready to take the next step on the path to becoming members of the Mages of High Sorcery.

Rovina hands each character an ornate scroll and a spellbook emblazoned with the symbol of the Mages of High Sorcery. She says the books are meant for the characters, either to use as spellbooks or to fill with their discoveries. The scrolls are meant for the mage who will lead the characters on the next step of their journey: a black-robed mage named Wyhan who resides in the city of Kalaman near Vogler. The characters have already received their invitation to Ispin Greenshield's funeral, and Kalaman is conveniently nearby.

Rovina tells the characters they must take their scrolls to Wyhan. She emphasizes that they must not open the scrolls under any circumstances, as their contents are meant for Wyhan only. More details about Wyhan and the characters' next step on the path to joining the Mages of High Sorcery can be found in chapter 4. Rovina will answer any other questions the characters have about the Mages of High Sorcery. After that, she congratulates them once more and bids them good luck on their travels.

Scales of War

An army carrying the banner of Takhisis the Dragon Queen marches to war, its ranks filled with monstrous, dragon-like beings that revel in destruction. This Dragon Army now encroaches on Solamnia, where its agents already strike beyond the nation's borders, and several farms and garrisons have been sacked.

Running This Prelude

The characters witness the aftermath of a vicious attack by draconian servants of the Dragon Army. This prelude is appropriate for characters of all backgrounds and classes.

Frantic Farmer

The prelude begins on the road to Vogler. At some point during travel, the characters encounter Rhys, a young human **commoner** who barely survived a recent attack on the caravan he was traveling with.

Read or paraphrase the following text to start this prelude:

> As you travel down the road, you hear quivering scream from around the next corner. "Please, help!" a young man shouts as he rushes around a bend ahead and races toward you.

This young man is Rhys. He's terrified and barely coherent in his frantic pleas for help. If a character spends a minute trying to calm Rhys down, he finally realizes he's not being chased by anything. Once this happens, Rhys reveals the following information:

- Rhys works at a nearby farm and was hired by a group of soldiers to travel with them and care for their horses.
- Rhys doesn't know much about the soldiers. He heard them talk about enemy troops supposedly afoot in the region.
- Just moments ago, the soldiers Rhys was with were attacked by black-cloaked figures.
- Rhys didn't get a good look at the cloaked attackers. He hid in the brush and escaped while the soldiers fought them off.

If the characters are visibly armed, Rhys urges them to help the soldiers, fearing his employers might fall against their attackers. He can lead the characters to where the caravan was attacked, about a half mile down the road.

Rhys doesn't know this, but the soldiers who hired him weren't merely solders—they were Knights of Solamnia who were deployed to investigate reports of recent attacks by strange creatures in the region.

Fallen Caravan

Rhys leads the characters down the road. Once they approach the place where Rhys and the soldiers were ambushed, Rhys refuses to go any farther. He tells the characters the soldiers should be just ahead.

The ambush site is a few hundred feet ahead. Read the following text when the characters arrive:

> A wrecked wagon lies toppled, surrounded by armored corpses. Strange figures pick through the remains. From beneath the figures' dark cloaks jut scaly wings and sharp, reptilian features

The mysterious raiders are a **kapak draconian** and four **baaz draconians** (see appendix B for both stat blocks). They wear armor emblazoned with the symbol of Takhisis, which any character can recognize by succeeding on a DC 12 Intelligence (Religion) check.

A TERRIFYING NEW ENEMY INFILTRATES THE SHADOWS OF SOLAMNIA: DRACONIANS.

OLIVIER BERNARD

If the characters want to remain hidden, have them roll Dexterity (Stealth) checks against the kapak draconian's passive Wisdom (Perception) score of 13. If the draconians don't notice the characters, they pick the wagon clean of valuables and leave shortly after.

If the draconians notice the characters, the kapak draconian orders two of the baaz draconians to attack, then slips away with the other two into the surrounding forest. The baaz draconians are battered from the fight with the knights and have half their normal hit points. The retreating draconians won't fight the characters under any circumstances; they have orders to immediately rejoin the Dragon Army elsewhere and report on the knights' fate.

Murdered Knights. By the time the characters arrive, the three soldiers who hired Rhys have been killed. They are beyond the aid of a *revivify* spell. A character who examines the dead soldiers' armor and succeeds on a DC 12 Intelligence (History) check recognizes them as Knights of Solamnia.

If the characters search the remains, they find correspondence that states the knights were investigating reports of nearby farmsteads being raided by strange creatures that match the draconians' descriptions.

Treasure. The three soldiers each wear plate armor with filigree and horned helmets distinctive to Knights of Solamnia, but each suit bears vicious claw marks that make it unusable. Among the wreckage are also three longswords, eight days of food and water for one person, and 40 gp.

CONCLUSION

Shortly after the draconians are defeated, Rhys rejoins the characters and asks them what those monsters were. He has no idea, and the characters likely don't either. This is one of the first times draconians have made their way into Solamnia, but it won't be the last.

If battle turns against the characters, another group of travelers can be heard approaching on the road. Not wanting to risk a larger fight, the wounded draconians retreat, leaving the characters to be saved by these travelers, who are also headed to Vogler.

CHAPTER 3

WHEN HOME BURNS

A T THE EDGE OF THE SOLAMNIC PROVINCE OF Hinterlund lies the quiet fishing village of Vogler. Home to humans, kender, and hill dwarves, Vogler is the last stop on the road to nowhere. To the village's north, scattered woods and shady brooks give way to the deadly badlands known as the Northern Wastes. Across the Vingaard River to the south stretches a land of grim legends and opportunity: the province of Nightlund, whose nearby port of Kalaman welcomes traders from long-forgotten lands. Vogler's people know little of the evil afoot in the world. On the day the characters arrive, the people of Vogler are concerned with two things: kicking off the annual Kingfisher Festival and putting a local hero to rest.

Before running this chapter, make sure each character has a reason for attending the funeral of Ispin Greenshield and experienced a fateful event during their journey to Vogler, as detailed in chapter 2.

RUNNING THIS CHAPTER

The events of this chapter unfold in two parts. First, the characters are introduced to the quaint village of Vogler during its annual Kingfisher Festival, where they meet many of the town's inhabitants. Familiarize yourself with the "Vogler Gazetteer" section in this chapter, which introduces many of the people and places in the town.

In the second part of the chapter, war comes to Vogler. The characters must survive a mercenary company's betrayal and ultimately help the townsfolk flee an invasion by the Red Dragon Army.

CHARACTER ADVANCEMENT

In this chapter, level advancement is handled as follows:

- The characters start this chapter at 2nd level, having gained a level after the events in chapter 2.
- They advance to 3rd level after the Battle of High Hill.
- They advance to 4th level at the end of the chapter, after evacuating Vogler.

Arriving in Vogler

The characters arrive on the day of Ispin Greenshield's funeral, which is scheduled to take place in the evening. Read or paraphrase the following text when you're ready for the adventure to begin:

> The fishing village of Vogler clings to a spit of land reaching into the Vingaard River. Wooded cliffs overlook the community, and the only path from the north descends past the ivy-covered remnants of a crumbling stone keep. The village's modest wooden buildings cluster around a quaint central circle and along the riverbank.
>
> Jutting into the river—out of place and seemingly out of time—stands an incomplete stone bridge of incredible artisanship. The structure clearly dates to before the Cataclysm, eclipsing its modern peers in size and sturdiness. The bridge crosses less than half the river's width before giving way to a series of ropes and tethered rafts serving as ferries.
>
> On the river itself, dozens of small boats drift along the slow, murky waters as the fishers of Vogler ply their trade.

The characters can explore Vogler as they please. Individuals or small groups could peruse the market, observe villagers preparing for the Kingfisher Festival, or find the rooms that—per their invitations—await them at the Brass Crab.

Use the "Vogler Gazetteer" section to help characters get acquainted with the village. Once they're done exploring it, they should meet at the Brass Crab for the funeral. From there, proceed with the "Final Farewell" section.

Vogler Gazetteer

The Solamnic village of Vogler rests at the foot of a partially built bridge on the Vingaard River. Fishers, lumberers, hunters, and farmers live here peacefully, only occasionally interrupted by bandits or predators from the Northern Wastes. In addition to a volunteer militia maintained by Mayor Raven Uth Vogler, the village is ostensibly under the protection of Hinterlund's capital, Maelgoth. This protection takes the form of a retired Knight of Solamnia, Becklin Uth Viharin, who's stationed at the crumbling Thornwall Keep—now more a historic landmark than a true fortification.

The Kingfisher Festival

The characters' visit to Vogler overlaps with the kickoff of the Kingfisher Festival, an annual celebration commemorating Solamnia's victory over the forces of Istar during a clash near the town centuries ago. The festival takes its name from the kingfisher, a symbol of the Knights of Solamnia and a bird the fishers of Vogler consider lucky. Festivities culminate with the locals' reenactment of the Battle of High Hill, a clash between Istarian and Solamnic soldiers.

Locations in Vogler

While in Vogler, the characters might visit any of the locations in this section. These sites are marked on map 3.1.

The Brass Crab

The Brass Crab is a modest single-story inn on the village wharf, and its exterior vaguely resembles its namesake. Its proprietor, an Ergothian woman named Yalme (neutral good, human **commoner**), has an odd love of bad storytellers and inept musicians. One wall of the circular common room features a faded mural of two enormous crabs locked in combat, inlaid with brass details. The mural's origins are lost to time, but if asked, Yalme says she named the crabs Fancy and Gorgeous George. Four short halls branch off the common room, each lined with rooms for rent.

The Fishbowl

After a long day on the river, many of Vogler's fishers gather at the Fishbowl to tell tales, quench their thirst, and indulge in baked fish pies. The cramped but well-kept tavern is known for its savory baked goods more than its weak ale. The Fishbowl's proprietor is the elderly Elthar (neutral good, human **commoner**), whom most locals call Uncle.

High Hill

High Hill stands a mile north of Vogler. Centuries ago, Solamnic and Istarian forces clashed here, and legends claim the spirits of fallen knights haunt the hill and watch over the town. Each year, the Kingfisher Festival's reenactment of the battle serves as a reminder of the village's history and nominally honors any spirits lingering at the battlefield.

Market

Across from Vogler's busy wharf spreads the village market. Amid this collection of stalls, vendors sell fresh river fish, fishing supplies, crafts, the bounty of local farms, and all manner of mundane equipment. One notable stall is that of Froswin (chaotic good, kender **commoner**), who sells intricate fishbone puppets she designs in the shapes of animals and sea serpents.

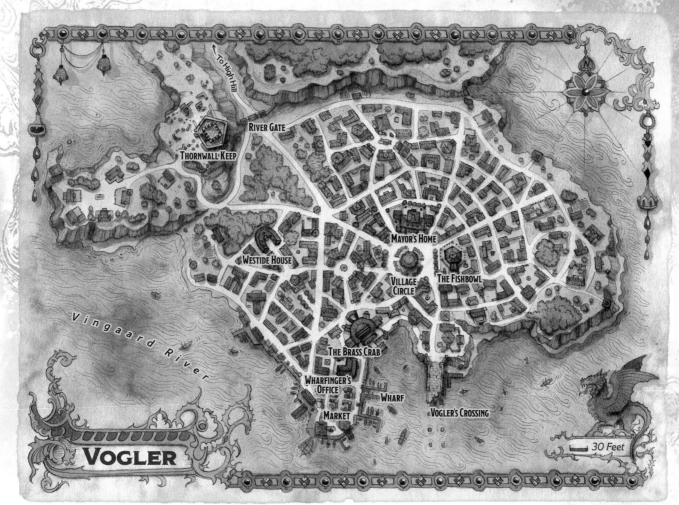

MAP 3.1: VOGLER

MAYOR'S HOME

Vogler's down-to-earth mayor, Raven Uth Vogler (neutral good, human **scout**), lives in a two-story house on the village circle. Raven is a practical, empathetic leader in her thirties who grew up on the river. She keeps a pair of guest rooms—lavishly decorated with mounted fish—where she frequently hosts villagers going through tough times.

MERCENARY CAMP

Along the road north of Vogler, a mile past High Hill, lies a mercenary camp. Known as the Ironclad Regiment, the soldiers here are under the command of Captain Ridomir "Cudgel" Ironsmile (introduced in the "Final Farewell" section). Cudgel is a friend of the deceased Ispin Greenshield and many others in town, and she brought her company to Vogler a week ago to attend Ispin's funeral. She volunteered her band to take part in the annual reenactment of the Battle of High Hill—her attempt to lift the village's spirits after their loss.

During the day, Cudgel remains in the camp with her lieutenants—the half-ogre Gragonis and the human Jeyev Veldrews—along with several dozen mercenaries. The soldiers spend most of the day participating in drills. At night, they keep

to themselves, lounging and playing dice. They're under strict orders from Cudgel not to interfere with the locals.

RIVER GATE

Those who enter Vogler from the north pass through the unguarded River Gate, a 15-foot-tall wooden archway carved with two leaping fish on its frame. Over the years, locals have etched the coin-sized scales of these fish with prayers for bountiful fishing. Two large wooden doors stand within the arch, but they haven't been closed for years and are embedded in the surrounding dirt.

THORNWALL KEEP

The ruins of an ancient Solamnic keep perch on a rocky rise at the western edge of town. Thornwall Keep's steward, the knight Becklin Uth Viharin (introduced in the "Final Farewell" section), maintains the keep. Partially ruined walls surround the keep's three-story tower. The tower's ground level holds a small library and a collection of local relics: over forty pieces of rusty tools and armor. The second floor holds the quarters of Becklin's squire, Darrett Highwater (introduced in the "Parting Gift" section later in this chapter). Becklin's austere room lies on the uppermost story; from there, a ladder leads to the keep's crenelated roof.

Vogler's resident tinker gnome, Than, built an elaborate catapult-like contraption on the roof of the keep. A friend of Becklin and Darrett, Than occasionally drops by to fine-tune this device, called a gnomeflinger (detailed in appendix A). Though it looks like a weapon of war, the contraption is a mode of rapid transportation originally devised by the tinker gnomes of Mount Nevermind. Becklin tolerates the gnomeflinger—and the noise of Than's occasional early-morning tinkering—because she sees the catapult-shaped device as a deterrent against attack.

VILLAGE CIRCLE

The homes and shops in Vogler cluster around a grassy patch shaded by an ancient tree. This green is encircled by a dirt road that branches off into streets leading north out of the village and south to the ferry across the Vingaard, and others radiating out into the town. The village circle serves as a public space, meeting spot, and festival ground. An iron bell hangs atop a tall pole near the mayor's house. In times of need, anyone who vigorously rings the bell summons the mayor and 2d12 volunteer militia members (**guards**) who arrive in about 5 minutes. The local militia is largely composed of retired farmers and fishers who exhibit more zeal than skill in the village's defense, but they all take the bell's sounding very seriously.

VOGLER'S CROSSING

South of Vogler, an incomplete stone bridge begins to stretch across the Vingaard River. Half-constructed before the Cataclysm using techniques lost in the ages since, the bridge looks like a glorified pier—a remnant of once-promised glory. A simple ferry system of ropes and winches follows the bridge's supports and connects with posts on the opposite shore. Simple rafts and skiffs allow travelers and even small wagons to cross the river. The process is safe but slow, taking approximately 10 minutes for a raft to cross the broad river. Travelers can make use of the crossing themselves or hire a ferrier to aid them for 1 sp.

WESTIDE HOUSE

The horseshoe-shaped structure known as Westide House is only slightly larger than the other homes in Vogler, but its owner speaks of it as if it were an opulent country manor. This is the home of Lord Bakaris Uth Estide (neutral evil, human **noble**; detailed in chapter 4) and his son, Bakaris the Younger (introduced in the "Heckler" section later in this chapter). Lord Bakaris is a Solamnic noble who claims to be living in exile after raiders burned his family home in Estwilde. In truth, Lord Bakaris and his son were driven from the region and sought anonymity in Vogler. They've been in the village for over a year, throwing their wealth around and treating the people of Vogler as backward yokels.

WHARF

Local fishers crowd these docks each dawn and dusk, rowing out with empty nets and returning with the day's catch. At the end of the southernmost pier, a centuries-old wooden post bears an eroded carving of a bird with a fish in its mouth. Many locals rub it for luck before seeking the morning catch. A cleric of Habbakuk or a character who succeeds on a DC 12 Intelligence (Religion) check recognizes the carving as a phoenix—a symbol of the god Habbakuk, deity of animal life and the sea.

WHARFINGER'S OFFICE

Wharfinger Umpton Lanth (lawful neutral, human **guard**) wakes up earlier than any other fisher in Vogler to inspect boats docked at the wharf and impose fines on those in poor repair. Fishers and traders seeking to use the wharf must register with Umpton at his stuffy two-story office across from the market. The office is usually staffed by Umpton's son Nesau (chaotic neutral, human **commoner**), who—to his father's consternation—is quick to forgive fines and forgo docking fees when his father isn't present, making him quite popular in the village.

FINAL FAREWELL

Once the characters have reconnected with one another and explored Vogler to their liking, it's time to assemble at the Brass Crab for the funeral of Ispin Greenshield. Becklin Uth Viharin, who sent the characters their funeral invitations, catches up to the characters prior to the funeral.

MEETING BECKLIN

Becklin is hard to miss, as she's dressed in the full-plate armor and horned helmet of the Knights of Solamnia. Though she's never met the characters before, she recognizes one or more of them from Ispin's descriptions. Becklin introduces herself, offers her condolences, and invites the characters to come with her to the Brass Crab if they aren't already there. She explains that the service is meant to be a celebration of Ispin's life, and people will be encouraged to share over-the-top stories about him—like the inflated tales he was known for sharing.

BECKLIN UTH VIHARIN

Becklin Uth Viharin (lawful good, human **knight**) is a Solamnic Knight of the Order of the Crown who, in her earlier years, adventured with Ispin Greenshield and Cudgel Ironsmile. For the last decade, she has served as castellan of Thornwall Keep in Vogler. This posting is not only an official charge from her superiors but also a quiet retirement for her. Becklin takes her role seriously, maintaining her skills and equipment as she remains alert for danger. In her considerable free time, she indulges her passion for studying the past by excavating the ruins of Thornwall Keep.

The region's commonfolk generally don't hold the Knights of Solamnia in high regard, most believing the knights had a hand in causing—or, at least, not preventing—the Cataclysm. However, the people of Vogler accept Becklin, as her skill at arms has kept the village safe from bandits and dangerous beasts for years.

Personality Trait. "Did you know Vogler was an island before the Cataclysm? Let me tell you about it!"

Ideal. "We can learn much from the past if we look for it."

Bond. "My honor was my life. It's still important to me, but no code accounts for all the challenges of living."

Flaw. "I romanticize the past. That's when people had the chance to become legends."

SENDING OFF A FRIEND

The funeral takes place at dusk on the stage and dock extending from the rear of the Brass Crab. Becklin encourages the characters to linger near the dock, while many mourning locals in small fishing craft assemble in the nearby water. When you're ready for the funeral to begin, Becklin takes the stage next to a simple boat, within which rests the body of Ispin Greenshield. Read or paraphrase the following:

> Those who were closest to Ispin Greenshield gather on the dock overlooking the Vingaard River. There, Ispin's body rests in a small boat, his body wrapped in a shroud. A musician plays a soft song as the knight Becklin Uth Viharin steps forward in her ornate Solamnic armor. She smiles gently at those assembled, and her voice carries clearly across the water.

BECKLIN UTH VIHARIN

LAUREN WALSH

CUDGEL IRONSMILE AND
BECKLIN UTH VIHARIN SEND OFF
THEIR FRIEND ISPIN GREENSHIELD.

> "You all knew Ispin as a friend, and there were
> none like him. Before he died, he told me this: 'There
> should be tales, not tears, for an old scoundrel like
> me. Make sure everyone knows my stories when I
> head off on the greatest adventure of them all.'"
>
> Becklin nods, and villagers carry the boat containing
> Ispin's body to the dock's edge, where she and Cud-
> gel lowered it into the water. "So, let us do just that,"
> Becklin continues as the tiny vessel drifts out onto the
> Vingaard River. "On the eve of the Kingfisher Festival,
> we celebrate you, Ispin. Good travels, friend. Until we
> meet again."

With that, the boat bearing Ispin's body drifts down
the river and eventually out of sight. After a moment
of silence, Becklin invites all assembled into the
Brass Crab for a reception and opportunity to share
stories about the departed.

TALES REMEMBERED

The funeral reception is a simple but crowded affair.
Yalme, the Brass Crab's proprietor, keeps bread,
cheese, and local ale coming for the dozens of attendees. Practically everyone in the village makes
an appearance at the reception, and the characters
can find anyone they've already met in the village
with whom they might want to talk.

Soon after the reception begins, Becklin calls
for everyone's attention and shares one of Ispin's
favorite stories: the tale of the time the High Sub-
Senior Artillerist of Mount Nevermind launched her
pet weasel all the way from the gnome enclave to
Sancrist Island, then hired Ispin to recover the crit-
ter—or, at least, to note its trajectory. Becklin tells
several other charming stories about Ispin, then invites attendees to share other tales Ispin might have
told them.

Characters are invited to participate in this comic
tale telling. They're welcome to improvise their
own tales about Ispin, taking cues from what they
know about their relationship with the adventurer
(as determined in chapter 2). The crowd nods along
to nearly any tale a character tells, whether hearing
it for the first or the thousandth time. If you or a
player wants a story prompt, roll on or choose an
option from the Ispin's Stories table. Award inspiration to characters who tell a particularly creative or
touching story.

LAUREN WALSH

ISPIN'S STORIES

d6	Story
1	For three days, a trireme crewed by minotaur pirates had been chasing Ispin's ship across the Blood Sea of Istar, when finally ...
2	Ispin spent the night in a roc's nest high in the Vingaard Mountains, but when the sun rose ...
3	The Lord of Palanthas ordered Ispin arrested after the adventurer shaved the lord's twin Solamnic poodles, but Ispin talked his way out of it by ...
4	Ispin weathered a week locked in the dungeons of the mountain dwarf nation of Kayolin, but he secured his release by promising to ...
5	One night, Ispin shared a campfire with a befuddled old man who disappeared before dawn, never to be seen again. Ispin always remembered the strange advice the traveler offered ...
6	Once, Ispin saved an entire village by using his shield to ...

HECKLER

During the storytelling, after one or two characters or others have told tales, a finely dressed local named Bakaris the Younger lets out an exaggerated yawn. If left to continue, he eventually blurts out, "We've heard this a thousand times!" or "You're telling it worse than he did!" Bakaris cares nothing for Ispin's death or the locals' mourning—he's only here for the free ale, which he claims is the worst he's ever tasted. The other mourners grumble, but nobody directly confronts the heckler.

Establishing Bakaris. Use this interaction to establish Bakaris the Younger as a cowardly cad. He and his father are local annoyances, and they'll further antagonize the characters later in the adventure. This encounter with Bakaris shouldn't come to violence, but it should give the characters an accurately negative impression of him.

Confronting the Heckler. A character who confronts Bakaris the Younger can convince him to stay quiet by roleplaying or succeeding on a DC 12 Charisma (Intimidation or Persuasion) check. After any confrontation, Bakaris the Younger scoffs and complains no one in Vogler can take a joke, then leaves of his own volition.

BAKARIS "THE YOUNGER" UTH ESTIDE

Bakaris (neutral evil, human **noble**) shares the same name as his father, his father's father, and so on for generations. Bakaris places inordinate value on his good looks, fashionable clothes, and athleticism, but he's known more for his arrogance, pettiness, and short temper. He cares nothing for his

family name, but he defers to his father—partly from unbroken childhood habit, and partly because all his privilege depends on his father's wealth. Bakaris also has a violent streak. While living in Estwilde, he murdered the son of a local leader during a duel, and he and his father to Vogler to escape the consequences. Bakaris takes quiet pride in that killing, and he fantasizes about one day winning respect via the point of his sword. He loathes being called "the Younger," a diminutive his father encourages.

Personality Trait. "My blood, my looks, my skill; everything about me is better than you."

Ideal. "I'll force the world to recognize how great I am."

Bond. "I've wasted too much time already; I owe it to myself to claim what I deserve."

Flaw. "What I can't get with my looks, I'll take with my sword."

MEETING CUDGEL

During the funeral reception, Ridomir "Cudgel" Ironsmile jovially introduces herself to the characters as an old friend of Ispin Greenshield and the leader of the Ironclad Regiment—mercenaries currently camped outside Vogler. Cudgel asks the characters how they knew Ispin and where they traveled from. She talks openly about herself and her plans to participate in tomorrow's reenactment of the

BAKARIS THE YOUNGER

ROBSON MICHEL

Battle of High Hill. Cudgel has no agenda other than to chitchat with out-of-town guests, as they likely have more in common with her than the local fishers. Early in the evening, Cudgel excuses herself to check on her company at the mercenary camp (detailed in the "Vogler Gazetteer" section).

RIDOMIR "CUDGEL" IRONSMILE

Cudgel Ironsmile (neutral, hill dwarf **veteran**) hails from the dwarven nation of Kayolin, south of Solamnia. For most of her life, she adventured with Becklin and Ispin, earning the nickname Cudgel along the way. She now commands her own company of mercenaries known as the Ironclad Regiment. Though small, the company has built a reputation for beating the odds, thanks in large part to her adroit leadership. Beyond a life of fighting, the middle-aged dwarf is a gifted card player. She also has a soft spot for Vogler, which she swears serves the best fish pies in Solamnia.

Personality Trait. "The person with the loudest voice usually wins the argument."

Ideal. "I like a well-thought-out plan, but a well-executed one is sublime."

Bond. "Money motivates, but the right cause inspires."

Flaw. "I can be slow to leave the comforts of an inn or tavern."

MYSTERIOUS MOURNER

A particularly somber guest—a blue-skinned Silvanesti elf named Leedara—keeps to the fringes of the reception. No one in town knows anything about her except her name, that she arrived a day before the characters, and that she claims to be a performer who knew Ispin. Characters who approach Leedara find her politely aloof and evasive about how she knew Ispin—yet she expresses sympathy for the characters, claiming she's lost many loved ones in her long life. A character can convince Leedara to perform by succeeding on a DC 16 Charisma (Persuasion) check, in which case she sings a heartbreakingly beautiful Silvanesti song in Elvish. Soon after, Leedara leaves the reception, retiring to her room in the inn.

Leedara has a role to play later in the adventure (see chapters 4 and 7). Use this scene to introduce this mysterious character, but don't reveal anything of her agenda (detailed below).

LEEDARA

Leedara died during the Cataclysm over three hundred years ago. Once an elven priest, Leedara witnessed her companion and fellow priest, Isolde, drawn into the grim fate of the wicked Knight of Solamnia, Lord Loren Soth (detailed in chapter 4). When Soth failed his gods-given quest to prevent the Cataclysm, he became cursed to exist forever as a death knight. As part of his curse, Leedara and several of her companions returned as deathless spirits devoted to ensuring Soth never finds peace.

Leedara has spent centuries tormenting Lord Soth in his accursed castle, Dargaard Keep, endlessly reminding him of his failures and losses. Now that the Dragon Queen has summoned Soth, Leedara works to stymie the death knight however she can. She followed Soth's trail to this area and is in Vogler looking for ways to subtly oppose him.

Leedara is neutral-aligned and typically appears as a living Silvanesti elf. She has the statistics of a **ghost** with the following action:

Change Shape. Leedara magically assumes the appearance she had in life, and her creature type changes to Humanoid, while retaining her other game statistics. This transformation ends if Leedara is reduced to 0 hit points or uses an action to end it.

AFTER THE FUNERAL

After each character who wants to has shared a story or mingled with the locals, the reception winds down. Before the characters retire for the evening, Becklin approaches, thanks them for coming, and says she has something Ispin left for them. She won't say what it is but asks the characters to call on her at Thornwall Keep in the morning.

PARTING GIFT

The morning after Ispin's funeral, the characters can take Becklin up on her invitation to Thornwall Keep. They have plenty of time to visit in the morning, as the Kingfisher Festival celebrations don't kick off until midday.

MEETING DARRETT

As the characters head across town toward Thornwall Keep, they meet Becklin's squire, Darrett Highwater, along the way. Read or paraphrase the following:

> The town is abuzz with festive energy this morning as locals set up stalls and hang decorations. Ahead, the road to Thornwall Keep climbs a low hill toward an ancient edifice, ghostly in the morning mist.
>
> "Good morning, Becklin's friends," comes a cheerful voice. "I'm glad I caught you." From a shop doorway steps a young man, no more than twenty years old. He has a sword at his hip and a cloth sack in his arm. "I'm Darrett, Becklin's student. I hope you haven't had breakfast already."

Darrett Highwater is Becklin's pupil, though Becklin would refers to him privately as her squire. As much as Darrett respects Becklin and hopes to one day become a true Knight of Solamnia, he knows the people of Vogler frown on the knighthood and would see his aspirations as naive fantasies.

Becklin sent Darrett to fetch baked hand pies from the Fishbowl for the two of them and their guests. He encourages the characters to come with him on his errand. Darrett gets few opportunities to speak with travelers and is eager to do so, but he doesn't press if the characters want to go straight to Thornwall Keep.

If the characters join him on the short walk, Darrett tells them he grew up in Vogler. He peppers the characters with questions about themselves, their travels, their weapons, and anything else about the world beyond Vogler. He knows all about the Kingfisher Festival and shares the following details:

- The annual festival celebrates the victory of a Knight of Solamnia, Lord Decater Vogler, over the forces of the Empire of Istar. This battle occurred hundreds of years ago, long before the Cataclysm, and sparked the village's founding.
- Today's festivities include music, food, and games associated with the town's founding.
- Mercenaries of the Ironclad Regiment—Cudgel Ironsmile's band—are training Vogler's small militia. They're also participating in a reenactment of the Battle of High Hill this afternoon.

Once Darrett stops at the Fishbowl and purchases hand pies for everyone, he leads the characters to Thornwall Keep.

Establishing Darrett. Throughout this adventure, Darrett will be the characters' earnest friend and ally. He's clever, eager to please, and a little starstruck by the characters. He always has their best interests in mind. Portray him as reliable and with whatever quirks your players are likely to find charming. Establish Darrett's trustworthiness now so the characters know they can rely on him when it matters later.

DARRETT HIGHWATER

Darrett Highwater (lawful good, human **knight**) is a fastidious, aspiring knight who serves Becklin Uth Viharin. His parents abandoned him in town over a decade ago, after which Darrett spent years as a ward of the community before coming under Becklin's wing. In the years since, his good heart and aptitude for strategic thinking led Becklin to train him for induction into the Knights of Solamnia one day. Darrett is well-read and courteous, though he sometimes catches himself talking in ways he considers less than knightly, for which he apologizes profusely.

DARRETT HIGHWATER

Personality Trait. "My mind sometimes works faster than I can talk, and I often second-guess myself."

Ideal. "My honor is my life."

Bond. "As Becklin's student, I'm trying to learn everything I can from such a hero."

Flaw. "Though I understand military strategy, I'm inexperienced at command and have a hard time delegating."

THORNWALL KEEP

> Veins of bronze-colored ivy cling to Thornwall Keep's ancient three-story stone tower, the tallest structure in Vogler. From its crenelated roof rises an elaborate device resembling a catapult. Crumbling ruins of walls and other fallen structures surround the keep, and amid them lie several shallow square pits and covered excavation sites.

Though it's no longer a working fortress, Thornwall Keep remains a sturdy structure and an emblem of Vogler's past. As the characters arrive, Becklin meets them at the door in a simple shirt and breeches, welcoming them inside to her first-floor library.

If Darrett is with the characters, he distributes the hand pies he bought for breakfast. If he's not, he arrives soon after the characters and does the same. Becklin readily makes small talk about the keep, the excavations she's conducting on the grounds, and the device on the roof—all detailed in the "Vogler Gazetteer" section.

THE GREEN SHIELD

After their breakfast, Becklin steps away to her quarters for a moment. When she returns, read the following:

> Becklin reenters the room carrying a shallow wooden box, approximately three feet to a side. She sets it down gently on a table. "Ispin left this for all of you," she explains. "But it comes with a condition. Since he won't be attending the Kingfisher Festival this year, he wanted you all to participate for him. Specifically, he hoped you'd take his place during the reenactment of the Battle of High Hill. Every year, he looked forward to participating—and dying—in an even more ludicrous way than the year before."
>
> Becklin smiles at the memory as she opens the box, revealing a round green shield.

The box contains Ispin's signature shield, a *+1 shield* carved with a scarred broadleaf tree and painted a mossy green. The characters all recall hearing Ispin's story of being given the shield by a unicorn in the far-off forest of Darken Wood. None can say if this is true or another of Ispin's tall tales.

Becklin gives the characters the shield only if at least one of them agrees to participate in the Battle of High Hill reenactment. She leaves it to the group to decide which character keeps the shield or how they share it.

If the characters have been pleasant, Becklin is happy to chat some more before she tells them she has to prepare for the Kingfisher Festival. Darrett eagerly suggests going to the festival alongside the characters.

THE KINGFISHER FESTIVAL

When the characters return to town after visiting Thornwall Keep, the Kingfisher Festival is in full swing. Happy villagers drift from their homes toward the sounds of laughter and upbeat music at the village circle. The characters arrive at the center of town, by following either Darrett's lead or the flow of traffic, just in time to hear Mayor Raven Uth Vogler address the crowd:

> Colorful banners and paper decorations shaped like kingfishers decorate the village circle. Temporary stalls sell food and colorful crafts, and in the center of the circle, an ancient tree provides shade for happy picnickers. From a temporary stage, a band of local musicians brings a spirited song to a close as Mayor Raven Uth Vogler takes the stage.
>
> "Welcome, friends!" the mayor begins, raising her arms high. "Welcome to the Kingfisher Festival!"
>
> Cheers and applause fill the circle. The mayor smiles widely. "Today is a day of not only revelry but also reflection. We are all here thanks to the courage of heroes who came before us. Let us honor our founders, our family, and all those who can't be here to celebrate today. Enjoy your festival, Vogler, with good spirits, good times, and good friends! And look to the kingfishers for good luck!"
>
> An energetic round of cheers follows the mayor's words. With that, the Kingfisher Festival is officially underway.

Vogler's village circle is the heart of the Kingfisher Festival's events. Here, townsfolk share food and drink while a rotating series of enthusiastic local musicians take to the stage and encourage the crowd to dance. From the various stalls in the circle, characters can buy a variety of fish-filled pastries, sweet drinks, and kingfisher-shaped crafts for 3 cp each.

FESTIVITIES

Traditional Kingfisher Festival events commemorate Vogler's founding and history. Characters might participate in an annual competition, the season's inaugural fish catch, where fishers try to catch the biggest fish during a set period. Darrett and other friendly locals encourage the characters to participate.

Characters can also carouse in the village circle, volunteer to perform on the festival stage, or socialize with locals. Any villager from the "Vogler Gazetteer" section might interact with the characters at the festival.

Whenever you please, transition to the "Battle of High Hill" section.

FISH CATCH

Traffic flows steadily from the village circle to the wharf. Here, the fish catch pits amateur fishers against the community's best anglers, all competing to catch the largest fish. Characters who go to the wharf are invited to participate in this popular event and, if they accept, are lent fishing poles and bait.

THE PEOPLE OF VOGLER CELEBRATE DURING THE KINGFISHER FESTIVAL.

At the end of each 30-minute contest, participants are given charming but valueless trophies; bragging rights are the real prize at stake.

Should characters choose to participate, they find one of Vogler's best fishers, Mayor Raven, is in their group, along with a dozen other locals. Read the following description when the characters have their fishing gear prepared and are ready to start:

A fishing pole resting on her shoulder, Raven takes her place as one of the competitors and beckons other participants to line up with her along the docks. "It's time to find out who among us kingfisher fisherfolk is the fisher king!" the mayor says as she casts her line into the Vingaard River. The competitors receive her pun with good-spirited groans and laughter, then cast their lines as well.

Running the Contest. The contest plays out in three 10-minute rounds. After a character spends 10 minutes fishing, roll on the Fish to Catch table to determine whether a fish tugs on their line and, if so, the DC of the Wisdom (Survival) check required to catch it. The character then makes a Wisdom (Survival) check, catching the fish if they succeed and losing it if they fail. A character has advantage on this check if they brought their own fishing gear to the contest rather than borrowing gear. If a character fails this check by 10 or more, they are pulled into the water and are out of the contest.

Repeat these rolls for every 10 minutes a character participates in the fish catch. After 30 minutes, the contest ends and a winner is determined.

FISH TO CATCH

d20	Catch DC	Fish
1–3	—	No fish
4–7	8	Tiny river eel (1 ft. long)
8–11	10	Tiny cuirassed carp (1 ft. long)
12–15	11	Mature river eel (1½ ft. long)
16–18	12	Mature cuirassed carp (3 ft. long)
19	15	Greater cuirassed carp (5 ft. long)
20	18	Benebog the Line Breaker (8 ft. long)

Benebog the Line Breaker. This enormous cuirassed carp is a Vogler legend. Even sighting Benebog is considered good luck, and catching it makes a fisher an instant town legend. Benebog can be caught only once. If a character rolls a 20 on the Fish to Catch table after Benebog has been caught, a greater cuirassed carp tugs on their line instead.

Contest Winner. The winner is determined by totaling the length of all fish each participant caught.

LINDA LITHEN

Mayor Raven's catch totals 7 feet, followed by a villager whose catch totals 5 feet. The participant with the highest total is the winner. Participants then receive prizes.

Contest Prizes. All contest participants receive tiny wooden carvings of kingfishers, while the winner receives their choice of a blue knit cap or a fishing fly made from blue feathers. These prizes are charmingly made but have no significant value. Should a character catch Benebog, the mayor gives the character an exceptionally crafted fishing pole carved with kingfishers, worth 50 gp. Additionally, for the rest of the day, the villagers laud the character with congratulations and free drinks.

Repeat Contests. Characters can participate in the fish catch as many times as they like. On future rounds, the best villager catches fish totaling 1d4 + 3 feet. Mayor Raven doesn't participate again.

Bad Sport. Lord Bakaris drinks heavily during the festival and spends much of his time on the wharf, watching the fish catch and grumbling about how boring it is. He stands near the most competent-looking character participating in the contest and mockingly asks why they enjoy such a ridiculous pastime. (The "Castle Kalaman" section in chapter 4 presents more information on roleplaying Lord Bakaris.) For as long as Lord Bakaris is present, the character he's haranguing has disadvantage on Wisdom (Survival) checks made during the fish catch. Characters can make Lord Bakaris go away by roleplaying or succeeding on a DC 14 Charisma (Intimidation or Persuasion) check.

BETRAYAL AT HIGH HILL

The Kingfisher Festival culminates in the annual reenactment of the Battle of High Hill, held at a hill located about a 30-minute walk north of the village. The reenactment, which also serves as a drill for Vogler's militia, is followed by a feast at the Brass Crab.

The event is scheduled to begin in the afternoon. About an hour before, Mayor Raven rallies Vogler's militia in the village circle. The militia then leads a haphazard parade from town to High Hill, followed by dozens of spectators and a wagon filled with drinks for participants.

Darrett, Becklin, or another villager finds the characters as the parade begins and encourages the party to walk with them. If the characters agreed to honor Ispin's last wishes, they easily find the other participants gathering at High Hill, either at the direction of this villager or by following momentum from the parade.

BEHIND THE BATTLE

This year's reenactment is a little different than in past years. Should the characters chat with Darrett or other locals during the walk to High Hill, they learn the following information:

- This mock battle reenacts the Knights of Solamnia's ancient victory over enemy forces from the eastern nation of Istar. The battle was led by Lord Vogler, a noble knight and the village's founder.
- This year, Mayor Raven arranged for a friend of the town, the mercenary leader Cudgel Ironsmile, to participate. Cudgel's Ironclad Regiment is playing the part of the invading Istarian forces. The mayor claims it's a happy coincidence Cudgel's band was in the area during the event.
- Mayor Raven has given the village's militia a lot of attention recently. Some villagers think she hired Cudgel to visit Vogler and help with this event—possibly because of vague rumors of war in the east. With trained mercenaries on the opposing side, this year's reenactment could be more of a challenge for the militia than in past years.

BETRAYAL

Unbeknownst to anyone in the village, Cudgel's lieutenant in the Ironclad Regiment—Gragonis (neutral evil **half-ogre**) has betrayed his leader. He has paid off many of the mercenaries under his command, and with the exception of Cudgel and a few mercenaries who aren't attending the reenactment,

RAVEN UTH VOGLER

the entire company secretly plans to attack lethally during the mock battle

Agents of the Red Dragon Army—part of the greater army waging war in eastern Ansalon—hatched this plan when they learned the mercenaries would join in the mock battle. The commanders of the Red Dragon Army bought Gragonis's loyalty, and they seek to take Vogler quickly as part of a greater scheme.

A contingent of the Red Dragon Army slipped into the lands near Vogler and crossed the Vingaard River in recent days. The draconians the characters might have encountered in chapter 2 were part of this force. If Vogler can be taken by the traitorous members of the Ironclad Regiment, all the better. If it can't, the Dragon Army plans to bring its own devastating forces to bear.

PREPARING FOR BATTLE

When the characters and people of Vogler arrive at High Hill, read the following description:

> Passing through woods and fields, Vogler's parade of militia members and reenactment spectators finally reaches High Hill. The grassy slope is spotted with trees and crumbled stone fencing. Near the base, several dozen soldiers in matching armor stand in even formation. The contrast is striking between these mercenaries of the Ironclad Regiment and Vogler's militia—with their mismatched armor and crooked helmets—but it does nothing to dampen the spirits of those assembled for the Kingfisher Festival's climactic reenactment.

The parade follows a trail to the top of the hill, where Mayor Raven and Cudgel Ironsmile meet and discuss final preparations for the event. Soon, reenactment participants and spectators break up, with the former taking up wooden weapons while the latter settle down to watch the reenactment.

Encourage all characters to participate in the reenactment, if for no other reason than to honor Ispin Greenshield's last wishes. If a character refuses, Mayor Raven offers to pay them 5 gp to be a judge during the battle, making sure no one uses real weapons and calling for aid if someone gets hurt.

To prepare for the battle, Mayor Raven calls out to those assembled, explaining the mercenaries will charge up the west side of the hill while the militia and other participants charge down. The two groups will clash midway in a mock fight, with the mercenaries' Istarian forces eventually retreating. Participants are encouraged to use their own armor but are given wooden spears with padded tips to

prevent them from dealing damage. The mayor reminds everyone not to use real weapons during the reenactment so nobody gets hurt.

Mercenaries of the Ironclad Regiment use the **guard** stat block. Members of the Vogler militia also use the **guard** stat block, but their spears are padded and deal no damage.

BATTLE BEGINS

When the characters are ready, Darrett or a militia member guides them into line with the other Vogler troops. Read the following description:

> After much laughter and jostling, the mayor, Cudgel, and other spectators walk to a nearby vantage to watch. As they do, the militia takes up its position atop High Hill—the same hill Solamnic troops held centuries ago. They face the mercenaries of the Ironclad Regiment at the base of the hill, arrayed as the forces of Istar once were. Although the event is only a reenactment, a tingle of excitement fills the field. Somewhere on the line, a reenactor hoots and yells, "Let's send those Istarian rats running!"
>
> A moment later, a trumpet blast signals the start of the battle. "For Istar!" yells the mercenaries' leader, a tall half-ogre among several mounted soldiers. The mock Istarian troops assault the hill. Around you, the Vogler militia charges to meet them.

As the two groups charge, have each character make a Wisdom (Perception) check. The character who rolls the highest notices the sun glinting off the mercenaries' spear tips and their half-ogre leader gesturing with a steel axe. Regardless of how the characters react to this, it's too late to stop the attack. The mounted mercenaries lead their forces in a charge up the hill. When they clash with the militia members, an actual battle begins.

BATTLE OF HIGH HILL

> The unexpected sound of metal clashing on armor rings across the field, silencing laughter and melodramatic boasts. A ribbon of red splashes over the grassy hill, followed by shocked screams. Any pretense of a reenactment shatters—High Hill is the site of a true battle once more. Within moments, all around you, armed mercenaries attack unprepared villagers fighting for their lives.

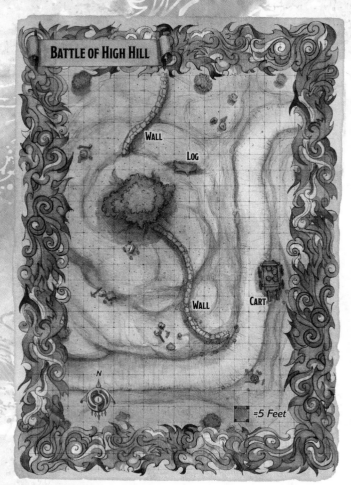

BATTLE OF HIGH HILL

WALL

LOG

WALL

CART

N

=5 Feet

MAP 3.2: BATTLE OF HIGH HILL

The characters find themselves in the middle of a battlefield. Map 3.2 depicts the characters' location during the conflict; they start the battle adjacent to the log at the north of the map. The "High Hill Battlefield Features" and "High Hill Battlefield Events" sections note elements of this battle.

The characters have little opportunity to aid the villagers being attacked as three hostile mercenary **guards**, each mounted on a **warhorse**, appear on the road at the southwest edge of the battlefield and focus their attacks on the characters.

If Darrett or another well-liked NPC accompanied the characters to the hill, they may be wounded during combat but should survive the battle. Other spectators, like Mayor Raven and Cudgel, are far enough away that they won't reach the battlefield until after the fight ends.

After these mercenaries are defeated, proceed with the "Gragonis Arrives" encounter.

HIGH HILL BATTLEFIELD FEATURES
The battlefield, shown on map 3.2, has the following features:

BATTLEFIELD ENCOUNTERS
The "Battle of High Hill" section presents the first of several battlefield encounters in this adventure. These are events that take place on active battlefields. During these scenes, the wider battle is abstracted, allowing the characters focus on specific, tide-turning conflicts.

At the edge of each mapped battlefield encounter and beyond is a region called the Fray. The Fray is an interpretation of the dangers of combat, from clashing combatants to deadly spells. It is also the source of additional threats. Each battlefield encounter explains the Fray's effects and presents additional dangers that might occur at the end of each round of combat. A battlefield encounter ends when noted in the text.

Fray. The 15-foot-wide area marked by the design at the edge of the map represents dozens of clashing combatants. This area and the battlefield beyond the map are difficult terrain. A creature that enters the Fray for the first time on a turn or starts its turn there must succeed on a DC 16 Dexterity saving throw or take 7 (2d6) slashing damage from opportunistic foes. The Fray can't be damaged and remains until the battle ends.

Wall and Cart. Both the stone walls and the supply cart are difficult terrain. They grant half cover to creatures behind them.

HIGH HILL BATTLEFIELD EVENTS
During this encounter, roll on the High Hill Battlefield Events table each round at initiative count 0. Also consider rolling on the table if a character enters the Fray or otherwise tries to leave the battlefield.

HIGH HILL BATTLEFIELD EVENTS

d4	Events
1	A volley of arrows falls on a random player character's position. That character and each creature within 10 feet of them must succeed on a DC 12 Dexterity saving throw or take 3 (1d6) piercing damage.
2	Two terrified, riderless warhorses bolt from the Fray. One random player character must succeed on a DC 14 Dexterity saving throw or be knocked prone. The horses then dash off the battlefield.
3	An injured member of Vogler's militia (a **guard** with 1 hit point) crawls onto the battlefield and begs for help, appearing in an unoccupied space adjacent to the Fray nearest a random character.
4	A hostile mercenary **guard** with 6 hit points appears in an unoccupied space adjacent to the Fray nearest a random mercenary on the battlefield. The guard takes their turn on initiative count 10.

Gragonis Arrives

As the characters prevail against the mounted guards, or whenever it feels appropriate, read or paraphrase the following:

> A hulking figure swinging a formidable battleaxe leads a band of mercenaries through the chaos. He cuts through the few remaining members of Vogler's militia as he draws closer.

The **half-ogre** Gragonis emerges at the west edge of the battlefield adjacent to the Fray, along with four mercenaries (use the **guard** stat block). As he does, he points at the most formidable-looking character and laughs to his allies, "Look here! We got one who still thinks this is all a game!" Gragonis and the mercenaries then attack.

Aftermath

After Gragonis and his four guards are defeated, the remaining mercenaries scatter and the battlefield encounter ends.

The mercenaries' retreat is further motivated by the arrival of their horrified commander, Cudgel Ironsmile, along with Mayor Raven, Becklin, and several burly spectators. The group has already seen some fighting, as treacherous mercenaries tried and failed to kill Cudgel at Gragonis's orders.

Anyone who accompanied the characters to the hill, like Darrett, also survived the battle, but almost all of Vogler's militia was wiped out.

If all the characters are defeated, Darrett or other surviving members of Vogler's militia drag them from danger and revive them. The characters awaken outside of battle with 1 hit point each just as Cudgel, Becklin, and Raven arrive.

Response

Mayor Raven thanks the characters for defending her people, fearing things would have gone far worse if they hadn't. She promises to reward the characters, but at the moment, she's focused on treating the wounded and getting everyone back to Vogler safely.

Cudgel Betrayed

As the characters and Mayor Raven speak, Cudgel Ironsmile seeks answers. While the battle was taking place, one of her own mercenaries appeared and attacked her, only to be killed by Becklin. The typically unflappable mercenary commander is livid. It doesn't take her long to find one of her mercenaries who was wounded but survived the battle—possibly Gragonis, if the characters spared him. She angrily shakes and yells at the wounded mercenary. If the characters don't act first, Mayor Raven calms Cudgel and has the traitor bound for the walk back to Vogler where they can be interrogated (see the "Mercenary Interrogation" section).

Healing the Wounded

Most of Vogler's militia died during the battle, but if the characters search for wounded, they find a few souls in need of aid. A character who succeeds on a DC 12 Wisdom (Medicine) check can bring a villager back from the brink of death. A character can also use healing magic to save a wounded villager by restoring 1 or more hit points. Any healed villager thanks their savior, giving the character a piece of jewelry or lucky charm worth 20 gp.

If a character openly uses the power of a god to save a villager, locals who see this are awed and consider it nothing less than a miracle. A villager saved in this way is particularly thankful and seeks to learn more about the character's deity.

Back to Vogler

After the wounded are tended to, Mayor Raven and Becklin urge the villagers to return to Vogler so they can organize a proper response. Raven and Becklin ask the characters to escort the villagers home safely in case of further threats, but the somber return trip to Vogler proves uneventful.

Character Advancement

The characters advance to 3rd level after the battle at High Hill.

Back in Vogler

After returning to Vogler, Mayor Raven, Cudgel, and Becklin ask the characters to join them at the Brass Crab as Darrett and other villagers tend to the wounded. The Kingfisher Festival's levity is abandoned as worried locals seek refuge or mill about the village circle, uncertain how to help.

The Brass Crab's owner, Yalme, had prepared the tavern's common room for a night of celebration, but those plans are quickly abandoned when the characters arrive with the village leaders. Mayor Raven leads the conversation, prioritizing the following points:

- Raven already instructed trusted villagers to tend to the wounded and to recover the bodies of those murdered at High Hill.
- Raven wants to understand why the Ironclad Regiment attacked. Clearly Cudgel was betrayed, but why? The captive mercenary might have answers to these questions.

- Vogler's leaders need to know whether other dangerous mercenaries are afoot.
- If one of the characters used magic—particularly healing magic or other evidence of a god's power—Raven asks if the character can use their talents to help her people.

Cudgel has only one concern: discovering the fate of the rest of her troops. She plans to return to her camp once the mercenary has been interrogated. She won't be deterred, and she refuses to let anyone go with her; if her mercenaries have betrayed her, she doesn't want anyone else walking into danger.

Let the characters pose their own concerns and plans, but ultimately the mayor urges everyone—except Cudgel—to stay in the village tonight as they try to learn more. In the meantime, Raven encourages the characters to join Cudgel in interrogating the surviving mercenary.

MERCENARY INTERROGATION

Unless the characters previously spared the life of a specific mercenary (such as Gragonis), the mercenary captured during the Battle of High Hill is a low-ranking **guard** of the Ironclad Regiment named Svilnt Sunderlit.

Mayor Raven gives Cudgel and the characters leeway in conducting the interrogation. Raven doesn't oppose the use of coercive magic, but she refuses to let anyone harm the captive. Cudgel initially tries to lead the interrogation, but she struggles to contain her anger at her betrayal. She soon retreats to watch from a distance as the characters lead things—though she occasionally interjects at particularly angering news.

The captive mercenary is brought in with their chest and arms bound by a fishing net. At first, the mercenary only mocks the characters and refuses to reveal anything but their name. By coercing the captive through roleplaying or by succeeding on a DC 12 Charisma (Intimidation or Persuasion) check, the characters learn the following information:

- Gragonis planned to kill Cudgel and take control of the Ironclad Regiment.
- Several days ago, Gragonis headed into the woods west of the mercenary camp, then returned with a considerable amount of gold.
- Afterward, Gragonis hired his most loyal mercenaries to attack the Vogler militia during the reenactment. He planned to then raid Vogler.
- The mercenary doesn't know who gave Gragonis the gold he used to pay off the mercenaries.
- A few mercenaries remained at their camp, including Jeyev, Cudgel's other lieutenant. The mercenary thinks the others at the camp are loyal to Cudgel—the ones Gragonis paid accompanied him to the reenactment.

If Gragonis is the mercenary being interrogated, he claims not to know who his benefactor was, other than they were hooded and wore black and red armor.

A TENSE EVENING

When the characters are done questioning the mercenary, the captive is placed under guard in a nearby shed. Cudgel heads out soon after, intent on verifying the mercenary's story at her camp. She promises to return by the following dawn. The "Cudgel's Report" section details what Cudgel learns.

Mayor Raven is eager to learn more about Gragonis's meeting in the woods west of town, despite not wanting anyone else to leave the village. She plans to send out local hunters in the morning, but she responds with gratitude if the characters offer to investigate the woods instead. Raven offers to send Darrett with them as a guide—a task he eagerly agrees to.

SIGHTING THE ENEMY

Either the night of or morning after the attack at High Hill, the characters (or experienced hunters from the village) head into the woods west of Vogler where Gragonis met with a mysterious sponsor. If villagers conduct this reconnaissance, they report back by midmorning with dire information, having learned everything the characters would in the following expedition.

If the characters go, they find a small wooded area an hour west of the village. A character who spends an hour searching the woods finds strange tracks. Some of these tracks are boot prints, while others are clawed reptilian feet the characters can't identify. The tracks wind north through the woods.

Following the tracks takes more than an hour, leading the characters from the woods into rugged hills. In a valley, they see the following:

> The woods give way to a ledge overlooking a shallow valley. In the distance, dozens of low fires illuminate hundreds of red tents. Among them move patrols of shadowy, humanlike figures. Over a thousand soldiers occupy the camp—a whole army.

This is a camp of Red Dragon Army soldiers. Should the characters attempt to approach the camp, a patrol of three **baaz draconians** and two **Dragon Army soldiers** draws near (see appendix B for both stat blocks). The draconians are hooded and look like Humanoid soldiers from afar, but a character who engages in melee combat with them discovers their true nature. If attacked, one draconian attempts to flee to camp and raise an alarm.

Use more draconians to prevent the characters from drawing close to the camp. Even if the camp is alerted to the characters' presence, the draconians don't follow the characters to Vogler.

Ultimately, when the characters or other scouts return to Vogler, they should have learned the following information:

- A significant military force is camped several miles northwest of the village.
- The force looks well organized and has vigilant patrols.
- The soldiers are a mix of humans and other hooded figures. If the characters encountered them up close, they know these hooded figures have wings and reptilian features.

A Fateful Morning

Mayor Raven spends the night and next morning conferring with members of the community in the common room of the Brass Crab. The morning after the battle at High Hill, two things happen:

- The characters (or local scouts) return with news of an armed camp.
- Cudgel Ironsmile returns with information from the mercenary camp.

Camp Reconnaissance

When the characters or other scouts return to Vogler, they're directed to report to Mayor Raven, who has been at the Brass Crab with Becklin and other concerned villagers all night. Raven is shocked by the report about the enemy camp. She wants to know more about the nature and disposition of this force, and she's aware Vogler can't defend itself against anything more than a few raiders. She's eager to hear advice from the characters and others about how to address this potential threat.

At the outset, Raven is inclined to draft a letter to the commander of the camp to declare Vogler's neutrality in all conflicts, ask the mysterious army's intentions, and welcome them to meet with the mayor. But before the mayor can develop a plan further, Cudgel returns.

Cudgel's Report

Cudgel Ironsmile returns to Vogler accompanied by the lieutenant of her scouts, the human Jeyev Veldrews. Cudgel shares the following information:

- She believes Jeyev and her remaining troops are loyal to her—they could have easily overpowered her if they weren't.
- On her return, Cudgel found Jeyev and other loyal mercenaries had heard of the events at High Hill. They had restrained several soldiers loyal to

Gragonis but who didn't have orders to participate in the reenactment.
- During the night, Jeyev's scouts came across a large military force to the northwest of the village, much too large and organized to be a mere mercenary band. This is the same army the characters likely spotted, and Jeyev's scouts can confirm everything from the "Sighting the Enemy" section.

Vogler's Response

Allow the characters, in consultation with the village leaders, to determine how Vogler should respond to the mysterious army. Becklin, Cudgel, and Raven take the following positions:

Becklin Uth Viharin. The knight is deeply concerned. She's heard rumors of strange armies in the east, and now there's a strange army close to her home. As the most experienced military leader in the room, she expects the worst, but she's trying not to panic anyone.

Cudgel Ironsmile. Cudgel feels responsible for everything at High Hill. She gives the village the complete support of the Ironclad Regiment. She favors a peaceful response to the mysterious army, but one backed by her mercenaries' spears.

Mayor Raven Uth Vogler. The mayor will do anything to keep her people safe. However, she wants more information before acting.

JEYEV VELDREWS

To further complicate the situation, Lord Bakaris joins the group mid-conversation, insulted that he hasn't been involved in what are clearly important discussions. However, he has no idea what the discussions are about. Bakaris cares nothing for the safety of the village, but he posits ideas that make him look important without requiring any actual effort.

Allow the characters to guide the decision of Vogler's leaders, who will largely support any plan that doesn't involve a preemptive strike or bringing battle into the village.

VOICE OF WAR

However the characters choose to respond to the army near Vogler, their plans are derailed by unexpected visitors. As the characters prepare, a messenger in black-and-red armor arrives at the River Gate. Villagers are the first to spot the messenger, and they alert the mayor and the characters.

When Mayor Raven and the characters arrive at the River Gate, read the following text:

> Beneath the carvings of leaping fish etched into Vogler's open wooden gate, a human in black-and-red scale mail sits astride an armored warhorse. She holds out a rolled parchment and calls out, "Who among you speaks for this village?"

This **Dragon Army soldier** (see appendix B) astride a **warhorse** is a messenger from the Red Dragon Army. If a character doesn't speak up first, Raven steps forward and takes the messenger's letter. The message reads as follows:

> People of Vogler,
>   By the orders of Belephaion, the Voice of Takhisis, you will quarter the soldiers of the invincible Red Dragon Army this night. Refuse and die.
>   This is the Dragon Queen's will.

Characters proficient in Religion recognize the name Takhisis as one of the gods of Krynn. A cleric of Takhisis or a character who succeeds on a DC 12 Intelligence (Religion) check recognizes a spiral symbol on the messenger's armor as a symbol of Takhisis, the greatest of the evil gods, who is also known as the Dragon Queen. This same symbol appears on all Dragon Army armor.

The messenger demands the village prepare to be occupied by Dragon Army troops that evening. In the meantime, nobody can leave the village. If the characters press the messenger for more

information, she provides none. If threatened, the soldier holds her ground and gives a signal. Atop the 30-foot-tall cliffs to the east of the gate, four **Dragon Army soldiers** appear (see appendix B). They use their javelins to attack anyone who threatens the messenger or who tries to leave the village.

Mayor Raven seeks to avoid bloodshed and encourages the characters to withdraw.

RESISTANCE

The appearance of the Red Dragon Army soldiers answers many questions about the force near Vogler. Back at the Brass Crab, Mayor Raven consults with the characters, Becklin, and Cudgel. Raven sees no other option than to do as the message demands and welcome the Dragon Army. Becklin and Cudgel immediately oppose this, having witnessed the horrors of occupying forces.

Let the characters propose plans to keep the Dragon Army at bay. If they don't suggest using the Ironclad Regiment to defend the town, Cudgel suggests it. As the mercenaries are camped north of the village, bringing them to Vogler without alerting the Dragon Army likely requires getting rid of the Dragon Army soldiers at the gate—a challenge while the soldiers hold the upper ground.

If the characters wish to sneak up on the Dragon Army soldiers, they have two options, both described in the sections that follow.

ON THE CLIFFS
The simplest way to reach the Dragon Army soldiers is to climb the northeastern cliffs and sneak up on them. Taking a boat downriver, landing, and sneaking back is also a viable option.

The area atop the cliffs is wooded, but an open field lies below and behind the soldiers' position. Scaling the 30-foot-tall cliffs is simple enough, but unless they are distracted, the soldiers notice anyone climbing the cliff or approaching from another direction. If the characters reach the top of the cliff, they find four **Dragon Army soldiers** (see appendix B).

THE GNOMEFLINGER
Thornwall Keep sits directly across from the Dragon Army soldiers' clifftop vantage. Atop Thornwall Keep sits the creation of the tinker gnome Than: a people-launching device called a gnomeflinger (described in appendix A). If using the gnomeflinger comes up, Becklin or Darrett suggests consulting with Than first.

Than is overjoyed to let the characters use the gnomeflinger. They're so delighted that they forget they also have several safety devices called nary-crashes (see appendix A). Than mentions the nary-crashes only if a character raises concerns about landing after using the gnomeflinger. Than has enough narycrashes for each character to get one.

Should the characters use the gnomeflinger, it proves surprisingly effective and quiet, allowing the characters to surprise the four **Dragon Army soldiers** (see appendix B) atop the cliffs.

DEALING WITH THE SOLDIERS

If the characters confront the Dragon Army soldiers on the cliffs, the messenger attempts to retreat to the Dragon Army camp on her warhorse rather than aiding her allies. With the Dragon Army soldiers gone, Cudgel is eager to ride out to meet her mercenaries. She plans to bring them back to a defensible position just north of the village. If the characters don't attack the Dragon Army soldiers on the cliffs, skip to the "Preparing for the Worst" section.

PREPARING FOR THE WORST

Whether the characters drive off the Dragon Army soldiers or make other plans within town, Mayor Raven eventually seeks the characters' council in determining how best to protect the villagers. During this conversation, Becklin, Cudgel, and Raven take the following positions:

Becklin Uth Viharin. Becklin has grown quiet. She wants to speak privately to the characters and Darrett after they've conferred with Mayor Raven and Cudgel (see the "Becklin's Fear" section).

Cudgel Ironsmile. Cudgel wants only to get her troops and bring them back to Vogler. Even if they're outnumbered, fighting is the only option in her mind.

Mayor Raven Uth Vogler. If the characters attacked the Dragon Army soldiers, Mayor Raven is grappling with the fact they just started a war. Otherwise, she's frustrated by the situation and seeks advice on how to protect her people by nightfall. She refuses any suggestion involving fighting in the village.

If the characters suggest they prepare to evacuate Vogler, the mayor initially dismisses the idea, but a character who succeeds on a DC 12 Charisma (Persuasion) check convinces her it's in the village's best interest. Becklin agrees and shares the information in the "Becklin's Fear" section. The mayor doesn't like it but grudgingly accepts it's the only option.

If not deterred, Cudgel and Jeyev either ride or sneak out of Vogler to rally their mercenaries.

BECKLIN'S FEAR

If the characters don't suggest preparing Vogler for evacuation, Becklin pulls them and Darrett aside for a private conversation. She shares the following concerns:

- Becklin has heard about war and unstoppable armies in the east. She fears these Red Dragon Army soldiers are part of that greater force.
- She's lived in Vogler for decades and knows its people aren't soldiers. They'd need weeks of training and a hundred more professional soldiers to stand a chance in any conflict.
- She suggests readying the villagers to evacuate at a moment's notice in case other plans fail.
- Evacuees can follow the river to safety in Kalaman (detailed below).

Becklin asks the characters to help convince Mayor Raven of this idea. If the characters already suggested this idea to the mayor, Becklin supports them, adding the points here to the argument. If both the characters and Becklin advocate for evacuating the village, Mayor Raven begrudgingly agrees.

Characters who succeed on a DC 12 Intelligence (History) check or who ask a resident of Vogler about the city of Kalaman can any of the information from the "Knowledge of Kalaman" section at the start of chapter 4.

GNOMEFLINGER

Planning to Evacuate

Once the village leaders agree to prepare for evacuation, the people of Vogler have much to do. Becklin focuses on getting information about the Red Dragon Army and shoring up local defenses. Mayor Raven asks for the characters' and Darrett's help organizing the evacuation, tasking them with the following:

- Help her inform the villagers of the situation by collecting everyone in the village circle.
- Assess how many ships the village has and roughly how many villagers they can carry.
- Instruct the villagers how to get to safety.
- Keep the villagers calm.

Mayor Raven and Darrett cooperate with any plans the characters have, as long as they clearly help prepare for escape and don't risk any villagers' lives. However, the mayor doesn't want to start the evacuation until absolutely necessary, allowing villagers time to prepare and safely evacuate together.

Informing the Villagers

The characters can easily summon most of Vogler's people to the village circle, likely by going door to door or by ringing the village circle's bell. When the villagers have gathered, Mayor Raven addresses the crowd. Read the following text:

> Colorful Kingfisher Festival decorations still cover the village circle and the festival stage. Unlike the day before, the people collected in the village center are somber, muttering in worried tones as Mayor Raven takes the stage.
>
> The mayor doesn't mince words: "A dangerous army is headed for Vogler. The Ironclad Regiment will do what it can to defend Vogler, but we must be ready to flee."
>
> Following the mayor's report, the locals stand in stunned silence. Then their questions come in a wave of shouting, anger, and fear.

With a successful DC 12 Charisma (Intimidation or Persuasion) check, the characters can help the mayor regain control of the crowd by speaking in support or explaining evacuation plans. Otherwise, it takes the mayor over an hour to placate the community and get evacuation preparations underway.

At your discretion, Lord Bakaris or Bakaris the Younger might speak out and try to undermine the mayor and the characters. If so, the villagers reject the evacuation plans until a character counters Bakaris by roleplaying or succeeding on a DC 14 Charisma (Intimidation or Persuasion) check.

Once the villagers have accepted the evacuation plans, they assist Mayor Raven, Darrett, and the characters in preparing to evacuate to Kalaman, understanding time is short.

Short Ship Supply

A character who spends an hour inspecting the ships in Vogler's wharf estimates the vessels there could transport only two hundred of the village's four hundred residents. Let the characters concoct ways to solve this problem. If they don't initially have ideas, characters can make skill checks to identify solutions like the following. A character proficient with water vehicles makes these checks with advantage.

Boat Made of Boats. A character who succeeds on a DC 16 Wisdom (Survival) check formulates a plan to use rope and rings of small boats to corral floating masses of logs, creating several large rafts capable of holding two hundred more villagers. With the help of locals, this simple plan takes three hours to complete.

Personal Fleet. If a character asks Vogler's fishers for help and succeeds on a DC 14 Charisma (Persuasion) check, the character can convince the villagers to lend their personal vessels to the evacuation: boats in need of simple repairs, boats collecting dust in villagers' sheds, and even boats serving as decorations in homes. Given two hours, the villagers can find enough boats to fit one hundred more people.

Repurposed Ferry. A character who succeeds on a DC 12 Intelligence (Investigation) check notices the ferry crossing on the Vingaard River has a series of rafts and small boats on a pulley system. The mechanism can be broken down in two hours, freeing up vessels for one hundred people.

Battle Plans

Early in the afternoon, Cudgel returns to Vogler. She shares the following information:

- Cudgel has directed the Ironclad Regiment to hold a position north of the village. The mercenaries believe they can, for a time, defend against a larger force.
- She hopes they won't have to fight. With any luck, a show of force will convince the Dragon Army that Vogler isn't an easy target.
- Just in case, her soldiers set up a small rear command tent near the River Gate. She's posted a

messenger there so the village can send word to her troops as needed.

- She asks Becklin to join her at the front. She hopes if a Knight of Solamnia appears on the field, the enemy will hesitate to provoke the knighthood.

Mayor Raven and Becklin support Cudgel's choices, and the knight agrees with her friend's plan.

Defenders of Vogler. This plan leaves the village and its escape operation undefended except for the handful of remaining militia members and a few tough fishers. Becklin and Cudgel ask the characters and Darrett to remain in the village with the mayor. They want to ensure that if any enemies get past the Ironclad Regiment, the villagers have protection.

BECKLIN'S REQUEST

During the conversation about battle plans, the character with the highest passive Wisdom (Insight) score realizes Becklin is keeping something back. She won't say anything in front of Cudgel, Mayor Raven, or Darrett, but if approached in private, she thanks the character and asks them to do her a favor. A large wooden box is under her bed in Thornwall Keep. She doesn't tell them what it holds but asks the characters to fetch the box and give it to Darrett once he safely escapes town.

The characters can easily retrieve the box from Becklin's quarters at any point before the "Invasion Encounters" section. The sturdy wooden box weighs about 70 pounds and bears no markings other than a simple kingfisher emblem on the lid. If the characters open the box, they find it holds a suit of Solamnic plate armor.

If the characters follow Becklin's instructions, they won't give the box to Darrett until after the evacuation. If they instead do so before leaving town, see the "Darrett's Armor" section in chapter 4.

THE ENEMY SIGHTED

After Cudgel has returned and the characters have organized Vogler's evacuation, a local farmer rides into the village circle. The farmer reports seeing hundreds of soldiers on the road, headed toward Vogler. The adventure unfolds in one of two ways from here:

With Mass Combat. If you are using the *Dragonlance: Warriors of Krynn* game along with this adventure, consult the "Warriors of Krynn: Scenario 1" sidebar.

Without Mass Combat. If you aren't using the *Dragonlance: Warriors of Krynn* game, continue with the "Invasion of Vogler" section.

WARRIORS OF KRYNN: SCENARIO 1

With the Red Dragon Army on its way, Becklin Uth Viharin summons the characters to Cudgel's command tent at the village's edge. When they arrive, read the introduction to scenario 1 in *Dragonlance: Warriors of Krynn*, then play that scenario. This scenario details an organized defense of Vogler and the characters' desperate attempt to get the villagers to safety.

If the characters attain a win or hold during this scenario, each character gains inspiration. Additionally, after the people of Vogler have reached safety, they recognize the characters as honorary members of the village and the mayor gifts them one of the community's few treasures: a folded paper kingfisher that functions as a *Quaal's feather token* (bird). Characters gain no rewards for a loss.

At the end of the scenario, Darrett is reeling from Becklin's defeat and returns with the characters to Vogler. You can run any encounters from the "Invasion of Vogler" section as the characters escape the village, or you can skip ahead to "The Final Boat" section.

INVASION OF VOGLER

Before Becklin and Cudgel leave Vogler to join the Ironclad Regiment, Becklin shares a brief, formal goodbye with Darrett. She then thanks the characters for all they've done, saying, "Ispin was right to call you friends. I'm glad I've had the chance to do the same." Becklin and Cudgel then ride out.

An hour passes before news arrives. In the meantime, keep the characters occupied with the evacuation's preparations, such as finding missing villagers and corralling ships.

NEWS FROM THE FRONT

When you're ready to begin this section, give the characters a reason to be near the River Gate, such as fetching Becklin's box from Thornwall Keep or looking for a lost villager. When the characters are within earshot, read the following:

> Pounding hooves sound from the direction of the River Gate as a mercenary of the Ironclad Regiment rides toward the village circle. As she nears, she yells, "They're coming! Evacuate now! The Dragon Ar—" The message is cut short as a squat, hooded figure launches from the nearby clifftops and slams into the rider's back, sending horse and rider tumbling.

The rider is a **scout** sent by Becklin to alert Vogler to evacuate immediately. When the characters arrive, the rider's horse is dead and she is locked in battle with her attacker, a **baaz draconian** (see appendix B). The draconian kills her if the characters don't intercede.

If the characters save the rider, she announces that an attack is imminent—the Dragon Army has split into two prongs. One went to engage the mercenaries, while the second is headed to the village.

PERILOUS EVACUATION

It's up to the characters to decide how to handle the incoming invasion. Unless the characters made other plans, Mayor Raven and Darrett are at the village's wharf with most of the villagers. After learning the scout's news, Mayor Raven orders the evacuation to begin. Read the following description:

> The villagers remain eerily quiet as they begin lowering themselves into the boats. Panic washes over the crowd as cloaked figures emerge at the edge of the cliff above Vogler. The figures linger for a moment, then step off the edge. Wings sweep from beneath their cloaks, slowing their descent into the village.

As invaders sweep over the cliff into Vogler, Darrett draws his sword and asks the characters to help him defend the escaping villagers.

INVASION ENCOUNTERS

Vogler is swiftly overwhelmed by Dragon Army draconians. Roll on or choose encounters from the Vogler Invasion Encounters table. Set these encounters anywhere in the village you wish.

After the second encounter, the characters hear loud clanking sounds from the north—something large and metal is moving toward them. This is the boilerdrak they'll encounter in the "Escape from Vogler" section. Before the characters can investigate the noise, a third encounter distracts them.

When you've run at least three of these encounters, proceed with the "Escape from Vogler" section.

VOGLER INVASION ENCOUNTERS

d10	Encounter
1–2	A family of four **commoners** gets separated from the other evacuees. Unless escorted to the wharf, they try to hide from the invaders.
3	An abandoned cat leaps onto one of the characters. It is terrified and refuses to leave them during the invasion.
4–5	Airborne Assassin (see below)
6–7	Direct Attack (see below)
8	Ominous Riders (see below)
9–10	Vogler Militia (see below)

AIRBORNE ASSASSIN

A **kapak draconian** (see appendix B) glides overhead from the cliffs, intent on dropping onto one of the characters. Only characters who have a passive Wisdom (Perception) score of 14 or higher notice it. Unless alerted, the other characters are surprised when the kapak attacks.

DIRECT ATTACK

> From between buildings sprint four cloaked invaders, their clawed feet gouging the dirt. They wave torches and fierce blades above their reptilian heads.

Five **baaz draconians** (see appendix B) charge toward the wharf, intent on setting buildings ablaze and murdering escaping villagers. In their frenzied state, the draconians fight to the death.

OMINOUS RIDERS

The character who has the highest passive Wisdom (Perception) score glimpses the following scene during the invasion:

> A distant flash of light catches your attention. Atop the cliffs north of town, three figures on motionless horses sit in the shadows of the trees. You make out the glint of light on plate armor, but before you can alert your companions, the figures vanish.

Three mysterious knights watch the battle, but they disappear as soon as they're spotted. If the character who noticed them succeeds on a DC 16 Intelligence (History) check, they recognize the figures as wearing the antiquated armor of Knights of Solamnia. Who these knights are—skeletal knights, Lord Soth and his retinue, or the spirits of Lord Vogler and his knights—is up to you.

VOGLER MILITIA

> The sound of clashing metal draws your attention. Two of Vogler's remaining militia members struggle to hold their own against reptile-headed invaders. The scaled soldiers bait the militia members, hissing cruel laughter.

The two militia members (**guards**) are outmatched by five **baaz draconians** (see appendix B). If the characters don't intervene quickly, the militia members are slaughtered. If the characters help and a militia member lives, this survivor gives the characters a *potion of healing*.

Escape from Vogler

When you're ready to bring the invasion of Vogler to its climax, proceed with this encounter. No matter where the characters are in the village, screams ring out from the wharf. When the characters draw close, read the following:

> The screams of villagers, still evacuating onto boats, ring through the smoke of burning buildings. Among the screams rises an unbelievable word: "Dragon!"
>
> Then it comes into view. Pitching this way and that, its scales clanking like steel plates, a black beast draws near the wharf, flanked by reptilian invaders. Flames crackle from the beast's gaping maw.

Despite its appearance, the thing nearing Vogler's wharf isn't a dragon—it's a boilerdrak, a gnomish siege engine invented for the Red Dragon Army (see appendix A). The boilerdrak is crewed by four **baaz draconians** (see appendix B).

This battle takes place in front of Vogler's wharf, depicted on map 3.3. The "Vogler Battlefield Features" and "Vogler Battlefield Events" sections detail elements of this battle. The boilerdrak is positioned on the scorched ground. The characters start the battle anywhere on the wharf.

On the first round of battle, three draconians use their actions to load, aim, and fire the boilerdrak at the Wharfinger's Office—the structure at the north of the map. The building rapidly catches fire.

Characters who succeed on a DC 12 Wisdom (Perception) check or who come within 5 feet of the boilerdrak recognize it isn't a dragon, but a mechanical device.

After the baaz draconians are defeated, proceed with the "Fewmaster Gholcag" encounter.

Vogler Battlefield Features

The battlefield includes the following features:

Burning Building. The Wharfinger's Office is on fire. A creature that enters the burning structure for the first time on a turn or starts its turn there must succeed on a DC 16 Constitution saving throw or take 5 (1d10) fire damage.

Fray. The 15-foot-wide area marked by the design at the edge of the map represents draconians facing off against Vogler's remaining defenders. This area and the village beyond the map are difficult terrain. A creature that enters the Fray for the first time on a turn or starts its turn there must succeed on a DC 16 Dexterity saving throw or take 7 (2d6) slashing damage from opportunistic foes. The Fray can't be damaged and remains until the battle ends.

Vogler Battlefield Events

During this encounter, roll on the Vogler Battlefield Events table each round at initiative count 0. Also consider rolling on the table if a character enters the Fray or otherwise tries to leave the battlefield.

Vogler Battlefield Events

d6	Events
1	Two Vogler fishers (**guards**) come to assist the characters. They appear in unoccupied spaces adjacent to the Fray nearest a random character.
2	A blinded **bozak draconian** (see appendix B) with 1 hit point staggers from the Fray and across the battlefield. It doesn't attack, but it explodes in its Death Throes if killed. The draconian appears in an unoccupied space adjacent to the Fray nearest a random character.
3–4	A draconian gliding overhead throws a fiery flask at one random player character, who must succeed on a DC 10 Dexterity saving throw or take 3 (1d6) fire damage.
5–6	Villagers on the docks shout their support. A random player character has advantage on their next attack roll.

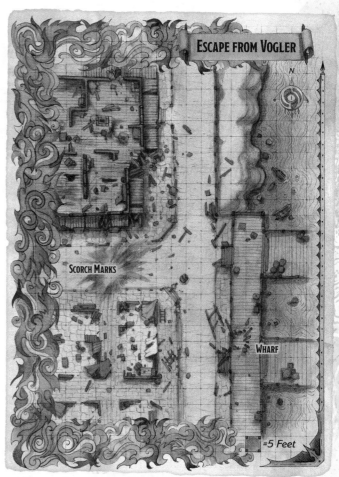

Map 3.3: Escape from Vogler

FEWMASTER GHOLCAG

After the boilerdrak's baaz draconians are defeated, the commander of the draconian assault arrives. Read or paraphrase the following:

> An exterior wall of the Brass Crab shatters outward. A ten-foot-tall brute in black scale armor emerges from the inn. Holding a barrel of fish under one arm, the hulking figure fills her mouth with a fistful of wriggling fish.
>
> From behind her, two reptilian soldiers emerge. "Them next," the ogre says, gesturing in your direction. The soldiers move forward obediently.

Fewmaster Gholcag is a low-ranking commander in the Red Dragon Army and the leader of the raid on Vogler. She and two **baaz draconians** (see appendix B) arrive adjacent to the Fray along the northernmost road. Fewmaster Gholcag uses the **ogre** stat block, but she wears scale mail and has AC 14. She and the draconians fight to the death.

After Gholcag and the draconians are defeated, the battlefield encounter ends.

FEWMASTER GHOLCAG

THE FINAL BOAT

Most of the draconians remaining in Vogler focus on looting the village, giving the villagers enough time to evacuate. At the end of the pier, only Mayor Raven, Darrett, and a few others have yet to board a boat. The remaining boats have enough space for them and the characters.

Before the characters head to their boats, read the following text:

> "Hold the boat!" a voice rasps from the smoke-shrouded street. A man runs through the haze toward the wharf, clad in the armor of an Ironclad Regiment mercenary and gripping a horned helmet in his hand.

Characters recognize this man as Jeyev Veldrews, Cudgel's lieutenant. He says he's been sent by Becklin to pass on the following information:

- The battle with the Red Dragon Army went poorly, but a few of the Ironclad Regiment escaped.
- Becklin sent him to help everyone in the village safely evacuate and to ensure nobody waited for her and the mercenaries.
- More Dragon Army forces are on his heels, and the villagers have to flee now.

A character who looks at the helmet he carries recognizes it's the helmet of a Knight of Solamnia. Jeyev won't say more until they've boarded the ship. See the "Lost in Battle" section for more details.

LAST GLIMPSE OF VOGLER

The characters escape Vogler on the last boat, a small fishing vessel barely large enough for the characters, Darrett, Mayor Raven, Jeyev, and a few other locals. Read or paraphrase the following as the characters leave Vogler behind:

> Vogler is in flames. Amid the columns of smoke rising from the village, invaders loot what remains. The villagers traveling with you don't look away, watching until their home is nothing more than a red-black smear along the river's edge. The evacuation boats carry all that remains of Vogler down the Vingaard, toward an uncertain sanctuary in Kalaman.

LOST IN BATTLE

It's up to you to determine how Becklin and Cudgel's battle against the Red Dragon Army unfolded and what Jeyev knows. In any case, Vogler's defenders were defeated and an enemy force marches on the town. The characters' allies might have suffered any of the following fates:

Assassination. Jeyev is actually a neutral evil **bandit captain** who was bought off by the Dragon Army just like Gragonis was. He's been hired to assassinate the Solamnic knights in Vogler—Becklin and Darrett. He murdered Becklin during the battle and is now using her helmet to get close to Darrett.

Capture. Becklin sent Jeyev to warn the villagers that the defense failed and not to wait for their defenders. She sent her helmet as proof that Jeyev's words come from her. As Jeyev fled, he saw Becklin captured. You can determine where Becklin is being held, perhaps in one of the Dragon Army encampments detailed in chapters 4 or 5.

Scattered. Becklin and Cudgel orchestrated a retreat from the Dragon Army. Either of them might reappear in Kalaman in later chapters after evading their foes. As in the previous possibility, she sent Jeyev to warn the villagers.

Witness. If the characters already know about Becklin's defeat, Jeyev was separated from the rest of Vogler's defenders, knows specifics of her last battle, and recovered her helmet. He might still be an assassin or know the information in any of the other entries here.

Regardless of your choice, Darrett takes Becklin's helmet and promises to keep it safe. If you choose to have Becklin return after the battle, she becomes a valued adviser to the military leaders of Kalaman (detailed in chapter 4).

NEXT STEPS

As the Vingaard River carries the flotilla of boats from Vogler toward Kalaman, a journey that takes most of the night, the characters advance to 4th level. After the horrors the villagers have faced, everyone is relieved their journey downriver is uneventful. Chapter 4 begins with the refugees' arrival outside Kalaman.

RALPH HORSLEY

Kalaman's defenders march forth to confront the Dragon Army.

CHAPTER 4

SHADOW OF WAR

VOGLER IS GONE, DEVASTATED BY THE RED Dragon Army. After escaping the village by following the Vingaard River, the characters and other survivors seek refuge in the city of Kalaman. They carry with them a warning: war is coming for Kalaman. The city's leaders recruit the characters to help identify and resist the threat of the Red Dragon Army. As the characters travel the lands around Kalaman, they learn more about the Dragon Army's goals and the terrifying shadow behind this war.

RUNNING THIS CHAPTER

This chapter begins with an overview of the city of Kalaman. After familiarizing yourself with the "Kalaman Gazetteer" section, continue the adventure with the characters and Vogler's refugees arriving near the city. Once the characters ensure the villagers' safety, encourage them to follow Darrett Highwater's lead by joining—or at least collaborating with—Kalaman's military. The military provides the support and direction necessary to face the Red Dragon Army and its supernatural allies for the rest of the adventure.

CHARACTER ADVANCEMENT

In this chapter, level advancement is handled as follows:

- Characters start this chapter at 4th level, having gained a level after evacuating Vogler.
- Characters advance to 5th level before retaking Wheelwatch Outpost.
- Characters advance to 6th level after defeating the skeletal knight Zanas Sarlamir at the end of the chapter.

Kalaman Gazetteer

Kalaman, the Beacon of the East, is one of the largest cities in Solamnia. Far from the nation's heartland and the capital of Palanthas, the city is a bastion of trade and safety at the edge of the province of Nightlund. This section provides an overview of the city. Flesh out its locations and residents however you please. The city will be the party's home for the rest of this adventure, and their connections to the city will encourage them to defend it against the Dragon Army threat.

Knowledge of Kalaman

Characters who are from Kalaman or succeed on a DC 12 Intelligence (History) check know the following details about the city:

Capital City. Kalaman is the capital of the Solamnic province of Nightlund.

Ancient Bastion. Kalaman is a thriving trade city known for its strong walls, castle, and harbor beacons, all of which predate the Cataclysm.

Rulers. The city is led by a governor, a council of prominent guild leaders, and a military marshal.

Military. Kalaman maintains a significant military force to deter raiders from Estwilde and monsters from the Dargaard Mountains.

Vingaard Port. The city sits at the mouth of the Vingaard River, about thirty miles downriver from Vogler.

Power in Kalaman

Kalaman is led by the following three groups:

Governor. The head of Kalaman's government is Governor Calof Miat (lawful neutral, human **noble**). He represents the city's people and speaks on their behalf during council sessions.

Guild Leaders. A council composed of the leaders of the city's five most prominent guilds—the Cartographers' Guild, Dockhands' Guild, Fishers' Guild, Masons' Guild, and Shipwrights' Guild—oversees the city's broad business interests and runs varied public services. The guilds' leaders are neutral human and hill dwarf **nobles** who are prone to bickering and jockeying for influence.

Marshal. Kalaman's military guards the city and defends eastern Solamnia. The military is robust, as the city can't afford to solicit aid from the Knights of Solamnia, headquartered in the west, every time raiders from Estwilde or other threats cross the border. Kalaman's military is commanded by the pragmatic Marshal Nestra Vendri (lawful neutral, human **knight**).

Kalaman Locations

While in Kalaman, the characters might visit any of the locations in this section. These sites appear on map 4.1.

Castle Kalaman

A symbol of the city, the age-old fortress of Castle Kalaman rises atop rugged cliffs, visible from anywhere within the city walls and for miles beyond. The city's governor dwells within the castle, and the ruling council holds its meetings here. Castle Kalaman also serves as the headquarters of Kalaman's military, and its barracks can house hundreds of troops. Extensive catacombs run beneath Castle Kalaman, but the entrances to these tunnels were closed long ago and remain magically sealed.

City Market

Merchants from across Ansalon do business in Kalaman's thriving bazaar. Characters can purchase any equipment from the *Player's Handbook* here. Vendors from far-off lands—like Ergoth or Mount Nevermind—often bring rare curios here to trade.

Hammerstrike Forges

Twin forges stand across the street from one another, run by the dwarven cousins Kadmos and Tiria Hammerstrike (both lawful neutral, hill dwarf **veterans**). While both are competent smiths, Kadmos specializes in armor and Tiria excels with weaponry.

Harbor Beacons

The walls of Kalaman extend several hundred feet into the city's harbor. The tower at each end holds a prominent beacon surrounded by an array of lenses. These beacons were created before the Cataclysm by the city's Istarian founders, and the light from their flames cuts through the densest fog.

Kalaman Harbor

At any time, dozens of ships are anchored along the busy docks of Kalaman's harbor. Small local fishing ships vie for harbor space alongside mighty seafaring vessels, some from far-off lands. Every day there's a 10 percent chance a merchant ship from a distant land puts into port here, its crew eager to sell unique wares and tell tales of danger on the sea.

Meulara's Oddities

Meulara's Oddities is a small shop piled with trinkets. Its shopkeeper, Meulara (chaotic good, kender **commoner**), is a silver-haired woman with a bright smile. Meulara claims to know every kender in the city, and most kender new to town are directed to her so they can swap stories and news from their travels.

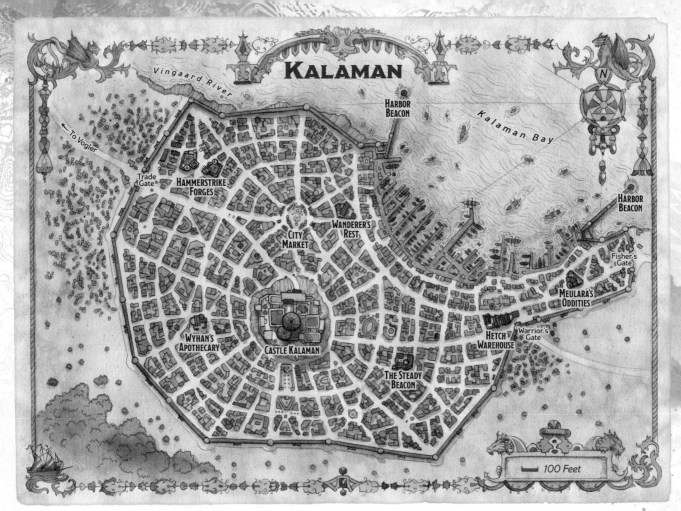

KALAMAN

Vingaard River

HARBOR
BEACON

Kalaman Bay

N

To Vogler

Trade
Gate

HAMMERSTRIKE
FORGES

HARBOR
BEACON

CITY
MARKET

WANDERER'S
REST

Fisher's
Gate

MEULARA'S
ODDITIES

WYHAN'S
APOTHECARY

CASTLE KALAMAN

HETCH
WAREHOUSE

Warrior's
Gate

THE STEADY
BEACON

100 Feet

MAP 4.1: KALAMAN

THE STEADY BEACON

The Steady Beacon is a tavern that boasts a large taproom, a fish-focused menu, and modest lodging. Its decor features the broken weapons of defeated bandits. The tavern is a favorite of Kalaman's soldiers, and most evenings, dozens of off-duty troops relax here. The inn's owner, Jesen Thold (neutral good, human **veteran**), is a friend of Marshal Nestra Vendri, head of Kalaman's military.

TRADE CAMPS

Outside the city to the east and west sprawl trade camps. These expanses of ramshackle buildings began as campgrounds for caravans. Over time, the tents were replaced by simple buildings aligned along muddy streets. They now house hundreds who can't find lodgings within the city's walls.

WYHAN'S APOTHECARY

Wyhan (lawful evil, human **mage**) is a black-robed Mage of High Sorcery. Though supposedly retired, she keeps a shop that deals in wares few in Kalaman need. Wyhan's Apothecary sells the occasional good-luck charm, but those who know what to ask for might gain access to the apothecary's back room, which houses esoteric spell components. The "Message for a Mage" section later in this chapter provides more details on Wyhan and her shop.

ARRIVING IN KALAMAN

By dawn the morning after evacuating from Vogler, the characters and Vogler's surviving villagers arrive within sight of Kalaman. Read the following text when you're ready to start this part of the adventure:

> The walled city of Kalaman rises in the distance, spreading across the southern shore of a wide bay. Ships sail to and from the city's walled harbor, their courses lit by a pair of towering beacons.
>
> On the shore ahead, where the Vingaard River meets Kalaman Bay, dozens of survivors from Vogler have pulled their mismatched boats ashore and begun making camp.

The characters are among the last to arrive from Vogler, likely accompanied by Darrett Highwater and other allies. When they reach the survivors' camp, they find villagers organizing to assess their numbers, reunite separated families, and build fires to prepare meals.

REFUGEES AT THE SHORE

As the survivors of Vogler pull their ships ashore, the reality of their situation sets in, and minor troubles begin confounding the refugees. Roll on the Survivor Camp Hardships table to determine what challenges the survivors need help with. After you've run as many of these encounters as you like, proceed with the "Darrett's Armor" section.

SURVIVOR CAMP HARDSHIPS

d4	Situation
1	Youngsters struggle to land their boat. The boat is 20 feet from the shore and drifting away. A character who swims to the boat can pilot it in by succeeding on a DC 14 Wisdom (Survival) check.
2	An older refugee slipped in the shallow water and sprained an ankle. A character can provide relief by succeeding on a DC 12 Wisdom (Medicine) check, expending one use of a healer's kit, or using any magic that restores hit points.
3	A couple sits shivering beside an unlit stack of firewood, staring off in the direction of Vogler. Lighting the fire through any means calms the couple and earns a wordless nod of thanks.
4	Two rowdy youths take advantage of the chaos to try to rob a disliked neighbor. A character can stop them with a successful DC 12 Charisma (Intimidation or Persuasion) check.

DARRETT'S ARMOR

If the characters collected the box Becklin Uth Viharin asked them to fetch from Thornwall Keep in chapter 3, they can present it to Darrett Highwater after escaping Vogler.

Inside the box is a suit of plate armor filigreed with Solamnic knotwork, perfectly sized for Darrett's use. There's no note or any other instructions with the armor. If the characters explain Becklin asked them to give it to him, Darrett's touched and thanks the characters profusely.

From this point on, Darrett wears his Solamnic armor often and does his best to comport himself as he believes Becklin would have. If a character is affiliated with the Knights of Solamnia, he strives to emulate their virtuous deeds and might even adopt them as a mentor.

DELEGATION TO KALAMAN

Soon after arriving on shore, the character with the highest passive Wisdom (Perception) score realizes two prominent villagers are missing: Lord Bakaris and his son, Bakaris the Younger. If the characters

ask around, a villager who reached the shore before them mentions that Lord Bakaris and his son headed to Kalaman hours ago, intent on addressing the city's leaders, but no one's heard back from them since. If the characters don't head to Kalaman to investigate, Mayor Raven asks them and Darrett to do so, giving them authority to make whatever arrangements are necessary to secure the safety of Vogler's people.

ENTRANCE TO KALAMAN

The trek from the villagers' landing spot to Kalaman spans two miles. As the characters and Darrett approach the city, read the following:

> Statues of titanic soldiers line Kalaman's mighty walls. These ancient stone knights stare into the distance, daring invaders to dash themselves against defenses that withstood even the Cataclysm. A disorganized neighborhood of tents and ramshackle structures lines the road to the city's nearest gate, where soldiers in blue-and-yellow uniforms question all who enter.

The gate guards halt the characters and ask their business, but admit them to the city as long as the characters aren't hostile. If a character asks about Lord Bakaris or a representative from the Vogler refugees, the guards point the way toward Castle Kalaman. The guards recall their captain leading a man matching Bakaris's description to the castle some time ago. Castle Kalaman is a towering structure and easy to find without directions, and the guards can also direct the characters to any site in the "Kalaman Locations" section.

CASTLE KALAMAN

When the characters and Darrett arrive at Castle Kalaman, read the following:

> Even if the imposing Castle Kalaman didn't stand atop hundred-foot cliffs, it would still tower over every other structure in the city. The path to it rises up the cliffside, overlooked by gigantic statues matching those that line the city's walls. At the path's end, guards stand before an open gate.

The guards at Castle Kalaman ask the characters to state their business. If the characters explain that they're representatives of Vogler's people, a guard leads them across a courtyard toward a council chamber where Lord Bakaris is speaking with the city council.

Encounter with Bakaris

While the characters are making their way to the council chamber, read the following text:

> As you cross Castle Kalaman's paved courtyard, a familiar figure intercepts you with an arrogant smile—Bakaris the Younger.
>
> "My father has matters well in hand. We'll be sure to send for you and the rest of the fish-folk once we've determined what's best for them."

Bakaris the Younger halts the group. He insists the characters shouldn't be allowed to disturb his father's audience with Kalaman's leaders.

Establish Bakaris the Younger not just as a bully, but as a threat to people in need. He and his father are putting their own ambitions before the needs of the people of Vogler—a trend that continues for the rest of this adventure. A character can make Bakaris the Younger step aside through roleplaying or by succeeding on a DC 10 Charisma (Intimidation) check. Alternatively, a character convinces the guard they're with to ignore Bakaris by succeeding on a DC 14 Charisma (Persuasion) check. Afterward, Bakaris hurls weak insults and slinks off.

Council Meeting

When the group arrives at the council chamber, the guard escorts the characters inside and explains who they are. After this, read the following:

> Eight serious-looking people sit around a broad table in the middle of a spacious hall. At the table's end, a tall man with plaited blond hair and a velvet vest of blue and gold stands to greet you.
>
> "Welcome, guests. I'm Governor Calof Miat. Your leader has briefed us on the situation in Vogler, his bold defense, and his eagerness to strike back against these invaders." As Miat says this, he nods to a man near him—Lord Bakaris, who glares at your intrusion.
>
> "Tell us," the governor continues, "are your people still preparing for battle?"

Along with Lord Bakaris and Governor Miat, the meeting includes guild leaders and Marshal Vendri (detailed in the "Kalaman Gazetteer" section).

It's clear from the governor's words and Lord Bakaris's expression that Bakaris is trying to advance his own agenda. Lord Bakaris told the council the villagers are taking up arms to retake their home. The characters know this isn't the case, though. Mayor Raven is focused on ensuring the villagers

LORD BAKARIS UTH ESTIDE

have food, security, and support in the days to come. And the characters are certain the refugees didn't appoint Lord Bakaris their leader.

Lord Bakaris Uth Estide

Lord Bakaris Uth Estide (neutral evil, human **noble**) is an arrogant man with a lesser title among the Solamnic nobility. In ages past, his family was known for its wealth and generations of membership in the Knights of Solamnia. While Lord Bakaris retains a considerable amount of wealth, he has lived his entire life on stories of honor and great deeds, none of which are his own. Now Lord Bakaris sees the situation in Kalaman as his chance to win glory for himself. At heart, he's comically cowardly, full of bluster and inflated words. He has neither the spine to stand up to opposition nor the experience to lead.

Personality Trait. "I was born for greatness, and I'll take what I deserve."

Ideal. "My brilliance and worthiness are clear to everyone intelligent enough to deserve my time."

Bond. "My deeds will be the grandest chapter in the Estide family legend."

Flaw. "My blood makes me a leader. If commoners can do it, how hard can it be?"

Retaking Vogler

During the conversation with Kalaman's leaders, the characters might ask about retaking Vogler. Lord Bakaris is eager to do this, while Darrett prioritizes ensuring the villagers' safety. For the time being, the city council is more interested in gaining information about the enemy than running headlong into battle. If necessary, use Darrett to temper characters' desire for immediate revenge.

Clarifying the Situation

It's up to the characters to correct Bakaris's misinformation. Kalaman's council listens to what the characters say, asking probing questions until the truth of what happened in Vogler comes out. As the characters speak, Lord Bakaris contradicts them, trying to bolster his own fictitious position as the village leader who deserves accolades for bravely facing the Red Dragon Army. Through roleplaying or by succeeding on a DC 14 Charisma (Intimidation) check, a character can silence Lord Bakaris.

After the characters explain the current situation of those who escaped Vogler, read the following:

> Governor Miat frowns. "This is all dire news. My heart goes out to your friends and families, but I hope you can understand our reticence to welcome you all through our city's gates. These aren't normal times. Marshal?"
>
> The governor gestures to a stern woman wearing armor embellished with the blue and gold colors of Kalaman. She nods and begins, "I am Marshal Vendri, commander of Kalaman's military forces. I'm afraid your situation is far from unique."

Kalaman's Concerns

Marshal Vendri goes on to explain that Vogler isn't the only community in the region to face peril. She shares the following details:

- Small villages and farms to the south and east of Kalaman have been burned in recent weeks.
- Vogler is the largest community to be attacked and the only one with many survivors.
- Experienced patrols of armored Kalaman soldiers have been found cut down, in some cases with mysterious clawlike gashes in their armor.
- Lord Bakaris and the characters have provided the clearest information on the enemy that Kalaman has received to date.

Marshal Vendri knows nothing of draconians, the Dragon Queen, or the Dragon Army. Her experience is considerable, but it involves battling raiders from Estwilde and ogres from the Taman Busuk.

Everyone here has heard rumors of war in the eastern nation of Khur, but until now, they hadn't considered that far-off nation's struggles relevant.

Marshal Vendri is eager to hear anything the characters know about the enemy. She's even more impressed if the characters have physical evidence of draconians or Dragon Army soldiers.

Once the characters have heard the marshal's report, the governor asks the characters and Darrett to step outside while the council discusses what they've learned. Lord Bakaris isn't asked to leave.

Awaiting a Decision

Darrett and the characters are ushered into the hall outside the council chamber. Use this opportunity to have Darrett reemphasize how important it is for Vogler's people to have Kalaman's support and protection. A character who listens at the council chamber door and succeeds on a DC 14 Wisdom (Perception) check hears a frustrated Marshal Vendri repeatedly interrupt Lord Bakaris.

Kalaman's Decision

After half an hour, the council meeting adjourns. Read the following text:

> The chamber's doors open, and most of the council members file past you without a glance. Marshal Vendri beckons to you from the door, while inside, Governor Miat and Lord Bakaris remain seated.

When the characters reenter the council chamber, the governor bids them sit. After they're settled, read the following text:

> In a decisive tone, Governor Miat says, "The citizens of Kalaman are prepared to offer your people shelter in the neighborhoods outside the city walls, the protection of our soldiers, and—while we can spare it— food from our tables." He folds his hands and fixes his eyes on you. "There is a condition, though."

Governor Miat explains the following points:

- Kalaman's leaders are concerned about the threat posed by the enemy that attacked Vogler.
- The city has woefully little information about this foe, and the scouts sent to learn more have all disappeared.
- The characters, however, both faced this foe and saved an entire village from its attack.
- In return for Kalaman protecting the people of Vogler, Kalaman's leaders want the characters and Darrett to report to Marshal Vendri as special operatives in the Kalaman military.

Let the characters discuss this offer. Marshal Vendri provides the following clarifications as needed:

- Only one of the characters needs to swear themself to serve Kalaman's military—though all are welcome—and only until the threat to the region is over.
- Sworn characters will become esquires of Kalaman and be paid 5 gp per week.
- Sworn characters and their companions will receive free lodging at Castle Kalaman.
- Sworn characters will be given a palm-sized emblem with the blue-and-gold symbol of Kalaman etched into its face. This is a symbol of their special rank, which is akin to a lieutenancy (higher than soldiers but lower than commanders).

If the characters refuse, Darrett asks to speak with them for a moment. He plans to accept the governor's terms and attempts to convince the characters to join him. He wants their aid not only to protect his people, but to counter the terrifying threat of the Dragon Army. If the characters still resist, Darrett suggests the characters could work for him as aides rather than working directly for the military—a proposal Kalaman's leaders are willing to accept.

If the characters and Darrett accept, Governor Miat is pleased and orders that Vogler's people be provided with food and supplies. Marshal Vendri dispatches guards to help the refugees relocate to lodgings outside the Trade Gate.

With that, the meeting with Kalaman's leaders concludes. Marshal Vendri asks Darrett and the characters to come to her office on the second floor of Castle Kalaman when they're ready to learn more about their position and their first duties. Until then, they should ensure their people are safe and familiarize themselves with the city.

REPORTING BACK

When the characters return to where Vogler's survivors are camped, Mayor Raven meets them. If the characters gained the city's support, she thanks them profusely. If they didn't, she's eager to brainstorm ways to do so.

After hearing that Darrett—and likely some of the characters—agreed to aid Kalaman's military, Raven says she and the survivors of Vogler's militia intend to offer their assistance as well. She also asks the characters to stop calling her mayor—so long as Vogler is in Dragon Army hands, she's just Raven.

Lord Bakaris and his son don't return to the camp, instead paying for rooms at the Steady Beacon.

REINFORCEMENTS

A couple hours later, several wagons and a contingent of soldiers from Kalaman reach the survivors' camp with food and supplies. They aid the people most in need first, eventually assisting everyone in relocating to an unoccupied group of simple wooden buildings north of Kalaman's Trade Gate. The survivors find dry, safe housing and pitch in to make everyone's lodgings more comfortable. They also establish a communal cookhouse and infirmary.

Encourage the characters to use skills like Wisdom (Medicine) or any artisan's tools they might have to support Vogler's people and make their accommodations more welcoming. If they wish, the characters can also find bunks here for the evening, but staying at Castle Kalaman would be more comfortable—and free up more space and resources for the other evacuees. Once the characters see to the safety of Vogler's survivors, they're free to explore Kalaman as they please.

MESSAGE FOR A MAGE

If a character has a scroll to deliver to Wyhan, the Mage of High Sorcery (see the "Eye in the Sky" section in chapter 2), they can find her at Wyhan's Apothecary. If no characters are interested in joining the Mages of High Sorcery, skip this section.

The characters can easily find Wyhan's Apothecary. Foggy windows obscure a selection of charms and occult trappings for sale. The shop is open only during the day. If the characters enter during business hours, read the following description:

> Wyhan's Apothecary smells of licorice and pepper. The modest shop has a few meager tables displaying good-luck charms, odd animal bones, and vials advertising various remedies. At the rear of the shop, a human woman with raven hair and a dark dress with feathered, winglike sleeves stands behind a counter heaped with open books. She looks up from her reading, eyes you with disinterest, then goes back to her book.

The shopkeeper here is Wyhan (lawful evil, human **mage**), a black-robed Mage of High Sorcery. Although self-interested and disdainful of non-mages, Wyhan is a dedicated member of her organization.

If a character interested in joining the Mages of High Sorcery introduces themself, Wyhan asks if they have a scroll for her. If the character delivers the scroll, Wyhan immediately opens it.

A Test Completed

Delivering the scroll to Wyhan is part of a test informing her which robed order of the Mages of High Sorcery might be a good fit for the character. After receiving the scroll, Wyhan magically knows the alignment of the character tasked with delivering it—and whether they opened the scroll. The Scroll Predictions table determines which robed order Wyhan predicts the deliverer will join, based on the character's alignment and whether they opened the scroll before delivering it.

Don't share this with the character immediately—Wyhan's estimation comes up later in their conversation with her.

Scroll Predictions

Alignment	Opened Scroll	Didn't Open Scroll
Good	Red robes	White robes
Neutral	Red robes	Red robes
Evil	Black robes	Red robes

Wyhan's Recommendation

Wyhan is skeptical of any character who expresses an interest in joining the Mages of High Sorcery. She asks them the following questions:

WYHAN

- Why do you think you're worthy of using magic?
- Do you serve your magic, or does your magic serve you?
- How will you change the world with your magic?
- If you were to lose your magic, what would you do?

Regardless of the character's answers, Wyhan responds with pragmatic criticism. Have her engage spellcasting characters in a philosophical conversation about the role of magic for as long as you want. Afterward, Wyhan does the following:

- She recommends which order of the Mages of High Sorcery she thinks the character is suited to (revealing her prediction from the previous section).
- She agrees to contact her fellow Mages of High Sorcery and petition for the character's inclusion in the organization.
- She promises to contact the characters when she hears back from the Mages' leaders at the Tower of High Sorcery in Wayreth.
- She agrees to aid the character in obtaining transport to Wayreth so they can undertake the Test of High Sorcery (detailed in the "Mages of High Sorcery" section of chapter 1).

Wyhan is willing to answer a couple more questions about the Mages of High Sorcery, but after that, she insists the characters buy something or get out.

Any character interested in joining the Mages of High Sorcery hears back from Wyhan regarding their Test of High Sorcery at the beginning of the next chapter.

Reporting for Duty

Once the characters are ready to begin work with Kalaman's military, they can report to Castle Kalaman. If they look for Darrett among the other Vogler survivors, he's nowhere to be found, as he has already reported to the castle.

When the characters arrive at Castle Kalaman, any guard can direct them to Marshal Vendri's office on the second floor (see "Within the Castle" for more information on the castle's layout). When the characters arrive at Vendri's office, an aide has them wait a few moments, then escorts them inside. Read the following description:

> Marshal Vendri's office is spare. It holds little more than a desk heaped with documents, shelves filled with rolled scrolls, and a board on which is pinned a map of the surrounding province of Nightlund. Vendri stands as you enter. "Thank you for coming. I won't mince words: we're in the dark regarding the dangers I fear are fast approaching our gates, and your role will be to change that. But first, you must have questions."

OLGA DREBAS

Vendri patiently answers any questions about Kalaman, the city's military, and the characters' duties. Along with the details previously noted in the "Kalaman's Decision" section, Vendri shares the following particulars:

- The characters are expected to serve as a specialized squad dedicated to meeting challenges other troops can't address.
- Each week's military salary is paid in advance. Characters who agreed to join can pick up their first payment of 5 gp from Vendri's clerk today.
- Characters in need of equipment can freely take any mundane weapons, light armor, or medium armor they please from the armory on the castle's first floor.
- Several people from Vogler have offered to lend Vendri their aid. She's currently determining how best to use these enthusiastic conscripts.
- Vendri is still working out the details of the characters' first assignment. In the meantime, they should familiarize themselves with the castle and their lodgings on the fourth floor.
- She doesn't bring up Darrett or his role. If the characters ask about him, she smiles and says she'll let him tell them himself shortly (see the "Darrett's Orders" section).

WITHIN THE CASTLE

Once the conversation with Marshal Vendri is complete, a guard guides the characters to the fourth floor while sharing details about the castle. Built centuries ago, the castle was long used by the Knights of Solamnia. Many of its large halls are decorated with images of Solamnic knights and the gods and animals they honored. The guard goes on to describe the castle's layout as follows:

First Floor. The city council and governor meet and hold events on the first floor. Various government offices, a small library, and the armory are also here.

Second Floor. Military command and officer lodgings fill the second floor.

Third Floor. Castle guards lodge on the third floor. Most other soldiers reside elsewhere in the city or in the castle's ancillary structures.

Fourth Floor and Towers. Much of the castle is vacant and in disrepair, including most of the fourth floor and towers. The characters have been assigned lodgings in an unused ballroom on the fourth floor.

Basement. The basement is used for storage, though it also holds long-sealed doors to the castle's ruined dungeons.

CASTLE LODGINGS

When the characters reach their lodgings, read the following description:

> This room was once a small ballroom. A row of pillars, sculpted with knotwork and images of knights, supports a vaulted ceiling. Light shines into the room through tall windows facing the mountains to the south. One corner of the hall holds a collection of plain cots and empty chests, and nearby stands a large wooden table.

Each character has a cot and an empty chest assigned to them. Three small private rooms connect to this hall, which the characters may use as they please.

SOLAMNIC STATUARY

Throughout Castle Kalaman, including within the characters' chambers, stonework and statues depict the warrior-god Kiri-Jolith, patron of the Solamnic Knights of the Sword. Clerics of Kiri-Jolith recognize these depictions, as do characters who succeed on a DC 12 Intelligence (Religion) check.

DARRETT'S ORDERS

As the characters settle into their lodgings, Darrett enters. After greeting them warmly, he shares the following information:

- He spent much of the morning demonstrating his training to Marshal Vendri and her commanders.
- Vendri was pleased and ordered him to work with her to train a new unit of Kalaman soldiers.
- Vendri also assigned him to work with the characters. He's not their commander, but he'll serve as Vendri's envoy, delivering her orders to them—and if needed, he can advocate for the characters with Vendri and Kalaman's leaders.
- He was given lodgings on the third floor among the castle's guards.
- He thanks the characters for all they've done for him and Vogler. He hopes to continue to learn from and support them.

Darrett answers any questions the characters have, but he doesn't know much about Kalaman or missions to come. He's earnest in his desire to help the characters and excited to be in a castle where Knights of Solamnia once walked. He's eager to learn from this experience and hopes it'll one day help him become a true Knight of Solamnia.

After this, the characters have the rest of the day to do as they please. They'll receive their first mission in the morning.

The First Mission

The next morning, Darrett meets the characters and relays the following orders from Marshal Vendri:

- Kalaman's leadership is disturbed to hear about the dragon-like invention the Red Dragon Army deployed in Vogler. They want to know more about it.
- Twelve miles south of Kalaman lives a gnome inventor named Tatina Rookledust.
- Vendri wants the characters to go to Rookledust's home and see if she knows anything about this device or similar ones.
- Even if Rookledust knows nothing, Kalaman's forces would like to meet with her in the city to recruit her as an advisor.
- Darrett won't be joining them on this mission.

Darrett doesn't know much more than this, but he provides the characters with accurate directions to Rookledust's home.

Journey down Esker Brook

The lands around Kalaman consist of open fields, rolling hills, and scattered woods. The map of the Kalaman region in appendix E illustrates this area.

To the south rise the Dargaard Mountains, constantly cloaked in dark clouds that often spread their gloom across the surrounding land. A character who succeeds on a DC 12 Intelligence (History) check knows the Solamnic province of Nightlund, which encompasses both the Dargaard Mountains and Kalaman, is widely said to be a land of eternal twilight where the sun never shines. In reality, the area is gloomy and sees frequent drizzle, but hardly suffers from accursed darkness.

During the party's travels, roll on the Hinterlands Encounters table to see what sights they come across.

Hinterlands Encounters

d4	Encounter
1	Light rain falls for an hour, and distant lightning is visible over the Dargaard Mountains.
2	A band of 2d4 **bandits** heads northwest, paying the characters no mind. The bandits have no interest in fighting; they're following rumors of well-paying mercenary work.
3	The characters see a small, burned farmhouse. A character who investigates and succeeds on a DC 14 Wisdom (Survival) check finds no evidence of visitors, but the fire clearly started on the roof.
4	A **kender skirmisher** (see appendix B) named Trapspringer approaches and asks if the characters have seen any dragons. He's heard rumors about dragons near Kalaman but hasn't seen any.

Rookledust's Workshop

As the characters come within sight of Rookledust's home, read the following text:

> On a hill stands an unusual structure that resembles both a cottage and a metal fortress. The building bristles with steaming pipes and whirring devices, and it is currently under siege.
>
> Amid clanging metal contraptions, goblins try to breach the structure, impeded by gadgets that spin, snap, and thrash in the yard. Every few moments, a gnome appears from an open clockface above the door and hucks a new clockwork calamity at the attackers while cackling and yelling insults.

The home of the gnome Tatina Rookledust is under attack by ten **goblins** and—standing well back from the chaos—their **hobgoblin** leader. The goblinoids wear dark armor with a spiral symbol—the same colors and symbol of Takhisis commonly worn by Red Dragon Army troops.

Characters who move adjacent to a goblin expose themselves to the out-of-control clockwork devices. These devices are Small objects with AC 15, 8 hit points, and immunity to poison and psychic damage. On initiative count 0, roll on the Clockwork Chaos table for each character adjacent to a goblin to determine how the devices react to that character.

Clockwork Chaos

d6	Device Effect
1–2	No devices threaten the character.
3	A contraption that looks like a big set of teeth tries to bite the character (+3 to hit, 1d6 bludgeoning damage on a hit).
4	A bundle of thrashing cords whips around the character, who must succeed on a DC 10 Dexterity saving throw or be restrained until the end of the character's next turn.
5	A device fires a dart filled with glowing green fluid at the character (+4 to hit, 1 piercing damage on a hit). On a hit, the fluid is injected with an ominous hiss—but it proves harmless.
6	A mechanical chicken fires tin eggs at the character (+4 to hit, 1d4 bludgeoning damage on a hit). On a hit, the egg bursts in an oily mess, and the character has disadvantage on attack rolls until the end of the character's next turn.

The goblins flee after half their number are defeated. The hobgoblin tries to make the goblins hold their ground but also flees if he finds himself outnumbered by the characters.

The inventor Tatina Rookledust defends her home from Dragon Army goblins.

Taken Alive

If the characters capture and interrogate one of the goblinoids, a character who succeeds on a DC 14 Charisma (Intimidation or Persuasion) check learns the following:

- The goblinoids are members of the Red Dragon Army.
- Their commander sent them here to get a weapon.
- They don't know much about their leaders—only that most are humans and they pay well. One is a woman whose eye glows like an ember.
- The army is to the north, near a burned village. The goblins are supposed to take the weapon there.

The village the goblinoids are referring to is Vogler, but they don't know its name.

Meeting Rookledust

Once the characters defeat the goblinoids, the gnome—Tatina Rookledust—appears through an aperture above her workshop's door. She asks the characters who they are, what they want, and if they're with the Dragon Army. Once she's convinced the characters pose no threat, she comes outside and speaks with them while she cleans up the devices in her yard.

RALPH HORSLEY

Tatina Rookledust

Tatina Rookledust (neutral good rock gnome) moved to Nightlund decades ago from the distant gnome homeland of Mount Nevermind. She uses the **acolyte** stat block, but the effects of her Spellcasting manifest from various tools and tiny devices she always carries with her. Rookledust talks rapidly and is always formulating new ideas for her next overdesigned contraption. Though many of her creations are dangerous, she doesn't build them with violence in mind. She's particularly interested in devices for long-distance communication and inventions that mechanize the work of farm animals.

Personality Trait. "The faster I talk, think, and invent, the faster I can improve my designs."

Ideal. "Not only can I make that, I can make it better!"

Bond. "Through invention, we make a more interesting world."

Flaw. "I can make it for ya! Who are you again?"

Talking with Rookledust

Rookledust is eager to speak with the characters once she knows they're not affiliated with the Dragon Army. Use the following topics to guide the conversation with Rookledust:

- Rookledust is an inventor. She lives in seclusion so as not to disturb her neighbors with her experiments.
- Several weeks ago, a stranger in red-and-black armor asked to purchase her weed-clearing device, but with some modifications to make it resemble a mythical dragon. She agreed. (Unbeknownst to her, the stranger was a Dragon Army agent and the device was the boilerdrak used in Vogler.)
- The stranger also hired her to design another device, which he was supposed to pick up today. Instead, the goblinoids showed up and demanded she turn over "the weapons."
- Realizing the stranger was using her devices for malign reasons, she refused to hand over her inventions. The goblinoids then attacked.
- She's happy to come with the characters to Kalaman and insists on giving them her newest invention (see "The Fargab").

Rookledust regrets her weed-clearing device was misused, but she doesn't dwell on the past. She's ready to leave with the characters whenever they want to go; she just needs to grab her invention.

THE FARGAB

Rookledust calls her newest invention the "fargab" (see appendix A). She was supposed to design a new weapon for the Red Dragon Army, but she got distracted and instead created this long-distance communication device. She currently has one paired set of fargabs, which she gives to the characters—and, by extension, Kalaman's defenders.

BACK TO KALAMAN

After giving the characters the fargabs, Rookledust accompanies them to Kalaman. The journey back to the city is uneventful.

The city leaders welcome Rookledust as their guest and give her comfortable lodgings. In the coming days, she advises them on what little she knows about the Dragon Army and spouts ideas for inventions to aid Kalaman.

MISSIONS FOR KALAMAN

In the days following the characters' arrival in Kalaman, war looms ever closer. The missions in this section represent the growing threat to the region. Use some or all of these missions in any order you please, with as much time between missions as you wish. After you've established the Red Dragon Army's threat, continue with the "Wheelwatch Outpost" section.

CLARIFYING THE THREAT

As the characters complete these assignments, it becomes clear the Dragon Army is more than a group of raiders. Gradually reinforce the following facts:

Dangerous Recruits. Bandits and mercenaries have been coming to the region to join the Dragon Army. It's said the Dragon Army pays well.

Draconians. Dragon Army forces include bipedal creatures with dragon-like features. Dragon Army soldiers refer to these creatures as draconians.

Enemy Armor. Dragon Army troops wear black armor with red flourishes and the symbol of Takhisis the Dragon Queen.

The Highmaster. The Red Dragon Army leader is Dragon Highmaster Kansaldi Fire-Eyes. Her soldiers fear her and claim she can see through lies.

Additionally, if the characters capture a prisoner and succeed on a DC 14 Charisma (Intimidation or Persuasion) check, they learn one of the following pieces of information:

Dread Servants. Draconians serve the Dragon Queen fanatically and fearlessly.

Flying Steeds. The Dragon Army uses wyverns and dragonkin called dragonnels as flying steeds.

Magical Threats. Some draconians can cast spells, control the minds of others, steal the form of foes they've killed, or even explode when they die.

MISSIONS

Through Darrett, the leaders of Kalaman might send the characters on the following missions. Use the random encounter table in appendix B if you'd like to add more encounters with the Dragon Army.

AMBUSHING THE ENEMY

The characters are tasked with investigating a farmstead eighteen miles east of the city, after fleeing residents report the farm was overrun by soldiers. When the characters arrive, they find the farm ransacked and a **Dragon Army soldier** (see appendix B) training six **hobgoblin** mercenaries. The Dragon Army soldier orders the hobgoblins to attack, telling them, "Here's your final test. Dispatch these fools and earn your place in the Dragon Army!" The hobgoblins fight until their commanding Dragon Army soldier is killed or half their number are wiped out.

Treasure. The soldiers' gear includes 200 gp and five suits of black chain mail emblazoned with the symbol of Takhisis. The Dragon Army soldier also carries the following message:

> The Highmaster requires soldiers, not thugs. Figure out which you have, then dispatch the ones not suited to the task. This is the Dragon Queen's will.

DRACONIAN BLOCKADE

Word reaches Kalaman of soldiers attacking travelers on the roads leading toward farmlands near the Estwilde border. The characters are ordered to follow the road east and see what they find.

Twenty miles east of Kalaman, where the road crosses the Raiding Rill, the characters find two empty, toppled wagons. A character who succeeds on a DC 12 Wisdom (Survival) finds clawed footprints leading to woods to the south. If the characters follow the path, they come on a camp of five **baaz draconians** led by a **bozak draconian** (see appendix B for both stat blocks). The draconians fight to the death.

Treasure. The draconians have stolen 120 gp, food equivalent to 60 days of rations, and a *driftglobe*.

MISSING SCOUTS

The characters are sent to track down a pair of scouts keeping tabs on Dragon Army movements north of the Vingaard River, twenty miles northwest of Kalaman and six miles east of Vogler. The characters are told to find the scouts' lookout post in a stand of gray birch, trees uncommon in the area.

Once the characters arrive in the area, they find the lookout post in fifteen minutes if a character succeeds on a DC 15 Wisdom (Survival) check; otherwise, finding the post takes three hours. Regardless of when the characters arrive, they find one **scout** tied to a tree in the center of the camp, being harassed by two **baaz draconians** (see appendix B); the other scout lies dead nearby. A **kapak draconian** (see appendix B) hides in the trees above the camp and tries to ambush the characters after combat begins.

Development. If the scout is freed, they report that the Dragon Army has split its forces to attack communities across Hinterlund and Nightlund. The army seems intent on isolating Kalaman from the Solamnic cities of Maelgoth and Palanthas in the west. The scout asks the party to help them return safely to Kalaman with this report. If the characters do so, Kalaman's leaders are pleased and reward them with a bonus of 100 gp each.

TROOPS RETURN

While the characters are completing another mission, they catch sight of a small group of armed soldiers marching toward Kalaman. These soldiers are at least a mile away and don't bear the colors of either Kalaman or the Dragon Army. If the characters draw closer, it's clear the soldiers are exhausted and have recently seen battle. If the soldiers spot the characters, their leader calls a halt and approaches the characters. Characters quickly recognize Cudgel Ironsmile (introduced in chapter 3).

> ### WARRIORS OF KRYNN INTERLUDES
>
> If you are using the *Dragonlance: Warriors of Krynn* board game alongside this adventure, consider running scenarios 2 and 3 during the "Missions" section of the adventure. These scenarios are optional, but they provide further insight into what Kalaman's troops are doing to combat the Dragon Army threat.

Reuniting with Cudgel. Cudgel is delighted to see the characters survived the evacuation of Vogler. She explains she and the troops here are all that remains of her mercenary company, the Ironclad Regiment, after they engaged the Dragon Army outside Vogler. Since their defeat, they've taken a winding route to avoid the enemy as they make their way to Kalaman. Cudgel seeks to rest and find work in the city. If it comes up that the characters are working for Kalaman's military, she asks the characters to introduce her to Marshal Vendri. Even if the characters don't make this introduction, in the coming days, Cudgel allies herself and her remaining troops with Kalaman's military.

Other Survivors. At your discretion, other folk from Vogler who were lost during the Dragon Army's attack, like Becklin (see the "Lost in Battle" section in chapter 3), could also return with Cudgel's group.

CHARACTER ADVANCEMENT

After completing this section—and before proceeding with the "Wheelwatch Outpost" section—the characters advance to 5th level.

WHEELWATCH OUTPOST

Wheelwatch, Kalaman's southernmost outpost, has been taken by Red Dragon Army forces. Darrett requests the characters participate in retaking it. Start this section only after you've run any desired events in the "Missions for Kalaman" section.

PREPARING FOR THE MISSION

Darrett brings the characters word that the Dragon Army has taken one of Kalaman's border forts. He has the following information:

- Wheelwatch Outpost stands near the border with the land of Estwilde. The fort supplies Kalaman's forces that patrol the border.
- The fort, which lies twenty-four miles southeast of the city, has been taken by the Dragon Army.
- Raven has been aiding Kalaman's military. She was given command of a force to retake the outpost, but that force is small and inexperienced.
- Darrett asks the characters to join Raven and support her in retaking the fort.

Darrett arranges a meeting between the characters and Raven later that day. During the meeting, Raven provides a sketch of Wheelwatch Outpost featuring the information on map 4.2. Raven also informs the characters of the following:

- The fort's tall northwest tower is a watchtower with a commanding view of the surrounding land.
- All four corner fortifications are equipped with horns that sentries use to raise an alarm.
- Raven doesn't know how many Dragon Army soldiers occupy the fort.
- After Raven and her troops leave Kalaman, it will take them eight hours to get in position in a secluded grove a mile from the fort.

Raven suggests the characters slip into the fort and open a gate without raising the alarm. However, she's amenable to any plan that doesn't risk the lives of her troops or destroy the fort.

RECONNAISSANCE

Wheelwatch Outpost lies south of where the streams known as the Gravel Run and the Raiding Rill meet. Read the following description when the characters come within sight of the fort:

> In the distance, a squat stone fortress rises from one of the last patches of green before the rocky scrubland of Estwilde. Its tall wooden gates are flanked by crenelated battlements and solid watchtowers. Torchlight shines through the fort's windows, and every so often, armored figures make their way along the walls.

If a character spends eight hours observing the fort, they determine that patrols in the corner towers switch watch duty every six hours, and they can make a DC 14 Intelligence (Investigation) check to estimate how many Dragon Army soldiers are in the fort. On a successful check, the character accurately estimates about twenty Dragon Army soldiers are in the fort. On a failed check, they estimate double this number. If the check fails by 10 or more, the character is spotted, and after 10 minutes, a squad of six **Dragon Army soldiers** (see appendix B) leaves the fort to investigate the character's position. If the soldiers find the character or don't return, the fort goes on alert (see the "Wheelwatch Alert" section).

WHEELWATCH ALERT

The Dragon Army troops occupying Wheelwatch Outpost are on the lookout for danger. Use the following details to guide when the Dragon Army soldiers go on alert and how that affects their behavior.

ALARM HORNS

Each of the outpost's corner guard posts (areas W2, W3, and W4) is equipped with an alarm horn. If a sentry in one of these areas notices enemies or unusual activity, they attempt to sound an alarm horn 1 round later on their turn. Once an alarm horn is sounded, the fort goes on alert.

ALERT

If a threat is detected, the eight **Dragon Army soldiers** (see appendix B) in area W5 rush to meet it (or gather in area W1 if the source is unclear). While on alert, Dragon Army troops have advantage on Wisdom (Perception) checks. Troops remain on alert for twelve hours after spotting an enemy or finding other clear signs of enemy activity. In the case of other threats, troops remain on alert until the danger passes or is identified as a false alarm.

IMPOSTORS

Characters who wear Dragon Army armor have advantage on Charisma (Deception) checks made to pass as Dragon Army soldiers.

DRAGONNEL RIDER

The Dragon Army has a secret weapon in area W8: a **Dragon Army dragonnel** and its **Dragon Army officer** rider (see appendix B for both stat blocks). If the characters don't discover the pair first, the dragonnel and its rider take to the air and attack at a dramatic moment—likely after the characters have overcome most of the fort's forces or as they work to open the gates in area W1.

WHEELWATCH FEATURES

Wheelwatch Outpost has the following features:

Ceilings. The ceilings in the outpost's interior chambers are 10 feet high.

Gates. The outpost's 15-foot-tall, reinforced wooden gates can be opened or closed only by the gate controls nearest them (see area W1 for a description of these controls). Each gate door is a Huge object with AC 17, 80 hit points, and immunity to poison and psychic damage.

Light. Torches provide bright light throughout the fort, except for area W5, which is dimly lit.

Walls. The walls of Wheelwatch are 20 feet high, with towers and fortifications adding an additional 10 feet for each floor. A character can climb the walls by succeeding on a DC 14 Strength (Athletics) check. The windows in these walls are 6-inch-wide arrow slits.

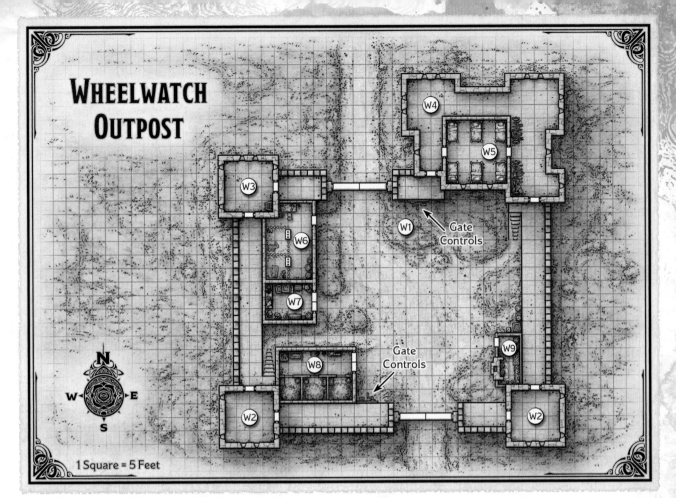

MAP 4.2: WHEELWATCH OUTPOST

WHEELWATCH LOCATIONS

The following locations are keyed to map 4.2.

W1: COURTYARD

> The fort's courtyard holds several small structures with wooden roofs. Stairs climb from the dirt yard to the fort's west and east battlements. To the north and south stand solid wooden gates reinforced with iron bands. Along the wall next to each gate is a metal mechanism with a prominent winch.

At any given time, three **Dragon Army soldiers** (see appendix B) are in the courtyard patrolling, training, or running errands.

Gate Controls. The north and south gates each have a mechanism to open and close that gate. Unlocking a gate mechanism requires using one of the outpost's three gate keys or succeeding on a DC 14 Dexterity check using thieves' tools. Once unlocked, the winch on the controls moves freely. It takes 1 minute to fully open or close the gates using the controls. Opening a gate attracts the attention of all creatures in areas W1, W2, W3, and W4.

W2: SOUTH GUARD TOWERS

> Two soldiers stand at this stone room's narrow windows. A horn hangs on the wall between the doors.

The south guard towers are identical. In each, two **Dragon Army soldiers** (see appendix B) watch the surrounding land.

W3: NORTHWEST GUARD TOWER

> Narrow windows line the walls of this bare stone room. In the southeast corner, a ladder climbs to the floor above. On the wall next to it hangs a metal horn.

The northwest tower is the largest of Wheelwatch's guard towers. Its second floor is identical to the first, accessed by the ladder here.

On the first floor, a **sivak draconian** (see appendix B) stands guard in human guise. It's using its Shape Theft reaction to take the form of a Kalaman soldier it killed. If slain, it shifts back to its true form.

Two **Dragon Army soldiers** (see appendix B) guard the second floor. Their alarm horn hangs on the south wall by the ladder.

W4: Northeast Fortification

> A U-shaped hall lined with narrow windows runs around this fortification. Along a wall bearing racks of weapons and a horn hanging from a leather strap, doors lead into an interior room.

Two **baaz draconians** (see appendix B) keep watch in the hall here. Their alarm horn hangs from the north weapon rack. If battle breaks out here, the Dragon Army soldiers in area W5 come to investigate after 2 rounds.

Treasure. The weapon racks hold dozens of weapons that belonged to Kalaman's forces before the fort was taken. One rack also has a hoopak staff (see appendix A) taken from Elgo (who's imprisoned in area W6). Mounted over the south rack is a shiny lance etched with images of dragons; made of tin, this decoration is useless in combat.

W5: Barracks

> Soft lantern light dimly outlines six two-level sets of bunk beds filling this modest barracks. A footlocker sits beneath each set of bunks.

At any given time, eight **Dragon Army soldiers** (see appendix B) rest here. They swap places with on-duty guards throughout the day. If they hear battle in area W4 or an alarm horn sounds, they rush to support their allies after 2 rounds.

Treasure. Under each of the sets of bunks is a simple wooden footlocker. Each holds two sets of common clothes and 10 gp. One footlocker also contains a silvered longsword, while another contains a holy symbol of Takhisis and a key for the gate controls in area W1.

W6: Prison

If the alarm hasn't been raised, a **Dragon Army officer** (see appendix B) named Ardlic Vanse is seated at a desk, writing a report. He commands the forces here. He is terrified of his commander, Kansaldi Fire-Eyes, and will sacrifice his life and the lives of his troops to keep control of the fort.

North Cell. This locked cell holds a neutral human **Kalaman soldier** (see appendix B) named Lanal Brint. He was sleeping off a night of drink in this cell when the outpost was taken. He tells the characters anything they want to know about the fortress—such as how the gate mechanisms work—but only after he's separated from Elgo (see below).

South Cell. This locked cell holds Elgo Duck-ditcher, a chaotic good **kender skirmisher** (see appendix B) who considers herself a famous explorer and avoider of fowl. The Red Dragon Army imprisoned her here after she insisted she be allowed to explore the fort. In the days since, she has told Lanal every story she knows twice and has declared him her adopted cousin. She's convinced his name is Flannel, though, and she won't hear otherwise—she knows her own cousin's name. If freed, Elgo won't leave until she recovers her hoopak (found in area W4).

Treasure. The papers on the desk include Commander Vanse's daily reports, along with orders to hold Wheelwatch at all costs, signed "Dragon Highmaster Kansaldi Fire-Eyes." A desk drawer holds thieves' tools confiscated from Elgo and 200 gp.

Commander Vanse carries an iron ring with keys to the cells in this area and to the gates in area W1.

W7: Storage

The storage room's barrels contain enough food, water, and other supplies to sustain the outpost for a month. A character who spends 5 minutes searching the supplies and succeeds on a DC 16 Intelligence (Investigation) check finds a dusty case containing six flasks of alchemist's fire.

W8: Stable

A character who listens at the door to the stable and succeeds on a DC 14 Wisdom (Perception) check hears something large moving inside.

> Filled with stalls and supplies for horses, this stable stinks of large animals and blood. The ground is covered with the scattered skeletons of two horses. Looming over them, something large, red, and reptilian picks through their bones.

A **Dragon Army dragonnel** and its rider, a **Dragon Army officer**, are in this stable (see appendix B for both stat blocks). If the characters enter, the dragonnel recognizes them as intruders and attacks. This is likely the first time the characters have seen a creature this similar to a dragon. A character who succeeds on a DC 14 Intelligence (Arcana or Nature) check knows the creature is a dragonnel, a wild lesser cousin of the storied dragons that disappeared from Krynn.

If the dragonnel and its rider already took flight (see "Wheelwatch Alert"), this area is empty.

W9: Kitchen

> Cooking supplies fill this room. Opposite a table covered in cutlery and scrawny carrots, a human soldier wearing a stained apron over his armor minds two pots bubbling on a lit stove.

A **Dragon Army soldier** (see appendix B) prepares a meal here: a watery soup, heavy on pepper.

Treasure. The cook's prized possession is a pair of salt and pepper shakers worth 20 gp. They're lovingly carved to resemble black and white dragons.

COMPLETING THE MISSION

Once the characters open Wheelwatch's gates, Raven sends in her troops to clear out any remaining Dragon Army resistance. She suggests the characters rest and recuperate, then return to Kalaman with a letter from Raven informing Marshal Vendri of their victory.

Any Dragon Army soldier taken captive during the mission makes one of the following claims:

Futile Victory. The Dragon Army is certain to re-take Wheelwatch at any time. Kalaman's defenders should surrender now.

Gathering Threat. The Red Dragon Army's leader, Dragon Highmaster Kansaldi Fire-Eyes, is still preparing her forces. Her troops will subdue the region before turning to greater conquests.

Messenger. The dragonnel stationed here was a mere messenger. When war truly comes to the region, red wings will darken the skies.

BATTLE AT STEEL SPRINGS

The trip from Wheelwatch back to Kalaman is uneventful. On their return to Castle Kalaman, the character with the highest passive Wisdom (Perception) score notices the castle is unusually quiet. When the characters report to Marshal Vendri's office, an aide informs them the marshal is away from Kalaman and shares the following facts:

- After the characters left Kalaman, the city council got word that a contingent of Dragon Army troops had broken away from the larger force.
- Tired of measured steps, members of Kalaman's leadership—spurred by Lord Bakaris—demanded Kalaman's military ride out to seize a victory.
- With Marshal Vendri away leading troops further west, Governor Miat approved the strike.
- Lord Bakaris and his son are leading the attack. Darrett is serving under them.
- They plan to ambush the Red Dragon Army near a crossing of the Inkwater called Steel Springs, thirty miles west of Kalaman.

The aide knows nothing more, but before the characters leave, the aide discreetly slips them a sealed note signed by Darrett that reads as follows:

> Come at once. Bakaris is leading us to ruin at Steel Springs. He's the commander of this mission, and I can't disobey. I'll do what I can, but I need your help.

If the characters seek out Governor Miat, he's busy conducting other business with the city's guild leaders and won't be available for hours. Even if the characters find him, he isn't a military leader, doesn't understand the characters' concern, and can do little now the troops have been sent.

FLIGHT TO STEEL SPRINGS

Assuming the characters head to Steel Springs, they arrive as Kalaman's forces engage the Dragon Army. However, Kalaman received faulty intelligence, and its troops are badly outnumbered. Rather than joining the Kalaman forces in their advance, the characters find themselves defending a retreat.

The adventure unfolds in one of two ways:

With Mass Combat. If you're using the *Dragonlance: Warriors of Krynn* game with this adventure, consult the "Warriors of Krynn: Scenario 4" sidebar.

Without Mass Combat. If you aren't using the *Dragonlance: Warriors of Krynn* game, continue with the following section.

RETREAT FROM STEEL SPRINGS

When the characters complete the thirty-mile trip to Steel Springs, read the following text:

> As the brook called the Inkwater comes into view, smoke rises over the tree line beyond it. Wounded Kalaman soldiers stagger from the trees, heading toward a narrow crossing that lies in your direction. Dragon Army soldiers give chase on horseback.

This battlefield is represented on map 4.3. As the characters arrive, six **Kalaman soldiers** (see appendix B), each with 8 hit points, flee south from the battle occurring up the road. They've reached the islet at the center of the map. Four **Dragon Army soldiers** (see appendix B) on **warhorses** gallop in pursuit along the road at the north of the map.

WARRIORS OF KRYNN: SCENARIO 4

The characters reach the battlefield as the conflict turns against Kalaman's forces. Read the introduction to scenario 4 in *Dragonlance: Warriors of Krynn*, then play that scenario. This scenario details the characters' attempt to organize a retreat from this losing battle.

If the characters attain a win or hold during this scenario, Kalaman's soldiers henceforth know them as the Saviors of Steel Springs, and each character has advantage on their next Charisma (Deception or Persuasion) check made to influence a member of Kalaman's military. Characters gain no benefit for a loss.

When this scenario concludes, proceed with "The Lord's Arrival."

The Dragon Army soldiers ride to the edge of the northern stream, throwing javelins at the retreating Kalaman soldiers. The Dragon Army soldiers shift their attention to the characters if attacked.

The Kalaman soldiers continue their retreat south instead of engaging. They move only 15 feet per round (see "Steel Springs Battlefield Events"), staying in a group and aiding the wounded among them.

After all enemy forces are defeated, proceed with the "Commanders' Retreat" section.

STEEL SPRINGS BATTLEFIELD FEATURES

The battlefield includes the following features:

Rocks and Scrub. Rocks and vegetation on the map are difficult terrain.

Stream. The chilly stream is 4 feet deep and is difficult terrain. The crossings aren't difficult terrain.

Fray. The 15-foot-wide area marked by the design at the edge of the map represents directions from which creatures from the nearby battle might arrive, as detailed in the following section.

STEEL SPRINGS BATTLEFIELD EVENTS

During this encounter, as long as there are still Dragon Army soldiers on the battlefield, roll on the Steel Springs Battlefield Events table each round on initiative count 0. Also consider rolling on the table if a character enters the Fray or a Kalaman soldier is killed. After you roll on this table, the wounded Kalaman soldiers move 15 feet south along the road unless an event says otherwise.

STEEL SPRINGS BATTLEFIELD EVENTS

d8	Event
1–3	One of the wounded Kalaman soldiers collapses. The soldier and other Kalaman soldiers within 10 feet of that soldier don't move this round.
4–5	Arrows arc over the trees to the north. A random player character and each creature within 10 feet of that character must succeed on a DC 14 Dexterity saving throw or take 10 (3d6) piercing damage.
6	Another wounded **Kalaman soldier** (see appendix B) with 8 hit points appears adjacent to the Fray nearest a random Dragon Army soldier. This wounded soldier moves only 15 feet per round and tries to retreat south like the other Kalaman soldiers.
7	A dragonnel flies overhead, dropping a screaming Kalaman soldier next to a random player character as it does. The soldier dies on impact. This event is unsettling but has no other effect.
8	A hostile **Dragon Army soldier** (see appendix B) mounted on a **warhorse** appears in a space adjacent to the Fray nearest a random player character. This event occurs only once during the battle; re-roll on this table if it is rolled again.

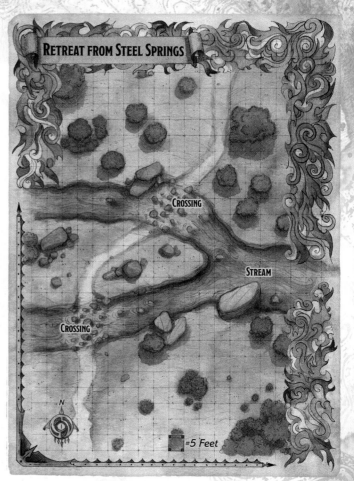

MAP 4.3: RETREAT FROM STEEL SPRINGS

COMMANDERS' RETREAT

After the Dragon Army soldiers are dealt with, read or paraphrase the following text:

> A dozen mounted soldiers gallop from the tree line, rushing south toward the crossing. Kalaman's colors are visible on these soldiers' armor, despite the dents and stains of battle. It's easy to pick out Darrett among these riders in his distinctive Solamnic armor. Another figure sits behind Darrett, sharing his steed.

This group of twelve mounted Kalaman soldiers includes several commanders who drew off the Dragon Army forces so their allies could retreat farther to the east. Darrett rides with Lord Bakaris behind him, sharing his mount.

Darrett spots the characters and tells them the Dragon Army's forces overwhelmed Kalaman's troops and are in pursuit. He urges the characters to follow him to a fallback point to the east. If the characters seek to fight the Dragon Army, Darrett reinforces that hundreds of enemy soldiers are inbound and the wounded Kalaman troops need the characters' help. Lord Bakaris is clearly in a state of shock and doesn't speak during the conversation.

SAFE FOR NOW

Darrett leads the characters six miles east of Steel Springs, where Kalaman's soldiers have retreated to. Once there, Darrett explains the following details:

- Lord Bakaris ordered an assault on the Dragon Army forces, unaware of Dragon Army reinforcements nearby. The battle swiftly swung against Kalaman's forces.
- Darrett and other commanders ordered a swift withdrawal, saving many lives.
- In the retreat, forces commanded by Bakaris the Younger were overwhelmed. Bakaris the Younger is unaccounted for and believed dead.
- Lord Bakaris is in a state of shock.
- The Dragon Army doesn't seem to be pursuing the retreating troops.
- Darrett has word that Marshal Vendri's forces are traveling from the west to protect the city.

Darrett, the de facto leader of the retreating forces, lets the troops rest overnight. He suggests the characters rest along with them. The next morning, he encourages the characters to ride ahead to Kalaman to inform Governor Miat of what happened while the surviving troops rendezvous with Marshal Vendri on the way to Kalaman.

THE LORD'S ARRIVAL

This section presents a surprise attack on Kalaman's leadership and reveals a new threat hidden within the Dragon Army. Before the characters begin this section, make sure they're rested. There is no timeline for how the following events unfold, but encourage a sense of urgency; the characters are all that stand between Kalaman and tragedy.

RETURNING TO KALAMAN

As the characters near the gates of Kalaman, read the following text:

> A crowd mills at the gate ahead, dozens of commoners murmuring and excitedly looking past the closed portcullis. "There's nothing to see!" shouts a guard, "Please move along."

The characters learn the following from a gate guard or anyone in the crowd:

- An hour ago, a retinue of Knights of Solamnia entered the city and headed to Castle Kalaman.
- The knights aren't well-liked in Kalaman, but at this point, any allies are welcome.

- The lead knight's name was Knight Caradoc. He was a charming man with a message for the governor.
- Knight Caradoc entered with at least a dozen heavily armored knights, like something out of a story.

While learning about the knights' arrival, a character can press a local for more details by making a DC 14 Charisma (Persuasion) check. On a successful check, the local says they were surprised by some of the knights' armor; it was tarnished in a way the Knights of Solamnia from old stories would surely have avoided.

When the characters identify themselves, the guards raise the gate's portcullis and admit them into the city.

SOLAMNIC KNIGHTS MYSTERIOUSLY ARRIVE IN KALAMAN.

KATERINA LADON

Castle Kalaman's Visitors

The gates of Castle Kalaman are closed when the characters arrive, but the guards recognize the characters and admit them. The guards confirm a contingent of knights is meeting with the governor and the city councilors in the main council chamber, but a couple of the knights remained in the castle's courtyard if the characters wish to meet them.

Once the characters enter Castle Kalaman's courtyard, read the following:

> Castle Kalaman's courtyard is largely deserted, as most of the city's defenders remain with the troops west of the city. Near the covered cloisters leading to the city council's conference rooms are two heavily armored Knights of Solamnia on horseback. One of them holds a banner bearing a prominent rose emblem.

The two knights here are Undead soldiers. They use the **wight** stat block with the following changes:

- They wear plate armor and have AC 18.
- They don't have the Sunlight Sensitivity trait.

The wights refuse to speak, and their armor and other clothing disguise their nature. Any character with a passive Wisdom (Perception) score of 16 or higher notices the knights' armor is covered in spots of ash and rust, as if exceptionally old.

These Undead knights block the entrance to the castle. They attack anyone who tries to slip past or to remove part of a wight's disguise. After a wight takes 10 points of damage, its disguise is undermined, revealing the skeletal form below.

Council Massacre

When the characters approach the council chamber, read the following text:

> As you near the chamber where the governor and city council are meeting with the Knights of Solamnia, the halls are empty. The council chamber's door stands ajar, and its guard is absent. Though the room usually buzzes with conversation, everything is silent.

In the council chamber, the characters find the following scene:

> A scene of slaughter spills across the council chamber. Several guards wearing the colors of Kalaman soldiers lie tangled amid skeletal remains in tarnished Solamnic armor. The bloody bodies of Kalaman's council members slump in high-backed chairs and across the room's large table. At a position of honor opposite the door, Governor Calof Miat's body is transfixed to his chair, a gleaming longsword piercing his chest.
>
> Next to the governor's body, a man in Solamnic armor rocks back in a chair. He props his booted feet on the table as he balances a scroll on one finger.

The governor, all of Kalaman's council members, and six castle guards lie dead here. They are beyond the aid of a *revivify* spell.

The man here is **Caradoc** (see appendix B), an Undead spirit who has been possessing a Knight of Solamnia (use the **knight** stat block) for over a week. Charming but utterly amoral, Caradoc is Lord Loren Soth's seneschal. He served as the mouthpiece of Lord Soth and his Undead troops, gaining them access to Kalaman's rulers under the guise of being helpful Knights of Solamnia. During their audience with the city's rulers, Lord Soth, Caradoc, and their Undead knights murdered the city's leaders. Soth then went on to his actual objective in the catacombs beneath the castle, while Caradoc remained behind to prevent any interference.

Caradoc

Caradoc (see appendix B) died during the Cataclysm alongside Lord Soth over three hundred years ago. In life, Caradoc gained his station among the Knights of Solamnia due to his noble pedigree and his family's money. Cowardly but charming, Caradoc befriended and came to serve his fellow knight, Lord Soth, often advising the bold knight about the subtleties of courtly intrigues. Soth made Caradoc his seneschal, and the knight serves him still.

When Soth rose as an Undead, Caradoc was similarly cursed, returning to life as an incorporeal spirit. Caradoc can't leave the grounds of Dargaard Keep except within a body he has possessed. Now, he delights in jumping from body to body, using and disposing of the living as he pleases.

Personality Trait. "I might be dead, but there's no reason I can't live it up a little."

Ideal. "The safest place to be is behind the toughest warrior in the room."

Bond. "In life and in death, I'm the only one who matters."

Flaw. "Who can resist a little drama?"

CAUGHT IN THE ACT

When Caradoc sees the characters, read the following text:

> Noticing you, the knight stands, clears his throat, and bombastically declares, "Hail, friends, and fear not—your heroes have arrived!
>
> "I, Knight Caradoc, bring word that the Knights of Solamnia are, at this very moment, en route with all manner of pomp and mustache wax and whatever else they bother with these days." He gestures at the corpses about the room, "Do try to contain yourselves better than this lot did."

Caradoc delights in mocking the characters and disrespecting the dead. As he's buying time for Lord Soth, Caradoc converses with the characters for as long as he can, sharing the following information:

- He's Caradoc, a Knight of Solamnia.
- No, of course the Knights of Solamnia aren't actually coming, but saying so did allow him to get his lord's retinue through the city gates.
- No, he won't say who his lord is.
- No, he doesn't serve the Red Dragon Army—not quite. He serves his lord, and his lord serves a higher power.
- His lord was here, but he had to go attend to business with a musty old friend.

A character who succeeds on a DC 18 Intelligence (History) check recalls Caradoc was the name of an obscure knight of the Order of the Rose who died during the Cataclysm.

Blood Trail. While speaking with Caradoc or after defeating him, the character with the highest passive Wisdom (Perception) score notices a blood trail leading to a small, shattered door at the rear of the room. Beyond it, a hall leads to the sealed staircase detailed in the "Path Below" section.

Fighting Caradoc. When the characters attack Caradoc or try to leave the room, Caradoc pulls his sword from Governor Miat's corpse and attacks. He's reckless in battle and mocks the characters as they fight. Once his knight form is defeated, Caradoc rises in his true incorporeal form. On the first round after emerging from the knight's body, he automatically succeeds on the saving throw his Bound Haunting trait requires him to make. He continues to attack the characters with his Possession and Withering Touch actions until he's destroyed or his Bound Haunting trait spirits him back to Dargaard Keep. Before vanishing, Caradoc promises the characters he'll see them again.

KNIGHT CARADOC CARRIES A MESSAGE TO KALAMAN'S LEADERS.

Lost Knight. If the knight Caradoc has been possessing drops to 0 hit points, allow the knight to make death saving throws, as the characters may wish to heal him. His name is Durstan Rial (neutral, human **knight**), and he has little memory of the last few weeks since he was ambushed while traveling near the Dargaard Mountains. He helps the characters defeat Caradoc if the spirit is present, but he ultimately wishes to return to his home in Maelgoth.

Treasure. Once Caradoc is defeated, a character can get a better look at the scroll he was holding. Its slightly scorched parchment is sealed by black wax with a rose emblem stamped into it. If they open the scroll, the characters see the following words burned into the page:

> People of Kalaman,
>
> I exert my rightful claim as ruler of the province of Knightlund. Submit or flee.
>
> Lord Loren Soth, Knight of the Rose

A character who succeeds on a DC 14 Intelligence (History) check recalls the following information about Lord Soth:

Knight and Ruler. Lord Soth was a Knight of Solamnia of the Order of the Rose. He ruled the province of Nightlund when it was known as Knightlund.

Failed Redemption. The gods gave Soth the opportunity to redeem himself and prevent the Cataclysm, but he didn't complete his quest, and the Cataclysm occurred.

Tarnished Reputation. Soth's failure contributed to the widespread distrust of the Knights of Solamnia.

Cursed Castle. Soth's fate is a mystery, but his home, Dargaard Keep, is known to be a cursed, haunted ruin.

LEEDARA'S WARNING

Moments after Caradoc is defeated, Leedara (detailed in chapter 3) appears. Read the following text:

> The musician Leedara steps forward from a corner of the chamber, though you could've sworn it was empty a moment ago. A look of urgency tightens her features. "You must hurry on," the elf says, pointing to a shattered door at the rear of the chamber. "There's a secret beneath this castle—one the old lord can't be allowed to possess."

Leedara won't elaborate on her words or why she's present, insisting it might already be too late and the characters must hurry. At some point while the characters are all distracted or otherwise don't have her in their line of sight, Leedara vanishes. If the characters later search for her in Kalaman, they don't find her.

PATH BELOW

Beyond the broken door in the council chamber lies a narrow corridor used by servants. Several plain doors lead to other parts of the castle, but at the far end of the passage shines a faint violet light. Characters who seek out the light see the following:

> A doorframe sculpted with somber knights stands in an alcove along this corridor. The doorframe was once sealed, but shattered bricks now lie scattered across the floor. Beyond the opening, a steep flight of stairs descends below ground. Violet light and the sound of crackling flames emanate from below.

This passage descends into the catacombs beneath Castle Kalaman.

RAIDED CATACOMBS

When the Knights of Solamnia held Castle Kalaman, the structure was more than a fortress—it was also a temple, beneath which fallen knights were entombed in a place of honor. During the Cataclysm, waves of divine wrath raged across the land. While the flames receded following the disaster, in a few cursed places this Cataclysmic fire remained. One such place is the catacombs containing the tomb of Knight Sarlamir beneath Castle Kalaman. The Knights of Solamnia locked these tombs away, and when others later took control of the castle, the catacombs were sealed entirely. Now Lord Soth has come to these catacombs following the Dragon Queen's will.

KNIGHT SARLAMIR'S CURSE

Among the dead entombed beneath Castle Kalaman lies the body of Knight Zanas Sarlamir. A respected knight of the Order of the Crown, Sarlamir received a divine quest from the god Paladine years before the Cataclysm. Paladine told him the Kingpriest of Istar had created a magical wonder in the east—a flying city (detailed in chapter 6)—and in so doing, the kingpriest had enraged the metallic dragons that had long remained hidden on Krynn. Paladine tasked Sarlamir with going to this flying city, assuaging the dragons' fury, and convincing the kingpriest to return the city to the land. Sarlamir agreed. The knight knew his task was daunting, though, and decided to hedge his bets. He took his family's greatest treasure with him: an ancient *dragonlance*.

Sarlamir and his fellow knights reached the kingpriest's flying city and stood before a flight of righteously furious metallic dragons. When the kingpriest refused to land the flying city, the dragons refused to leave. As the conflict escalated, Sarlamir used his *dragonlance* to slay the dragons' leader, the gold dragon Karavarix. As soon as Karavarix's blood touched the *dragonlance*, the weapon rusted away in Knight Sarlamir's hand. The dragons attacked, slaying Sarlamir and crashing the flying city.

A handful of Sarlamir's loyal knights escaped, and they brought his body and his cursed *dragonlance* back to Kalaman. Both were interred beneath the city, where they remained.

LORD SOTH'S CURSE

The characters are preceded through Castle Kalaman's catacombs by Lord Soth, a villain whose vices allowed the Cataclysm to occur.

LORD SOTH'S LEGEND

In the years before the Cataclysm, Loren Soth was a Solamnic Knight of the Order of the Rose. He ruled the province of Knightlund from Dargaard Keep. However, his fall from grace began when he rescued a company of Silvanesti elves from raiders, including the priest Isolde and her attendants. Though Lord Soth was married, he fell in love with Isolde—and shortly after, Soth's wife died. He and Isolde married days later. For disrespecting his dead wife's memory, the Knights of Solamnia cast Soth from their orders.

Soon after, the gods called Soth to redeem himself by preventing the Cataclysm, but Soth failed in his quest, and the gods rained destruction on the world. The Knights of Solamnia fell into disgrace in the aftermath of the Cataclysm, and Dargaard Keep became a cursed, haunted ruin.

The Rest of the Story

When Lord Soth began his gods-given quest to avert the Cataclysm, he encountered Isolde's attendants, who blamed him for leading Isolde from her holy path. The attendants played on his jealousy, falsely accusing Isolde of being unfaithful. Enraged, Soth ignored the gods' direction and returned to Dargaard Keep to murder her. As he did, the gods unleashed the Cataclysm on the world. With Isolde's dying breath, she cursed Soth to suffer one lifetime for every life lost in the Cataclysm.

For his defiance of the gods, Soth became a death knight, while his followers were similarly reanimated as other Undead. Meanwhile, several of Isolde's attendants became spirits devoted to ensuring Soth never finds peace.

Cataclysmic Fire

Though the signs of the gods' rage have receded from the world, violet flames from the Cataclysm continue to burn in Sarlamir's tomb. This magical fire lingers as a mark of disgrace on one who failed the gods and the world. Lord Soth has come to the catacombs seeking the Cataclysmic fire for its magical properties, which can be harnessed through rituals whispered to him by the Dragon Queen. These phantom flames respond to the memories of the dead and re-create illusory scenes from the moments that haunt their souls.

Visions in Fire

As Soth moves through the catacombs, the Cataclysmic fire limning the tombs re-creates tragic scenes from his life. These scenes represent Soth's memories of events—which don't always match the actual events. Every time the characters enter a new area, the illusory flames create figures of violet flame, play out a scene, then harmlessly fade. After reading the description of each room, paraphrase the next scene from the following list:

CATACLYSMIC FLAMES REVEAL GLIMPSES OF LORD SOTH'S MEMORIES.

Meeting. A Knight of Solamnia saves a group of elf travelers from ogre raiders. An elf woman falls into the knight's arms. Behind him, the silhouette of a human woman turns and fades away.

Disgraced. The knight from the previous vision is cast out from a group of other knights. The scene fades into a wedding between the knight and the elf woman from the previous vision.

Quest. The knight receives a vision from a beam of divine light. As his wife pleads with him, he dons his armor and mounts his steed, then heads off.

Distraction. The knight's encounters the attendants of the elf woman from the first vision. They taunt him and point back the way he came. The knight slays them and turns back home in a rage.

Confrontation. The knight slays his wife as the world around him crumbles and burns. The knight burns as well, but he doesn't fall. His armor fuses with his body; his eyes blaze with flames; and he becomes a terrifying, deathless figure.

If the characters enter a room after all these scenes have played out, skeletal visages leer at them from the flames, then vanish. Characters who recalled Lord Soth's legend in the "Caught in the Act" section recognize that these scenes relate to his tale. If no characters succeeded on that check, they can make the DC 14 Intelligence (History) check again with advantage after seeing the first two scenes. On a success, they recall everything in that section.

Though the full truth of Lord Soth's tale remains vague, the characters might learn more when they encounter Leedara again in chapter 7.

RAIDED CATACOMBS FEATURES

The catacombs beneath Castle Kalaman have the following features:

Cataclysmic Flames. Illusory violet flames fill the catacombs with dim light. These flames create no heat and don't harm creatures that touch them.

Ceilings. The ceilings throughout the catacombs are 15 feet high.

Doors. The doors throughout the catacombs are made of stone. They can be opened only by creatures with a combined Strength of 20 or higher.

RAIDED CATACOMBS LOCATIONS

The following locations are keyed to map 4.4.

R1: HALL OF KNIGHTS

> Stairs descend into a stone chamber engulfed in violet flames. In the fire stand four dignified statues of Knights of Solamnia. At the east end of the room lies an antechamber before a stone double door. There, a fifth statue depicts a bison-headed warrior.

The statues depict four historic leaders of the Knights of Solamnia and the bison-headed god Kiri-Jolith. A cleric of Kiri-Jolith or a character who succeeds on a DC 14 Intelligence (Religion) check recognizes the statue of Kiri-Jolith, god of honor and war.

The flames are Cataclysmic fire (see the "Cataclysmic Fire" section). Once the characters enter, the first scene from the "Visions in Fire" section plays.

R2: CRYPTS

> This long chamber blazes with violet flame. The walls are lined with alcoves, within which lie bodies wrapped in yellowed cloth. A brazier rests at the end of the hall. A section of wall has been smashed to the southwest, creating a crude tunnel to the catacombs beyond. To the southeast stands a closed stone door.

As the characters enter this area, the next scene from the "Visions in Fire" section plays out.

Burial Alcoves. Fifteen forgotten Knights of Solamnia are buried here, each with their now-rusted plate armor and longsword. If any of the bodies are disturbed, two **wraiths** that look like spectral Knights of Solamnia emerge from crypts and attack. The wraiths vanish if a character returns any stolen goods and makes an earnest apology.

Broken Passage. Lord Soth smashed through the catacomb's wall to venture directly toward area R7. A character with the Stonecunning trait can tell this tunnel was created only a short while ago.

R3: TOMB OF VAUNTED STEEL

> Violet flames engulf this room, dancing across walls with faded mosaics of blacksmiths forging gleaming weapons. Bars seal off alcoves to the north and south. To the west, weapons hang on the walls. A crude tunnel has been punched through the south wall there.

As the characters enter this area, the next scene from the "Visions in Fire" section plays out.

Sealed Tombs. The two tombs commemorate honored Solamnic weaponsmiths. Their burial places are sealed behind iron bars, which are Medium objects with AC 19, 20 hit points, and immunity to poison and psychic damage.

The north tomb contains a skeleton clutching a *berserker axe*.

The south tomb is empty except for an iron amulet shaped like a smith's hammer. A cleric of Reorx or a character who succeeds on a DC 14 Intelligence (Religion) check recognizes this as a holy symbol of Reorx, god of craft.

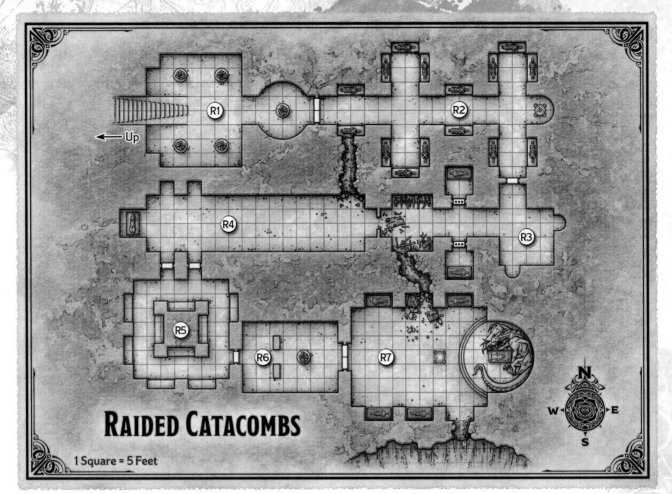

Map 4.4: Raided Catacombs

Broken Passage. Lord Soth destroyed a door and a section of wall here to reach area R7. Characters with the Stonecunning trait or who succeed on a DC 14 Wisdom (Perception or Survival) check can tell this destruction occurred recently and the narrow passage is dangerously unstable. The first creature to pass 5 feet along this passage must make a DC 16 Dexterity saving throw as the south end of the path collapses, blocking the way to area R7. On a successful save, the creature safely dodges back into area R3. On a failed save, it takes 4d6 bludgeoning damage and is forced into area R3.

Treasure. The weapons to the west are the armaments of heroic Solamnic knights and their allies. Most are rotted or rusted through, but characters can find a *+1 longsword*, a *mithral breastplate*, and a *Kagonesti forest shroud* (see appendix A).

R4: Hall of Steeds

> Mosaics of knights riding armored stallions cover the walls of this room and are limned in violet flames. To the east lies a shattered stone door, and north of it gapes a tunnel that leads back to the catacomb entrance. At the west end of the room stands a statue of a rearing horse and two stone doors leading south.

As the characters enter this area, the next scene from the "Visions in Fire" section plays out. After the scene completes, two **warhorse skeletons** manifest at the west end of the hall. These are the remains of the heroic warhorses Xheriev and Steelwind, which attack. However, if a character is wearing the armor of a Solamnic knight or succeeds on a DC 16 Wisdom (Animal Handling) check, the skeletons stop, bow, and vanish. That character then gains the following charm (a type of supernatural gift detailed in the *Dungeon Master's Guide*).

Favor of the Heroic Steed
Supernatural Gift (Charm)

Two heroic steeds find you worthy and agree to serve you. This charm has 2 charges. As an action, you can expend 1 charge to summon a **warhorse** wearing plate barding (AC 18). The warhorse serves you for 24 hours, then vanishes.

R5: Monument of the Lost

> This chamber blazes with violet flames. In the middle of the room, steps lead up to a sleek marble monument etched with hundreds of lines of text. Doors lead from the room to the north and east.

As the characters enter this area, the next scene from the "Visions in Fire" section unfolds.

Marble Slabs. The monument in this room records the Knights of Solamnia who served at Castle Kalaman and died with honor. A character who reads the monument finds the names of Knight Vogler and Knight Jandin (whom the characters meet in area R6).

R6: Shrine of the Honored

> A statue of a saluting Knight of Solamnia stands in this room, along with two tall marble slabs etched with text. All three crackle with violet flames, and the spirit of a Knight of Solamnia kneels before one of the slabs. A door leads to the west, and a double door leads to the east.

As the characters enter this area, the next scene from the "Visions in Fire" section plays out.

Marble Slabs. The marble slabs here bear the names of honored heroes and leaders among the Knights of Solamnia who served at Castle Kalaman. A character who reads the names finds Knight Sarlamir on the list.

Knight Spirit. The kneeling spirit is incorporeal and harmless. If attacked, she fades away and doesn't reappear.

This spirit was among those knights who journeyed with Knight Sarlamir. If the characters converse with her, she introduces herself as Knight Jandin, a knight of the Order of the Sword who died during the Cataclysm. She shares the information from "Knight Sarlamir's Curse" at the start of this section, along with the following information:

- When Jandin returned Sarlamir's body to Kalaman, she twisted the truth, reporting Sarlamir died defending people from rampaging evil dragons. Sarlamir was entombed a hero.
- Jandin regrets this, knowing Sarlamir's disobedience and deeds contributed to the gods' disfavor—and ultimately to the Cataclysm. She believes herself complicit in her fellow knight's disgrace.
- She asks the characters to take the weapon entombed with Sarlamir in the next chamber. Perhaps in their hands, it can find redemption and the gods' favor.
- The flames blazing through the tombs are fire from the Cataclysm. They used to be confined to Sarlamir's tomb, but now they run rampant. Jandin doesn't know why (she's unaware of Lord Soth's presence).

After relating this information, Knight Jandin wishes the characters luck and fades away.

R7: Tomb of Heroes

> Violet flames outline the tombs set into the walls of this spacious crypt. A heavy stone brazier sits empty near the room's center. A sarcophagus to the north lies in pieces at the mouth of a crumbling tunnel. A wall to the southeast is similarly broken.
>
> At the far end of the tomb, a flaming dais holds a sarcophagus sculpted with the image of a knight. A life-sized sculpture of a dead dragon impaled with a spear curls around the sarcophagus.
>
> Something within this sarcophagus moves, slamming against the lid, as the unnatural flames on the dais blaze with wild intensity.

When the characters enter this room, any remaining scenes from the "Visions in Fire" section unfold. Read the following text after all the scenes have played out and the characters are in this area:

> The violet flames waver, forming ominous images once more. The terrifying knight from the last vision steps through the wall. He approaches the brazier at the room's center, above which roils a flaming orb. The knight holds up a scepter sculpted with screaming faces. Once touched to the ball of flame, the scepter ignites and the orb vanishes. The knight admires the flaming scepter, then points it at the ornate tomb and statue at the end of this room. Both burst into flames that spread throughout the crypt. The figure then moves to the south wall and vanishes.

Lord Soth was here minutes before the characters and claimed a portion of the Cataclysmic fire that cursed this tomb. He then shattered the south wall, creating a passage high in the cliffs beneath Castle Kalaman. After this scene plays out, another violent blow shakes the tomb surrounded by the sculpted dragon.

Sarlamir's Tomb. Sarlamir's tomb rests to the east and bears the words "Zanas Sarlamir, Knight of the Crown." A creature can open it with a successful DC 12 Strength check. Within lie the knight's animate remains (see below). If the characters don't open the crypt, Sarlamir shatters the lid and emerges 3 rounds after they enter the room.

Knight Sarlamir. Lord Soth used the Cataclysmic fire to reanimate Sarlamir as a **skeletal knight** (see appendix B). The Undead knight wears ancient Solamnic armor and wields a blade blazing with violet flame. He attacks the characters as soon as he emerges and fights until destroyed.

KNIGHT SARLAMIR

OLIVIER BERNARD

Sarlamir speaks as he attacks, making it clear he's compelled by Soth's magic. In a hollow voice, the armored skeleton proclaims the following:

- The cursed knight, Lord Soth, calls to Sarlamir through the haunted flames of the Cataclysm.
- Lord Soth commands Sarlamir to slay those who would oppose Soth.
- Soth beckons Sarlamir to follow him north—back to the place of his dishonor, the place in the Northern Wastes Soth calls the City of Lost Names.

As soon as Sarlamir is defeated, the violet flames around his weapon and elsewhere in the catacombs dim, then vanish. Make sure Sarlamir mentions the City of Lost Names and the Northern Wastes, even if it's as a final gasp. The characters will learn more about these places in chapter 5.

North Passage. If the broken passage in the north wall hasn't already collapsed, it does so if a creature proceeds more than 5 feet down it. See area R3 for details on how the passage collapses. Characters caught in the collapse are forced into area R7 rather than R3.

South Passage. This crude passage emerges 80 feet up a sheer cliff beneath the walls of Castle Kalaman. Below are paved streets and the rooftops of buildings. There is no sign of Lord Soth, who has already met with any of his surviving Undead knights and ridden from the city. See the beginning of chapter 5 for details on where Soth heads next.

Treasure. Inside Sarlamir's tomb is the distinctive head of a rusty spear—all that remains of his *dragonlance*. A *detect magic* spell reveals an aura of evocation magic, though the spearhead has no obvious properties. A character who tries to attune to the item and succeeds on a DC 12 Intelligence (Arcana or Religion) check discovers that the spearhead is magical but that divine power has rendered its magic inert. The other tombs in this room are empty except for bones and rusty armor.

NEXT STEPS

After defeating Knight Sarlamir, the characters advance to 6th level. Once the Cataclysmic flames fade, the catacombs return to normal.

SOTH'S ESCAPE

Lord Soth has vanished, taking a scepter blazing with haunted flames along with him. If the characters try to pursue him, he and his Undead knights have already departed the city, their objectives complete. No one is certain where they headed after leaving, though this is revealed at the start of the next chapter.

SANCTUARY SHATTERED

By the time the characters emerge from the catacombs, the council room's carnage has been mostly cleared.

Several hours later, Darrett arrives in Kalaman with Marshal Vendri, Lord Bakaris, and the bulk of the city's martial forces. They're shocked to learn what happened. Marshal Vendri moves swiftly to keep order in the city and ensure no more attacks are forthcoming. At the same time, Darrett seeks out the characters to learn more. He pays particular interest to what they have to say about Lord Soth and the City of Lost Names—two names that guide the characters in the following chapter.

Soldiers from Kalaman struggle
to survive amid the treacherous
canyons of the Northern Wastes.

CHAPTER 5

THE NORTHERN WASTES

BURIED BENEATH THE MAGICALLY SCARRED reaches of the Northern Wastes lies an ancient ruin now known as the City of Lost Names. In a bygone age, the city was named Onyari. Built by the Kingpriest of Istar, it soared through the heavens, but it was brought low by enraged dragons who discovered its grim secret: its flight relied on the innate magic of the draconic graveyard it was built on. Now, Onyari's ruins draw the attention of the Red Dragon Army, whose leaders believe they can raise the city into the heavens once more. The black-robed mage Lohezet and the priest Belephaion lead an expedition to claim the city as a massive weapon of war. The death knight Lord Soth joins them, following whispers from the Dragon Queen to use the Cataclysmic fire from the depths of Castle Kalaman to raise the dead dragons buried in Onyari's foundations and bring them to her service.

RUNNING THIS CHAPTER

This chapter begins as the characters follow Lord Soth into the Northern Wastes, accompanied by troops from Kalaman. Once there, the characters must explore several mystical sites to discover the location of the City of Lost Names.

CHARACTER ADVANCEMENT

In this chapter, the characters advance from 6th to 8th level as they traverse the Northern Wastes. This chapter features multiple adventuring locations that can be explored in any order, so it's up to you to decide when the characters gain these levels. Consider using two of the following suggestions:

- The characters gain a level after completing three adventuring locations in the Northern Wastes.
- The characters gain a level if they accomplish an extraordinary feat, such as rescuing the bronze dragon egg from Camp Carrionclay.
- The characters gain a level once they find the passage leading into the City of Lost Names.

KIERAN YANNER

Desperation in Kalaman

Soon after the characters emerge from the catacombs beneath Castle Kalaman, Darrett Highwater and Marshal Vendri return to Kalaman with their troops. As they learn about the attack on the city, Darrett urges the characters to rest. He sends scouts to learn where Lord Soth and his retinue went after fleeing the city. The following day, Darrett meets the characters with the following news:

- Marshal Vendri is working to maintain order in Kalaman until new civilian leaders are appointed.
- She wants to speak with the characters soon.
- Darrett's scouts have reported the Red Dragon Army has split its forces. A contingent is inexplicably heading into the Northern Wastes.

Darrett doesn't know much beyond this at the moment. When the characters are ready, he leads them to meet with Marshal Vendri.

Group Debriefing

The meeting with Marshal Vendri takes place in a small meeting room. Read the following:

> Marshal Vendri has claimed a modest meeting room down the hall from the council chamber marred by Lord Soth's attack. The room holds little more than a long table covered in reports, though tall windows offer a stunning view of the city and harbor beyond.
>
> The marshal stands by a window, gazing toward the horizon. From a seat at the table, Lord Bakaris glances at you and then bitterly observes, "Here they are now, Marshal. Perhaps if we hadn't put our faith in sellswords, my son would be at my side and the governor would still be alive."

Let the characters respond to Lord Bakaris if they please. Soon after, Vendri invites him to leave, and the noble grudgingly complies. Afterward, Vendri asks the characters to explain what happened the day before, including how the governor died. Guide the conversation using the following points:

- Vendri trusts the characters.
- She says Lord Bakaris is spreading rumors that the characters could've saved Kalaman's leaders. Some locals are looking for someone to blame for the terrifying slaughter.
- If characters mention Lord Soth's interest in the City of Lost Names in the Northern Wastes, the marshal knows nothing about the location and notes that the Northern Wastes is nothing but a deadly wasteland. If Soth is heading there, she believes he presents no further threat.

- If characters present the broken *dragonlance*, neither Vendri nor Darrett is familiar with the weapon, and they see it only as an ancient relic.
- Though Darrett doesn't understand Lord Soth's cryptic goals, he believes the characters' discoveries are important.
- The marshal feels otherwise, believing Kalaman's military should focus on fighting nearby Dragon Army forces and restoring Kalaman's government.

With Darrett's support, encourage the characters to make the case that Lord Soth is a threat and the Dragon Army's plans in the north shouldn't be taken lightly. Vendri eventually relents.

Darrett then asks Vendri to let him take the characters and a contingent of troops into the Northern Wastes to investigate whatever the Dragon Army wants there. While Vendri isn't confident the move is strategically sound, she thinks it's a good idea for the characters to get out of Kalaman for a while to avoid the ire of its citizens. She asks the characters to leave while she and Darrett discuss details, suggesting they visit the castle's small library and learn what they can about the Northern Wastes.

Learning about the Wastes

A character who spends at least one hour researching the Northern Wastes in Castle Kalaman's library learns that after the Cataclysm, the Northern Wastes became a barren, deadly region prone to flash floods. If a character succeeds on a DC 14 Intelligence (History) check, they also learn that grand ruins predating the Cataclysm litter the region, though few explorers survive attempts to seek them.

Darrett's Negotiations

Allow the characters to research the Northern Wastes or conduct any business in Kalaman. Afterward, Darrett seeks out the characters and relates the following information:

- Marshal Vendri has agreed to send Darrett and the characters to the Northern Wastes to investigate the Dragon Army's agenda there.
- Darrett will be given command of a few hundred soldiers.
- To avoid drawing the attention of the Dragon Army, Vendri has ordered a few ships to ferry Darrett's troops across Kalaman Bay at night.
- A secluded cove called Wrecker's Edge lies at the southeastern shore of the wastes. This is where the forces will disembark.
- From there, the characters and Darrett's troops are to discover the Dragon Army's plot, thwart it, and then return to the ships.

Darrett answers any questions, then encourages the characters to prepare for the trip. He wants to depart the following night but is willing to delay a day.

Message from Wyhan

If any of the characters are interested in joining the Mages of High Sorcery and delivered a scroll to Wyhan, the black-robed mage sends the characters an invitation to meet her at her apothecary.

When they arrive, Wyhan shares the following information:

> "My contacts at the Tower of High Sorcery in Wayreth have denied your request to travel there and participate in the Test of High Sorcery. The threat of the Dragon Army is too great, and the orders don't want to be perceived as taking sides in the conflict. However, the head of the conclave, the mage Par-Salian, has granted you a special exception."
>
> Wyhan offers you a simple wooden brooch studded with black, red, and white stones: the symbol of the Mages of High Sorcery. "He has allowed you to practice magic as a provisional member of the Mages of High Sorcery. The time of your test will be decided after the Dragon Army's threat has passed. Until then, this token represents the conclave's blessing. Congratulations, provisional mage."

Wyhan doesn't know when the characters will be able to take the Test of High Sorcery. She knows the Mages of High Sorcery are wary of attracting the Dragon Army's ire, so the sooner the Dragon Army is defeated, the sooner the characters can progress with their magical studies.

After this, she urges the characters to either make a purchase or let her return to her research.

Leaving Kalaman

Once the characters are ready to sail to the wastes, Darrett arranges to meet them that evening at a section of Kalaman's docks used by the military.

When the characters arrive, they find Cudgel Ironsmile and Tatina Rookledust have volunteered to join the journey. Rookledust—who has dyed her hair a vibrant violet hue—is excited at the opportunity to field-test her fargabs (see appendix A).

When the characters board one of the ships ferrying the troops, read the following:

> Water sloshes and wood creaks as ships depart from Kalaman's docks in the dead of night. Citizens gathered to bid farewell to loved ones soon fade from view. The ships cuts through the dark waters of Kalaman Bay, sailing to perilous shores under cloudy skies.

Into the Wastes

The rest of this chapter takes place in the Northern Wastes, a region where the Cataclysm's destruction is still evident centuries later. This section contains general information about the region and the challenges the characters face as they traverse it. Map 5.1 depicts this region, sites that might be discovered by explorers, and various named environmental features. A version of this map appropriate to share with players appears in appendix E.

Movement in the Wastes

Broken by canyons and sheer plateaus, the entirety of the Northern Wastes is considered difficult terrain for the purpose of travel. As a result, characters move at half speed through the wastes, as summarized in the Northern Wastes Land Travel table.

This means that if characters move at a normal pace, they can move 2 hexes on map 5.1 per day.

Northern Wastes Land Travel

| | Distance Per ... | | |
Pace	Hour	Day	Effect
Fast	2 miles	15 miles	–5 penalty to passive Wisdom (Perception) scores
Normal	1.5 miles	12 miles	None
Slow	1 mile	9 miles	Able to use Stealth

Movement with an Army

Darrett's troops have a challenging time navigating the Northern Wastes. They move at a slow pace, covering about nine miles a day. Darrett encourages the characters to move ahead of the troops and rendezvous with them at predetermined points. He relies on the characters to help him determine where to head next.

Running Travel in the Wastes

The Northern Wastes span hundreds of miles. Instead of roleplaying every minute of the party's travel, use the encounters from the "Wastes Encounters" section later in this chapter as often as you please—usually once per day. After the characters have spent several days in the wastes and learned about its dangers, consider making encounters less frequent.

The hexes on map 5.1 measure distance, but characters don't need to explore every hex. Feel free to skim over days of travel to reach new locations or return to already-visited ones. The Dragon Army also faces the challenges of the wasteland, so the characters don't need to rush to prevent their enemies from fulfilling their plots by a certain time.

THE WASH

Travelers in the Northern Wastes must contend with both the broken, canyon-riddled land and the Wash. Tides driven by Krynn's three moons cause floodwaters from the Turbidus Ocean to sweep through the region. These unpredictable flood tides are known as the Wash, and their harsh, salty water threatens creatures in the canyons. Sometimes the Wash leaves the Northern Wastes' canyons parched for weeks at a time; other times, the waters sweep in and out multiple times in a few days.

Each day the characters travel the Northern Wastes (or whenever you please), roll on the Nature of the Wash table to see how the floodwaters affect the region. At your discretion, the Wash might unexpectedly change during other encounters in the region, making them more dangerous.

NATURE OF THE WASH

d10	Wash Effect
1–3	The Wash is low. Canyons are dry.
4–6	The Wash is high. It fills the canyons.
7–10	The Wash remains at the same level as the previous day.

DANGERS OF THE WASH

When the Wash fills the Northern Wastes, the characters must make a DC 12 group Wisdom (Survival) check. On a successful check, they notice signs of water beginning to fill the canyons, giving them time to reach safe ground. On a failed check, the characters are caught in a flash flood.

FLASH FLOOD

During a flash flood, turbulent Wash waters flood the canyons in the area the characters are traveling through. If the characters are in a canyon, its walls are 2d4 × 10 feet high.

When the flood starts, have the characters and nearby creatures roll initiative. Each round, on initiative counts 10 and 0, the water level rises by 10 feet (up to the height of the canyon) and travels 100 feet horizontally. On each of these initiative counts, creatures in the water and moving along with it must make a DC 15 Strength saving throw as they're smashed by large chunks of debris. A creature takes 2d6 bludgeoning damage on a failed save, or half as much damage on a successful one.

The water level continues to rise and move this way for 2d4 rounds, then stops.

WASTES ENCOUNTERS

Countless threats loom in the wild, dangerous Northern Wastes. Whenever you want a random encounter to occur—usually once per day—roll on the Northern Wastes Encounters table.

NORTHERN WASTES ENCOUNTERS

d20	Encounter
1–10	No encounter
11–14	Dragon Army Patrols (see below)
15	Malfunctioning Gate (see below)
16–20	Wastes Predators (see below)

DRAGON ARMY PATROLS

Hostile Dragon Army patrols scour the Northern Wastes for pre-Cataclysm ruins to exploit. Roll on the Dragon Army Patrol table to determine which patrol the characters encounter (see appendix B for the patrol members' stat blocks). If the characters are defeated or surrender, they're taken as prisoners to Camp Carrionclay (detailed later in this chapter).

DRAGON ARMY PATROL

d4	Encounter
1	8 **baaz draconians** and 2 **Dragon Army soldiers**
2	1 **sivak draconian** and 5 **Dragon Army soldiers**
3	2 **kapak draconians** and 2 **Dragon Army officers**
4	3 **Dragon Army officers** riding 3 **Dragon Army dragonnels**

MALFUNCTIONING GATE

The characters find a stone archway lined with sigils. This gate used to be a teleportation gate—part of a magical transportation system created by Istarian mages. It once stood in Onyari before the city fell. As soon as a character approaches, magical energy swirls within the arch. The magic kicks up nearby debris that animates as a hostile **clay golem**.

Golem. The golem resembles a proud-looking human with fine robes and an aura of sunbeams around its head. The magic that animates the golem was designed to safeguard the gate, but it has malfunctioned. The golem goes berserk (as per its Berserk trait). The golem remains in that state as long as other creatures are visible.

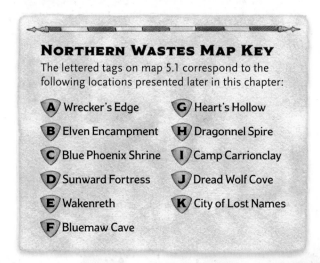

NORTHERN WASTES MAP KEY

The lettered tags on map 5.1 correspond to the following locations presented later in this chapter:

A Wrecker's Edge	G Heart's Hollow
B Elven Encampment	H Dragonnel Spire
C Blue Phoenix Shrine	I Camp Carrionclay
D Sunward Fortress	J Dread Wolf Cove
E Wakenreth	K City of Lost Names
F Bluemaw Cave	

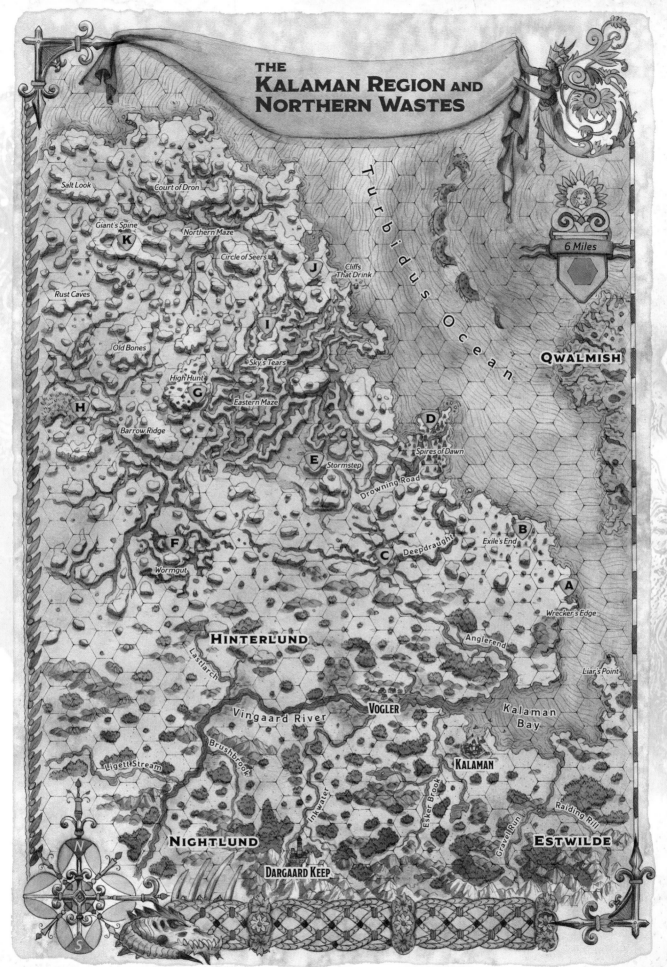

THE KALAMAN REGION AND NORTHERN WASTES

Salt Look

Court of Dron

Giant's Spine

K

Northern Maze

Circle of Seers

J

Cliffs That Drink

Rust Caves

I

Old Bones

Sky's Tears

High Hunt

G

Eastern Maze

H

Barrow Ridge

E Stormstep

Spires of Dawn

D

Drowning Road

B

Exile's End

C Deepdraught

F

A

Wormgut

Wrecker's Edge

Anglerend

Liar's Point

HINTERLUND

Lastlarch

VOGLER

Kalaman Bay

Vingaard River

Brushbrook

KALAMAN

Ligett Stream

Inkwater

Esker Brook

Raiding Rill

NIGHTLUND

Gravel Run

ESTWILDE

DARGAARD KEEP

Turbidus Ocean

QWALMISH

6 Miles

N

S

MAP 5.1: THE KALAMAN REGION AND NORTHERN WASTES

FRANCESCA BAERALD

Stabilizing the Gate. Magical energy flickers in the gate. After the golem is defeated, a character with the Pact Magic or Spellcasting feature can spend one minute investigating the gate to learn how to stabilize the gate's malfunctioning magic. If a character spends a spell slot of 1st level or higher or succeeds on a DC 18 Intelligence (Arcana) check, the gate stabilizes and serves as a permanent teleportation circle linked to its partner gate, which can be in any hex on map 5.1 you please—perhaps near Wrecker's Edge (location A) or High Hunt, the plateau that hosts Heart's Hollow (location G).

Sigil Sequence. Characters can learn the sigil sequence on the gate so they can teleport to it with the *teleportation circle* spell.

WASTES PREDATORS

Roll on the table below to determine what predators the characters encounter. Each entry provides a different threat depending on whether the Wash is high or low (as noted in parentheses).

FEW CAN SURVIVE THE FLOOD-PRONE CANYONS OF THE NORTHERN WASTES.

WASTES PREDATORS

d10	Encounter
1	The bones of a Humanoid or Beast, infested with harmless spiders or tide-pool creatures (high or low)
2–3	6 **giant octopuses** (high) or 3 **giant scorpions** (low)
4–5	4 **merrow** (high) or 6 **giant spiders** (low)
6–7	3 **plesiosauruses** (high) or 3 **manticores** (low)
8–9	2 **giant sharks** (high) or 3 **wasteland dragonnels** (low; see appendix B)
10	1 **purple worm** spotted a mile away (high or low)

KALAMAN TROOPS

Traveling alongside Kalaman's troops presents challenges, but it is also safer and will eventually help the characters face the Dragon Army.

ARMY IN TOW

During this part of the adventure, the characters are guiding Kalaman's troops toward battle with the Dragon Army. The characters should frequently split from the troops, then meet back up with them, serving as scouts and handling missions while the army advances. Darrett won't send his soldiers into uncertain danger, such as caves or ruins.

COMBAT ENCOUNTERS

Avoid involving Kalaman's troops in encounters meant for the characters. If combat breaks out while the characters are with Kalaman's troops, use five **Kalaman soldiers** (see appendix B)—or however many you deem appropriate—to represent allied soldiers who are quick to aid the characters.

KALAMAN ARMY CAMP

As they travel the wastes, Darrett and his troops establish temporary camps. These camps offer characters a safe place to rest, replenish supplies, and interact with allies. A camp includes the following features, which you can arrange as you please:

Characters' Tents. The characters can rest in their tents.

Command Tent. A large table is set up in this sizable tent. Here, the characters can meet with Darrett to discuss strategy and troop movement.

Cudgel's Tent. Cudgel's tent features an impressive weapons collection. If the characters need to talk to the dwarf, they likely find her here.

Darrett's Tent. Darrett's tent is spartan and well kept. If the characters ever need to talk to him in private, they're likely to find him here.

Rookledust's Tent. Rookledust's tent is filled with strange contraptions and unfinished projects. The gnome is often here, tinkering with the fargabs (see appendix A) and other inventions.

Other Tents. Guard posts, hospital tents, supply tents, and other accommodations fill out the camp.

Exploring the Wastes

As the characters venture into the Northern Wastes, they might want to explore the following areas.

A: Wrecker's Edge

After crossing Kalaman Bay, the ships carrying the characters and their allies arrive near Wrecker's Edge (location A on map 5.1). As the ships drop anchor near a rocky coast, read the following text:

> Waves crash against jagged rocks along the shore. Beyond, red-hued canyons carve their way through a harsh landscape. In the distance, mountainous crags and strange formations jut skyward.

Darrett asks the characters to take a rowboat and find a place where the troops can disembark safely.

Hidden Cove

After about an hour of exploring the shore, the characters spot a narrow cove. This time is halved if a character is proficient with water vehicles or is a ranger whose favored terrain is the coast.

A few rotten wooden buildings abandoned by smugglers line this cove. Additionally, a small ship is anchored near a clear beach inside the cove.

Elven Ship

The ship belongs to a group of elven wizards who found Wrecker's Edge a few months ago. Characters who grew up in an elven society or who succeed on a DC 14 Intelligence (History) check identify the ship as being of Silvanesti elven origin.

The ship is small but seaworthy, with enough room for a dozen crew members. It has nothing of value on its deck or in the communal bunks below deck. However, two **air elementals** on the deck defend the vessel against intruders. They attack any non-elf that sets foot upon the ship.

If the characters haven't met Dalamar yet (see the following section), he's nearby when they board the ship, and an *alarm* spell cast on the deck alerts him to their intrusion. He might approach them anytime after they defeat the elementals (see the following section).

Meeting Dalamar

Dalamar approaches the characters soon after they defeat the elementals or Kalaman's troops start disembarking. Dalamar is curious about the adventurers' motives and whether they align with his. Speaking with him reveals the following information:

- Dalamar is part of a contingent of Silvanesti elves.
- The ship is the elves' conveyance.
- Dalamar is surveying the coast for ancient ruins. He knowns there are none here, but his leader, Zhelsuel, wants him to search thoroughly anyway.
- If the characters mention the City of Lost Names, he pretends not to recognize the name until he knows more about the characters (see the "Mutual Understanding" section). A character who succeeds on a DC 14 Wisdom (Insight) check believes Dalamar knows more than he says.
- Dalamar invites the characters to return with him to his group at the elven encampment (location B on map 5.1).

Dalamar

An ambitious elf magic-user, Dalamar (neutral elf **mage**) has an insatiable thirst for knowledge. This often puts him at odds with other Silvanesti mages, whose conservative methods wear on his patience.

Dalamar participated in the ill-fated defense of Silvanesti against the Dragon Armies. His desperate actions were part of the reason he and the other mages were sent to the Northern Wastes. Despite resenting his people's small-minded decisions, he sees this mission as a chance to prove himself and potentially strike back against the Dragon Armies. Dalamar studied pre-Cataclysm magic long before being sent here, and he believes something of magical value might be hidden in the region. He wants to find it swiftly, return to his people, and continue working toward joining the Mages of High Sorcery.

Personality Trait. "Everybody wants something. I'm certain we can help one another."

Ideal. "Magic is meant to be used."

Bond. "I'll do anything to recover my home."

Flaw. "I'm overconfident, sometimes to the point of putting myself or others in danger."

Reporting Back

If the characters return to their ships and give Darrett directions to Wrecker's Edge, he orders the ships to shore. He's curious about Dalamar and the elves. He suggests the characters investigate the elven encampment and determine whether they can be trusted.

While the characters are away, Kalaman's troops unload the ships and set up their first camp as detailed in the "Kalaman's Army Camp" section earlier in this chapter.

B: Elven Encampment

Dalamar leads the characters to his expedition's encampment about twelve miles northwest of the hidden cove. The journey takes the better part of the day, during which Dalamar charmingly banters with the characters, trying to learn more about why they're in the region. He offers little in return but is eager to hear about recent events in Kalaman.

Expedition Members

The elven camp lies next to some small ruins on a plateau overlooking the wastes, with a dozen or so tents arranged in a spiral pattern. Ten elves are present in the camp when the characters arrive, including their leader, Zhelsuel. Others roam the wastes in search of information. They all use the **mage** stat block.

Silvanesti's Exiles

Once a beautiful woodland nation with sculpted trees and towering spires, the elven land of Silvanesti lies in ruins after being invaded by the Dragon Armies. The elves struggled to defend their homeland and were ultimately forced to retreat to the island of Southern Ergoth to seek a new home.

   The elves here in the Northern Wastes were among the defenders of Silvanesti. When they failed to protect their homeland, they were sent on an expedition to the wastes following centuries-old legends of Silvanesti magic lost in the region. They hope recovering such magic might help them save their homeland and redeem themselves in the eyes of their people.

Zhelsuel

Zhelsuel, a once-respected member of House Mystic—an elven clan known for magical prowess—is reaching a venerable age even by elven standards. He's keenly aware this expedition is a fool's errand analogous to exile, and he believes his homeland is lost to him forever. But if he must spend the rest of his days in this bleak expanse, he's determined to spend them as an exemplar of thoroughness and scholarship. He drives his subordinates to catalog every foot of the Northern Wastes in search of the barest scrap of Silvanesti magic.

   Personality Trait. "I know what's best for my people, and I lead with logic and precision."

   Ideal. "I take pride in work done to perfection."

   Bond. "I'll show my people what I can do. My name won't be forgotten."

   Flaw. "I won't accept any course of action that doesn't put the best interest of Silvanesti first."

Meeting Zhelsuel

Zhelsuel confronts Dalamar and the characters when they arrive. He wants nothing to do with outsiders and sees them as an obstacle to the elves' progress. He tells the characters he and the rest of the elves are conducting research, but he refuses to elaborate.

A character who speaks to Zhelsuel in Elvish or succeeds on a DC 16 Charisma (Persuasion) check convinces him to converse, though most of Zhelsuel's responses are cutting and brief:

- Zhelsuel shares any of the information from the "Silvanesti's Exiles" or "Zhelsuel" sections.
- If characters bring up the Red Dragon Army's attack on Kalaman, it clearly gives him pause, but he quickly dismisses the conflict as irrelevant to his people.
- If the characters mention they're in pursuit of the Dragon Army, Zhelsuel scoffs at their eagerness to rush to their deaths.

Zhelsuel ultimately demands the characters leave and not return. He commands the expedition, specifically Dalamar, to focus on their survey of the region. He then tells Dalamar to escort the characters away and return to his work.

Mutual Understanding

Dalamar is frustrated that Zhelsuel seems content to spend the rest of his days—and those of the other expedition members—turning over rocks in the Northern Wastes. After being told to see the characters away, he shares that the elves recently spotted Dragon Army soldiers headed north. He doesn't know their destination, but he suspects they're not just wandering. He suggests that perhaps the Dragon Army, the elves, and the characters have similar interests in this land's hidden magic.

Finding the City of Lost Names

If the characters asked Dalamar about the City of Lost Names, he tells them he learned of the city from the Silvanesti writings that led him and the other elves to this region. Though he doesn't know its location, he's interested in finding it, as it reportedly was a magical marvel that might hold valuable secrets.

Once Dalamar reveals this shared interest in the City of Lost Names, he proposes an arrangement that would allow him to advance his research without technically disobeying Zhelsuel. He points the characters to sites in the Northern Wastes he has already identified as being related to or of a similar age to the City of Lost Names. With the characters' insights and reports about whatever magic remains at those sites, he should be able to glean more information about the city's location. The following

locations (detailed later in this chapter and shown on map 5.1) are of particular interest to Dalamar:

- Blue Phoenix Shrine (location C)
- Sunward Fortress (location D)
- Wakenreth (location E)

Mark these sites' hexes on the players' map of the region in appendix E after Dalamar notes their locations.

If the characters agree to work with Dalamar, he's pleased. They can explore the locations in any order they wish. Dalamar plans to convince Zhelsuel to let him meet the characters at Wakenreth. Once they've relayed their findings to him, he hopes he'll be able to determine the location of the City of Lost Names (see the end of the "E: Wakenreth" section for details). With this, Dalamar sends the characters on their way, wishing them fruitful investigations.

C: Blue Phoenix Shrine

Carved into a labyrinthine gorge is the Blue Phoenix Shrine, an ancient shrine to Habbakuk—god of the seas and animal life. The entrance to the shrine is completely engulfed by water when the Wash is high, but it is visible during low tide.

Disrupted Pilgrimage

Every year, a group of Dimernesti sea elves from Thoradin Bay travels to the Blue Phoenix Shrine to honor the Sea Lord for his bounty. While most sea elves have forgotten the name Habbakuk, they faithfully continue this annual pilgrimage.

Though the Wash changes chaotically, the sea elves swim to the shrine following reliable rivers that flow through ravines. This year, however, the pilgrimage went awry when the sea elves crossed paths with the Red Dragon Army. Four sea elves were captured—including their leader, the priest Yearkal—and many others perished in the confrontation (the characters can rescue three of the captured sea elves at Camp Carrionclay, while Yearkal was taken to the Sunward Fortress). Six survivors reached the shrine, but they managed to hold on to only one offering: a pouch of blue deep-sea pearls.

Approaching the Shrine

When the characters arrive, the Wash is low. The sea elves have set up camp near the shrine's entrance. They periodically leave to scout for signs of the Dragon Army or missing comrades.

The Sea Elves

After their recent ordeal, the sea elves are on alert for large groups of people. If the characters approach them with Kalaman's troops in tow, the sea elves retreat. Their current leader, Ishvern

Stargazer, approaches only if it's clear no one's pursuing them with hostile intent.

Ishvern and the sea elves use the **scout** stat block with the following changes:

- They have advantage on saving throws against being charmed, and magic can't put them to sleep.
- They have darkvision out to 60 feet.
- They have a swimming speed of 30 feet and can breathe air and water.

ISHVERN STARGAZER

Ishvern (neutral good, sea elf **scout**), the de facto leader of the Dimernesti group in their priest's absence, is pious, curious, and insightful. Having survived in the deadliest depths of the Turbidus Ocean for over a century, he knows better than to venture into mysterious places unprepared. He isn't eager to risk his companions' lives without the priest Yearkal's guidance. However, Ishvern fears Yearkal might be lost forever. If others might aid him in fulfilling her spiritual mission, he's eager for their help.

Personality Trait. "Embrace the world's wonders, but be wary of its dangers."

Ideal. "Life and nature are marvels that must be protected at all costs."

Bond. "I will find my missing companions."

Flaw. "I can be indecisive when choosing between options with uncertain outcomes."

ISHVERN

ISHVERN'S PLEA

Ishvern tries to get a sense of the characters' motivations for traveling the Northern Wastes. He explains the nearby shrine is a sacred place, dedicated to an old deity the sea elves now remember only as the Sea Lord. If the characters approached the camp respectfully, he also tells them how the sea elves were attacked by the Dragon Army.

Even if he is suspicious of the characters, Ishvern sees value in their presence—especially if there's a cleric among them. He requests the characters help him make the group's offering in the name of their lost priest, Yearkal. The elves seek to make this offering in keeping with their peoples' centuries-old traditions, but they know little of the deed's religious ties or the god Habbakuk. If the characters agree, Ishvern leads them to the shrine's entrance.

Yearkal's Return. If the characters know of Yearkal's fate or return her to the group (see the "D: Sunward Fortress" section), the elves encourage the characters to come with them into the shrine. If Yearkal is with them, she knows all the threats and secret passages in areas C1 through C4.

SHRINE FEATURES

The shrine has the following features:

Ceilings. The ceilings in the shrine are 15 feet high.

Light. All areas of the shrine are brightly lit by blue *continual flame* spells cast on seashells and other objects embedded in the walls.

Walls and Doors. The shrine's walls and doors are made of solid stone. Except for the door in area C1, the doors throughout the shrine open easily.

Water. The Wash is low when the characters reach the shrine, but each room is filled with 2 feet of standing water, except for area C5. Areas with standing water are difficult terrain.

SHRINE LOCATIONS

The following locations are keyed to map 5.2.

C1: SHRINE ENTRANCE

The shrine's entrance is carved in the escarpment of the ravine. Once the characters reach the entrance, read the following text:

> An ancient, algae-covered double door made of white granite stands here. It is etched with an eroded image of a majestic bird with outstretched wings.

A follower of Habbakuk or a character who succeeds on a DC 12 Intelligence (Religion) check recognizes the bird on the door as a blue phoenix, the symbol of the god Habbakuk, god of the seas and animal life.

Shrine Door. Ishvern explains Yearkal opened this door by saying a specific prayer, but he doesn't know it. If a character says the name "Habbakuk" within 10 feet of the door, it swings open magically. Casting the *knock* spell also opens the door.

The door is a Large object with AC 17, 40 hit points, and immunity to poison and psychic damage.

C2: Altar Room

> A long room stretches ahead, its walls carved with motifs of rolling waves. A ceiling supported by twin pillars glows with faint blue light.
>
> At the rear of the chamber stands an altar carved with coral-like designs. Behind it rises a sizable gran-ite sculpture depicting the bird from the shrine's en-trance, its outstretched wings wreathed in flames.
>
> An archway opens into a chamber to the west, while a simple stone door stands in the wall to the east.

Upon entering this chamber, Ishvern directs the characters to the west archway leading to area C3. He encourages them to cleanse themselves with the water there before proceeding deeper into the shrine.

Altar Guardians. If a character comes within 10 feet of the altar without having washed themself in area C3 within the last 24 hours, three **water weirds** rise from the water between the pillars. They are hostile toward any Humanoid who doesn't openly bear the symbol of Habbakuk. The water weirds cease attacking and vanish if a creature in the room uses an action to apologize to Habbakuk or speak a prayer to the god's name.

C3: Cleansing Room

> In the center of this room rests a three-foot-high brass basin filled with clear water. A relief ornaments the walls, depicting great sea birds dipping into the waves alongside leaping fish and whimsical creatures.

On entering this room, Ishvern reminds the characters to cleanse themselves with the pool's water before proceeding deeper into the holy place. He then spends a minute washing his own face and hands.

Characters who follow suit feel refreshed. The first time a creature washes itself with water from the basin, it gains 5 temporary hit points.

C4: Hall

This passage is empty, but its north door bears an inscription in Elvish: "Honor those who came be-fore, and walk on." Ishvern can translate this text if needed.

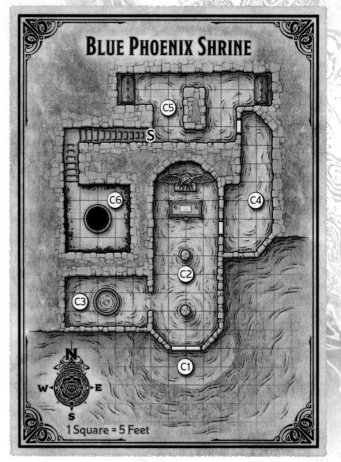

MAP 5.2: Blue Phoenix Shrine

C5: Crypt

> Alcoves to the west and east of this chamber hold waist-high stone sarcophagi sculpted with images of shells and graceful sea creatures.

This crypt is the resting place of followers of Habba-kuk who tended to this shrine.

Tombs. The sarcophagus to the west bears an in-scription in Elvish: "Herzon, who built this prayer in stone." A character who has a passive Wisdom (Per-ception) score of 16 or higher notices a design on its lid resembling the layout of the shrine. Although the crypt has no other visible exits, the room on the map corresponding to the crypt features a second passage leading to the southwest.

The sarcophagus to the east bears a differ-ent inscription in Elvish: "Awinthel, our devoted first priest."

A character who succeeds on a DC 17 Strength check can open either sarcophagus—though Ishvern strongly objects. The corpse within each sarcopha-gus is immaculately preserved, but the burial places contain nothing of value.

Secret Door. This crypt is seemingly a dead end. A character who has a passive Wisdom (Perception) score of 20 or higher notices the secret door if they come within 5 feet of it. The *detect magic* spell also reveals the secret door.

The secret door magically opens if a character obeys the inscription on door in area C4 and prays or makes an offering at either sarcophagus. Casting the *dispel magic* or *knock* spell also makes it easy to push the door open. The door is a Large object with AC 17, 40 hit points, and immunity to poison and psychic damage.

C6: Offering Chamber

> Steps ascend into a room covered in thick, black algae. At the center of the room stands a well, from which emanates the sound of distant waves and the cries of sea birds.

Here, initiates of Habbakuk once made offerings to honor their god.

Shrine Guardians. If a character who didn't wash in area C3 or who opened a sarcophagus in area C4 comes within 10 feet of the well, the algae on the walls coalesces into three **black puddings** that immediately attack the offending character as well as other creatures that attack the puddings.

Ishvern's Offering. So long as there are no obvious threats in this room, Ishvern moves to the side of the well, softly speaks a brief prayer in Elvish, then empties several dozen blue pearls from a pouch into the well (he retains 750 gp worth of pearls just in case). After he does so, each character in the room who washed themselves in area C3 and who didn't disturb the sarcophagi in area C4 gains the charm Habbakuk's Blessing (a type of supernatural gift detailed in the *Dungeon Master's Guide*; see below). With this done, Ishvern thanks the characters for helping him complete his party's task and prepares to depart.

Habbakuk's Blessing
Supernatural Gift (Charm)

Habbakuk blesses your travels through the Northern Wastes. This charm grants you advantage on Wisdom (Survival) checks made to notice the Wash's waters filling chasms.

Additionally, while traveling, you and up to 5 other creatures with you ignore difficult terrain outdoors in the Northern Wastes, allowing you to move at double the pace listed on the Northern Wastes Land Travel table (see the "Into the Wastes" section earlier in this chapter).

This charm vanishes 24 hours after you leave the Northern Wastes.

Leaving the Shrine

Dalamar needs to know only that the Blue Phoenix Shrine is a holy place sacred to the god Habbakuk.

As the group leaves the shrine, if the characters haven't already rescued the sea elves at Camp Carrionclay, a sea elf scout approaches Ishvern to tell him they've found where their captured companions were taken. The sea elves have been imprisoned at a Dragon Army camp in the middle of a murky lake (see the "I: Camp Carrionclay" section). These sea elf scouts provide directions to area I on map 5.1. Mark this hex on the players' map of the region in appendix E.

Ishvern asks the characters to find and free these captives. In return, he offers them what remaining treasure he has: a few blue pearls worth 750 gp.

D: Sunward Fortress

The Red Dragon Army has unearthed the centuries-old Sunward Fortress, a pre-Cataclysm monument to the god Sirrion. While most of its ruins have sunk beneath the ground, a crumbling, lighthouse-like spire pierces the surface and marks the location of the ruins below.

Shard of Chaos

When Dragon Army scouts discovered the ruins of the Sunward Fortress, the black-robed wizard Lohezet ordered an outpost established there. A servant of the Dragon Queen and a fervent antiquarian, Lohezet sought to discover the forgotten ruin's secrets. Dragon Army soldiers and captives worked tirelessly until they unearthed a mysterious stone in the ruins' depths. Soon after, workers at the site began transforming into scaled monstrosities. Unbeknown to everyone, the shard was imbued with the power of the Spawning Stone—the source of the vicious monsters called slaadi.

The Dragon Army evacuated the ruin, but not completely. The evil cleric Belephaion, Lohezet's peer, was fascinated with the phenomenon. He ordered a bozak draconian named Virruza to stay behind and claim the Spawning Shard's magic in the Dragon Queen's name.

Approaching the Fortress

Read the following when the characters approach the Sunward Fortress:

> Amid the natural stone formations of the Northern Wastes, a broken, hundred-foot spire lies half buried. The massive spire's base and toppled pinnacle would be easy to miss were it not for the excavation sites and abandoned tents surrounding them.

The Sunward Fortress was once a hermitage for those seeking to commune with Sirrion's greatest flame: the sun. The structure was akin to a great lighthouse, the upper reaches of which burned in the god's honor. It toppled down during the Cataclysm and has been abandoned ever since.

TOPPLED RUINS

The Sunward Fortress's pinnacle remains unexcavated, but characters who investigate it find only several crumbled, half-buried floors. A character who examines these ruins and succeeds on a DC 16 Intelligence (History) check can tell this was a holy site whose upper levels were constructed to burn like a massive beacon.

DRAGON ARMY EXCAVATION

At the base of the spire's remains stand a dozen ragged canvas tents in the red and black colors of the Red Dragon Army. Dozens of empty or shattered crates are scattered amid the camp. Nearby, an earthen ramp cuts through the clay and leads to an opening into the ruined spire's foundation. This opening leads to area D1.

Abandoned Gear. Characters who spend 10 minutes investigating the tents find enough dried meat to sustain one person for ten days, twelve dirty shovels, an overturned wheelbarrow, and a suit of leather armor bearing the Dragon Queen's symbol.

Mysterious Markings. A character who has a passive Wisdom (Survival) score of 16 or higher notices two types of clawed footprints amid the camp. Some are roughly human-sized, while others are twice that size. Characters who have seen draconian footprints before recognize the smaller prints as draconian. The characters likely have no way of knowing the larger prints are slaadi tracks.

Resting near Camp. If the characters take a long rest in the camp or within a mile of the Sunward Fortress, there is a 50 percent chance they are attacked by two **red slaadi** that fight to the death.

SUNWARD FORTRESS FEATURES

The ruin has the following features:

Ceilings. The ceilings in the ruins are 10 feet high.
Light. The ruins are not illuminated. The current occupants rely on darkvision to see. Area descriptions assume the characters have a light source or other means of seeing in the dark.
Tracks. The floors throughout the ruin are covered in clear footprints of booted Dragon Army soldiers, captives wearing foot-wrappings, draconian claws, and slaadi claws. They go in every direction and don't suggest individual paths.

SUNWARD FORTRESS LOCATIONS

The following locations are keyed to map 5.3.

D1: ENTRY CHAMBER

> A ramp of packed clay descends from the surface through a gap in the ancient stone wall. It emerges into a chamber thick with dust and old air. Atop a low dais to the north stands an altar carved with candle sconces, a shallow basin, and stylized flames. To the south, a spiral stairwell winds downward. To the east, an archway leads to another chamber.

This room once served as a place of worship for the hermits who occupied the spire.

Altar. A cleric of Sirrion or a character who succeeds on a DC 14 Intelligence (Religion) check recognizes the symbols on the altar as holy to Sirrion, god of creativity and change. A character who speaks an earnest prayer to Sirrion causes flames to spring to life within the altar's candle sconces and a thick, red liquid to fill its basin. This liquid is a *potion of fire breath*. After creating this potion, the altar won't do so again until one month has passed.

Stairs. The stairs here descend to area D3.

D2: ABANDONED DORMITORIES

> Battered bed frames and straw mattresses clutter this room, interspersed with fragments of ragged clothing.

The Dragon Army's prisoners rested here before slaadi destroyed the room. A character who spends five minutes searching the debris finds bits of clothing, two sets of manacles, and a blue pearl worth 150 gp.

D3: LOWER CHAMBERS

> The stairs descend into an space surrounded by a series of halls and cramped rooms. A thick, rotten smell permeates the air. Digging equipment and crates have been crammed into every corner and alcove.

This floor once served as lodging for the fortress's residents. Characters who enter the east hall see the barricaded door leading to area D4.

Equipment. The crates hold dozens of tools. A character who spends ten minutes searching the equipment finds three bullseye lanterns, six flasks of oil, 100 feet of hempen rope, four vials of acid, and three sets of mason's tools.

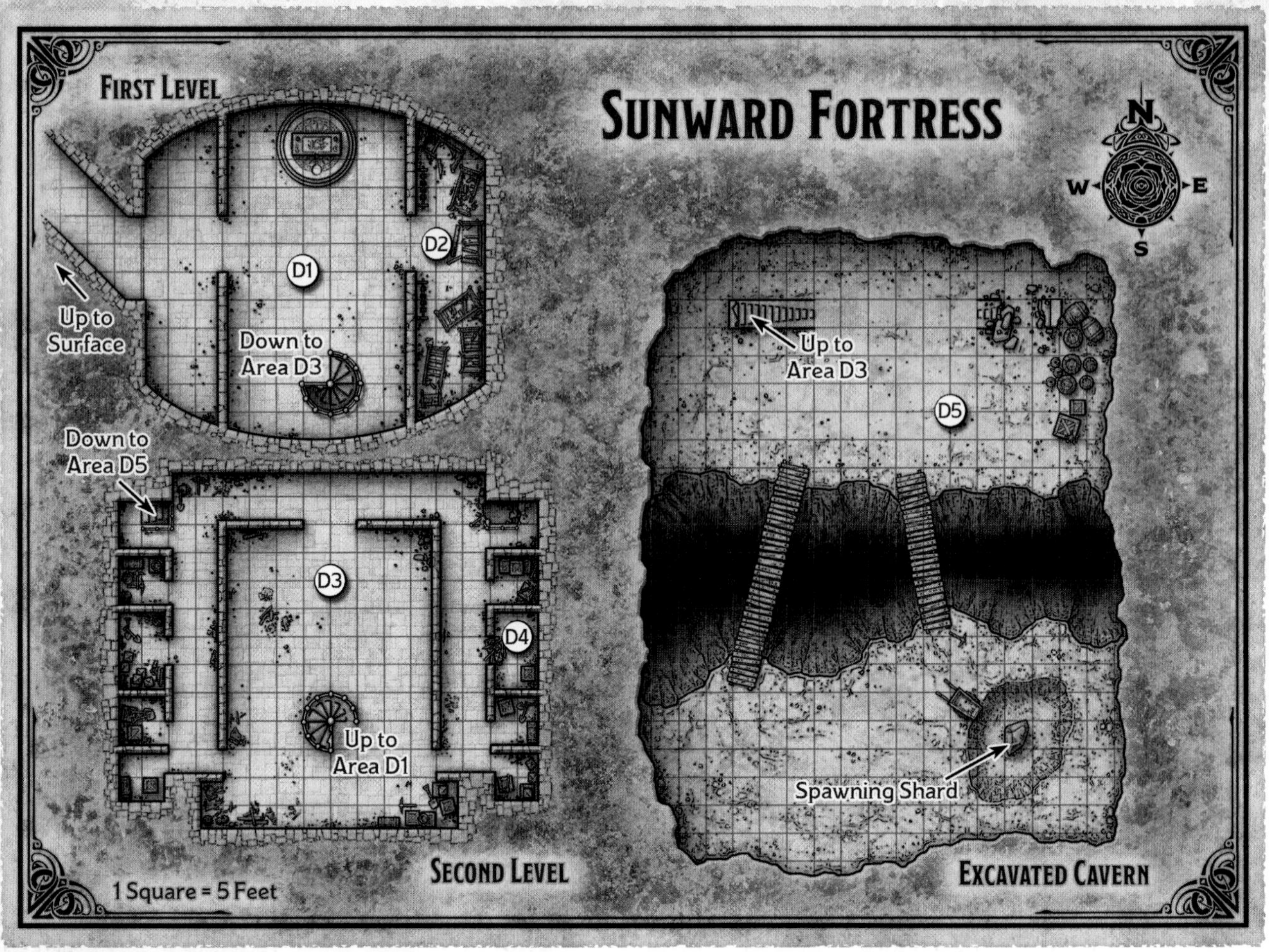
Sunward Fortress
First Level
D1
D2
Up to Surface
Down to Area D3
Down to Area D5
D3
D4
Up to Area D1
Second Level
1 Square = 5 Feet
D5
Up to Area D3
Spawning Shard
Excavated Cavern
N
W
E
S

Map 5.3: Sunward Fortress

Dracophage Subjects. Four mutated draconian-slaad hybrids lurk in the east hall. They look like bloated draconians with bright-red skin and wide, frog-like mouths. These creatures use the **kapak draconian** stat block (see appendix B), but replace their Dagger attack with the following attack:

Claw. *Melee Weapon Attack:* +5 to hit, reach 5 ft., one target. *Hit:* 5 (1d4 + 3) piercing damage plus 7 (2d6) poison damage. If the target is a Humanoid, it must succeed on a DC 12 Constitution saving throw or be infected with a disease—a minuscule slaad egg.

A Humanoid host can carry only one slaad egg at a time. Over three months, the egg moves to the chest cavity, gestates, and forms a slaad tadpole. In the 24-hour period before the tadpole is born, the host feels unwell; its speed is halved; and it has disadvantage on attack rolls, ability checks, and saving throws. At birth, the tadpole chews its way through vital organs and out of the host's chest in 1 round, killing the host in the process.

If the disease is cured before the tadpole's emergence, the tadpole disintegrates.

Stairs. In the northwest corner of the level, stairs descend to area D5.

D4: Barricaded Room

The entrance to this room is barricaded by heavy mining equipment. Inside are two Dragon Army captives who escaped the initial slaadi attack and Virruza (see area D5 for details). A character can unblock the door by succeeding on a DC 17 Strength check, but doing so alerts the hybrid draconians in area D3. If the characters try to speak through the crates, Yearkal answers them in a whisper, urging them to keep quiet.

Survivors. The Dimernesti sea elf Yearkal (neutral good, sea elf **acolyte**; see the "C: Blue Phoenix Shrine" section for details on sea elves) hides inside the room with the unconscious Rone (neutral, human **scout**), a hunter from Heart's Hollow. Rone has been infected with an ailment Yearkal doesn't know how to treat (see "Rone's Fate" below).

Yearkal is scared but unharmed. Once she confirms the characters aren't monsters, she removes the barricade and shares the following facts:

- When Yearkal was captured and brought here, the Dragon Army made her join the workers unearthing this ruin. The camp's commander had orders to recover whatever relics or magic lie within.
- They eventually dug up a large, glowing stone. Soon after, violent, toad-like terrors emerged.

Mike Schley

- Yearkal and Rone fled but were recaptured by Virruza, a magic-using draconian.
- Virruza seeks to use the magic of the stone to transform people into draconians. However, his actions caused more monsters to emerge.
- Since then, Yearkal and Rone have been hiding here. Rone has felt unusual for the last few days, but he's grown increasingly ill in the last day.
- Yearkal knows there are other sea elves at the Blue Phoenix Shrine and Camp Carrionclay. She wishes to reunite with all of them.

Rone's Fate. Rone is infected with a slaad tadpole. Due to Virruza's experiments, the tadpole matured rapidly and is about to hatch. A character who succeeds on a DC 18 Intelligence (Arcana or Medicine) check realizes Rone is infected by a dangerous parasite that will soon kill him, though a *lesser restoration* spell or similar magic could heal him.

If the characters don't heal Rone, a **slaad tadpole** emerges 1 hour after the characters encounter him, killing him. If the characters do heal Rone, he thanks them and offers them a 1,000 gp reward if they take him home to Heart's Hollow.

D5: Spire Depths

> This level of the fortress hasn't been fully excavated. A thirty-foot-wide chasm splits it in two, spanned by makeshift wooden footbridges. On the far side of the chasm, digging implements surround an eight-foot-tall crystal glowing with a noxious orange light. On the near side of the chasm, a hulking red form covered in squirming shapes digs through broken crates.

The creature is a **red slaad** covered in five **slaad tadpoles**. These monsters attack as soon as they spot the characters. A character who succeeds on a DC 16 Intelligence (Arcana) check recognizes the monsters as slaadi, denizens of the plane of Limbo.

Hidden in the shadows south of the chasm is the mutated draconian Virruza (see below). He doesn't attack until someone tries to cross the chasm.

Chasm and Bridges. The chasm drops 70 feet to an uneven stone floor below. A creature that falls into the chasm takes 24 (7d6) bludgeoning damage.

The bridges crossing the chasm look treacherous but are stable. If Virruza hits a creature on a bridge with his Hurl Flame attack, the bridge begins to smolder, igniting at the beginning of his next turn. After a bridge ignites, a creature that enters the bridge for the first time on a turn or starts its turn there must succeed on a DC 14 Dexterity saving throw or take 3 (1d6) fire damage. A bridge falls into the chasm 3 rounds after it ignites.

Virruza. Changed by days of strange experiments involving draconian blood and exposure to the Spawning Shard, Virruza now looks like a tumescent draconian with warty green skin and an overly large mouth. Use the **green slaad** stat block for Virruza, but replace the Shapechanger trait with the following trait:

Death Throes. When Virruza is reduced to 0 hit points, he turns into a puddle of acid and splashes acid on those around him. Each creature within 5 feet of him must succeed on a DC 12 Dexterity saving throw or be covered in acid for 1 minute. A creature can use its action to scrape or wash the acid off itself or another creature. A creature covered in the acid takes 7 (2d6) acid damage at the start of each of its turns.

Virruza is hostile, is unable to communicate intelligibly, and fights to the death.

Spawning Shard. This enormous orange gem weighs over a ton and sheds dim light for 10 feet. A *detect magic* spell reveals it emanates an aura of transmutation magic. A character who inspects the Spawning Shard and succeeds on a DC 18 Intelligence (Arcana) check determines the gem's magic can corrupt creatures and turn them into slaadi.

A creature that touches the gem must succeed on a DC 15 Constitution saving throw or become infected with a disease called chaos phage. While

A RED SLAAD
COVERED IN
SLAAD TADPOLES

MARK BEHM

infected, the target can't regain hit points, and its hit point maximum is reduced by 10 (3d6) every 24 hours unless the target is cured by magic such as the *lesser restoration* spell. If the disease reduces the target's hit point maximum to 0, the target instantly transforms into a red slaad or, if it has the ability to cast spells of 3rd level or higher, a green slaad. Only a *wish* spell can reverse the transformation.

Treasure. Virruza carries a pouch containing 900 gp worth of nonmagical orange gemstones—they aren't related to the Spawning Shard, though they look similar. He also carries a *+1 wand of the war mage* he has forgotten how to use.

Characters who search the south side of the chamber find Virruza's personal notes on scattered pieces of parchment. A character who spends ten minutes reading them learns the following details:

- Virruza was following orders from a Dragon Army commander named Belephaion.
- His mission was to investigate the monster-creating stone unearthed here.
- He was optimistic he could use the stone's magic to create a disease to turn people into draconians.
- Virruza notes that exposure to what he calls the "Spawning Shard" has begun to change him.
- After this, the notes grow sloppy and nonsensical.

LEAVING THE FORTRESS

Once the characters have investigated area D5—and potentially claimed Virruza's notes—they have all the information about this site Dalamar requires.

If the characters want to seal the entrance to the Sunward Fortress or otherwise bury the Spawning Shard, the equipment left around the ruins allows them to collapse the ramp leading to area D1 with four hours of effort. Destructive magic hastens this work.

E: WAKENRETH

The funerary obelisk of Wakenreth—"House of Silence" in Elvish—was constructed by Silvanesti elves in the Istarian city of Onyari shortly before the city took flight. The tower served as an emblem of peace between the people of Istar and Silvanesti. However, as with all of Onyari, Wakenreth met a tragic end, and it's now haunted by the spirits it used to keep safe. Dalamar is unaware Wakenreth was once part of the City of Lost Names—he knows only that Silvanesti writings speak of a magical tower rising from the wasteland.

THE DOOMED MAUSOLEUM

In addition to being a symbol of peace between Silvanesti and Istar, the tower of Wakenreth served as a crypt for the elves who lived in Onyari—though it saw little use before the city's destruction. When Onyari began its slow fall across the skies of the Northern Wastes, the monolith broke from its foundations, toppling toward the ground far from where the rest of the city eventually crashed. As the structure fell, Wakenreth's caretaker desperately invoked the tower's magic in hopes of transporting it to the Feywild. However, the magic of the displaced tower went awry and partially transported the tower to the Shadowfell. Though this helped Wakenreth survive, the portal within the tower has corrupted the spirits of those who rested within and trapped the site in a state of perpetual dissolution.

APPROACHING WAKENRETH

As the characters near the ruined tower, read the following text:

> Ahead, a pale stone tower juts from the rust-colored landscape. Carved with the likenesses of a thousand elven warriors, the tower has relatively intact lower levels, but as it climbs toward its eighty-foot height, the upper levels deteriorate. Rather than falling, the crumbling stone hangs in the air, the tower's disintegration frozen unnaturally. A rusty iron double door at the tower's base hangs ajar.

Exposure to Shadowfell magic has caused the upper levels of Wakenreth to deteriorate. Caught between that plane and the Material Plane, the ruin is locked in a perpetual state of frozen dissolution. Although the upper levels are crumbling, the shattered stone walls are still bound tightly enough to prevent creatures from slipping inside.

The ancient door here opens into area E1.

WAKENRETH FEATURES

The mystical tower has the following features:

Ceilings. Wakenreth's ceilings are 20 feet high.
Doors. All doors are made of rusty iron. They are unlocked and open easily, though noisily.
Lighting. Areas E1 and E2 are brightly lit by *continual flame* spells cast on wall sconces. In areas E3 and E4, these glowing sconces are affected by Shadowfell magic that causes them to produce only dim light and shine with an eerie green glow. Area E5 is dimly lit by a gloomy gray sky.

Wakenreth Locations

The following locations are keyed to map 5.4, except for area E5, which is unmapped.

E1: First Level

> This round chamber is illuminated by white flames flickering in magical sconces on the walls. In the room's center stands a gleaming obsidian statue of a solemn elf warrior. Around the statue's pedestal, hundreds of silver coins lie scattered in the dust. Beyond, a staircase ascends, curving along the tower's north wall.

If a character examines the coins or statue, have them make a DC 14 Intelligence (History) check. Silvanesti elves have advantage on this check. On a successful check, the character recognizes that the statue is a guardian common to Silvanesti burial sites and that the silver coins represent souls shining as stars in the night sky. The character also knows Silvanesti tradition dictates each visitor must leave a silver coin on the statue's pedestal.

Cursed. A character who proceeds up the stairs without leaving a coin on the pedestal or who takes a coin from the room becomes cursed for as long as they remain within the tower or until the curse is removed by a *remove curse* spell or similar magic. While cursed, the character has disadvantage on all ability checks and saving throws.

Stairs. The stairs here climb up to area E2.

Treasure. There are 451 silver coins in this room, which a character can collect by spending ten minutes. However, a character who removes a coin from this room becomes cursed as noted above.

E2: Second Level

> Heaps of rubble have fallen from this chamber's partially collapsed ceiling. The room holds two stone crypts, while the walls are sculpted with empty burial niches. A door stands to the southeast. Sconces on the walls shed light tinged a faint green.

The characters draw the attention of two hostile **wraiths** that lurk inside the crypts here. Once each wraith is defeated, it turns into an incorporeal elven spirit. One spirit quickly fades away, while the other—a woman with light-gray hair and pale eyes—floats through the ceiling and out of sight.

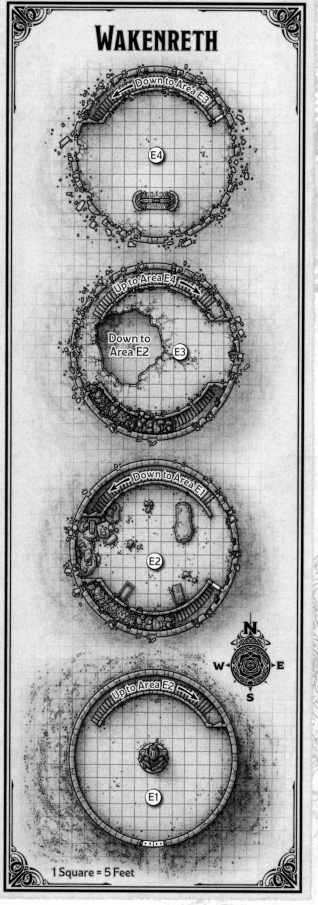

Map 5.4: Wakenreth

Stairs and Ceiling. The door here leads to stairs once used to access area E3. However, the stairs are blocked by rubble that would take hours to clear. The hole in the ceiling 20 feet above is the fastest way to access area E3.

Treasure. The two crypts each hold a desiccated elven body. One body wears a *cloak of protection*, while the other wears the nonmagical white robes of a Mage of High Sorcery.

E3: THIRD LEVEL

> The room's shattered walls stand frozen in time, hovering a heartbeat away from falling apart.
>
> A sizable hole gapes in the room's floor. To the south, rubble blocks a staircase leading down, while to the north, another staircase climbs to the level above. Dismal gray-green light shines from flickering wall sconces, eerily illuminating yellowed bones fallen from burial niches and scattered across the floor.

If the characters defeated the wraiths in the previous level, the elf spirit is here.

Regretful Spirit. The woman's spirit repeatedly tries to pick up a sword from the remains on the floor, failing every time. She doesn't notice the characters until she's addressed directly, at which point she shares the following information in a distant, hollow voice:

- Her name is Jentida. She was a guard in a Silvanesti delegation sent to the Istarian city of Onyari.
- She doesn't know what the City of Lost Names is (as she's unaware Onyari was later called that).
- She has no memory of how she got here, but she feels perpetually angry—and it feels like her anger is being fueled by something higher in this tower.
- She asks if the characters know her sister Tenadria, an elf diplomat who disappeared from the delegation. There's no way the characters can know Tenadria, but her remains appear in chapter 7.

After conversing with the characters, Jentida fades away.

Stairs. The stairs leading down are blocked by rubble. The stairs leading up have a door at the top, which opens to area E4.

Treasure. The sword the spirit was trying to pick up is a *dancing longsword*. In addition, characters who search the remains in this room find six onyx gemstones worth 200 gp each.

E4: FOURTH LEVEL

> The door opens into a room that hovers in a starless night sky. Though the floor is stable, shattered wall fragments float in the air, their sconces emitting a faint, sickly green light. Beyond the broken walls lies an endless black expanse.
>
> Across the platform stands a stone archway sculpted with sharp runes and the heads of five dragons. Within the arch swirls dense gray mist.

The darkness beyond this room's broken walls is only an illusion. This room stands at the top of the tower, not in an extraplanar space.

Portal. The archway was created to connect the tower with a friendly realm within the Feywild. When Wakenreth toppled from Onyari, though, its magic was disrupted. Now the portal connects to the Shadowfell.

A character who inspects the portal and succeeds on a DC 14 Intelligence (Arcana) check recognizes the sculpted dragon heads as those of green dragons, while the runes relate to the natural magic of the Feywild. They also notice the runes can rotate, likely as a means of controlling the portal, but their function is unclear. A character who attempts to adjust the runes without instructions from Veriel in area E5 must make the saving throw detailed in the "Restoring the Tower" section, and they can't close the portal yet.

A creature that steps through the portal appears in area E5 (an endless expanse not depicted on map 5.4). If no character steps through the portal, Veriel (see area E5) appears amid the mist in the arch and converses with the characters.

E5: SHADOWFELL EXPANSE

> You find yourself atop a broken tower of jet-black stone, standing in a barren, unfamiliar landscape. Jagged peaks of colorless rock stretch for miles, and the wind howls mournfully.
>
> Behind you, faint light shines from an identical version of the stone archway you just passed through.

Once the characters enter the portal, they're in the Shadowfell, and they can see the door behind them shining like a beacon of light. Characters can freely pass back and forth through the portal between area E4 and E5, and they can speak through its mist to creatures in the other area.

Veriel. An elf spirit appears and greets the characters, introducing himself as Veriel (lawful neutral **ghost**), Wakenreth's caretaker. He explains to the characters what happened to the tower (detailed in "The Doomed Mausoleum" at the beginning of the "E: Wakenreth" section). He knows nothing about the City of Lost Names or its location (as he's unaware Onyari was later called that). Veriel asks for the party's help in severing the link between Wakenreth and the Shadowfell, a feat that can be accomplished only from the other side of the portal. His time spent in the Shadowfell has linked him to this plane, and he can't pass through the portal.

Undead Beast. As Veriel relays this information, an **anhkolox** (see appendix B) climbs into view from the tower's edge, drawn by the activity here. Hungry for the characters' life essence, the creature attacks. It ignores Veriel, who stays out of the fight.

The Shadowfell. The Shadowfell is detailed in the *Dungeon Master's Guide*. Any exploration of the plane beyond the portal's immediate vicinity is beyond the scope of this adventure.

RESTORING THE TOWER

After the anhkolox is defeated, Veriel continues his explanation. To cut Wakenreth off from the Shadowfell, the runes on the portal in area E4 must be restored to their intended order, which Veriel shares with them.

The runes on the portal can be adjusted only in area E4. The process takes five minutes and requires a character to make a DC 14 Constitution saving throw as Shadowfell energies tug at their life essence. On a failed check, the character takes 17 (5d6) necrotic damage and gains 1 level of exhaustion, then the portal closes. On a successful check, the portal closes without harming the character. Either way, the portal's connection with the Shadowfell is severed.

Once Wakenreth is cut off from the Shadowfell, the supernatural darkness in area E4 fades, the torch sconces throughout the structure shed bright light, and the walls are restored.

CONFERRING WITH DALAMAR

As the characters leave Wakenreth, Dalamar arrives at the ruin. Whether the characters were successful in restoring the monolith or whether they simply share what they've discovered, the mage is pleased with their findings.

Once the tower is cut off from the Shadowfell and cleared of threats, Dalamar takes an hour to investigate the portal. After doing so, he relates the following information:

- Wakenreth was clearly built elsewhere and somehow fell here. He believes he can use the portal's magic to pinpoint where Wakenreth originally stood.
- To do so, Dalamar must research the magical ley lines underpinning the region and how they're influenced by other sources of magic.
- If the characters haven't done so already, he encourages them to investigate the Blue Phoenix Shrine and the Sunward Fortress—two sources of unique magic in the region.
- Once he knows more about the nature of those places and what magic lingers there, he believes he can use Wakenreth's magic to discover the location of the tower's foundations.
- This should provide him with the general location of the City of Lost Names.

Once the characters learn (if they haven't already) that the Blue Phoenix Shrine is a holy place of the god Habbakuk and that the Sunward Fortress holds the slaadi Spawning Shard, Dalamar needs 24 hours to evaluate that information and complete his research. Afterward, he directs the characters to a mesa at the northern edge of the wastes called the Giant's Spine (area K on map 5.1), where he believes they'll find the City of Lost Names.

A SECOND QUEST

Once the location of the City of Lost Names is revealed, Dalamar is willing to conclude his business with the characters. However, during his research using the portal here, he's discovered a powerful source of magic to the north. He asks the characters to escort him there, not knowing the location is Dread Wolf Cove (area J on map 5.1). If they do, he promises to reward them with whatever they find there and a future favor.

F: BLUEMAW CAVE

Bluemaw Cave, an abandoned dragon's lair, owes its blue hue to its high concentration of blue salt crystals. The characters might stumble across Bluemaw Cave or learn about it from the "Heart's Hollow Quests" section.

NOT-QUITE-ABANDONED LAIR

The cave was carved by a blue dragon that abandoned it long ago. It now houses a family of dwarves who were captured in the south by the Dragon Army but have since escaped. They claimed the cave as a home away from the war.

In a stroke of terrible luck for the dwarves, the Dragon Army leader Belephaion recently identified the place as a possible dragon's lair and sent draconians to investigate.

APPROACHING THE CAVE

> A massive cave opens in the cliff ahead. Enormous sapphire-blue crystals line the cave's mouth.

Grasha recently finished a pit trap just inside the mouth of the cave. She has been hiding all day in a crevasse near the top of the cave's mouth, waiting to see if any draconians fall into it.

Pit Trap. The pit trap is concealed beneath rocky gravel that blends with the surrounding ground. As a character approaches the entrance, they must make a DC 15 Intelligence (Investigation) check. On a failed check, the character falls 20 feet into the pit, taking 2d6 bludgeoning damage from the fall and 2d10 piercing damage from the spikes at the bottom.

Whether the trap is triggered or not, Grasha hears the characters approaching, and after confirming they aren't draconians, she comes out of hiding.

GRASHA

GRASHA MIGAN

The leader of a dwarf family and an enthusiast of gnomish engineering, Grasha wears patchwork knit clothing and her hair in a long braid. Grasha is an accomplished inventor who's fascinated by the rare minerals she's found around Bluemaw Cave.

Personality Trait. "If being a mother's taught me anything, it's the importance of improvisation."

Ideal. "The best ideas are effective but also a little flashy."

Bond. "I'll protect my family—their today and their tomorrow."

Flaw. "Dangerous? My plans aren't dangerous—you just need to know where to stand."

AN HONEST MISTAKE

When Grasha approaches the characters, she isn't threatening. Unless the characters are hostile, she deeply apologizes and helps anyone who fell into the trap. Grasha warns against going into the cave, as it's crawling with monsters and draconians.

She explains that she and her clan came here after being captured by the Dragon Army. She encourages the characters not to linger near the cave entrance, lest they draw the attention of foes within. Grasha suggests guiding the characters to a safe spot where they can meet the rest of her clan, but she warns the way might be uncomfortable for larger folk.

THE MIGAN CLAN

If the characters agree to go with Grasha, she leads them to a small passage near the cave's entrance. Medium creatures must squeeze through the cave's narrow tunnels, and Large creatures won't fit.

After about 10 minutes of following Grasha's meandering path through the caverns, the characters finally arrive at the dwarves' cramped hideout. Other than Grasha, seven other dwarves are present: Reka, Blem, Grap, Lop, Oske, Trop, and Yula. Reka, Grasha's wife, steps forward to gently scold Grasha (in Dwarven) and question who the characters are (in Common).

MEETING THE DWARVES

Grasha has already decided the characters are the solution to the family's draconian problem. Reka distrusts strangers and is skeptical of the characters, but she wants the draconians to leave so the clan can reclaim the cave. If the characters are willing to help, Reka gives Grasha her blessing to lead them to the lair.

If the characters are hesitant to help the dwarves, Grasha emphasizes that the draconians have been retrieving enormous amounts of treasure from an abandoned dragon's lair in the depths of the cave.

PREPARING FOR THE MAW

If the characters agree to help the dwarves, Grasha casually adds that, in addition to the draconians, they might have to deal with monsters she calls "fang worms." Grasha doesn't know it, but the creatures are gricks agitated by the draconians' presence.

INTO THE CAVE

Once the characters are ready, Grasha takes them to the entrance of Bluemaw Cave. Grasha won't go beyond the cave's entrance, but she assures the characters she'll rearm the pit trap at the cave's mouth to ward off intruders.

BLUEMAW CAVE FEATURES

The cave is carved from igneous rock. Its entrance sports a cavernous 40-foot-high ceiling, and its lower chamber opens to the surface above. The lair also has the following features:

Blue Crystals. Glowing blue salt crystals line the cave's walls, most densely in area F1. Each 5-foot cube of crystal has AC 11, 15 hit points, immunity to poison and psychic damage, and vulnerability to thunder damage. The crystals are highly conductive to lightning energy, which a character can determine with a successful DC 13 Intelligence (Arcana or Nature) check. If a crystal is dealt lightning damage, it explodes in a dazzling blast, dealing 7 (2d6) lightning damage to creatures within 10 feet of it.

Lighting. Crystals fill the upper level of the cave with dim light. The lower level opens to the surface, allowing natural bright light in during the daytime.

BLUEMAW CAVE LOCATIONS

The following locations are keyed to map 5.5.

F1: CRYSTAL CAVE

> Blue crystal formations line the walls and floors of this cavern, so dense in places that they look engulfed in ice. The crystals glow sedately with a dim light.

Investigation reveals the crystals to be salt, though they have special properties (detailed in "Bluemaw Cave Features" above). The draconians in area F3 can be heard faintly from here, grunting and growling at each other in Draconic.

Grick Pack. The characters draw the attention of a pack of seven **gricks** hiding in cracks in the walls. They were riled up and ultimately scared off from the lower chamber by the draconians. They attack the first creature they see.

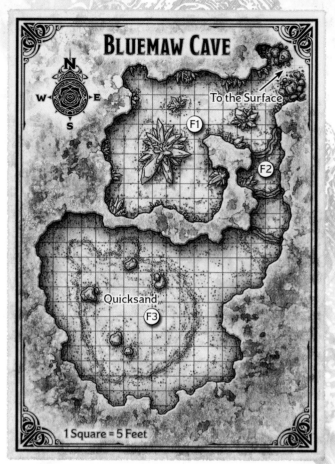

MAP 5.5: BLUEMAW CAVE

The draconians in area F3 have heard other draconians slaying gricks around the cave, so they ignore the sound of fighting above.

F2: DESCENDING CLIFFS

> The passage descends in a series of sheer cliffs, each one plunging farther than the last into the depths.

Three cliffs drop to the lower chamber. The first drops 30 feet, the second 40 feet, and the third 50 feet. Area F3 is visible from atop the last cliff.

F3: SAND PIT

> This chamber's ceiling opens to the sky above, and much of its ground is made of fine sand. The cavern walls are engraved with claw marks in intricate geometric patterns. Five draconians labor below, sifting the sand and placing treasures they find into half-filled sacks, while a winged draconian watches.

This sand pit is where the dragon spent most of its time. The markings on the walls are artistic renderings of Draconic words, including the name "Nadir."

Draconians. A **sivak draconian** and five **baaz draconians** occupy this room (see appendix B for both stat blocks). The baaz draconians drag treasure from the sand pit, placing it into sacks the sivak draconian can fly out through the cavern's open top. If a draconian spots the characters, they attack while shouting to alert the others.

Quicksand. Much of the sandy lair contains 15 feet of quicksand (see map 5.2), which the draconians are already aware of. A character who prods the floor or searches for hazards discerns the pit's dangers with a successful DC 13 Wisdom (Perception) check. When a creature enters quicksand, it sinks 3 feet into the pit and becomes restrained. At the start of each of the creature's turns, it sinks 3 feet again. As long as the creature isn't completely submerged, it can escape by using its action and succeeding on a Strength check. The DC is 10 plus the number of feet the creature has sunk. A creature that is completely submerged can't breathe.

A creature can pull another creature within its reach from the quicksand by using its action and succeeding on a Strength check. The DC is 5 plus the number of feet the target creature has sunk.

Grick Alpha. If combat breaks out, a **grick alpha** and two **gricks** that were dozing in the sand emerge in a random space adjacent to the quicksand. They indiscriminately attack any creatures in the room.

Treasure. The draconians have removed much of the hoard's treasure, but some remains in the sacks here and hidden beneath the sand. The draconians have gathered 700 gp in their sacks. Searching for and safely extracting what remains takes approximately six hours, unless the characters use magical means to move the sand, in which case the time can be reduced at your discretion. The remaining hoard includes 1,200 cp, 8,000 sp, 2,300 gp, 60 pp, twelve assorted gems worth 50 gp each, an ornate chalice worth 1,000 gp, and a pair of *boots of levitation*.

VICTORY!

Once the draconians are dealt with, Grasha thanks the characters for their help. The dwarves start moving back into the cave and offer to feed and shelter the characters for as long as they like.

G: HEART'S HOLLOW

Heart's Hollow is a small but thriving community of a few hundred people living in the walls of a deep crater. No one in the village knows the community grew from the lair of Nezrah, a bronze dragon who has lived in hiding in the region for centuries. The first residents of Heart's Hollow were wanderers she rescued while disguised in human form. Over time, others lost in the Northern Wastes joined the community and carved dwellings into the cavern's walls, gradually creating a unique hidden village.

If the characters meet Kennah in Camp Carrionclay or Rone in the Sunward Fortress, they might seek Heart's Hollow themselves. Otherwise, use the encounter in the following section whenever you please. Make sure the characters meet Clystran, as he plays a role in later chapters.

THE DRAGON HUNTER

As characters near Heart's Hollow (or whenever you wish to introduce Clystran), the Wash rises in the region. The character with the highest passive Wisdom (Perception) score hears energetic cursing ahead. Read or paraphrase the following text:

> Water rushes into the canyon ahead, rising swiftly. The sudden flooding has spurred creatures to seek higher ground—including a human in rugged leathers rapidly climbing a rope out of the chasm, pursued by several horse-sized spiders.

Clystran (neutral good, human **scout**) is being pursued by five **giant spiders** as the canyon floods (see "The Wash" earlier in this chapter). You decide whether the characters are in the canyon as well or above it. The giant spiders turn their attention toward the characters if attacked, and they flee if three or more spiders are killed.

After the spiders are defeated, Clystran proves friendly—and tremendously excited to meet strangers in the Northern Wastes.

CLYSTRAN

Clystran has lived his entire life in the Northern Wastes and considers himself an expert on the region. He knows dozens of interesting hollows and rock formations around High Hunt, the plateau that Heart's Hollow occupies. He can share any of the local names for Northern Wastes regions, like "Wormgut" and "Giant's Spine," shown on map 5.1. He also considers himself an expert on the fauna of the Northern Wastes and takes a particular interest in the region's wasteland dragonnels. Clystran claims he saw an actual dragon in his youth, leading to a lifelong search of the wastes for where such elusive creatures hide. No one in Heart's Hollow takes his story or lifelong hunt seriously, though.

Personality Trait. "I know all there is to know about the Northern Wastes, except where the dragons live."

Ideal. "I'll become the best explorer in the wastes."

Bond. "Both the Northern Wastes and Heart's Hollow are my home. I'm loyal to both."

Flaw. "I can probably squeeze down that hole—there might be a dragon's lair inside!"

Talking with Clystran

So long as the characters aren't hostile to Clystran, he wants to know all about them. Use the following topics to guide the conversation with him:

- Clystran wants to know where the characters came from and—if the Kalaman forces are nearby—why their whole village is with them.
- He doesn't know about the Red Dragon Army in the region, but he has seen strange dragonnels with people riding them, and he's fascinated.
- He's happy to point the characters toward many landmarks in the Northern Wastes (see "Heart's Hollow Quests" for suggestions).
- Clystran scavenges for his community, looking for anything useful the Wash brings in.
- He offers to take the characters to Heart's Hollow; he's headed there now. However, he'd prefer their whole army not come as well.

Heart's Hollow Locations

Most structures in Heart's Hollow are carved out of the wall of a deep crater. Patchwork fabrics scavenged from the wastes decorate each home, and lanterns hang in every window. Detail the unique community of Heart's Hollow however you please, including the following locations and landmarks (appearing on map 5.6):

Breakwater Landing. Breakwater Landing serves as the town square and bartering place. A slate column marked with chalk serves as a community message board.

End's Odds. Run by Grandit "End" Pike (neutral good, hill dwarf **commoner**), End's Odds sells "slightly used" goods and equipment found in the wastes.

The Fort. Secrecy is Heart's Hollow's greatest defense, but the town also maintains the Fort, a communal warehouse and armory. Should danger arise, the locals arm themselves here.

Lavender's. Lavender Jalls (lawful neutral, human **mage**) is a renegade wizard who hasn't taken the Test of High Sorcery. He specializes in casting helpful cantrips and brewing alchemical tinctures.

The Mosaic. Spiraling through Heart's Hollow is the Mosaic, a sloped pathway lined with colorful stones. Every person who visits the village is invited to add a stone to the path, symbolizing the beautiful mark they leave on the community.

Salt Lick. The Salt Lick is a popular tavern suspended over open air by a web of sturdy cords. Ness (see "Nezrah" below) can often be found here at a table jokingly called "the Mayor's Office."

CLYSTRAN

Heart's Hollow Residents

The lively people of Heart's Hollow are mainly humans, hill dwarves, and kender. Most feel they were given a second lease on life when they were rescued from the wastes or found their way here. Nezrah's desire to keep her community a secret from other dragons has rubbed off on the residents, and they are wary of strangers. However, once someone proves they care for the community's needs as much as their own, locals welcome them for life.

Nezrah

The secretive dragon Nezrah (neutral good **adult bronze dragon**) goes by the name Ness. She uses her magic to disguise herself as a middle-aged human woman, and no one knows she's a dragon.

Nezrah has made it her life's mission to build and protect Heart's Hollow. Over a hundred years ago, she came to the Northern Wastes seeking clutches of good dragon eggs hidden in the region, but she hasn't found any yet. Although she focuses on protecting the people of Heart's Hollow, she still hopes to find dragon eggs in the wastes one day.

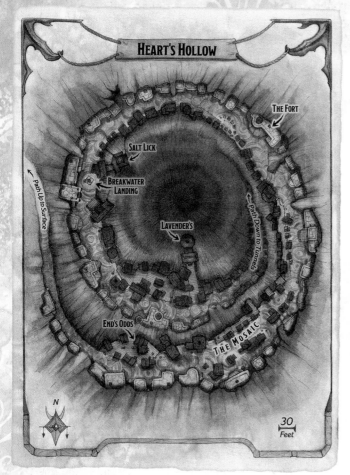

HEART'S HOLLOW

Path Up to Surface

THE FORT

SALT LICK

BREAKWATER LANDING

LAVENDER'S

Path Down to Tunnels

END'S ODDS

THE MOSAIC

N

30 Feet

MAP 5.6: HEART'S HOLLOW

HEART'S HOLLOW QUESTS

Heart's Hollow serves as a safe place for the characters to rest and resupply in the Northern Wastes. The locals also know much about the region. If the characters have missed any important information during their exploration, they might learn it from Clystran, Ness, or another resident of Heart's Hollow.

The people of Heart's Hollow don't know where the City of Lost Names is and have avoided the Dragon Army. They know the location of the Blue Phoenix Shrine, Sunward Fortress, and Wakenreth. They're also curious about other locations in the wastes and might ask for the characters' help—see the locations below.

BLUEMAW CAVE EXPLORATION

A group of scavengers have heard of Bluemaw Cave (location F on map 5.1), an out-of-the-way cavern where they've spotted dwarves living. They'd like to meet the dwarves and perhaps establish a friendly rapport. If the threats in the cave have not yet been defeated, the scavengers encourage the characters to clear them out, but they won't participate in combat themselves.

CARRIONCLAY DISCOVERY

No one in Heart's Hollow knows about Camp Carrionclay (location I on map 5.1). However, if the characters recover the dragon egg there and return to Heart's Hollow, Ness urgently seeks them out. She pleads for the egg, swearing to keep it safe. She'll even reveal her true nature to the characters if she needs to convince them she'll be a worthy guardian, but she won't threaten or harm them. If the characters agree to give her the egg, she rewards them with a suit of bronze *dragon scale mail* made from her own scales. She won't interfere in the conflict with the Dragon Army, though.

DRAGONNEL FEEDING

Clystran frequently takes dried meat to a flight of dragonnels he's been watching for years. However, he hasn't been able to visit for months and would like the characters' help delivering several packs of food to his dragonnel friends. Their den is at location H on map 5.1. If the characters help him, Clystran will work for the characters as a scout (see "Heart's Hollow Scouts").

HEART'S HOLLOW SCOUTS

The characters might convince residents of Heart's Hollow to aid them in their travels. If they do, the characters gain the following benefits:

Clystran the Guide. If Clystran guides the characters in the Northern Wastes, the characters can ignore difficult terrain during travel, allowing them to cover double the distance listed on the Northern Wastes Land Travel table earlier in this chapter. While with the characters, Clystran avoids combat and most dangerous situations.

Scavengers as Guides. A group of scavengers might temporarily join Darrett and his troops. These guides scout for the Kalaman forces through the Northern Wastes, allowing them to move at a normal pace of 12 miles (2 hexes on map 5.1) per day.

H: DRAGONNEL SPIRE

Twelve **wasteland dragonnels** (see appendix B) lair atop this rock formation, which looks like a dragon. Formations like this are common in the wastes, as if the spirits of the dragons killed during Onyari's fall reshaped the land.

The dragonnels avoid the characters unless Clystran is with them. Clystran respectfully lays out the dried meat he brought for the dragonnels and watches them from a distance. After an hour, he's ready to return home, his errand complete.

I: Camp Carrionclay

The Red Dragon Army established this outpost to serve as a waypoint for its supply lines as it travels across the Northern Wastes.

Characters might visit this location to rescue the sea elves they learn were captured in the "C: Blue Phoenix Shrine" section. Alternatively, if the characters are defeated by Dragon Army soldiers, they're brought here as prisoners.

Approaching the Camp

When the characters approach Camp Carrionclay, read the following:

> Ahead, the smells of rotting fish and burning flesh hang thick in the air. A fortified camp sits atop cliffs jutting from the center of a muddy lake. The camp is ringed by immense bone spurs, with makeshift wooden walls between. A wooden palisade surrounds a camp composed of tents, huts, and a crooked watchtower. Dozens of Dragon Army soldiers keep watch around the camp.

Camp Carrionclay Features

The camp has the following general features:

Walls. The 15-foot-high walls around the camp are made from driftwood. Each 10-foot section has AC 12, 30 hit points, and immunity to poison and psychic damage.

Sentries. Three **Dragon Army soldiers** (see appendix B) keep watch from the central tower in area I3.

Patrols. Two groups of soldiers patrol the camp, each including a **Dragon Army officer** and five **Dragon Army soldiers** (see appendix B for both stat blocks). One group watches the bridge outside the walls, and the other monitors the interior.

Infiltrating the Camp

It's difficult to infiltrate Camp Carrionclay. Here are some ways the characters might attempt to enter the camp unhindered:

Entering at Night. Most troops are asleep at night, except for those on the bridge and in the watchtower.

Posing as Soldiers. Characters can attempt to gain entrance by disguising themselves with magic or the uniforms of soldiers they've defeated. See area I2 for how such an attempt might unfold.

Camp Carrionclay Locations

The following locations are keyed to map 5.7.

I1: Wooden Bridge and Lake

> A wooden bridge crosses the marshy lake, which reeks with decay. The bridge ends at the camp's gate.

When the Wash is low, the lake surrounding the camp becomes a marsh filled with marine-animal carcasses and swamp plants, making the area difficult terrain. When the Wash is high, creatures can swim across the lake, but there is a 50 percent chance they are attacked by a **swarm of quippers**.

I2: Main Entrance

> A large, hastily made wooden gate blocks access to the camp. The area is guarded by three imposing figures with twisted draconic features.

The camp's only gate is watched by a **sivak draconian** and two **baaz draconians** (see appendix B for both stat blocks).

Gaining Access. If the characters disguise themselves as Dragon Army soldiers, they can attempt to deceive the draconians and enter the camp. The guards ask in Draconic where the characters are coming from. A character convinces the draconians to let them through with a successful DC 16 Charisma (Deception) check, made with disadvantage if the character doesn't speak Draconic.

I3: Watchtower

> The bare wooden beams of the camp's central watchtower support a makeshift platform with just enough room for four soldiers to stand comfortably.

The watchtower is occupied by three **Dragon Army soldiers** (see appendix B). Due to the high vantage point, the soldiers' passive Wisdom (Perception) score is 19.

Spotted. If a sentry atop the watchtower spots suspicious individuals—such as those not wearing Dragon Army uniforms—they blow a horn to alert the patrols and gate guards in area I2.

I4: Prisoner Cages

> Four dilapidated iron prison pens hold prisoners of the Dragon Army. Bloodstains spatter the ground beneath and around the cages.

The draconians keep prisoners in these cages. If the characters are captured, they're imprisoned in a cage with Kennah. The cages are guarded by three **baaz draconians** (see appendix B) and Urta, a **hobgoblin captain** who serves as jailer.

Cages. These cages are 10-foot cubes made of iron and locked with padlocks. Opening a lock requires the key held by Urta or a successful DC 17 Dexterity check using thieves' tools. A character inside a cage has disadvantage on this check.

Sea Elves. Two cages confine three Dimernesti sea elves, members of a group seeking the Blue Phoenix Shrine. Others in their group—including their leader, Yearkal—were taken to someplace called the Sunward Fortress. The sea elves know this name but not where it is. However, they can guide the party to the Blue Phoenix Shrine.

Bulette. One cage holds a recently captured **bulette**. It's hostile to everyone. If freed, it goes on a rampage, attacking anyone and retreating into the ground once reduced to 15 hit points or fewer.

Kennah. One cage houses Kennah, a **kender skirmisher** (see appendix B) with 1 hit point and no weapons. Kennah is from Heart's Hollow and was captured while scavenging the wastes. If freed, Kennah can take the characters to her settlement.

I5: ZIRROK'S HUT

> This hut is larger than the others in the camp. It's made of hides stretched over a wooden frame, with bone spikes protruding from the ground around it.

This hut belongs to Fewmaster Zirrok, the **hobgoblin warlord** in charge of the camp. Zirrok rarely leaves it. The hut is guarded by two **sivak draconians** (see appendix B). Inside is a cot, a desk, and an ornate chest.

Desk. The desk is covered in Dragon Army reports. A character who searches the desk finds letters from a commander named Belephaion talking about excavating the Sunward Fortress.

Ornate Chest. Opening this chest requires either the key held by Fewmaster Zirrok or a successful DC 20 Dexterity check using thieves' tools. The chest holds a bronze dragon egg, which will soon be claimed by an envoy of the evil cleric Belephaion (see "Wings of Death"). If the characters give the egg to Nezrah (see "Heart's Hollow Quests"), she rewards them.

Treasure. The desk holds two *potions of greater healing* and a pouch containing 300 gp.

WINGS OF DEATH

The following event occurs once the characters recover the bronze dragon egg or prepare to leave the camp. Read or paraphrase the following:

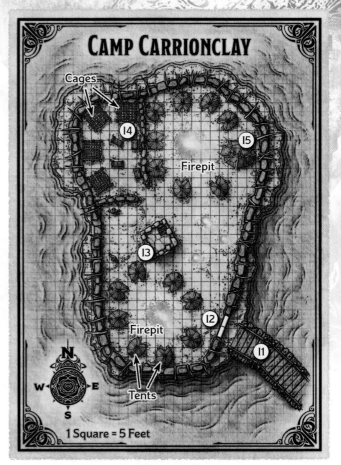

MAP 5.7: CAMP CARRIONCLAY

> Flapping wings sound above as a hulking creature with black scales descends, roaring as it lands atop the watchtower.

The creature is Akhviri, an **adult black dragon** tasked with retrieving the dragon egg for Belephaion. If the characters haven't left evidence of their presence, Akhviri waits for Fewmaster Zirrok to bring the chest from his tent to the watchtower.

True Dragon. On Krynn, chromatic and metallic dragons are considered creatures of legend, and Akhviri is likely the first dragon the characters have encountered. Characters who haven't encountered dragons before have disadvantage on saving throws against her Frightful Presence action.

Drawing Akhviri's Attention. Characters must succeed on a DC 21 group Dexterity (Stealth) check to avoid Akhviri's notice. If something is visibly amiss at the camp (such as dead soldiers or signs of battle), the DC for this check increases to 26. If Akhviri spots the characters and they're not disguised, she growls in Common from the tower:

> "Pitiful creatures, lurking in our domain with only your wretched lives to offer. I shall melt you to the bone!"

MIKE SCHLEY

At this point in the adventure, the characters aren't prepared to fight Akhviri and should be encouraged to flee. The dragon is proud and believes the adventurers are beneath her, so rather than pursuing them, she uses her Acid Breath once, then calls for any Dragon Army troops remaining in the camp to pursue the characters. Akhviri doesn't follow the characters beyond the camp.

J: Dread Wolf Cove

After the characters conclude their business at Wakenreth, Dalamar requests they escort him here.

Dread Wolf Cove is usually an unassuming inlet along the coast. However, the cove is lightly obscured by fog that billows from a nearby cave. If the characters enter, they encounter a wolflike **anhkolox** (see appendix B). Should the characters battle the monster, Dalamar (neutral elf **mage**) aids them.

Shard of Darkness. Once the anhkolox is destroyed, a character who searches the cave finds the source of the fog: a rounded piece of broken black glass. The fog ceases if the glass is touched, and it clears a minute later. A *detect magic* spell reveals the shard emanates an aura of enchantment magic. A character who succeeds on a DC 20 Intelligence (Arcana) check realizes the glass is a remnant of a destroyed *Orb of Dragonkind* (detailed in the *Dungeon Master's Guide*). The shattered, incomplete artifact has no properties in its current state.

Dalamar recognizes the shard immediately but pretends not to. He hasn't decided whether he wants it to aid his people or for his own studies. A character who succeeds on a DC 17 Wisdom (Insight) check realizes Dalamar recognizes the shard. If pressed, Dalamar reveals the shard's nature and his intention to have it. Dalamar won't attack the characters for the shard, but he will bargain for it now or concoct a way to steal it later. Dalamar's schemes don't have ramifications for the rest of the adventure, and you can develop them as you please.

After discovering the shard, Dalamar parts ways with the characters, returning to the elven encampment to plan his next move.

K. City of Lost Names

The characters learn the location of the City of Lost Names from Dalamar after completing the "E: Wakenreth" section. The characters know the City of Lost Names is the Red Dragon Army's destination. Before they head there, they should consider informing Darrett and their allies.

The Occupied City

As the characters approach the City of Lost Names, read the following text:

> A vast plateau rises from the wastes, its ancient cliffs soaring hundreds of feet high. A broad canyon splits the plateau's face, its passage blocked by an aged stone wall. Countless red tents spills from the canyon and its gate. Innumerable Dragon Army troops swarm the land, while patrols of dragonnels soar above.

The characters find the canyon leading to the City of Lost Names blocked by Dragon Army troops. The Dragon Army is an overwhelming threat the characters can't likely slip past, as Dragon Army mages see through magical methods of infiltration and dragonnel riders prevent any attempts to fly over.

The characters can learn more about the Dragon Army by interrogating captured soldiers or slipping into the camp. Doing so reveals the following:

- The canyon leads to the City of Lost Names.
- There, the army's leaders—the mage Lohezet and the priest Belephaion—seek an ancient weapon.
- They are accompanied by the terrifying knight Lord Soth and hundreds of other troops.
- The canyon to the city is blocked by a simple stone fortification—a remnant of a long-vanished people.
- The walls surrounding the ruined city are riddled with passages. One leads from the city to Wind's End, a landing point for Dragon Army dragonnels.

Wind's End is the characters' best chance to access the City of Lost Names. Wind's End teems with patrols of **Dragon Army dragonnels** and **Dragon Army soldiers** (see appendix B for both stat blocks). If the characters want to sneak into Wind's End, they'll need a significant distraction.

The Allied Army

If the characters reveal the location of the City of Lost Names to Darrett, he's prepared to head there whenever the characters please. If the characters haven't learned about the Dragon Army's camp yet, Kalaman scouts can reconnoiter the area and bring back the information from the previous section.

Let the characters discuss methods of slipping into the City of Lost Names with their allies. If the characters don't bring these points up themselves, Darrett notes the following:

- The Dragon Army forces outnumber Kalaman's, but Kalaman has the element of surprise.
- If Kalaman's forces attack the camp, Dragon Army reinforcements from within the city can reach them only through the narrow canyon.
- An attack would draw forces away from Wind's End and likely from the city.
- This would give the characters the opportunity to find the path into the city and strike at the Dragon Army leaders there.

Darrett believes such an attack is their strategy. He recognizes it'll come at a cost to Kalaman's forces, but he doesn't see another choice that would allow the characters to strike a decisive blow.

ASSAULTING THE DRAGON ARMY

Darrett will attack the Dragon Army, giving the characters the distraction they need to sneak into Wind's End, find the passage, and infiltrate the city. The adventure then proceeds in one of two ways:

With Mass Combat. If you are using the *Dragonlance: Warriors of Krynn* game along with this adventure, consult the "Warriors of Krynn: Scenario 7" sidebar instead of running the "Attack on Wind's End" section.

Without Mass Combat. If you aren't using the *Dragonlance: Warriors of Krynn* game, continue with the "Attack on Wind's End" section.

ATTACK ON WIND'S END

Darrett launches the attack on the Dragon Army whenever the characters choose. When the characters are in position and the Kalaman forces attack the Dragon Army camp, read the following:

> Ahead lies the outpost called Wind's End, a ramshackle enclosure pressed against massive cliff walls. Beside it, a strip of land has been cleared of rocks.
>
> Right on cue, shouts ring out to the southwest, quickly followed by smoke and alarm bells. In the distance, the silvery armor of Kalaman's soldiers cuts a swath through the unprepared Dragon Army camp.
>
> As chaos unfolds, most of the Dragon Army soldiers stationed at Wind's End rush their dragonnel mounts into the air, leaving the outpost vulnerable.

Three **Dragon Army officers** remain here with a **Dragon Army dragonnel** in a pen (see appendix B for both stat blocks). While the dragonnel is alert, the officers are distracted by the Kalaman forces and are surprised when the characters attack.

The "Wind's End Battlefield Features" section notes elements of this battle. Soon after the characters attack, dragonnels from the City of Lost Names fly overhead. Some might notice the characters, adding additional threats to this battle (see the "Wind's End Battlefield Events" section).

THE DRAGON ARMY BLOCKS THE PATH LEADING TO THE CITY OF LOST NAMES.

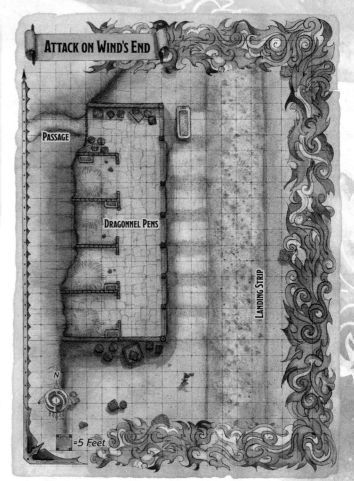

PASSAGE

DRAGONNEL PENS

LANDING STRIP

N

=5 Feet

MAP 5.8: ATTACK ON WIND'S END

WARRIORS OF KRYNN: SCENARIO 7

Darrett and the forces of Kalaman launch their attack on the Dragon Army. Things go well at first, but fate is against them, as an additional contingent of Dragon Army troops arrives soon after the battle begins. Read the introduction to scenario 7 in *Dragonlance: Warriors of Krynn*, then play that scenario. It details the attack on the Dragon Army forces at the walled canyon entrance to the City of Lost Names and the characters' search for a secret path through.

At the end of the scenario, proceed with chapter 6 as the characters infiltrate the City of Lost Names.

WIND'S END BATTLEFIELD FEATURES

The battlefield, depicted on map 5.8, has the following features:

Crates. Numerous crates lie in and around the dragonnel pens, filled with water and dried meat for the dragonnels.

Dragonnel Pens. A large cage encloses four spacious dragonnel pens and an equipment area. Its ceilings are 15 feet high.

Fray. The 15-foot-wide area marked by the design at the edge of the map represents areas from which danger might appear.

WIND'S END BATTLEFIELD EVENTS

During each round of this encounter, roll on the Wind's End Battlefield Events table on initiative count 0. Also consider rolling on the table if a character enters the Fray or otherwise tries to leave the battlefield.

WIND'S END BATTLEFIELD EVENTS

d10	Event
1–4	A **Dragon Army officer** (see appendix B) on a dragonnel flies overhead, firing a heavy crossbow at the character closest to the Fray. The attack has a +4 bonus to hit and deals 7 (1d10 + 2) piercing damage plus 5 (1d10) fire damage on a hit.
5–7	A dragonnel roars and strafes the battlefield, throwing up a cloud of dust. For the next round, the battlefield is heavily obscured.
8–9	Two **Dragon Army soldiers** (see appendix B) arrive, appearing in unoccupied spaces adjacent to the Fray near a random player character.
10	A dead dragonnel falls from the sky, crashing in a 10-foot area centered on a random player character who isn't in the dragonnel pens. Each creature in the crash area must succeed on a DC 14 Dexterity saving throw or take 33 (6d10) bludgeoning damage and be knocked prone. If all characters are in the dragonnel pens, reroll on this table.

PASSAGE

In a cargo-stuffed alcove at the north end of the dragonnel pens, several loose boards lean against the exposed cliff wall. The character with the highest passive Wisdom (Perception) score notices the gap behind these boards. The boards are easily moved, revealing a 5-foot-wide, 8-foot-high passage that winds into the cliff toward the City of Lost Names.

NEXT STEPS

The characters entering the passage in Wind's End concludes this chapter and makes a perfect cliffhanger. As the forces of Kalaman clash with the Dragon Army and the characters make their way toward the City of Lost Names, they advance to 8th level (if they haven't already done so).

The characters will discover what dangers lie beyond this passage in chapter 6.

The City of Lost Names has known
centuries of peace, but now the
Dragon Army claims its streets
and skies.

CHAPTER 6

CITY OF LOST NAMES

T HE GOAL OF THE RED DRAGON ARMY'S invasion is not only conquering Kalaman, but also obtaining a weapon to aid it in conquering all of Solamnia. A contingent of the Dragon Army's forces seeks to restore the ancient magic of the City of Lost Names, raising it as a devastating, flying battle platform. With these forces go Lord Soth, who—following whispers from the Dragon Queen—seeks to raise an army of Undead dragons from the draconic graveyard beneath the city. While the characters' allies distract the enemy forces outside the ruined city, the characters infiltrate the City of Lost Names to discover the Dragon Army's plots and foil them.

RUNNING THIS CHAPTER

This chapter begins as the characters venture through a hidden passage into the City of Lost Names. As they traverse this Path of Memories, they encounter an ancient magic-user who tells them much about the ruined city and the broken *dragonlance* they discovered beneath Castle Kalaman.

   Once the characters enter the City of Lost Names, they find it patrolled by Dragon Army forces. After exploring the city and learning of the army's goals, the party's quest leads the characters to the Threshold of the Heavens, where the black-robed wizard Lohezet and Belephaion, cleric of Takhisis, seek to restore the magic of the city and raise it into the air once more.

CHARACTER ADVANCEMENT

In this chapter, level advancement is handled as follows:

- Characters start this chapter at 8th level, having gained a level at the end of chapter 5.
- They advance to 9th level during their exploration of the City of Lost Names—likely after reforging the *dragonlance* at the Temple of Paladine.
- After escaping the Threshold of the Heavens and the city, they advance to 10th level.

History of the City

The tragic history of the City of Lost Names began long before the Cataclysm. The characters might learn parts of this history during their exploration.

Departure of Dragons

During a conflict called the Third Dragon War, many generations before the Cataclysm, the hero Huma Dragonbane defeated Takhisis and prevented her conquest of Krynn. When the Dragon Queen left the world, her wicked dragon servants went with her. To maintain the balance between good and evil, most of Krynn's metallic dragons agreed among themselves to retreat to hidden reaches of the world.

Built on Bones

Centuries passed. In that time, the last kingpriest rose to power in the land of Istar. This religious leader dreamed of an earthly paradise—a pleasure city to reward those he deemed righteous. The kingpriest and his servants created a great flying island. He named this aerial city Onyari, the City Without Sin, claiming it would be a place where he and his worthiest (and wealthiest) subjects might cast off mortal weakness and live like the gods.

But the kingpriest and his servants were loath to reveal how they created their paradise. The city was constructed on an ancient sacred site where, for millennia, dragons of Krynn had gone to die. The kingpriest harnessed the magical resonance of the dragons buried there, lifting the city into the sky.

Fall of Onyari

When the metallic dragons remaining on Krynn learned the kingpriest had desecrated the resting place of their dead, they were furious. Though some dragons urged a more moderate path, the gold dragon Karavarix refused to hold back. He led a contingent of metallic dragons to the soaring city, intent on forcing it to land. The god Paladine tasked the Knight of Solamnia Zanas Sarlamir (see chapter 4) with peaceably ending the conflict between the dragons and the kingpriest. However, Sarlamir's quest was a dismal failure, ultimately resulting in the knight attacking and killing Karavarix. The resulting battle between the dragons and Onyari's people ended in Sarlamir's death and the city's ruin. The flying city fell apart across the Northern Wastes, its bulk ultimately crashing in the hidden depression where it lies now.

Not willing to acknowledge his failure, the kingpriest suppressed all records of Onyari, and those who knew of the failed marvel refused to speak its name. In the wake of the Cataclysm, those few who remember Onyari at all know it only as the City of Lost Names.

Path of Memories

As the characters leave Wind's End (detailed in chapter 5), they follow ancient tunnels through the cliffs surrounding the City of Lost Names. The tunnels eventually breach the ruined city's foundation and wind through substructures of the eastern district. These tunnels and buried ruins are the Path of Memories, and they are far from abandoned.

When you're ready to start this part of the adventure, read the following:

> The passage from Wind's End runs through ancient stone, winding through darkness alive with skittering insects. After traveling for hundreds of feet, you pass a large seam in the wall, after which the rock's texture abruptly changes. Ahead, the tunnels stretch on.

The change in the rock marks the transition from the natural stone of the local cliffs to the foundation stone of the City of Lost Names. A character with the Stonecunning trait determines the passage ahead formed naturally, but the surrounding rock doesn't originate in the Northern Wastes.

The tunnel runs several hundred feet farther, then reaches area M1.

Path Features

The tunnels of the Path of Memories have the following features:

Ceilings. The ceilings of both the natural tunnels and buried chambers are 10 feet high unless otherwise noted.

Floors and Walls. The characters can clearly tell the difference between the natural tunnels and the worked marble of ancient Istarian structures.

Slope. All the chambers tilt slightly down to the southwest, due to the resting angle of the city's eastern district.

Darkness. The tunnels are not illuminated. Area descriptions assume the characters have a light source or other means of seeing in the dark.

Path Locations

The following locations are keyed to map 6.1.

M1: Hall of Betrayal

> As you approach a fork in the tunnel, the walls burst into green flame that rushes toward you. Spectral dragon heads erupt from the flames, and the corridor fills with furious, hissed words.

MAP 6.1: PATH OF MEMORIES

Dragon spirits haunt this area. They are illusory manifestations that can't attack or be damaged. In Draconic, they accuse the characters of trespassing, calling them desecraters and betrayers.

A character can calm the spirits by assuring them in Draconic of the party's innocent intentions. If the spirits aren't immediately calmed, each creature in the hall on the round after the spirits manifest must succeed on a DC 16 Wisdom saving throw or use its action to make a melee attack against a random creature within reach. If no other creatures are within reach, the creature does nothing this turn.

The spirits vanish 1 round after appearing. They reappear after 24 hours if creatures pass through the tunnel again.

M2: FALLEN SHOP

> Mismatched bones lie scattered around this large chamber. Though the cavern itself is natural, its ceiling has caved in—and with it, part of a building has fallen into the cavern. Inside the collapsed structure are strewn wooden heads and decaying hats.

A **stone golem** hides under a pile of shattered wood and feathery hats. Demelin (see area M9) created the golem and ordered it to attack any creature that disturbs the ruined structure. Any characters who near the ruin and have a passive Wisdom (Perception) score of 16 or higher notice the golem.

M3: FLOODED PASSAGE

> This chamber transitions from natural stone to walls and a floor of worked marble blocks. The passage tilts down to the southwest, where a carving depicts a dragon in flight. Half the dragon's body is submerged in dark water, and the hallway beyond it is completely flooded.

The flooded hallway, which leads to area M6, has partially collapsed. Creatures of Medium size or larger that attempt to swim through the tunnel will have to squeeze through the rubble. Creatures that attempt to squeeze through must succeed on a DC 16 Strength (Athletics) check to progress. If a creature fails this check by 5 or more, it gets stuck, is restrained, and risks drowning. A creature can free itself or a creature within reach by using an action to shift the rubble and succeeding on a DC 16 Strength (Athletics) check.

MIKE SCHLEY

M4: Wine Cellar

> A structure from above has collapsed into this cavern. Smashed barrels, shelving, and shards of colored glass clutter the chamber. A staircase that once led up to the east is blocked by rubble.

The ruined remnants of a wine cellar fill this chamber. A character who investigates the glass finds it comes from dozens of spiral-shaped wine bottles.

Treasure. A character who succeeds on a DC 16 Intelligence (Investigation) check locates 2d4 unbroken bottles. The blue wine within is spoiled, and a creature that drinks it is poisoned for 1 hour, but the intact Istarian bottles are worth 200 gp each to a collector.

M5: Bone Gauntlet

Enormous reptilian bones jut from the walls of this natural corridor. A character who examines the bones and succeeds on a DC 14 Intelligence (Arcana) check determines these are dragon bones.

When a character makes it halfway down the corridor, read or paraphrase the following:

> The tunnel fills with the sound of rattling as the bones in the walls begin to move, some lashing toward you. Chattering jaws hiss ancient words as incomplete skeletons burst forth.

Three incomplete dragon skeletons emerge from the walls, missing bones and entire limbs. These creatures each use the **bone naga** stat block but without the Spellcasting trait. They fight until destroyed.

Characters who speak Draconic understand the skeletons as they hiss accusations like "You fly on our backs" and "You soar on our bones." However, the skeletons don't understand or respond to anything the characters say.

Grasping Claws. Until all three skeletons are defeated, grasping skeletal claws reach from the ground, making the entire hallway difficult terrain.

M6: Flooded Tavern

The ceiling of this room is 20 feet high. The tunnel from area M5 opens into this room 10 feet above the surface of the water.

> Murals of dancing people cover the walls, and a small stone stage rises to the west. The lower southwest half of the room is flooded, with the remains of tables, chairs, and a bar barely protruding above the water's surface.

Murky water fills this room to a height of 3 feet, making the flooded area difficult terrain for creatures without a swimming speed.

A **green slaad** lurks on the stage, drawn to the tunnels by the chaotic magic of the city. If it notices a character, the slaad turns and hisses before using its Hurl Flame action against the character. If a character is in the water, the slaad ignites the flammable liquid (see below). The slaad fights until slain.

Firewater. The water flooding this room is covered by an oil slick. Characters with a passive Wisdom (Perception) score of 18 or higher notice the oil slick if they can see the water. If flames touch the water, the entire flooded area ignites, dealing 14 (4d6) fire damage to each creature in the water at that time. For the next minute, as the water continues to burn, a creature that enters the water for the first time on a turn or starts its turn there takes 14 (4d6) fire damage.

Flooded Passage. The passage to area M3 is partially collapsed and underwater—see that area for details.

M7: Ghosts of the Past

> Crumbled chairs lie toppled about the room. On the north wall hangs a long stone slab that features a bas-relief depicting dragons bowing respectfully over a large dragon corpse. A dragon skull is mounted on the east wall.

This room was once a lounge in an Istarian home. Characters with the Stonecunning trait or proficiency with mason's tools can tell that after the bas-relief was carved, a less skilled hand excavated it from its original stone and transported it here. In truth, the skull and relief were once part of a monument dragons erected to honor their kind—until the Istarians repurposed them for decoration.

Once multiple characters enter the room, green flames blaze in the skull's eyes, and beneath it, the incorporeal bones of a phantom brass dragon appear. The skull glares at the party and says the following in Draconic:

> "You built your degenerate throne on our graves and used our ancestors to fuel your ambition. But your gods abandoned you, and we struck you down. You return ... and so do we."

A character speaking Draconic can try to convince the dragon they mean no harm by making a DC 18 Charisma (Persuasion) check. On a successful check, the brass dragon nods and disappears. On a failed check or if a character doesn't speak to the dragon, the dragon's bones manifest around the skull as a complete skeleton. Together, they animate as a **lesser death dragon** (see appendix B) and attack.

M8: Wizard's Workshop

> This worked stone room is full of laboratory equipment: vials of colorful liquids, glass lenses, and live mice in cages. Books crowd shelves and overflow into the floor.

Demelin (currently in area M9) uses this chamber as a laboratory. Many of the books contain rare lore predating the Cataclysm. If a character spends 1 hour investigating the books here, they find references to a flying city called Onyari and learn all the information from the "History of the City" section. Additionally, they find a *spell scroll* of *arcane gate* and a book containing rituals for the *divination* and *phantom steed* spells.

M9: Demelin's Apartment

> This chamber is furnished as a luxurious apartment. Its lamps and stuffed chairs look old but well maintained.
>
> A hooded, crimson-robed figure steps through a door from the east and gives you a calm nod. From behind a bleached skull mask speaks a smooth voice: "Ah, welcome. Let's get to the assessment, then." The figure holds out a blue gem, which then shatters.

The robed figure is Demelin, high wizard of Onyari (detailed in the "Demelin" section). Members of the Mages of High Sorcery recognize her robes as those of the Order of Red Robes. Demelin has been using the *scrying* spell to monitor the characters and has judged they might be useful in ridding the ruins of the Dragon Army invaders.

The gem Demelin breaks is an *elemental gem*. An instant later, an **air elemental** with an outline resembling a dragon appears and attacks the characters. Demelin stands back and watches, taking the Dodge action until the elemental is defeated. Afterward, she holds up a hand and says the following:

> "Enough!" The robed figure pushes back her hood and removes her skull mask, revealing the features of an elven woman. "Forgive the rough welcome, but it was necessary to appraise your abilities. I'd like to speak now."

If attacked, Demelin uses her robes to cast the *dimension door* spell, retreating elsewhere in the Path of Memories. After letting the characters cool off, she approaches them again.

Demelin

Demelin (neutral, elf **archmage**) is hundreds of years old, one of a handful of Silvanesti elves old enough to have lived through the Cataclysm. She commonly wears a bone mask that resembles a skull, and her red robes serve as a *cape of the mountebank*. Prior to the destruction of the world, Demelin was a prominent member of the Mages of High Sorcery, the high wizard of Onyari, and—along with the Kingpriest of Istar—one of the magic-users responsible for raising the city into the heavens. When the city fell, Demelin learned a lesson in hubris. The dispassionate mage has since dwelled in the city's ruins, guarding the city to ensure it never takes to the skies again.

Personality Trait. "Here's your opportunity to learn from my mistakes."

Ideal. "The world's greatest mistakes must not be repeated."

Bond. "Onyari is my tomb. We must both stay buried."

Flaw. "My time is over. It's up to the people of the new world to avoid the sins of the past."

DEMELIN

TALKING WITH DEMELIN

Once the party agrees to hear Demelin out, she explains herself. Read or paraphrase the following:

> "I am Demelin, high wizard of Onyari. You're not the first visitors my fallen city has had in recent days. The world that forgot us has been flocking here, to the paradise of Istar. I fear that although my home has suddenly been remembered, its lessons have not."

Demelin wishes to evict all strangers from the City of Lost Names and ensure the city never flies again. Though the red-robed mage is unwilling to take on an entire army directly, she encourages the characters to drive off the militaristic intruders. She offers nothing but information about the city in return.

Use the following points to guide her conversation with the characters:

- Demelin is aware of the invasion of the city, but she doesn't know who these troops are or what plans they have.
- She shares what she's seen of the invaders' movements. Patrols of soldiers and monsters roam the city, focusing much of their activity on the Threshold of the Heavens at the city's center. Troops also frequently come and go from a sizable mansion that lies along the road to the Threshold. She suspects the latter is a command post.
- If asked, she explains the Threshold of the Heavens is where the city's flying magic was controlled.
- She won't accompany the characters into the city, but she gives them a basic overview of its geography (see the "Exploring the City" section).
- She shares the information from the "History of the City" section.

DEMELIN AND THE LANCE

If the characters ask Demelin about Knight Sarlamir's lance, she says she's seen it before. If the characters don't ask about it, she senses its presence. In either case, she tells them it's Sarlamir's *dragonlance*, which Paladine cursed after the knight slew the gold dragon Karavarix. She doesn't think its reappearance is a coincidence, and she encourages the characters to seek out the Temple of Paladine in the northeast of the city to reveal why the god has returned the lance to Onyari.

DEMELIN'S TEST

If any character seeks to join the Mages of High Sorcery, Demelin notes this before they leave and says the following:

> "Onyari isn't a place for novices. If you're going to continue, you should do so as a true mage. I was a master of the Tower of High Sorcery in Istar. If you're ready to earn your robes, I can administer the Test of High Sorcery."

If a character asks for more information before agreeing, Demelin explains she has administered the Test of High Sorcery countless times, and though these conditions are unusual, she can do so now. See "Mages of High Sorcery" in chapter 1 for details on the Test of High Sorcery.

If a character agrees to take the test, proceed to the following section.

After interested characters' tests are complete (or if no characters want to take the test) and the party is ready to enter the city proper, proceed to the "View of the City" section.

TEST OF HIGH SORCERY

The following section is an optional encounter for characters affiliated with the Mages of High Sorcery (detailed in chapter 1). The Test of High Sorcery is a personalized experience that assesses a potential member of the Mages of High Sorcery and determines the order they're most closely aligned with. If a character succeeds, they become a full member of the Mages of High Sorcery and are inducted into one of the group's orders. If a character fails, they're deemed unfit for the organization—if they survive the test.

PERSONALIZING THE TEST

The Test of High Sorcery is personalized for those who take it. Demelin's version of the test takes place in the participant's mind, casting them into a mental re-creation of Onyari's final moments. In this vision, the character faces a magical challenge and a moral choice that tests their values.

When personalizing the test and determining the challenge the character faces, consider the following questions:

- What is the character's alignment?
- What ambitions and goals do they have?
- What order did Wyhan recommend in chapter 4?
- What order of the Mages of High Sorcery has the character said they want to join?

To conduct the Test of High Sorcery, the mage Demelin conjures a vision of Onyari's fall.

BRUCE BRENNEISE

TEST RESULTS

The answers to the questions in the previous section might be straightforward and make it clear what order a character and their player want to join. If they aren't, use events during the test to determine what order the character is best suited to.

DURING THE TEST

The test should involve a clear choice between good, neutrality, and evil as represented by the orders of the White Robes, the Red Robes, and the Black Robes, respectively. As it unfolds, give the character the opportunity to choose any order they please. If the character makes a surprising choice, consider asking the player how they reconcile their choice with their character's values. If the character feels strongly about a choice that conflicts with their values or alignment, their player might use this as a pivotal moment for character growth.

ENDING THE TEST

As the test reaches its decisive moment, remind the character's player that their character's choices will result in them gaining membership in a particular order of the Mages of High Sorcery. If the player would like to change their choice, allow them to do so.

DYING DURING THE TEST

The Test of High Sorcery can be lethal, but only if that's part of the story the player wants to tell. A personal sacrifice within the vision that cements a character's beliefs should result in the test ending and the character regaining consciousness unharmed. However, if a character forsakes all magic or refuses to engage with the test, let the player know these choices could result in their character being consumed by magic and dying. If the player approves of this, proceed with the test's events. A character who dies during the test can be resurrected normally.

OTHER CHARACTERS AND THE TEST

Characters who aren't taking the test are generally unaware of what's transpiring in the test-taking character's mind. If you want to involve characters not taking the test, the test-taking character might create mental manifestations of their allies, which other players can control during the test. If you allow other characters to participate alongside a test-taking character, keep the focus of the encounters on the magic-using character. This should remain a character-defining moment for the spellcaster.

Running the Test

When a test-taking character is ready to begin the test, Demelin instructs them to move to the center of the room. Read or paraphrase the following text, addressing the test-taking character alone:

> Demelin raises her hands. The light in the room pulses, and spectral green flames trace the walls as she speaks.
>
> "In the old days, there would've been multiple tests. Casting every spell you know, spell battles, the like. But you've proven yourself by coming this far. This leaves just one trial—the most important question."
>
> The flames swirl around you both, rising to obscure everything but Demelin's glowing eyes.
>
> "Time to find out who you are ..."
>
> There's a flash of green light, and suddenly the ground shifts beneath you. Wind lashes your face, and the air fills with screams. Your vision clears, and you find yourself above the clouds, standing at the edge of an exquisite floating city of graceful marble spires. All around you, people flee as dragons dive from the sky, tearing swaths of destruction.

The character taking the test finds themself in this re-creation of Onyari's final moments before the flying city was destroyed. A moment later, a **young silver dragon** strafes the street ahead, freezing structures and people alike.

Consider the following suggestions as you develop this scene in a way that's influenced by the test-taking character's alignment.

Good Character

The dragon returns and attacks the fleeing people, including both a large group of innocents and a small group of people beloved by the character. There's likely time to save only one group. The character might prove themself suited for white robes by trying to save everyone, by sacrificing themself, or by desperately trying to negotiate with the dragon. If they prioritize what they want over the good of others, they might earn red robes.

Evil Character

The dragon returns, and the character's rival or a non-spellcasting ally steps between those trying to escape and the oncoming dragon. Unaware of the character, this rival uses the incredible magic of a glowing staff to hold off the dragon. If the character attacks their foe, tries to steal the staff, or otherwise prioritizes their own ambitions, they prove themself suited for the black robes. If they put the city and innocents first, they might earn red robes.

Neutral Character

Scholars struggle to evacuate a collection of ancient tomes (or something else the character highly values) from a crumbling structure. The dragon then returns, threatening both the scholars and a larger group of innocents. There's likely only time to save one group. If the character tries to save themselves or the lore-protecting librarians, they're probably suited for the red robes. If they protect the larger group of innocents, the character might be suited for the white robes. If the character tries to abscond with the books, they might be suited for the black robes.

Adjusting the Test

The test shouldn't be strictly a combat encounter. The point is to gauge a character's values and disposition. Consider the following suggestions to make the test more dramatic:

Altered Magic. Spellcasting or other class features could function differently during the test. For example, perhaps each time the character casts a spell using a spell slot, they take 6 (1d12) necrotic damage or gain 1 level of exhaustion that lingers until the test ends.

Dream Logic. Like a dream, the test doesn't need to make sense or be consistent from moment to moment. It's okay for the character's surroundings to shift dramatically or for unexpected individuals to show up. Don't let these changes make the character feel like their choices don't matter. Rather, change situations to heighten the drama—like by turning innocents into allies or childhood friends.

Timing. The test should last as long as feels dramatic and end after a character-defining moral choice. If it seems like things are going too fast, raise the stakes and make things worse to see if the character sticks with their choices.

Concluding the Test

When the test is complete, there's another flash of light, and the test-taking character finds themself back with Demelin. If the character forsook magic or refused to engage with the test, they fall dead. If they completed the test, their clothing transforms into the robes of their new order in the Mages of High Sorcery. Read or paraphrase the following:

> Demelin assesses your new robes. Nodding, she says, "Welcome to the order, fellow Mage of High Sorcery."

Mages of High Sorcery recognize the character's robes as legitimately gained and view the character as a member of their organization.

Demelin wishes the character the best and urges them to go explore the City of Lost Names.

VIEW OF THE CITY

A door in Demelin's apartment opens to a path leading up to the street above at the location marked "Path of Memories" on map 6.2. As the characters emerge outdoors, read or paraphrase the following:

> A glittering city of broken domes and jagged towers stretches before you. The nearby buildings and streets slope down into the basin of a vast, ruin-filled crater. Your vantage provides a view of the entire city, some of its broken districts scarred by fire and flooding. Here and there, crumbled structures and massive rocks bob gently in defiance of gravity. At the city's center, a delicate tower of sharp marble and graceful buttresses rises into the sky. It's made all the taller by its rocky foundation, which floats off the ground.

Give the players a few moments to ask questions about the city before continuing with the following section.

SHADOW OF SOTH

Lord Soth has brought the Cataclysmic flame from beneath Castle Kalaman to the ruins. In chapter 7, characters encounter the fruit of Soth's efforts to re-animate dead dragons. Foreshadow that threat after characters decide where they're headed by reading the following description:

> To the southwest, the crack of shearing stone sounds from a distant temple whose grounds teem with troops. On the temple's roof, a figure holds aloft a scepter crackling with familiar violet flame. A moment later, a skeletal dragon scales the temple and unleashes a screech that echoes across the city. It pauses before the figure, who climbs onto the undead terror's back. Together, they rise into the air and circle the city before flying south and out of sight.

The character with the highest passive Wisdom (Perception) score recognizes the Undead dragon's rider from Kalaman's catacombs—this is the knight Lord Soth, whose image they saw there.

The temple the characters see is detailed in the "Bastion of Takhisis" section.

Shortly afterward, if the characters have a fargab (see appendix A) with them, they get a call from Tatina Rookledust.

> "Are you okay?!" Rookledust asks, then she rapidly continues. "We just saw something come over the cliffs—a gods-cursed dragon skeleton! We're retreating, and the Dragon Armies are following. We'll keep them drawn out as long as we can. See if you can get at whoever's in charge in there!"

Rookledust encourages the characters to find the Dragon Army's leaders within the city rather than pursing Soth. The gnome is confident that Kalaman's forces can retreat safely, telling the characters she has a few tricks in store for their pursuers. Make it clear the characters don't need to rush their exploration of the city to return to their allies.

EXPLORING THE CITY

The City of Lost Names lies in a ruin-filled crater. The northwestern district punctured a subterranean aquifer in its crash, flooding its streets, while fire raged through homes in the southwestern district. The western pleasure gardens have become an untamed jungle where descendants of the city's monstrous menageries hunt amid vine-choked streets. Meanwhile, the eastern blocks lie propped against the crater rim, the whole district tilted at an angle.

MAKING A PLAN

Thanks to the party's initial vantage point on the rim of the crater and the information they learned from Demelin, the characters easily get a general sense of the city's layout. Provide them with a sense of the city's layout, informed by map 6.2. They can spot the Temple of Paladine across the crater, a glistening dome in the flooded northwestern district, along with the three points of interest listed in the "Dragon Army Activity" section.

DRAGON ARMY ACTIVITY

The characters see Dragon Army patrols moving through the city. Those who watch the patrols for ten minutes or more note activity at three locations:

Central Spire. A tower rises in the center of the city, surrounded by several dragonnels and smaller flying figures. The tower's foundation floats dozens of feet off the ground. (This tower is detailed in the "Threshold of the Heavens" section.)

Occupied Mansion. Small patrols come and go from a ruined mansion a third of the way across the city. (This building is detailed in the "Occupied Mansion" section.)

Sinister Temple. A foreboding temple stands at the south end of the city, its grounds teeming with soldiers. (This temple to the evil gods is detailed in the "Bastion of Takhisis" section. Discourage the characters from approaching it at this point.)

PRIORITIES

The characters can choose their priorities in the city, but they likely fall along the following lines:

Find an Outpost and learn what the Dragon Army is planning (see "Occupied Mansion").

Learn about the Dragonlance and how its curse might be undone (see "Temple of Paladine").

Investigate the Spire at the city's center and find the Dragon Army's leaders (see "Threshold of the Heavens").

Use the following sections to further detail the ruins as much as you please. This chapter concludes at the Threshold of the Heavens, so make sure the characters have investigated the city as much as they want before heading there.

CITY SIGHTS

As the characters explore the City of Lost Names, use the City Sights table to describe the ruins.

CITY SIGHTS

d6	Sight
1	A Humanoid skeleton lies under a fallen aqueduct. It holds a dagger, and the words "we deserve this" are scratched into a nearby cobblestone.
2	At the end of a boulevard stand two enormous marble feet—the rest of the statue is missing.
3	The partial remains of an adult bronze dragon lie in a heap between two structures.
4	A circular tower pierces a dome like a spear.
5	Vines climb a mural of the kingpriest—a stern man crowned with blazing light.
6	One side of a long fault line has risen 10 feet, shearing buildings in half.

CITY ENCOUNTERS

The City of Lost Names is full of Dragon Army troops and other threats. As the characters travel between locations, or whenever you please, roll on the Random City Encounters table.

RANDOM CITY ENCOUNTERS

d8	Encounter
1	Seven **ghasts** gnaw on dead Dragon Army soldiers.
2	Bridge Checkpoint (see below)
3	Three **ghosts** of bickering Istarians haunt the ruins of their shop.
4	Dragon Army Engineers (see below)
5	A curious **death slaad** wants to eat one of each type of draconian. If the characters help it hunt all five, it rewards them with a *ring of feather falling*.
6	Monster Hunters (see below)
7	Two **cyclopes**—a mother and her adult son—live in a library, burning its books for warmth.
8	Patrol (see below)

BRIDGE CHECKPOINT

Three **sivak draconians** (see appendix B) stand guard on a 25-foot-wide bridge spanning a 60-foot drop into a rocky fissure. They are quick to investigate any nearby noise or strange sights.

DRAGON ARMY ENGINEERS

One **Dragon Army officer** and three **sivak draconians** (see appendix B for both stat blocks) oversee ten **commoner** engineers repairing 30-foot-deep cracks in the city's streets. If the Dragon Army members spot the characters or the characters attack them, the engineers stay out of combat. The engineers can tell the characters they're making sure the city's foundations are solid, though they don't know why.

MONSTER HUNTERS

A **sivak draconian** and four **kapak draconians** (see appendix B for both stat blocks) have orders to seek out dangerous monsters lurking in the ruins. They've just found an **Istarian drone** (see appendix B) and are preparing to attack.

PATROL

Five **kapak draconians** (see appendix B) patrol the city. They follow a predictable route and, after an hour of walking, check in at their headquarters (see the "Occupied Manor" section).

INTERROGATIONS

A character who interrogates a low-ranking member of the Red Dragon Army and succeeds on a DC 14 Charisma (Intimidation or Persuasion) check learns one piece of information from the Dragon Army Interrogations table. On a failed check, the captive yells "As the Dragon Queen wills!" until silenced.

DRAGON ARMY INTERROGATIONS

d4	Information
1	Engineers work to shore up foundations and make sure the various districts are on solid stone.
2	The captive takes their orders from commanders at an occupied mansion near the city center.
3	The Temple of Paladine in the northwestern district is overgrown with dangerous vegetation. Patrols sent there haven't returned.
4	A black-robed wizard named Lohezet and the cleric of Takhisis named Belephaion lead the forces in the city. They spend their time in the Threshold of the Heavens, but no one can enter without a passphrase (which the captive doesn't know).

CITY OF LOST NAMES

Threshold of the Heavens

Temple of Paladine

Threshold of the Heavens

Path of Memories

Occupied Mansion

Bastion of Takhisis

N

1200 Feet

FRANCESCA BAERALD

Map 6.2: City of Lost Names

Bastion of Takhisis

At the south end of the ruins stands a temple once called the Bastion of Takhisis. Here, the people of Onyari established the holy sites of all the evil gods, unwilling to spread them across the city but also not wishing to disrespect the deities.

The Bastion of Takhisis has partially crumbled, leaving it a hollow frame within bare, intimidating walls. Lord Soth has claimed the temple as his own, tasking his Undead followers with creating a great brazier there to hold the Cataclysmic fire he stole from beneath Castle Kalaman. He plans to use this as a forge with which to animate the dragon remains buried beneath the city, turning them into death dragons (see appendix B). Using the remains of the dragon Karavarix, he's already created the first of these terrors.

Skeletal knights and other Dragon Army forces guard the temple. Use these forces and other Undead to deter the characters from visiting the temple at this time; they will explore it in chapter 7.

Occupied Mansion

The Red Dragon Army uses a ruined mansion as a field command post. Characters might determine this mansion is noteworthy by talking to Demelin or by observing Dragon Army soldiers.

Characters who wear Dragon Army armor or cloaks gain advantage on Charisma (Deception) checks made to pass as Dragon Army soldiers while in the mansion.

Occupied Mansion Features

The interior of the occupied mansion has the following features:

Ceilings. The ceilings are 10 feet high.
Doors. The doors to each room are unlocked, except for the door in the kitchen (area O6) leading to the pantry (area O7).
Lighting. Torches, candles, and fireplaces shed bright light throughout the mansion's interior.
Rubble. Portions of the mansion have collapsed. The rubble that remains is impassible.

Occupied Mansion Locations

The following locations are keyed to map 6.3.

O1: Exterior

> At the end of a row of ruins stands a partially intact manor. Most of the manor's east side has collapsed, but the rest of the house has been cleared and made serviceable. In the southeast corner, an attached carriage house stands next to the front entrance.

This command post buzzes with activity during the day, with human and draconian patrols coming and going. At night, only the draconian patrols continue.

Guards. Four **kapak draconians** (see appendix B) stand guard outside the mansion: one at the carriage house's east door, two at the front door, and one at the back patio door. If attacked, the draconians shout to alert the other draconians outside the house and in the area connected to the door they guard (area O3 or O4, whichever's closest).

Patrol. Roughly once per hour, a group of eight **Dragon Army soldiers** (see appendix B) arrives outside the mansion, checks in with the guards there, then departs. If the kapak guards aren't at their posts, the patrol ventures into the mansion to investigate.

O2: Foyer

> This foyer has an alcove studded with ornate coat hooks under a row of shelves. Stained rain cloaks currently overload the hooks, and several spears lean against the wall. Doors lead to the north and south.

When worn with the hood up, the cloaks here grant advantage on Charisma (Deception) checks made to pass as a Dragon Army soldier while in the mansion. There are also six spears here.

O3: Carriage House

Two sets of metal sliding doors lead into the carriage house. They make considerable noise when opened, alerting the creatures inside. A character who listens at these doors and succeeds on a DC 14 Wisdom (Perception) check hears snarling within. When the characters open a door, read or paraphrase the following:

> This carriage house features horse stalls to the east and an open space to the west. Two broad doorways lead to the street. A metal-reinforced prison cart sits in the northwest corner, occasionally shaking as something growls inside.

This carriage house serves as the base's prison.

Draconians. Three **kapak draconians** (see appendix B) stand guard here. One has the key to the prison cart.

Prison Cart. A wooden cart with an iron cage built into it holds a **wasteland dragonnel** (see appendix B) that had been lairing near the mansion. The troops captured the dragonnel, hoping to train it to serve as a mount. A character can free the caged dragonnel by using the key held by the room's guards or by succeeding on a DC 18 Dexterity check

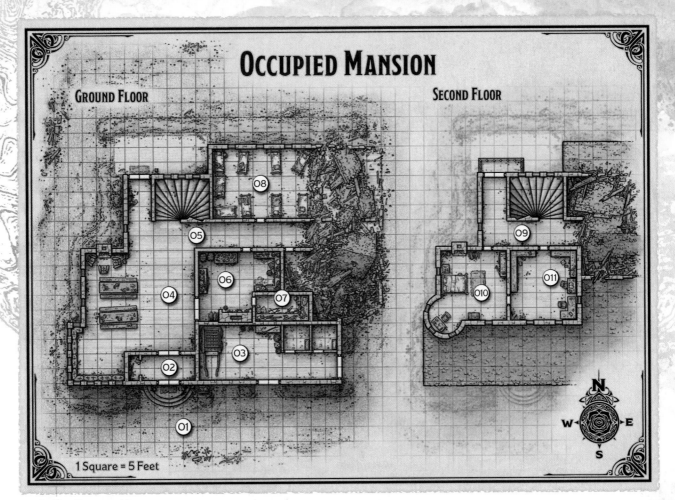

OCCUPIED MANSION

GROUND FLOOR

SECOND FLOOR

1 Square = 5 Feet

N W E S

MAP 6.3: OCCUPIED MANSION

using thieves' tools. If freed, the dragonnel is wary of the characters, avoiding them as it tries to escape to the street so it can fly away. It attacks any Dragon Army troops it encounters along the way.

O4: SALON

> A fire burns in the marble fireplace of this large salon. The room's tall windows have been boarded over, and its rotted furnishings have been shoved aside to make room for mismatched and gouged dining tables. On the north side of the room, a curving stairwell rises between the back door and a hallway. On the south side, one door leads to the south and another to the east.

The Dragon Army has converted this room into a mess hall. At any time, two **bozak draconians**, one **kapak draconian**, and three **Dragon Army soldiers** (see appendix B for these stat blocks) take meals here. They glance up at anyone who enters the room, but they pay no attention to characters dressed as Dragon Army troops.

If a fight breaks out here, the soldiers resting in area O8 respond after 2 rounds.

Stairwell. The stairs lead up to area O9.

O5: LOWER HALLWAY

This hall leads to areas O6 and O8, then ends in a heap of rubble where the east wing of the house collapsed long ago. The door at the east end of the hall opens into a collapsed room also filled with rubble.

O6: KITCHEN

> Next to a small pantry door, a fire burns in the kitchen's hearth. Above it, several large roasts hang from spits. Tables stand covered in flour and other ingredients. Additional doors lead to the west and north.

The command post's cook, Yurl, is a skeletally thin **hobgoblin captain**. His apron is covered with grisly stains, which grow by the minute as he hacks at a jackal carcass with an oversized cleaver. If Yurl detects intruders, he attacks with his cleaver (which uses the statistics for his Greatsword attack).

Yurl's apron pocket holds the key to area O7, along with a handful of animal teeth he's been collecting.

Pantry Door. The door to area O7 is locked. A character can unlock the door by using Yurl's key or succeeding on a DC 16 Dexterity check using thieves' tools.

O7: Pantry

This pantry is crammed with supplies, ranging from hardtack and clothing to weapons and armor. Although most of the crates are made of rough wood, a metal one is etched with designs of blue dragons.

Crates and weapon racks fill this room.

Trapped Chest. The metal chest, which belongs to the Dragon Army commander Belephaion, bears a magical trap that can be detected by a character who casts *detect magic* or who searches the chest and succeeds on a DC 16 Intelligence (Arcana or Perception) check. The trap can be disabled by the *dispel magic* spell. A character who tries to open the chest while the trap is active must make a DC 18 Dexterity saving throw, taking 27 (5d10) lightning damage on a failed save, or half as much damage on a successful one. The chest can be unlocked by a character who spends 1 minute and succeeds on a DC 20 Dexterity check using thieves' tools.

Treasure. The pantry holds enough food and water for fifty people to survive on for a month, along with twenty javelins, ten longswords, and ten suits of Dragon Army scale mail. Belephaion's trapped chest contains three *javelins of lightning* and a pouch full of sapphires worth 1,600 gp.

Captain Hask

O8: Drawing Room

Rows of identical cots and weathered packs crowd the floor of this room. Its walls are covered in ornate mosaics that have crumbled with age.

This parlor serves as a barracks for Dragon Army troops not on patrol. Eight **Dragon Army soldiers** (see appendix B) are resting here. If they haven't been alerted by noise in other rooms, they are surprised if the characters attack.

O9: Upper Hallway

The mansion's staircase connects this small hallway to area O4 on the ground floor. To the east, the hall ends in a collapsed wall. To the northwest, a door leads to a small balcony overlooking the patio.

O10: Master Bedroom

This bedroom is well preserved, with a four-poster bed, a desk, and a small chest. A round turret to the southeast—with glass intact in its windows—provides a panoramic view of the neighborhood's wreckage. A door leads to a room to the east, and another door opens to the hallway to the north.

Captain Hask, an **aurak draconian** (see appendix B), is writing reports at the desk. Hask knows all the soldiers in his unit, and the characters can convince Hask they're Dragon Army soldiers only with a successful DC 22 Charisma (Deception) check. If Hask believes he's being tricked, he stands and attacks while calling for the soldiers in area O11, who arrive after 1 round. Hask is a devout servant of the Dragon Queen and fights to the death.

Command Intelligence. The desk is covered in reports to Hask's superior, referred to as "Glorious Belephaion." A character who spends a minute reading the documents learns the following:

- Two Dragon Army leaders, Belephaion and Lohezet, work at the Threshold of the Heavens.
- The passphrase to gain entrance to the Threshold of the Heavens is "By her will: the world."
- Dragon Army engineers have completed the majority of their work, shoring up the foundations of the city's most intact districts.

Treasure. A key Hask carries opens the locked chest near the desk. The chest can also be unlocked by a character using thieves' tools who spends 1 minute and succeeds on a DC 18 Dexterity check. The chest contains a *pearl of power* and a 200-pound sack, labeled "Payroll" in Draconic, that holds 10,000 sp.

DAVID SLADEK

O11: Library

Most of this library's books have fallen to rot, but two desks beneath tall windows stand covered in papers and candles. One door leads to a room to the west, and another opens to the hallway to the north.

Three **Dragon Army officers** (see appendix B) work here as clerks, coordinating reports. If threatened, they shout to alert Captain Hask, who arrives from area O10 after 1 round. These officers are loyal to Captain Hask, and he counts as a Dragon for the purpose of their Draconic Devotion trait. Two of the three officers fight to the death. The last remaining officer surrenders when their allies are defeated.

Collecting Intelligence. The clerks know considerable information about the Dragon Army's plans. If a clerk is captured alive, a character can convince them to share the following information by succeeding on a DC 14 Charisma (Intimidation or Persuasion) check:

- The commander of the Red Dragon Army, Dragon Highmaster Kansaldi Fire-Eyes, isn't in the City of Lost Names. She remained with the bulk of the army near Kalaman.
- The commanders Belephaion and Lohezet lead this contingent of the Red Dragon Army. They don't get along.
- Belephaion is a terrifying fanatic who claims to speak for the Dragon Queen herself. Even Kansaldi listens to his advice.
- Lohezet is a scheming, black-robed Mage of High Sorcery. He's obsessed with ancient magic and venomous beasts, and his research led the Dragon Army to the City of Lost Names.
- Belephaion and Lohezet have worked at the tower called the Threshold of the Heavens for days, preparing to reactivate the city's ancient flying magic.
- The clerk knows nothing of Lord Soth and prefers it that way. The death knight supposedly receives orders directly from the Dragon Queen.

A character can also gather this information by spending an hour sifting through the reports in the room—though they might risk discovery by the patrol described in area O1.

RESTAFFING THE MANSION

Soon after the characters leave the mansion, a Dragon Army patrol discovers the intrusion (if they didn't already do so during the party's visit). The mansion is fully restaffed 24 hours after the characters leave, with all Dragon Army inhabitants of the mansion replaced with the same number and types of creatures.

TEMPLE OF PALADINE

The Temple of Paladine is among the most intact holy places to survive Onyari's fall. The characters are likely to come here at Demelin's behest, seeking answers regarding Sarlamir's broken *dragonlance*.

The temple lies in the city's flooded northwestern district. Buildings here rise like islands from streets clogged with water and pondweed. Although the streets around the temple are flooded, the structure sits atop a hill, keeping it out of the deepest water.

TEMPLE OF PALADINE FEATURES

The area in and around the Temple of Paladine has the following features:

Ceilings. Unless otherwise noted, the temple's ceilings are 10 feet high.
Flooded. Most of the Temple of Paladine and its grounds are flooded. Areas P3–P6 are flooded by 3 feet of water and are difficult terrain for creatures without a swimming speed.
Lighting. The temple and its grounds are lit by natural light alone. During the day, bright light fills the exterior areas and dim light fills the interior rooms. At night, all areas are in darkness. Area descriptions assume the characters have a light source or some other means of seeing in the dark.

TEMPLE OF PALADINE LOCATIONS

The following locations are keyed to map 6.4.

P1: CAUSEWAY

As characters near the temple's grounds, read or paraphrase the following:

Ahead, the water deepens into a broad pond broken by the rooflines of submerged buildings. An embankment rising just above the water is covered in a cluster of violet-leafed trees. The half-drowned ruins of a temple are visible beyond; a platinum triangle gleams on its leaning belfry.

The causeway rises over water that's 20 feet deep. From it, characters can see the temple grounds and the Temple of Paladine itself. A cleric of Paladine or a character who succeeds on a DC 12 Intelligence (Religion) check recognizes the platinum triangle as the symbol of the god Paladine.

Bodies. Characters with a passive Wisdom (Perception) score of 18 or higher notice hints of figures wearing red-and-black clothing among the tree branches ahead in area P2. These are Dragon Army soldiers killed by Duskwalker—but from this distance, characters can tell only that the soldiers are motionless, not that they're dead.

DUSKWALKER

P2: WOODED BERM

> The trees here stand shoulder to shoulder, forming a violet canopy as they climb a ring-shaped rise around the temple. Sloping stone stairs climb the rise, and on the other side, another set of stairs descends into the shallow water.

The neutral **treant** Duskwalker stands motionless amid trees whose branches bear dead Dragon Army soldiers. Before Onyari's destruction, Duskwalker served as its master gardener. The city's devastation left them deeply bitter, and the Dragon Army's invasion has newly angered the ancient creature.

Unless a character openly displays a symbol of a god of nature—like Chislev, Habbakuk, or Zeboim—or is otherwise clearly a servant of nature, Duskwalker uses their Animate Trees action to ambush the characters, then follows the trees into battle. During combat, Duskwalker slowly bellows, "Each defiler you send to my gardens meets the same end. Begone!" A character being attacked by a tree notices a dead Dragon Army soldier amid its branches.

Talking with Duskwalker. A character can convince the treant to negotiate by succeeding on a DC 20 Charisma (Persuasion) check as an action or by revealing a symbol of a god of nature. If

convinced to talk, Duskwalker reveals the following information:

- Duskwalker is the guardian of Onyari's gardens. The treant endured both the city's fall and the Cataclysm here.
- Recently, invaders have been trying to fell Duskwalker's trees for wood.
- The treant has killed—and will continue to kill—these "invasive species" that disturb Onyari's plants.
- Duskwalker will let the characters pass so long as they promise not to disturb the trees.

The treant refuses to aid the characters against the Dragon Army, wanting only to be left alone. If asked, Duskwalker removes the corpses of Dragon Army soldiers from nearby trees, allowing the characters to loot the bodies.

Treasure. Six Dragon Army corpses are lodged 20 feet up in the branches of nearby trees. Each body has a longsword, a suit of scale mail, and 10 gp.

P3: LAKE

> Inside the ring of trees, the ground lowers, creating a flooded bowl. Here, a roughly triangular temple rises from the water, its north side largely crumbled and its belfry leaning. The temple's doors, half covered with water, have begun succumbing to rot, but their platinum inlays of dragons still shine.

A hostile **marid** named Jamir has taken up residence in this area. Once bound by the kingpriest's wizards to power the city's plumbing, Jamir has taken great delight in Onyari's destruction and seeks to punish any who would reclaim the city. If alerted to the party's presence by noise from area P2, he conjures a **water elemental** and hides underwater, prepared to ambush the characters. Characters with a passive Wisdom (Perception) score of 16 or higher aren't surprised when Jamir attacks. If reduced to 20 hit points or fewer, he uses *plane shift* to escape at the first opportunity.

Doors. The doors to the temple are partially submerged and require a successful DC 13 Strength check to open.

P4: NAVE

> Murky water covers a triangular chamber. To the east, this large hall narrows to a raised area with an altar. The north side of the building is a tangle of fallen stone and beams. The south side holds two doors.

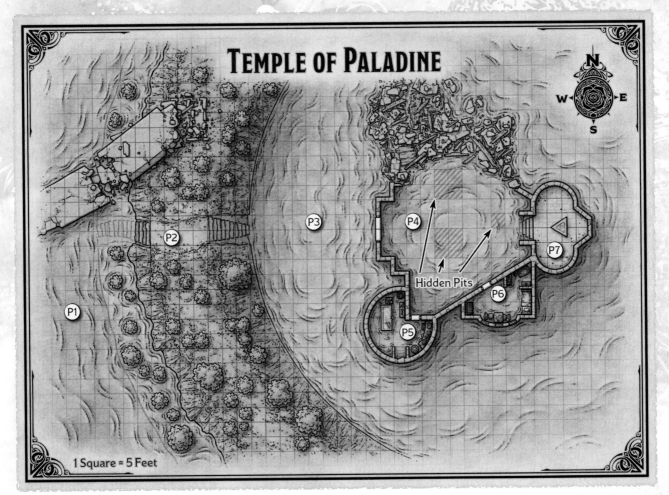

TEMPLE OF PALADINE

N
W • E
S

1 Square = 5 Feet

P1
P2
P3
P4
P5
P6
P7

Hidden Pits

MAP 6.4: TEMPLE OF PALADINE

The ceiling here is 20 feet high, and tall windows admit any light from outside.

Hidden Pits. The nave's floor has buckled, creating pits leading to the shattered crypts below. Only creatures that come within 5 feet of a pit and have a passive Wisdom (Perception) of 16 or higher notice a pit. A creature that steps into a pit sinks 20 feet to the bottom of the flooded hole. The water prevents them from taking damage. For creatures without a swimming speed, each foot of movement costs 2 extra feet as they swim out of the pit.

Disturbed Dead. If a creature falls into one of the pits, it disturbs the dead buried in the vault below. One round later, four slimy **mummies** emerge from the three pits. These lawful neutral Undead seek to defend the temple. They won't converse with characters, but they return to their soggy tombs if a character brandishes a symbol of Paladine toward them.

P5: PREPARATION CHAMBER

> A large stone table rises from the dirty water in this round, windowless chamber. Along the walls, shelves hold assorted bottles and vials, most of which have cracked and stained the walls with their drippings.

Here, the dead were prepared for burial in the crypts below the temple. These crypts have crumbled, and the stairs leading to them are filled with rubble and brackish water.

Treasure. A character who searches the shelves and succeeds on a DC 15 Intelligence (Investigation) check finds three intact *spell scrolls* of *gentle repose*.

P6: RECTORY

> This small living area is flooded like the rest of the temple, with moldering vestments hanging in a wardrobe and a bed blanketed in fungus.

This apartment once housed the temple's resident priest. A character who looks under the bed finds a rusty chest. Its rusted lock can't be picked, but a creature can break open the lock with a successful DC 17 Strength check. The chest is a Small object with AC 19, 15 hit points, and immunity to poison and psychic damage.

Treasure. The chest holds 400 gp, a platinum necklace featuring Paladine's symbol worth 150 gp, two *potions of healing* (superior), and a *periapt of proof against poison*.

MIKE SCHLEY

P7: Chancel

> Stone steps rise from the water to a dry platform bearing a triangular stone altar. Sculpted reliefs near the altar depict platinum dragons in majestic poses.

The altar here bears the symbol of Paladine, while the sculptures depict him in his draconic form. A cleric of Paladine or a character who succeeds on a DC 12 Intelligence (Religion) check recognizes the symbol.

Restoring the Lance. As each character enters this area, they gain the distinct impression the dragon sculptures are watching them. Good-aligned characters feel suffused with a warm sense of righteousness. If a character approaches the altar, a column of dim light rises from it.

If a character places Sarlamir's lance on the altar in this light, the lance shines with a silvery glow. The rust covering the lance bubbles and leaks a dark liquid that flows away from the altar and disappears. At the same time, the spear lengthens, growing into a whole, newly forged, pike-length *dragonlance* (see appendix A).

Before a character takes the reforged lance, read the following text:

> From nowhere and everywhere comes a powerful voice that inspires confidence and awe.
> "The last to wield this weapon was unworthy. His failure was a step along the path to the world's destruction. But this new age needs a new hope. Use this weapon to defend the destiny mortals have chosen. Banish the shadow of the Dragon Queen with the light of this most sacred weapon. With the blessing of the gods, ye champions, reclaim the *dragonlance*."

Any character with the Divinely Favored feat (from chapter 1) knows this is the voice of the god Paladine.

A moment later, a wave of light sweeps through the temple, healing each creature present as if by the *heal* spell. If any characters died during this chapter, they immediately come back to life as if by the *true resurrection* spell, their bodies appearing in the chancel if they're not already present. The light then vanishes.

Character Advancement

Once the *dragonlance* is reforged at the Temple of Paladine and the party explores the command post in the "Occupied Mansion" section, characters advance to 9th level.

Threshold of the Heavens

At the center of the ruins floats the section of the city bearing the Threshold of the Heavens, the tower that controlled the city's magical flight. The characters might decide to explore the tower because of their conversation with Demelin or their discoveries at the occupied mansion.

Before they infiltrate the tower, make sure the characters are 9th level and have done everything else they want to in the city. Events in the tower will prevent further exploration. If you need to deter the characters, a group of **sivak draconians** or **Dragon Army dragonnels** (see appendix B for both stat blocks) is conducting drills here when they arrive.

Reaching the Threshold

Though the rest of Onyari lost its capacity for flight, the island supporting the Threshold of the Heavens still bobs in the air. This island is 30 feet off the ground, requiring Dragon Army troops to fly to reach the tower. Characters might find a way to do the same. Alternatively, a character can ascend by leaping between a series of floating rocks and succeeding on three DC 14 Strength (Athletics) checks. A character ascends 10 feet with each successful check. If they fail a check, they make no progress. If they fail a check by 5 or more, they fall to the ground and must start the process over.

Threshold Features

The areas inside the Threshold of the Heavens have the following features:

Ceilings. The ceilings throughout are 30 feet high.
Doors. The doors are all unlocked. Though made of heavy stone, they open quietly.
Lighting. Magical lighting embedded in the ceilings fills the Threshold's rooms with bright light.

Threshold Locations

The following locations are keyed to map 6.5.

T1: Plaza

Once characters reach the floating island of the Threshold of the Heavens, read the following:

> Atop the floating island, a slender, gray obelisk rises nearly two hundred feet above the surrounding plaza. Four graceful flying buttresses curve up the tower's entire height, and crystalline windows punctuate its summit. At the tower's base stands a single stone door. Four hulking draconians guard the door, while armored dragonnels and their riders circle above.

An open plaza stretches for 100 feet on each side of the tower, ending at the island's edge.

Tower Patrol. Three **Dragon Army officers** mounted on **Dragon Army dragonnels** (see appendix B for both stat blocks) patrol near the tower. They ignore creatures wearing Dragon Army armor but confront anyone else on the floating island. If the tower's guards are attacked, this patrol arrives to aid their allies in 2 rounds.

Tower Guards. Four **sivak draconians** (see appendix B) guard the tower's entrance. They halt anyone who tries to enter, whether wearing Dragon Army armor or not, and demand they state the passphrase. If a character responds with the passphrase they learned in the "Occupied Manor" section ("By her will: the world") the draconians let the characters pass. If they don't speak the passphrase, a character must succeed on a DC 18 Charisma (Persuasion) check to fool the sivaks; otherwise, the sivaks attack. Characters wearing Dragon Army armor or similar garb have advantage on Charisma checks made to influence the tower's guards. The draconians ignore sounds inside the tower.

T2: Entry

> Murals of idyllic life in the flying city adorn this grand foyer's gray stone walls. One on the west wall depicts a handsome, long-haired man in flowing robes, radiating golden light. Fountains burble to the north and south. The east wall holds a single door to the north and a double door to the south.

The kingpriest insisted the Threshold was a holy place, but little besides the holy water fonts here remains of its religious trappings.

Guardians. A **bone devil** named Guelfost and his handler, a **bozak draconian** (see appendix B) named Orm, serve Lohezet and have been assigned to guard this level of the tower. Orm demands visitors state their business. A character must succeed on a DC 12 Charisma (Deception) check to convince Orm the characters have business in the tower.

Guelfost has orders to obey his handler, but they don't compel him to fight after Orm dies. If Orm is defeated, Guelfost ceases attacking. If not attacked further, he shares his name and the following facts:

- He is magically compelled to serve a black-robed wizard named Lohezet.
- He's wary of Lohezet's co-commander, Belephaion, who holds some secret power.
- If asked about dangers above, the devil notes the next floor has a chamber filled with dangerous energy. The characters can pass safely by speaking the Istarian word "cetteth."

After his draconian handler is defeated, Guelfost doesn't leave the room or act against the characters unless Lohezet orders him to.

Fonts. The two fonts are half-full of magically preserved holy water. Each font holds the equivalent of four flasks of holy water.

T3: TOWER MONITORING

> Two long consoles jut from the walls of this room, covered in levers, colored stones, and dull glass hemispheres. Etched into the floor between the consoles is an elaborate symbol radiating orange light.

This room monitors the tower's magic and its connection to the city beyond.

Consoles. A character who succeeds on a DC 14 Intelligence (Arcana) check discovers the consoles monitor a powerful source of magic elsewhere in the tower. They also determine that even though the magic is currently active, the controls indicate something is malfunctioning. If the character wishes, they can use the console to diminish the power of this magic, but they can't deactivate it completely.

Diminished Magic. If a character uses the console to throttle the tower's magic, the symbol in the center of the room turns red, and the Threshold's entire floating island plummets 10 feet. After this, a failsafe stops the island from falling, returns the rune to its original orange color, and disables the console. The experience is startling, but it doesn't harm the tower or creatures on the island.

If the tower drops in this manner, Lohezet commands the three **flameskulls** in area T7 to find the source of the problem. One minute later, the flameskulls find the characters (regardless of their location in the tower) and attack.

Symbol. The symbol on the floor sheds dim orange light out to 5 feet. A character who sees the symbol and succeeds on a DC 16 Wisdom (Perception) check realizes it looks like an aerial view of the tower and its exterior buttresses.

T4: ENERGY FIELD

> Nine blue crystalline columns crackle and hiss as lightning arcs unpredictably between them. A double door leads to another room to the north, and a smaller door leads to the stairs down.

This chamber functions as a defense for the tower and part of the tower's broader magical systems.

Lightning. When a creature enters this area for the first time on a turn or starts its turn there, it must succeed on a DC 16 Dexterity saving throw

or take 22 (4d10) lightning damage from lightning arcing between the columns. If a character says "cetteth" while on this level of the tower, they become immune to the lightning generated by this room for 24 hours.

Crystal Columns. The columns in this room are Large objects with AC 16, 18 hit points, and immunity to poison and psychic damage. If three or more of the room's nine columns are destroyed, lightning stops arcing between the columns, ending the effect described above. The first time a column in the room takes damage, a 10-foot-square panel opens in the floor near the door leading to area T5, releasing a hostile **Istarian drone** (see appendix B).

T5: DRONE MONITORING

> Stone columns inset with glowing crystal bands run along the north side of this room. Between the columns stand two still, insect-like constructs. Sporadicly, lightning arcs between a column and one of the constructs. To the southeast, an array of runes pulses on a console. In the middle of the south wall stands a small door and, to the west of it, a larger double door.

In this room, workers would charge and repair the tower's construct defenders. The two **Istarian drones** (see appendix B) are intact but powered down. They activate and attack in the room if a drone, a column, or the console is damaged.

Console. A character adjacent to the console who succeeds on a DC 20 Intelligence (Arcana) check can use an action to direct one of the Istarian drones in this room to move or attack a creature. The drone fulfills this order to the best of its ability, and will attack until its target leaves the room or is dead.

T6: CITY OVERVIEW

> In the middle of this room stands a three-foot-tall, circular metal pedestal. Atop it, hundreds of tiny illusory buildings glow in a pale yellow light, and in their center floats a miniature illusion of the Threshold of the Heavens. Four crystal globes mounted on the walls glow with the same light, projecting illusory images onto the pedestal. Doors lead to the north and west, and a third door leads to the stairs down.

The pedestal here is an illusory representation of Onyari prior to its crash. Sections of the illusion flicker, the structures fading in and out of existence. These flickering sections correspond to parts of the city that have been destroyed or radically changed.

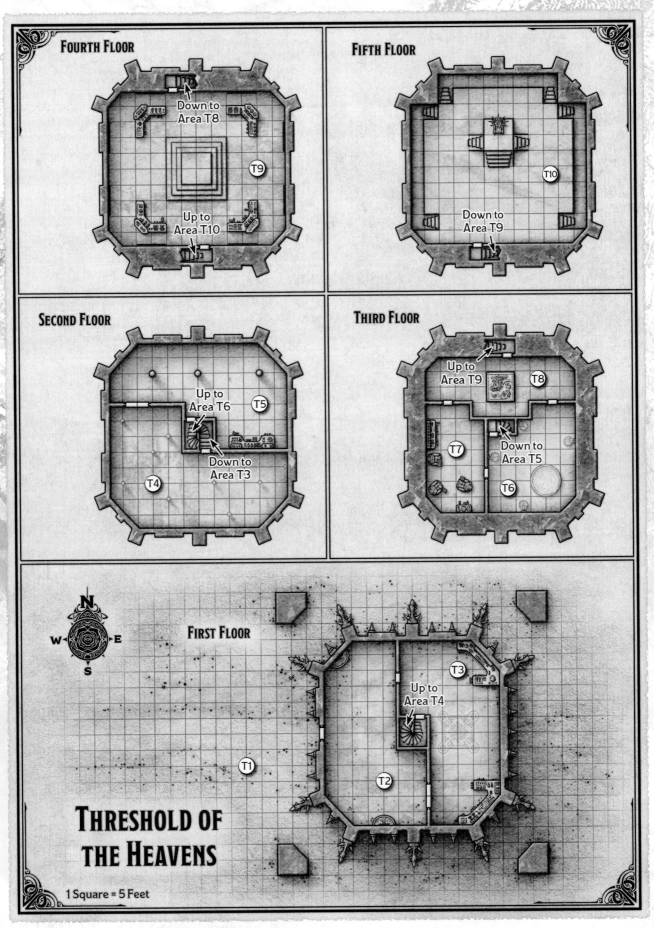

FOURTH FLOOR

Down to Area T8

T9

Up to Area T10

FIFTH FLOOR

T10

Down to Area T9

SECOND FLOOR

Up to Area T6

T5

T4

Down to Area T3

THIRD FLOOR

Up to Area T9

T8

T7

Down to Area T5

T6

N
W · E
S

FIRST FLOOR

T3

Up to Area T4

T1

T2

THRESHOLD OF THE HEAVENS

1 Square = 5 Feet

MAP 6.5: THRESHOLD OF THE HEAVENS

T7: Communications

> Three chairs are scattered across this room. Blackened consoles against the west and south walls buzz softly and occasionally emit sparks. Doors lead to the north and east.

The consoles once performed a magical function, but Dragon Army soldiers accidentally destroyed them. The consoles now buzz with misfiring magic. A character who succeeds on a DC 12 Intelligence (Arcana) check determines the consoles are broken beyond their ability to repair.

Flameskulls. Since whatever accident befell this room, Lohezet doesn't allow Dragon Army soldiers higher than this floor. Three **flameskulls** guard this room and attack any creature other than Lohezet that enters. The flameskulls are no longer present if they went to investigate area T3.

T8: Navigation

> A large table fills the center of this room, and beyond it, the north wall holds a door. Atop the table, a three-dimensional illusion depicts a vast, rocky expanse in meticulous detail.

Two **aurak draconians** (see appendix B) lean over the table, intensely studying it. They can be surprised by a character who succeeds on a DC 8 Dexterity (Stealth) check.

Magical Map. The magical map on the table changes as the city flies, accurately depicting the landscape for many miles around the city. A character who succeeds on a DC 14 Wisdom (Survival) check recognizes the map depicts the Northern Wastes, and they can pick out large groups of soldiers moving south of the city: Dragon Army forces and the Kalaman troops.

T9: Scrying Room

> Window-like crystal panels dominate the walls of this room, each displaying a different image. Three show crackling thunderheads, and the fourth depicts the city of Kalaman. In the center of the room, stone desks with magical consoles surround a raised platform. Doors lead to the north and south.

This chamber's scrying magic informed the city's navigators of storms and other approaching threats. The black-robed wizard **Lohezet** (see appendix B), who hunches over the southwest desk here, has been using his magic to alter the magical mirrors' focuses, fixing one on Kalaman.

Talking with Lohezet. Lohezet is surprised to see strangers. After discerning the characters' agenda, he tries to convince them he's been forced to serve the Dragon Armies. A character can determine he's lying with a DC 14 Wisdom (Insight) check. If the characters see through his lie, he tries to bargain and shares the following information:

- Lohezet doesn't care about the Dragon Armies' goals; they just support his research.
- He discovered the City of Lost Names's location while with the Black Dragon Army in the east.
- The Threshold of the Heavens is the control center of the city. He and the priest Belephaion have reactivated the magic here. They now await orders to raise the city into the sky.
- Belephaion, who is currently in the chamber above, is a fanatical worshiper of the Dragon Queen. If the characters slay Belephaion, Lohezet will leave the city without complaint.

Lohezet might make good on his word to leave, or he might ambush the characters later—he'll decide after seeing how they fare against Belephaion.

Scrying Mirrors. Lohezet has manipulated one of the mirrors to spy on Kalaman, looking down on the city as if from high above. A character who spends 10 minutes and succeeds on a DC 18 Intelligence (Arcana) check can restore the mirror to its original use. The mirrors can't be used to view any other locations. Each mirror is a Medium object with AC 13, 8 hit points, immunity to poison and psychic damage, and vulnerability to bludgeoning damage.

Treasure. Atop a console, Lohezet has placed Istarian relics he's investigating. These include six platinum tower components worth 200 gp each, a *gem of brightness*, and a *candle of invocation*.

T10: Bridge

> Enormous windows fill the walls of this room, granting a breathtaking view of the City of Lost Names. Lowered walkways line three walls like orchestra pits, while a dais in the center holds a bejeweled throne whose back is carved like the rays of the sun. Seated on the throne is a human man dressed in crimson robes and wearing a crown bearing the Dragon Queen's symbol.

AT THE THRESHOLD OF THE HEAVENS, BELEPHAION REVEALS HIS TRUE FORM.

Belephaion (see below) sits on the throne in this room. Two **bozak draconians** (see appendix B) attend him, one in the walkway to the southwest and the other in the walkway to the southeast.

When Belephaion sees the characters, read the following text:

> "It seems Lohezet has finally been dealt with." The man on the throne brings his hand down on a crimson jewel on the throne's arm. "No more need for his incessant human cautiousness. Glory will be mine alone. It is the Dragon Queen's will!"
>
> The jewels on the throne pulse. Beneath you, the floor lurches. Through the windows, the city's towers shudder, and the ruins begin to rise into the air.

Belephaion has activated the throne's magic, with dire ramifications for the city (see "Helm" below).

Belephaion. Belephaion, who's secretly a blue dragon, is currently in his **priest** form. He uses the **young blue dragon** stat block with the following action:

Alter Shape. Belephaion magically transforms into an **eagle** or a **priest**, while retaining his alignment, damage immunities, hit points, Hit Dice, and Intelligence, Wisdom, and Charisma scores. This transformation ends if he is reduced to 0 hit points or uses a bonus action to end it.

Belephaion mocks the characters and promises to send their souls to the Dragon Queen. As soon as the characters threaten or attack him, he orders the draconians to attack, transforms into his dragon form, and joins in battle. He fights to the death.

Helm. The throne is a *flying citadel helm* (see appendix A) attuned to Belephaion. As soon as the device activates, the entire city begins to hover. See "The City Rises" section for details.

Treasure. Belephaion carries a portion of his hoard with him in a *bag of holding* he wears. The bag contains 1,000 gp worth of ancient coins, a ruby holy symbol of Takhisis worth 250 gp, and an *Ioun stone* (insight). His crown is worth 3,500 gp.

Windows. Each of the four crystalline windows in this room is a Huge object with AC 13, 50 hit points, immunity to poison and psychic damage, and vulnerability to bludgeoning damage.

The City Rises

As soon as Belephaion activates the *flying citadel helm* atop the Threshold of the Heavens, the City of Lost Names lifts into the air. However, the device is damaged and can't effectively lift the shattered city. As a result, different parts of the ruins rise at different rates, tearing the city apart.

If Belephaion is killed, no one is attuned to the *flying citadel helm* and the Threshold's floating island ceases to rise. However, the rest of the city continues breaking apart and rising into the sky. Even if Belephaion is taken alive, he refuses to lower the city. The characters can't prevent the city from falling apart. Their only option is to escape, first from the tower, then from the city.

Threshold Evacuation

After Belephaion is defeated, read the following:

> The shaking underfoot continues. Outside the windows, boulder-sized chunks of the city tear free, rising into the air. Beneath them, whole districts shudder as mighty forces tug them skyward.
>
> Deep in the tower, something cracks. The floor under you slants as the tower begins to slowly lean.

A DRACONIAN FAILS TO ESCAPE THE CITY OF LOST NAMES.

The Threshold of the Heavens and the island it stands on are beginning to crumble. The characters have enough time to escape the tower, but encourage them to make a quick exit by describing cracking walls and stones dropping from the ceiling.

Characters who try to use the *flying citadel helm* can make a DC 10 Intelligence (Arcana) check. If they succeed, they realize it'd take several hours to attune to it and regain control of the city—and the tower isn't going to survive that long.

Soth's Ascent

As the party gets clear of the tower, read the following text:

> You find yourself amid disaster as ragged stone islands and crumbling buildings rise into the sky. Chaos confounds the Dragon Army troops throughout the city. Dragonnels dodge stones in the skies, while winged draconians race to escape cracking streets.
>
> To the south, violet flame lights the sky. At its center, a solid island rises, its stone foundations riddled with monstrous bones. The island bears an ominous temple, windows alight with otherworldly violet flame. As you watch, the undead dragon ridden by Lord Soth returns, and the two circle this blazing flying citadel.

This temple rising into the sky is the Bastion of Takhisis. Cataclysmic flame has awoken the dead dragons beneath the citadel, and their magic now holds it aloft similarly to how it once supported the whole city. While the rest of the ruins drift wildly, the Bastion of Takhisis rises as a flying citadel—a terrible weapon and the first of its kind.

Escaping the City

Allow the characters to choose their route to escape the city. The Path of Memories and the canyon to the south are both logical choices. If the party seeks out Demelin, the wizard is nowhere to be found.

As the characters flee, narrate the city crumbling around them. Use any of the following encounters to highlight the chaos of their escape.

Escaped Dragonnels

Four **Dragon Army dragonnels** (see appendix B) have been separated from their riders. A character can convince the dragonnels to let the characters ride them out of the city by succeeding on a DC 16 Charisma (Persuasion) check. Afterward, the dragonnels drop the characters off and depart.

Alternatively, if the characters saved the **wasteland dragonnel** (see appendix B) in the occupied mansion, it might return with other dragonnels to help them escape.

FLOATING ROCKS

The characters find their path impeded by a 30-foot ascent or descent between levels of the ruins. A character can jump between a series of floating rocks to navigate this obstacle. The character must succeed on three DC 14 Strength (Athletics) checks to leap from rock to rock. A character safely ascends or descends 10 feet with each successful check. If they fail a check, they make no progress. If they fail a check by 5 or more, they fall to the lower level.

ILL-FATED AMBUSH

A patrol of three **kapak draconians** and one **sivak draconian** (see appendix B for both stat blocks) spots the characters and attacks. At the end of the first round of combat, roll a die. If you roll an even number, a random draconian is affected as if by the *levitate* spell (save DC 15) for 1 minute. If you roll an odd number, a boulder falls on a random draconian, dealing 33 (6d10) bludgeoning damage to it.

ESCAPING THE ENEMY

Once the characters escape the City of Lost Names, they'll want to rejoin the Kalaman forces. They can use the fargab to learn where Darrett and their allies are; otherwise, soon after they escape the city, a small group of Kalaman soldiers finds them and leads them to the larger force.

The upheaval in the City of Lost Names has caused a momentary interruption in the conflict between the Red Dragon Army and Kalaman's forces. However, the Red Dragon Army is regrouping.

The adventure unfolds in one of two ways from here:

With Mass Combat. If you are using the *Dragonlance: Warriors of Krynn* game along with this adventure, consult the "Warriors of Krynn: Scenario 8" sidebar.

Without Mass Combat. If you aren't using the *Dragonlance: Warriors of Krynn* game, continue with the following section.

SWIFT RETREAT

When the characters reunite with Kalaman's soldiers, Darrett welcomes them back, but he keeps the conversation short. The Dragon Army is mustering and soon will strike at Kalaman's forces again. Darrett has lost a substantial number of troops after several skirmishes and hit-and-run attacks. He suggests retreating to the south as swiftly as possible.

WARRIORS OF KRYNN: SCENARIO 8

Soon after the characters reunite with their allies from Kalaman, the Dragon Army musters its scattered forces and prepares to pursue the fleeing Kalaman troops. Read the introduction to scenario 8 in *Dragonlance: Warriors of Krynn*, then play that scenario. This scenario details the flight of the Kalaman forces from the City of Lost Names.

If the characters attain a hold during this scenario, their allies hail them and share one *potion of healing* (superior) with each character. If the characters attained a win, the survivors also gift them a *ring of resistance* (fire) taken from a defeated Dragon Army officer. Characters gain no benefit for a loss.

At the end of the scenario, proceed with the "A New Threat" section.

A NEW THREAT

As the characters and Kalaman's troops slip away from the Dragon Army, read the following:

> As the cliffs surrounding the City of Lost Names grow distant, their red stone walls take on a violet hue. A floating island drifts over them, crowned by a terrifying temple smoldering with Cataclysmic flames. As the flying citadel takes up position over the rallying Dragon Army troops, you can make out crimson pennants fluttering on this terrible new weapon in the Dragon Queen's arsenal.

The flying citadel baffles and terrifies Kalaman's forces, but Darrett urges calm as the army focuses on escaping. He wants to know all about the flying citadel, but he delays that conversation until the army is well out of its sight. For the moment, his focus is ensuring the safety of his troops, escaping to the south, and alerting Kalaman's defenders about this terrible new weapon.

NEXT STEPS

After escaping the City of Lost Names, the characters advance to 10th level. Chapter 7 begins as the characters, Darrett, and the outmatched Kalaman troops depart the Northern Wastes. With time running out, they must prepare Kalaman to face the Dragon Army's newest threat.

With its flying citadel looming overhead, the Dragon Army prepares to lay siege to the city of Kalaman.

CHAPTER 7

SIEGE OF KALAMAN

THE RED DRAGON ARMY HAS FAILED TO raise the City of Lost Names into the heavens. The characters have deprived the Dragon Army of its city-sized battle platform, but as the smoke clears, a citadel flies free of the ruins, its course set for Kalaman.

RUNNING THIS CHAPTER

This chapter opens in the aftermath of the destruction of the City of Lost Names. The characters must make haste to prepare the people of Kalaman for the flying citadel's threat. A ship at the eastern coast of the Northern Wastes can swiftly sail them to the city—but first they have to reach the coast.

When the characters return to Kalaman, they apprise the city's leaders of the threat and help prepare for the coming siege. The characters have their hands full keeping Kalaman's people safe while taking the fight to the Dragon Army. With their allies' aid, the characters infiltrate the flying citadel and bring it down from within. Finally, the characters must face the Highmaster of the Red Dragon Army, Kansaldi Fire-Eyes herself.

CHARACTER ADVANCEMENT

In this chapter, level advancement is handled as follows:

- Characters begin this chapter at 10th level, having gained a level at the end of chapter 6.
- They advance to 11th level after completing the "Flight of the Dragonnels" section and reaching the flying citadel.

A Hasty Retreat

While the Red Dragon Army recovers from the destruction of the City of Lost Names, Darrett Highwater and the troops from Kalaman retreat and make camp a safe distance away. Begin this chapter as the characters join them by reading the following text:

> Kalaman's surviving soldiers made camp on a bluff east of the City of Lost Names—or what remains of it. In the distance, a constellation of rocks floats in the air, some the size of islands, others little more than boulders. However, the largest island advances south from the ruins, positioning itself above the reassembling Dragon Army forces. The island holds aloft a sinister temple with otherworldly violet light gleaming from its cracked walls. Its exposed foundations crawl with creatures of blackened bone and violet flame. As you watch, several of these skeletal dragons spread tattered wings, lurching into the sky to circle the citadel like gigantic vultures.

Characters who watch the flying citadel for ten minutes or more see dragonnels moving troops from the ground to the citadel. The flying citadel gives the

Dragon Army a powerful weapon, but it will take it days to move all of its forces aboard.

The flying citadel and the Dragon Army aren't immediate threats so long as the characters and Kalaman's forces keep their distance. If the characters draw near, they attract the attention of one or more **lesser death dragons** (see appendix B) that attack until the characters retreat.

Shadow of the Citadel

After the characters see the flying citadel, Darrett seeks them out. If they haven't already told him of their time in the City of Lost Names, he asks what occurred, anxious to learn about this new threat on the horizon. After the characters share what they know, Darrett relates the following information:

- Kalaman's troops aren't in any state to take on this flying citadel.
- Darrett suggests the characters hasten to Kalaman to apprise Marshal Vendri of this threat.
- Darrett sent word to the transports that ferried the group to the region to relocate. They should be waiting at Dread Wolf Cove to the east (location J on map 5.1).
- Darrett urges allies of the characters, like Cudgel and Rookledust, to go with them to help support their report to Kalaman's leaders.
- Darrett will stay and lead the troops back himself.

Darrett encourages the characters to rest, then set off for the coast as soon as they're ready. If Clystran (see chapter 5) is with Darrett's troops, he can guide them, hastening the characters' journey.

To the Coast

The journey to Dread Wolf Cove takes five days—fewer if the characters have Clystran's guidance or other methods of conveyance. Consult the "Movement in the Wastes" section in chapter 5 for details on moving through the region, but play the trek briskly; reporting to Kalaman about the flying citadel should feel like a race against time. If you wish, run one or more random encounters from chapter 5 during the journey. Shortly before the characters reach the cove, run the following encounter.

Dragonnel Down

When the characters are about a day from reaching the Kalaman ships at the coast, read the following:

> Three crimson dragonnels appear in the sky bearing riders in Dragon Army armor. They pursue a fourth dragonnel, but this one has no rider, and its scales are of a coppery hue. A Dragon Army rider whips a net at their desperately fleeing quarry, and the unfortunate creature tumbles from the sky, crashing near you.

Darrett Highwater
Wearing Solamnic Armor

The injured **wasteland dragonnel** (see appendix B) crashes to the ground 30 feet from the characters. It has 4 hit points remaining and is restrained by a net. The three **Dragon Army officers** and their **Dragon Army dragonnels** (see appendix B for both stat blocks) land nearby. They approach the injured dragonnel, planning to capture it and train it to serve as a mount. If the characters interfere, the Dragon Army troops attack them. The Dragon Army dragonnels flee if their riders are defeated.

Wasteland Dragonnel. The coppery dragonnel is entangled in a net. A character who warily approaches the dragonnel can remove the net by succeeding on a DC 10 Strength check. If the net is removed, the dragonnel locks eyes with whoever aided it, then clumsily flies away to the south.

Supply Camp

The characters find the Kalaman ships at Dread Wolf Cove. If the characters didn't already venture here in chapter 5, they find it as detailed there. The shore near the vessels is guarded by a small camp of Kalaman soldiers. One of the ship captains, a human man named Haldri Leddis, recognizes the characters and prepares a ship for their journey back to Kalaman. The other vessels wait here for Darrett and his troops.

If Clystran is with the characters, he bids the characters a fond farewell. He tells them he intends to return to Heart's Hollow, but he promises to send word if he finds a way to further aid them.

The characters' ship departs whenever they're ready. Thanks to strong winds in their favor, the voyage back to Kalaman takes only one day.

Return to Kalaman

When the characters reach Kalaman, the city looks much as they left it, but tension fills the streets. The Red Dragon Army has claimed much of the surrounding lands, and the city's forces have been locked in skirmish after skirmish.

If the characters don't go directly to Castle Kalaman to report to Marshal Vendri, one of her aides finds them within a few hours of their return and escorts them to the council chamber in the castle.

Grim Report

When the characters return to Castle Kalaman, Marshal Vendri is in a meeting with the city's newly elected leader, Governor Fuline Thren. However, the marshal has left standing orders to interrupt her if news comes from Darrett's forces. When her aide leads the characters into the castle's council chamber, read the following:

> This familiar conference hall and its large round table have seen significant repairs since last you were here. Marshal Vendri and Lord Bakaris sit at the table, along with various bickering strangers who wear the colors of Kalaman guilds. Opposite the door, a woman in simple clothes sits in the governor's chair, watching the proceedings with uncertainty.
>
> Marshal Vendri sees you and stands, surprise clear on her face.

Vendri calls for silence and welcomes the characters. Unless they recently contacted her via the *sending* spell or similar magic, she had thought they were lost. She's eager to hear their private report on what happened in the Northern Wastes.

Before Vendri can leave with the characters, though, Lord Bakaris demands the entire council hear whatever news they bring. Governor Thren hesitantly agrees, and Vendri reluctantly gestures for the characters to report. As the characters tell their story, consider interjecting criticism from Lord Bakaris or support from Marshal Vendri.

Any mention of the flying citadel captures the room's attention. Vendri, Thren, and others in the room pose the following questions:

- How many flying citadels does the enemy have?
- Could the enemy make more?
- How does the citadel fly?
- Where is it headed?
- How can it be destroyed?
- How can Kalaman stand against a fortress that soars over the city's defenses?

The characters are unlikely to have answers to all these questions, and Marshal Vendri doesn't expect them to, but the council grows more anxious with each unanswered question.

When the characters have answered what they can, Vendri bids them rest. The characters' quarters in the castle remain at their disposal.

Quiet Time

After finishing their report to Kalaman's leaders, the characters are free to spend the following days as they please. The Dragon Army will need at least a week to prepare its full force to march on Kalaman, so there's plenty of time for the characters to make final arrangements in and around the city. Encourage them to tie up any loose ends, as they'll have few opportunities once the Dragon Army attacks.

Kalaman remains as described in chapter 4, though rumors of a flying war machine now flood the streets, and there's a feeling of imminent crisis.

Meeting with the Marshal

If the characters seek out Marshal Vendri for further conversation, she's pleased to see them. Vendri shares that the war hasn't gone well in their absence. Kalaman's forces have held their own, but the Dragon Army has claimed much of the surrounding land. The enemy has conspicuously avoided Kalaman, and the bulk of its forces are camped near the ruins of Vogler, as if waiting for something. With the news of the flying citadel, Vendri now knows why. She has ordered all troops to return to Kalaman and shore up the defenses along the walls. However, she admits the city has little hope of defeating a flying fortress.

Day of Dread

When you're ready to proceed with this section, the characters hear a commotion in Castle Kalaman or the city streets. Scouts have returned to the city with news: A flying citadel has been spotted to the northwest of the city. Beneath it, the Red Dragon Army has begun to march toward Kalaman.

This news ushers in an uneasy day of waiting as the city braces for battle. As the day progresses, run the following encounters, using the Dread in the Streets table to set the mood as the characters venture across the city.

Dread in the Streets

d6	Event
1	A makeshift aid camp has taken over an alley, providing help to refugees recently arrived in the city.
2	A baker stands outside their bakery, handing out free bread to all passersby.
3	A lost child calls for their parents on a crowded street.
4	A sign hangs over a blacksmith shop: "Weapons out of stock. Sorry and good luck."
5	An old man with a pointed green hat sits on a bench, telling a group of children a story of the heroic knight Huma Dragonbane.
6	A person pulling a small wagon full of stray pets stops to pick up another lost critter.

Trouble at the Gates

A soldier discreetly seeks out the characters to report trouble at Kalaman's west Trade Gate. The soldier is concerned one of Kalaman's captains is preventing refugees from entering the city. Not wanting to make a scene or oppose a superior officer, the soldier hopes the characters can help.

If the characters follow the soldier, they find the following scene at the Trade Gate:

> The portcullis of the Trade Gate has been lowered. Dozens of anxious civilians gather outside it, banging on the gate and pleading for entry. Inside the gate, Kalaman soldiers stand with spears ready, nervously eyeing the gate and their stern captain.

The Trade Gate has been closed at the orders of Captain Oklid Narnhelm (neutral, human **veteran**). He's on the scene with his eight **Kalaman soldiers** (see appendix B). If questioned, Narnhelm shares the following:

- Dozens of travelers and residents of the trade camps seek refuge in the city.
- Narnhelm has heard draconians can take on the appearance of other people.
- When large groups started showing up, Narnhelm closed the gate to prevent disguised enemies from slipping inside.

A character can convince Narnhelm to open the gate through roleplaying or by succeeding on a DC 16 Charisma (Intimidation or Persuasion) check. If convinced, he orders the gate opened but tells his soldiers to remain on guard.

Strange Rider

Later in the day (likely while the characters are on the streets or walls), the character with the highest Wisdom (Perception) score spots a dragonnel ridden by two figures flying over the city toward the spires of Castle Kalaman. At a glance, the character doesn't see any Dragon Army colors on the distant figures.

The characters can learn more about this visitor by heading to the ramparts atop Castle Kalaman. When the party arrives, read the following text:

The riders are Clystran and Darrett. If the characters saved the dragonnel in the "Occupied Mansion" section in chapter 6 or in the "Dragonnel Down" encounter earlier in this chapter, they recognize it as the same creature.

Clystran and Darrett are pleased to see the characters and have the following information to share:

- Not long after parting ways with the characters, Clystran found this wasteland dragonnel. It was friendly and allowed Clystran to ride it.
- Clystran and the dragonnel managed to soar close to the flying citadel.
- Tunnels riddle the citadel's base. Eerie lights suggest they connect with the temple above.
- Clystran found Darrett and offered him a ride home once the Kalaman soldiers were safely aboard the ships.
- Several other friendly wasteland dragonnels followed Clystran and Darrett to Kalaman, but they broke off once the city came within sight.

Planning the Counterattack

Allow the characters to use the details Clystran and Darrett share to concoct a plan for infiltrating the flying citadel. If they miss particulars or need ideas, Darrett makes the following suggestions:

- Facing the Undead dragons and the Dragon Army troops directly on the surface of the flying citadel would end in disaster.
- The citadel is surrounded by flying foes, but their attention could be diverted by a distraction.
- Using the tunnels in the citadel's foundation, a group might sneak inside and find a way to destroy the flying citadel.
- Clystran might be able to find the other dragonnels in the region and bring them to aid the characters in reaching the flying citadel.

The characters can add their own embellishments to this plan, but the flying citadel will be vulnerable only during its attack on Kalaman. The tunnels in the flying citadel's foundations are the safest path for getting inside the fortress, and "The Flying Citadel" later in this chapter assumes the characters use these tunnels.

Once the characters and their allies agree on a plan, Clystran and his dragonnel rest briefly before heading off to find the other dragonnels and convince them to aid in Kalaman's defense.

Night of Terror

As dusk approaches, the defenders on Kalaman's western walls sound an alarm: the Red Dragon Army and its flying citadel draw near. All of Kalaman's soldiers are called to defensive positions. When the alarms ring out, Darrett finds the characters and takes them to the Trade Gate's ramparts. When they arrive, read the following description:

Marshal Vendri can spare only a moment for the characters. She has no immediate orders but asks them to stay on hand to solve whatever emergencies are sure to arise. She doesn't expect the Dragon Army will launch a full siege tonight, but Kalaman's defenders must be prepared for anything.

If the characters and Darrett have plans for attacking the flying citadel, Vendri supports them. Use her suggestions and orders to guide the characters toward infiltrating the flying citadel once they have the help of Clystran's dragonnels—a plan that becomes reality in the "Dragonnel Reinforcements" section.

No Sleep in Kalaman

The people of Kalaman face a long, anxious night waiting for the Dragon Army's attack. Use encounters from the Night Encounters table to reinforce the Dragon Army's menace throughout the night. When you're ready to conclude this section, move on to the "Bakaris Defects" encounter.

A SIVAK DRACONIAN
SWOOPS DOWN TO ATTACK.

NIGHT ENCOUNTERS

d4	Encounter
1	Six **kapak draconians** scale the walls and attack a group of **Kalaman soldiers** near the characters (see appendix B for both stat blocks).
2	Three Kalaman soldiers turn on their commander—in truth, these are four **sivak draconians** (see appendix B) disguised using Shape Theft.
3	Testing the Defenses (see below)
4	Highmaster's Message (see below)

TESTING THE DEFENSES

> A warning horn sounds from a group of soldiers crewing ballistae nearby. In the distance, a flight of Dragon Army dragonnels sweeps toward the city walls.

Four **Dragon Army dragonnels** carry a total of eight **bozak draconians** (see appendix B for both stat blocks). On the walls near the characters are three ballistae (detailed in the "Siege Equipment" section of the *Dungeon Master's Guide*) and six **Kalaman soldiers** (see appendix B).

The Dragon Army dragonnels are currently 360 feet from the city. In 3 rounds they will be 20 feet above the walls, and the eight bozak draconians will recklessly glide onto the ramparts and attack.

The characters can use the ballistae to attack the approaching dragonnels. A dragonnel struck by a ballista bolt panics and retreats with its two riders.

HIGHMASTER'S MESSAGE

This encounter occurs while the characters are outside, possibly on Kalaman's walls or the city streets. The character with the highest Wisdom (Perception) score sees a strange violet light in the sky. After they react, read the following text:

> A violet star plummets from the sky and crashes nearby, throwing up a cloud of debris. A breathless screech rises from the black-lit dust. An instant later, blackened fangs and violet flame burst forth in the form of a massive skeletal dragon.

This **lesser death dragon** (see appendix B) has come specifically for the characters. After its dramatic crash landing, it starts the battle with 160 hit points and fights to the death.

During the fight, the first character to deal damage to the death dragon notices a piece of parchment is pinned to the skeleton with a dagger. When the death dragon is defeated, the characters can retrieve the parchment, which bears this message:

> The Dragon Queen sees you, and I am the fire in her eyes. The end comes. It is the Dragon Queen's will.

The message was written by Kansaldi Fire-Eyes specifically for the characters. There is no signature, but the wording suggests the characters have become objects of the highmaster's ire.

BAKARIS DEFECTS

A messenger arrives, either seeking Marshal Vendri at the Trade Gate while the characters are present, or seeking the characters at Vendri's orders. The messenger reports the Warrior's Gate on the east wall is unguarded. Vendri urges the characters to quickly find out what happened.

When the characters arrive at the gate, read the following text:

> The Warrior's Gate stands open, though its portcullis remains closed. No guards are in sight, and beside the gate, the guardroom's door is ajar.
>
> On the other side of the portcullis, several figures wearing Dragon Army uniforms pace back and forth. As you near the gate, the portcullis begins to rise.

DAWN CARLOS

The portcullis rises jerkily. After 3 rounds, it will be high enough to admit a group of six **Dragon Army officers** (see appendix B) into the city.

The characters know the portcullis's controls are in the guardroom adjacent to the gate. There they find the anxious Lord Bakaris (**noble**), accompanied by six **knights** in Kalaman armor. One of the knights turns a winch, raising the portcullis outside.

Lord Bakaris is defecting to the Dragon Army and has convinced these knights to come with him. The cowardly lord is terrified of the invasion and is convinced everyone in Kalaman is about to be slaughtered. After a moment of shock at seeing the characters, he orders the five unoccupied knights to attack the characters—while trying to stay out of battle himself.

Portcullis. If the knight raising the portcullis isn't stopped within 3 rounds of the characters arriving at the Warrior's Gate, the Dragon Army officers join the battle and Lord Bakaris tries to flee from the city. If the characters prevent the portcullis from opening, the Dragon Army troops flee.

Bakaris's Defeat. Lord Bakaris panics if his escape plan falls apart. Desperate, he might try to climb over the city wall or employ another reckless scheme. He surrenders if he takes any damage or if his knights are defeated. Once Bakaris is defeated, a character who searches him finds the following message from his son:

> Father, the Dragon Army sends its greetings and a proposition: Avoid the doom in store for Kalaman. Meet our agents at the Warrior's Gate. Open the way, and they'll bring you to me. I've found a place here and have been promised a share of the glories to come. You can have the same if you embrace the Dragon Queen's will.

The letter is simply signed "Bakaris." The characters will face Bakaris the Younger in the "Flight of the Dragonnels" section, but they have no other information about the traitor at this time.

CONCLUDING THE NIGHT

After running the encounters in this section, the Dragon Army's attacks cease for a time. Have Darrett or another NPC urge the characters to rest before the coming day's battles. Give characters enough time to finish a long rest before starting the next section.

BATTLE OF KALAMAN

After a brief lull in the initial attacks on Kalaman, the Red Dragon Army unleashes its wrath on the city.

If the characters rested after the events of the previous section, their rest concludes to the sound of warning horns. Darrett or a messenger from Marshal Vendri urges them to hurry to the command post atop the Trade Gate. Once the characters arrive, read the following text:

> The siege of Kalaman has begun. Thousands of Dragon Army troops—humans, draconians, and other creatures—march on the city. Along the walls, Kalaman soldiers shout commands while ballistae fire in rapid percussion, their deadly bolts barely keeping the dragonnels wheeling overhead at bay. Beyond the dragonnel riders, the flying citadel looms like a thunderhead, drifting slowly but relentlessly closer.

At this point, there has been no word from Clystran or the dragonnels he went to track down.

BATTLE BEGINS

This section has no set timeline or specific goals beyond involving characters in Kalaman's desperate defense. Roll on or choose the encounters you want to run from the Defending the Wall table. These encounters are described below. Once you're ready for the characters to begin their infiltration of the flying citadel, proceed with the "Dragonnel Reinforcements" section.

DEFENDING THE WALL

d4	Encounter
1	Ballista Breakers
2	Daring Riders
3	Death Dragon Attack
4	Draconian Assassins

BALLISTA BREAKERS

A flight of dozens of sivak draconians soars from the flying citadel toward Kalaman. Many are shot down, but four **sivak draconians** (see appendix B) land on Kalaman's wall and attempt to destroy three ballistae 30 feet from the characters.

On each sivak's turn, it attacks a ballista unless the sivak was targeted before that turn by a character. A ballista is destroyed after sivaks attack it three times. If all three ballistae are destroyed, three dragonnels and their riders fly overhead, avoiding the wall's defenses. This provokes the "Daring Riders" encounter immediately after this encounter is resolved.

Daring Riders

Three **Dragon Army officers** mounted on **Dragon Army dragonnels** (see appendix B for both stat blocks) manage to get past Kalaman's walls. The riders throw alchemist's fire onto the city as they circle overhead. Characters on the wall can turn a ballista to fire over the city, but doing so takes an action and a successful DC 16 Strength (Athletics) check. If the ballistae near the characters have been destroyed, they can find an additional ballista 60 feet farther along the city wall.

Death Dragon Attack

A **lesser death dragon** (see appendix B) crashes against Kalaman's wall at least 90 feet from the characters. By the time the characters draw close, the death dragon has already used its Cataclysmic Breath to kill four Kalaman soldiers, transforming them into **zombies**.

Draconian Assassins

While the characters are at the Trade Gate command post or another vulnerable point, two **aurak draconians** (see appendix B) teleport nearby using the *dimension door* spell and attack a Kalaman commander (use the **veteran** stat block). This might be Marshal Vendri, Captain Narnhelm, or another Kalaman officer.

Dragonnel Reinforcements

When you're ready for the characters to turn their focus to the flying citadel, read the following text:

> A scout rushes to you with a message. Only minutes ago, a small group of coppery dragonnels landed in a grove southwest of the city. They didn't look like the kind the Dragon Army flies, and only one had a rider.

Warriors of Krynn: Scenario 11

Kalaman's defenders undertake an attack to distract the Dragon Army, giving the characters an opportunity to reach the dragonnels and fly to the flying citadel. Read the introduction to scenario 11 in *Dragonlance: Warriors of Krynn*, then play that scenario.

 If the characters attain a win or hold during this scenario, their dragonnels are energetic and well rested. During the "Flight of the Dragonnels" section, each dragonnel a character is riding has advantage on the first attack roll or ability check it makes. Characters gain no benefit for a loss.

 At the end of the scenario, skip the "Over Enemy Lines" and "Assault on Hawker's Grove" sections and proceed with "Flight of the Dragonnels."

From this description, the characters should recognize Clystran has returned with the dragonnels he sought. From here, the adventure proceeds in one of two ways:

With Mass Combat. If you are using the *Dragonlance: Warriors of Krynn* game along with this adventure, the characters are asked to report to Marshal Vendri. She plans to have her troops take to the field, providing cover for the characters to reach the dragonnels. Consult the "Warriors of Krynn: Scenario 11" sidebar.

Without Mass Combat. If you aren't using the *Dragonlance: Warriors of Krynn* game, continue with the "Over Enemy Lines" section.

Over Enemy Lines

Clystran found the dragonnels he went looking for and convinced them to follow him to Hawker's Grove, a wooded area southwest of the city. To rendezvous with Clystran, the characters must reach him amid the siege. The characters might come up with their own methods, but if they ask Darrett or another ally for suggestions, they're directed to the southwest city wall where Rookledust is posted.

 There, the characters find Rookledust and her new assistant, Than (introduced in chapter 3), have managed to convert a defunct catapult into a gnomeflinger (see appendix A). They created it to help get soldiers into the field or city rapidly, but thus far no commanders have incorporated the device into their strategies. The gnomes are delighted to let the characters use the gnomeflinger. They even provide each character a narycrash (see appendix A)—or two, if a character asks for a backup.

 Once the characters are ready, the gnomes happily launch the characters one by one from the southwest city wall and over the Dragon Army forces below. After flying several hundred feet, the characters land a short distance from the tree line and Hawker's Grove.

Assault on Hawker's Grove

Hawker's Grove is depicted on map 7.1. As the characters near Hawker's Grove, read the following text:

> Kalaman's scouts weren't the only ones to notice Clystran and his dragonnels. The grove ahead is in flames. From amid the smoke comes the sound of bestial screeching.

The **scout** Clystran has taken refuge in the grove and has set up a small camp where he waits for the characters. He's accompanied by his own coppery **wasteland dragonnel** (see appendix B) and one for each character. Just before the characters arrived, four **red dragon wyrmlings** pursuing the dragonnels used their breath to set part of the grove aflame. The red dragons now lurk in the smoke, preparing to attack. They fight until wounded by a *dragonlance* or reduced to 10 hit points or fewer. Clystran and his dragonnels stay out of battle unless attacked.

Unless the characters prepared another strategy, they begin this encounter adjacent to the tree stump at the southeast corner of the map.

The following section notes elements unique to this battle. The battle ends when the red dragons are defeated.

HAWKER'S GROVE BATTLEFIELD FEATURES
The battlefield includes the following features:

Burnt Ground and Trees. This area has recently been blasted with flames. It still smolders, and smoke heavily obscures this area. The smoke disperses after 5 minutes or if exposed to wind moving at least 10 miles an hour.

Fray. The 15-foot-wide area marked by the design at the edge of the map represents areas from which dangers might appear.

HAWKER'S GROVE BATTLEFIELD EVENTS
During this battle, roll on the Hawker's Grove Battlefield Events table each round on initiative count 0. Also consider rolling on the table when a red dragon is slain or if a character enters the Fray or otherwise tries to leave the battlefield.

HAWKER'S GROVE BATTLEFIELD EVENTS

d10	Event
1–3	A flight of dragonnels strafes the battlefield, the wind from their passage reigniting flames in the burnt ground. Each creature in this area must make a DC 14 Dexterity saving throw, taking 21 (6d6) fire damage on a failed save, or half as much damage on a successful one.
4–6	A stray ballista bolt fires into the grove. Roll any die. On an even roll, the bolt targets a random player character. On an odd roll, the bolt targets a random red dragon. The attack has +6 to hit and deals 16 (3d10) piercing damage on a hit.
7–8	A **sivak draconian** (see appendix B) arrives, appearing adjacent to the Fray near a random player character. If there is already a sivak draconian in the battle, no event occurs.
9–10	One of the red dragons roars a prayer: "Dragon Queen, grant us your flames!" Each red dragon recharges their Fire Breath action.

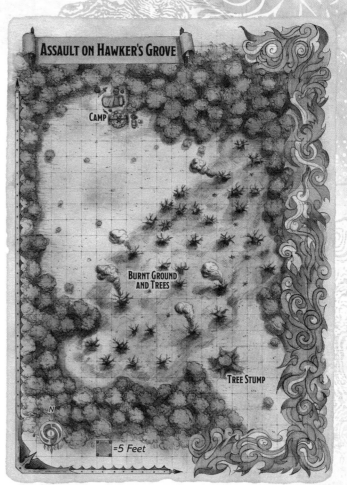

MAP 7.1: ASSAULT ON HAWKER'S GROVE

MEETING WITH CLYSTRAN
After the red dragons are defeated, Clystran greets the characters and introduces them to the **wasteland dragonnels** (see appendix B) he has convinced to aid them. Use the following topics to guide the conversation with Clystran:

- Clystran is eager to leave the grove before the Dragon Army attacks again.
- He hopes the dragonnels can slip past the Dragon Army's winged forces amid the chaos.
- He intends to lead the characters to the tunnels in the foundation of the flying citadel. He urges them not to attack during the flight or otherwise draw attention to themselves.
- Once the characters land on the citadel, it'll be up to them to find a way to bring it down.
- Clystran doesn't know how the characters will escape after destroying the flying citadel, but he promises to watch for them from a distance.

Once Clystran has answered any questions, he and the characters can mount their dragonnels and take off. The dragonnels are intelligent creatures and understand the stakes, so they allow their riders to direct their flight as long as their riders don't give life-threatening orders.

Flight of the Dragonnels

As Clystran and the characters fly above the battle-field, read the following text:

> The clash between the Dragon Army and Kalaman's defenders rages below. The city's walls hold, though smoke rises from the bombardment of enemy war machines and dragonnels. Flights of winged enemies circle between the city and, high above, the inky shape of the flying citadel. Clystran points toward the citadel and guides his mount to follow the path of a group of Dragon Army dragonnels returning from an attack.

As the characters near the flying citadel, they must succeed on a DC 14 group Dexterity (Stealth) check or a flight of six **Dragon Army dragonnels** (see appendix B) spots the party and approaches. If the characters have disguised themselves as Dragon Army soldiers, the dragonnels ignore them and fly on. Otherwise, the dragonnels attack. If the characters flee, the dragonnels break off after a short pursuit, but other foes notice the characters (see the following section).

Red Ruin

After the characters avoid or contend with the dragonnels, Clystran breaks away from the Dragon Army flight path he had been following, rushing the characters toward the base of the flying citadel. Read the following text as the characters approach:

> As you near the flying citadel, two shapes emerge from the dark clouds drifting in its wake. A pair of bright-red dragonnels slash through the air, their riders guiding them directly toward you.

The characters are spotted while they're approximately 600 feet above the ground. Coming for them is **Red Ruin**, the Red Dragon Army's ace dragonnel rider, and Bakaris the Younger (a **Dragon Army officer**). Both are mounted on **Dragon Army dragonnels** (see appendix B for all three stat blocks).

Red Ruin fights to the death, but Bakaris flees if reduced to 20 hit points or fewer. If Bakaris is knocked from his mount or slain, he falls and vanishes amid the chaos.

Clystran and his dragonnel stay out of combat.

Bakaris's Ego. During the battle, Bakaris removes his helmet and taunts the characters, claiming Kalaman is doomed and offering to find them jobs cleaning dragonnel stables if they surrender.

Falling in Battle. Red Ruin seeks to knock her foes from their mounts using her Lance attack. If a rider falls from a dragonnel, the rider falls toward the ground until the end of the following round. During this time, another rider who is mounted alone on a dragonnel can use movement to dive alongside the falling creature and try to catch that creature as an action. The rider catches the falling creature on the rider's dragonnel if the rider succeeds on a DC 12 Strength (Athletics) check. A falling creature that isn't rescued takes 70 (20d6) bludgeoning damage upon hitting the ground.

ENTERING THE CITADEL

Once Bakaris and Red Ruin are defeated, Clystran urges the characters to follow him directly to the citadel. Other Dragon Army dragonnel riders have noticed the battle and are turning from Kalaman to investigate, but they're still minutes away.

As the characters reach the flying citadel, read the following text:

> The flying citadel rises upon an inverted mountain of black stone and exposed dragon bones. Fissures riddle this foundation, creating tunnels that extend deep into the rock. Clystran guides his dragonnel close to one of these, a natural shelf with space enough to land. Beyond, a narrow cave cuts its way into the depths of the flying citadel.

Clystran urges the characters to land swiftly, dismount, and head into the cave before they're spotted. He'll take their dragonnels and lead off any pursuit. He doesn't know what's in the cave beyond the landing site, but he urges the characters to move fast and stay quiet, as untold numbers of Dragon Army troops occupy the land around the Bastion of Takhisis above. Soon after, Clystran and the dragonnels depart.

Before the characters enter the cave, have each character make an Intelligence check. The character with the highest result calculates that based on the flying citadel's current speed, at least three hours remain before the citadel reaches Kalaman's walls (at which point crashing it would destroy the city). The party shouldn't dally within the citadel, but they don't need to rush for the sake of bringing down the citadel quickly.

The tunnel here is narrow, and only Medium or smaller creatures can enter. It leads to area S1 in "The Flying Citadel."

CHARACTER ADVANCEMENT

When the characters arrive at the flying citadel, they advance to 11th level.

THE FLYING CITADEL

When the end came for the City of Lost Names, it came for everyone in equal measure except the followers of Chemosh, god of undeath. Chemosh's servants thrived in the ruins of the Bastion of Takhisis, Onyari's temple dedicated to forces controlled by the gods of evil. Led by the vampire Alstare Bellis, they assumed control of the temple and continued their worship. When Lord Soth claimed the temple, he carried Cataclysmic fire into heart of the temple, suffusing it with magical power. This power now animates the death dragons and gives Soth control over the Bastion of Takhisis.

GOALS IN THE CITADEL

It should be clear to the characters that the flying citadel must be prevented from reaching Kalaman, but they likely haven't yet determined exactly how. During their exploration of the flying citadel, characters like Leedara (see area S2) and Caradoc (see area S22) can reveal details that help the characters devise plans aligning with the possibilities below.

UNSEAT SOTH

The party's initial plan most likely hinges on destroying Lord Soth or otherwise removing him from the citadel. Soth is the absolute commander of the Bastion of Takhisis, and defeating him would render it inert. The characters need to be ingenious, as they can't hope to beat Lord Soth by direct confrontation.

DISCOVER LOST ELVEN MAGIC

Hidden in the depths of the temple is a magic item known as the *mirror of reflected pasts* (see appendix A). It can temporarily paralyze Lord Soth and halt the citadel. Multiple people point to the mirror as crucial to Soth's downfall, but on its own, it's only a temporary solution.

DESTROY THE CITADEL

Ending the magic that holds the citadel aloft means snuffing the Cataclysmic fire in the Mourning Sanctum, the heart of the citadel, or destroying the *flying citadel helm* (see appendix A) it empowers. Lord Soth will never allow this to happen, though, so he needs to be neutralized beforehand.

CITADEL FEATURES

Maps 7.2 and 7.3 depict the flying citadel. Unless otherwise noted, the following features are consistent throughout the dungeon:

Corridors. All corridors have 10-foot-high ceilings. Rooms have 20-foot-high ceilings.
Lighting. Except for natural chambers and areas that note otherwise, areas inside the flying citadel are dimly lit by the flickering flames of magical torches and candles.

CITADEL DEPTHS

The lowest levels of the flying citadel are unworked tunnels. The characters find an entrance to these depths through a fissure in the citadel's base.

S1: TUNNELS

As Clystran departs and the characters venture into the cave tunnels, read the following:

> The tunnels leading into the foundations of the flying citadel are completely dark. Occasional rumbles echo through the passages as the citadel's foundation shifts in flight.

The tunnels are 10 feet wide, occasionally opening into larger chambers. Switchbacks, dead ends, and sloping tunnels make these passages a maze.

To navigate the tunnels to area S2 without incident, the characters must succeed on a DC 16 group Wisdom (Survival) check. If more than half the characters fail the check, they find the passage leads through a 50-foot-wide, 70-foot-long, 50-foot-high cavern where a **lesser death dragon** (see appendix B) lurks. It attacks when it notices the characters. Once the dragon is defeated, the characters face no more dangers in the tunnels. They eventually find a 30-foot shaft rising to area S2.

LEEDARA

TEMPLE CRYPTS

The Bastion of Takhisis had countless enemies, many of whom were interred in the temple crypts (depicted on map 7.2). Lord Soth pays this level of the citadel little mind, as his cursory investigation turned up little of interest. Unbeknownst to him, several free-willed Undead linger here.

S2: ENTRY

> The tunnels that wind through the foundation of the flying citadel rise via a natural shaft into this rocky cavity. A gash in the rock forms a passage to the east, where a familiar, blue-skinned elf in a pale dress stands with a knowing smile on her face.

This chamber is a crooked seam in the rock. The passage to the east splits, with both routes connecting to area S3. One path enters area S3 through a broken crypt in that room's wall, while the other descends 15 feet and leads to a gouge in the floor of that area.

The elf waiting here is Leedara (a neutral **ghost** detailed in chapter 3) in her guise as a living Silvanesti elf. She's here to aid the characters in confounding Lord Soth's plans and imparts the following information:

- Lord Soth lurks in the ruins above. He's using the Cataclysmic fire from Kalaman's catacombs to control the flying citadel and reanimate dragon skeletons buried in the flying island's foundations.
- If the characters can quell the Cataclysmic fire, the Undead dragons will be destroyed and the flying citadel will fall.
- Leedara isn't certain how to quell the Cataclysmic fire. The flames were created by the gods, so it stands that the power of the gods could extinguish them.
- Lord Soth is a peerless foe. The characters won't be able to stand against him in battle.
- Hidden somewhere in the chambers ahead is an elven relic known as the *mirror of reflected pasts* (see appendix A). Those who view the mirror see glimpses of their past.
- Leedara believes the mirror can distract Soth, giving the characters a chance to extinguish the Cataclysmic fire.

Leedara also knows Lord Soth's past and relates all the information from "Lord Soth's Curse" in chapter 4.

The characters likely have many questions about Leedara herself: why she's here, how she knows so much about Soth, and so forth. If questioned, Leedara reveals her true, ghostly form. She explains that,

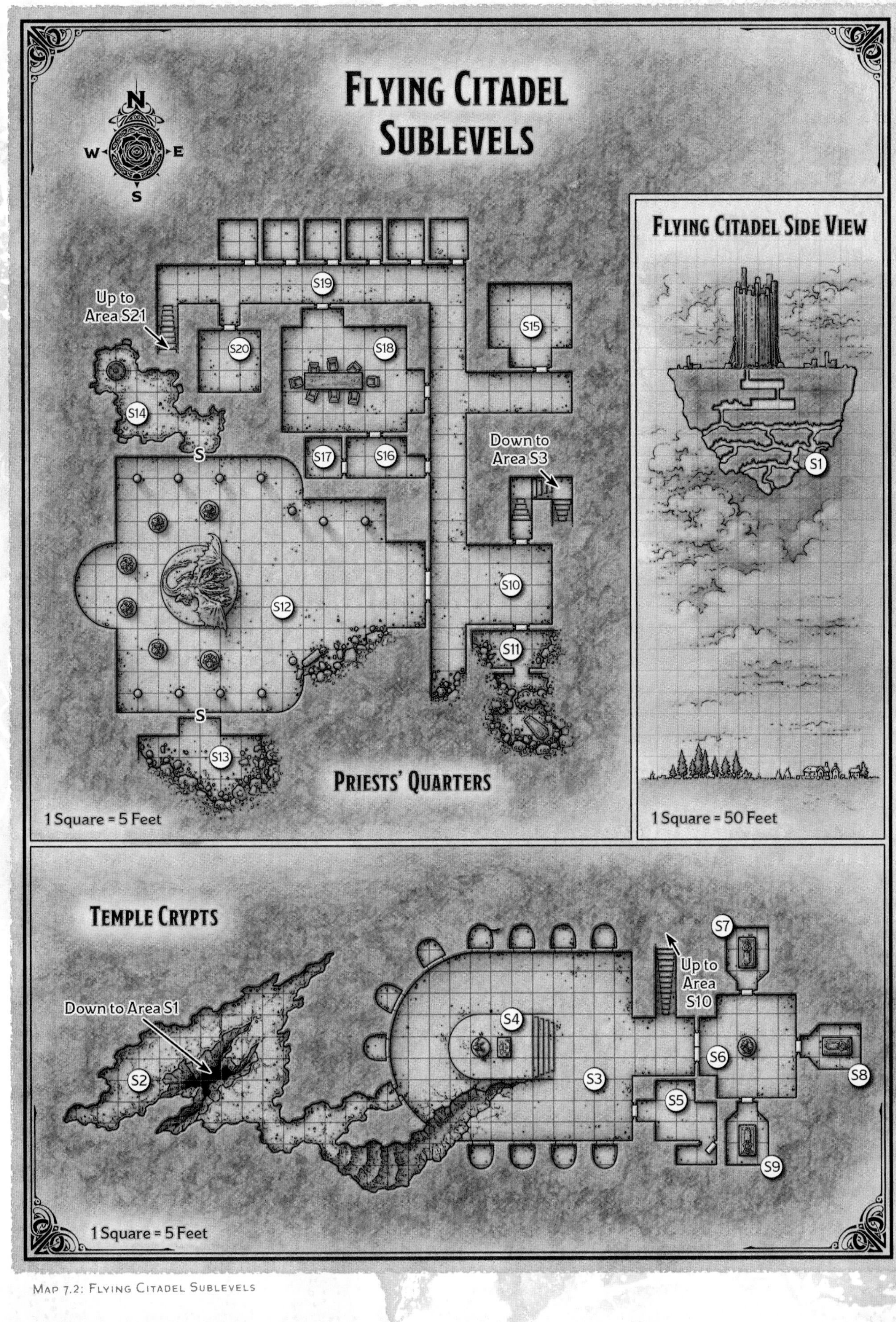

FLYING CITADEL SUBLEVELS

FLYING CITADEL SIDE VIEW

Up to
Area S21

S19

S20

S18

S15

S14

S

Down to
Area S3

S17

S16

S10

S12

S11

S

S13

PRIESTS' QUARTERS

1 Square = 5 Feet

S1

1 Square = 50 Feet

TEMPLE CRYPTS

Down to Area S1

S2

S4

S3

Up to
Area
S10

S7

S6

S5

S8

S9

1 Square = 5 Feet

MAP 7.2: FLYING CITADEL SUBLEVELS

MIKE SCHLEY

in life, she was one of the elven priestess Isolde's attendants and was among those who distracted Soth from his quest to prevent the Cataclysm. For her deeds, she's cursed to live as a ghost—but she's also a curse on Soth and works to stymie his ambitions. She can't stand against Soth alone and earnestly seeks to aid the characters. After sharing the information here and answering any questions the characters have about Lord Soth, she vanishes.

During the conversation with Leedara, if the characters attack or disbelieve her, the ghost vanishes, then reappears later to provide any of the information here as it proves helpful.

S3: BURIAL VAULT

> Spaced evenly about the perimeter of this chamber are numerous bricked-over stone archways. Plaques are set into many of these arches. At the room's center stands a raised stone dais bearing an ominous statue. A double door, a smaller door, and a stairwell stand at the east end of the room.

A fissure has opened in the wall of this vault, allowing access from area S2. Eleven sealed crypts line its walls. One crypt has been broken open, and a branch of the fissure connects it to area S2. The broken crypt bears a plaque reading "Acont, Prince of Minotaurs."

Two **skeletal knights** (see appendix B) and a **minotaur skeleton** stand guard in this room and attack intruders on sight.

Brickwork Seals. Each occupied crypt is bricked over. These brickwork seals are Large objects with AC 15, 30 hit points, and immunity to poison and psychic damage.

Crypts. Each crypt contains the remains of someone whose soul was remanded to Chemosh, God of Undeath. A simple plaque notes the occupant's identity. Use the Crypt Plaques table and Crypt Contents table to determine what the crypts' plaques say and what lies within each. If you roll the same name for a plaque more than once, the plaque is missing.

CRYPT PLAQUES

d10	Plaque
1–2	Scratches make the plaque unreadable
3–4	The plaque is missing
5	Minara of the Scarlet Robes
6	Nessa Coalcracker, Expert Engineer
7	Cecil Crownguard, Knight of the Dragon's Roar
8	Asa the Traitor
9	Lorry Wanwillow
10	Ohzren the Immortal

CRYPT CONTENTS

d10	Contents
1–3	Dusty Humanoid skeleton
4	Toppled jar of ashes
5	A **wight** that won't stop crying
6	Skeleton of an unidentifiable Beast
7	A **black pudding**
8	Gouged stone and a Humanoid skeleton with worn-down finger bones
9	Perfectly preserved Humanoid corpse
10	Humanoid skeleton wearing +2 leather armor. The crypt is empty if this result is rolled a second time.

S4: CHEMOSH'S SHRINE

> In the center of the crypt, a dais bears a statue of a robed figure with a grim skull for a face. Before the statue, a pair of skeletons kneel, holding an altar of polished black stone between them.

This shrine is under the effect of a *hallow* spell, with the additional effect that creatures other than Undead that attempt to ascend the dais are subject to the spell's fear effect (save DC 16).

Chemosh's Blessing. The first character who succeeds on the saving throw against the *hallow* spell and approaches the skull on the shrine hears the voice of Chemosh in their mind:

> "I find you worthy. Join me, and I will open the River of Souls to you."

If the character refuses the offer, the altar emits smoke that coalesces into a hulking figure. This hostile figure uses the **clay golem** stat block, but it is an Undead instead of a Construct. If the character accepts, they immediately become aware of how to use the altar to speak with the dead, and they don't need a holy symbol to do so.

Chemosh's Altar. A *detect magic* spell reveals an aura of necromancy around the altar. The altar can be used to commune with the dead. If a corpse's skull is placed on the altar, a creature wearing or holding a holy symbol of Chemosh can ask the skull five questions, as if by the *speak with dead* spell. Each skull can be questioned only once in this way.

If the characters question a skull from area S3, it can answer little beyond general questions about the temple's layout. If asked about the treasure vault's location, one of the skulls answers, "Treasure is found when Takhisis turns her ire south."

If the skulls from areas S8 and S9 are questioned, they provide the facts detailed in those sections.

S5: Vestry

> This bare room's only adornment is a half dozen dis-
> integrating robes hanging from pegs in the walls. A
> section of the wall has swung open, revealing another
> room once hidden behind a secret door.

The small room is strewn with shattered pottery,
a broken chest of empty drawers, and a moldering
pile of clothes. A successful DC 12 Intelligence
(Investigation) check shows this room has been ransacked; the chest of drawers and pottery have been
carelessly handled and the clothes tossed about.

Treasure. A character who searches the pile finds
a *portable hole* hidden among the clothing, folded
into a small triangle and tucked into the pocket of a
shirt sized for a Small creature.

S6: Elven Catacombs

> Statues adorn the north, south, and east walls. The
> north statue depicts an elf man reclining on a bench.
> The south statue depicts an elf woman doing the
> same—but the statue has been pushed aside, reveal-
> ing an open doorway behind it. The statue to the east
> features a noble elf man seated on a fine chair.

The Large statues mark the entrances to the tombs
of three elves: the Silvanesti ambassador Cithcillion
and his companions, Madar and Tenadria. All three
died as captives of the Temple of All Evil and were
interred here so their spirits could be further interrogated using magic mirrors in their tombs.

The statue to the south has been pushed aside,
revealing the entrance to a tomb behind it. Similar
entrances exist behind the other statues, which
can be pushed aside with a successful DC 20
Strength check.

S7: Madar's Tomb

The doorway to this tomb can be accessed by
pushing its statue aside with a successful DC 20
Strength check.

> A long, gray marble slab lies in the middle of this
> chamber. A shallow inset of similar dimensions is
> carved into the ceiling directly above the slab. Scat-
> tered about it are skeletal remains intermingled with
> shards of glass.

Close inspection of the floor reveals the shards of
glass are pieces of a mirror. The bones belong to

Cithcillion

Madar, one of Cithcillion's companions. Madar's
bones were thrown from the marble slab when the
City of Lost Names fell from the sky. The bones are
now scattered and shattered beyond repair.

S8: Cithcillion's Tomb

The doorway to this tomb can be accessed by
pushing its statue aside with a successful DC 20
Strength check.

> A long, gray marble slab lies in the center of this
> chamber. Scattered around it are the skeletal remains
> of an elf. An inset in the ceiling above the slab holds a
> mirror the same size as the slab.

A *detect magic* spell reveals the mirror on the
ceiling radiates an aura of necromancy. If the characters return Cithcillion's bones to the slab, the reflection in the mirror is of him as he was in life. His
reflected image opens its eyes and speaks:

> "I am Cithcillion of Silvanost. I came here with two
> dear friends, Madar and Tenadria. Do you know
> what's become of them?"

Cithcillion is aware he's dead, but he has no idea what became of his companions. The characters may realize the other tombs (areas S7 and S9) belong to Madar and Tenadria.

Cithcillion's Quandary. If the characters tell Cithcillion that Madar and Tenadria are also dead, his sadness is evident, and he requests the characters bring his friends' remains to his tomb so they can be reunited in death. He doesn't speak further or answer questions until the characters have done as he asks.

When Madar's and Tenadria's remains are brought to his tomb, Cithcillion is willing to talk with the characters, answering questions forthrightly. He doesn't know anything about the dungeons in which he is interred, the Cataclysm, the state of the City of Lost Names, or how much time has passed. He shares the following information with the characters:

- Cithcillion was a Silvanesti elf who, like many in Krynn, had grown concerned with the kingpriest's increasingly arrogant behavior.
- When rumors spread of the kingpriest desecrating a dragon burial ground, Cithcillion was sent as the Silvanesti ambassador to Onyari with his friends Madar and Tenadria. They hoped to persuade the kingpriest to return the bones to their proper resting place.
- They brought with them a gift, the *mirror of reflected pasts* (see appendix A). An elven relic used to help long-lived peoples recall happier times, the mirror was intended to help the kingpriest reflect on simpler expressions of faith and hopefully deter him from dramatic affronts to the gods.
- Their diplomatic visit ended with Cithcillion and his friends imprisoned and dying in the temple.
- Cithcillion doesn't know what happened to the mirror, but it's likely still in the temple somewhere.

If the characters use the *speak with dead* spell on Cithcillion's skull instead of using the mirror, he gives truthful answers about the above information.

S9: TENADRIA'S TOMB
The doorway to this tomb opens to area S6, as its statue was moved before the characters arrived.

> A long, gray marble slab lies in the middle of this chamber, and atop it lies a Humanoid skeleton. A shallow inset of similar dimensions is carved into the ceiling directly above the slab. Shards of broken glass litter the slab and floor.

Close inspection of the floor reveals the shards of glass are pieces of a shattered mirror. The skeleton on the slab belongs to Tenadria, an elf diplomat and one of Cithcillion's companions. Tenadria responds uncooperatively to the *speak with dead* spell.

Alstare Bellis. The neutral evil **vampire** and former high priest of Chemosh, Alstare Bellis, hides just above the entrance to the tomb in bat form. A character who succeeds on a DC 18 Wisdom (Perception) check notices the bat. If Alstare isn't detected, he waits for the characters to enter the tomb and drops behind them, changing into his Humanoid form and blocking the exit.

Alstare doesn't immediately attack the characters but instead questions them. If it becomes clear they're enemies of the Red Dragon Army, he offers a deal. In exchange for the characters destroying the draconians on the floor above—especially their gold-scaled leader (Drayan in area S12)—Alstare will reward the party with "treasures untold." Once the characters return to him with evidence they've completed this task, Alstare tells them how to access the treasure vault (area S13) using the statue in area S12.

If the characters agree to help Alstare, he also immediately shares how the altar in area S4 functions.

If refused or attacked, Alstare flees, then harasses the characters with hit-and-run tactics, seeking to make them his vampire spawn. This tomb is Alstare's resting place.

Alstare's Amulet. Alstare wears a medallion around his neck in the shape of a goat's skull, which he offers to loan to a character who wishes to use Chemosh's altar. A cleric of Chemosh or a character who succeeds on a DC 14 Intelligence (Religion) check recognizes this as a holy symbol of Chemosh, god of undeath.

PRIESTS' QUARTERS

The priests' quarters (depicted on map 7.2) are where many of the temple's faithful spent their lives. The Temple of All Evil's officiants and servants practiced their worship here, separate from the public spaces above. Now the draconians work feverishly to uncover its secrets while Lord Soth looks on through his Undead servants.

S10: CORRIDORS
The corridors on this level are guarded by two **skeletal knights** (see appendix B). The knights guard the door to the sanctuary (area S12), and they notice anyone using the southeast stairs to area S3.

S11: RUBBLE AND RUIN
Rubble chokes the southern half of this room where the wall and ceiling have collapsed. A character who examines the room and succeeds on a DC 12 Wisdom (Survival) check notices a set of bootprints from a Small Humanoid going north to south. At

the midpoint of the room, the Humanoid tracks stop and a set of rat tracks begin, leading directly into the rubble.

Exploration. Though the ruined area to the south has mostly collapsed, cramped passages allow space for a Medium or smaller creature to squeeze through to Lorry's lair.

Lorry's Lair. Past the rubble is a ruined chamber lit by black candles surrounding an open stone coffin. The body of a female kender lies in the coffin, her features placid and her hands folded over her heart.

Lorry Wanwillow (chaotic evil, kender **vampire**; her Shapechanger trait allows her to become a rat instead of a bat) rests in the coffin. The Humanoid and rat tracks in the room to the north were both hers. She appears dead, feigning as much until the characters draw near, at which point she tries to scare them by sitting up. Amused with herself, she then addresses the characters:

> "So, who are you then? Not hobgoblins or draconians. Not ghosts or ghoulies either. Oh, I know—you must be trespassers! That's fun."

Lorry has spent the last several days in rat form, surveilling the citadel's new residents. She'll happily parley with the characters as she's been unimaginably bored.

Lorry chatters at length and eventually provides the following information, only some of which is useful:

- Lorry came to the City of Lost Names about two hundred years ago, searching for treasure. Alstare Bellis caught her and turned her into a vampire. Fifty years later he bricked her up in the chamber, though she has no idea why (it's because she's a chatterbox).
- Lorry recently escaped her prison when the temple rising broke apart the bricks sealing her crypt.
- Alstare is a jerk, but he knows a lot about the temple. He's afraid of the black rose knight.
- A ghost named Caradoc is lurking around—it seems like he's up to no good. Lorry is thinking about destroying him and putting in for his job.
- Most of the dragon-people spend their time above ground, but some of the higher-ups have been spending time in the sanctuary (area S12).

Treasure. Lorry's backpack is tucked in the corner of the room. Among her possessions are a *potion of gaseous form*, a *ring of spell storing* with a *seeming* spell (save DC 16) stored in it, and a ventriloquist's dummy with a sharp widow's peak and a red satin cape. Lorry turns hostile if the characters try to take these items without her permission.

S12: SANCTUARY

> Crumbled frescoes lie along the walls of this dilapidated sanctuary. A twenty-foot-tall statue of the Dragon Queen dominates the west end of the room, with smaller statues arrayed behind it.

This chamber's vaulted ceiling is 50 feet high. Obsidian columns outline the walls, though a portion of the south wall has partially caved in, collapsing two of the columns. At the center of the room stands a statue of Takhisis in her five-headed form. Statues of the evil gods Chemosh, Hiddukel, Morgion, Nuitari, Sargonnas, and Zeboim (detailed in the introduction) form a semicircle behind Takhisis's statue. A character who is a cleric of a depicted deity or who succeeds on a successful DC 12 Intelligence (Religion) check recognizes the deity's statue.

Creatures. The **aurak draconian** Drayan supervises six **bozak draconians** (see appendix B for both stat blocks) in this room. The bozaks are busy dismantling the statues of the gods behind the effigy of Takhisis. If a fight ensues and the draconians are losing, Drayan uses the *dimension door* spell to flee to area S18, where she prepares to ambush the characters.

LORRY WANWILLOW

Statue. If the characters examine the statue of Takhisis, they notice depressions spaced along its base and a plaque reading, "Yield to Her Will." A character who inspects the depressions and succeeds on a DC 14 Intelligence (Investigation) check realizes they serve as handles to rotate the statue.

Though the statue is designed to move, it's still immensely heavy. It can be rotated to a new position by a character who succeeds on a DC 22 Strength check or by creatures with a combined Strength of 40 or higher.

If the statue is rotated to face north, the secret door to area S14 opens. If the statue is rotated to face south, the secret door to area S13 opens. If it is rotated to face any other direction, the statue's heads animate and breathe flame. Each creature in the chamber must make a DC 16 Dexterity saving throw, taking 35 (10d6) fire damage on a failed save, or half as much damage on a successful one. Once the statue has breathed flame, it rotates back to face east.

Secret Doors. There are secret doors in the north and south walls. A character can find one by searching that area and succeeding on a DC 16 Intelligence (Investigation) check, but there's no clear way of opening either door until the statue is moved.

S13: Treasure Vault

> Coins and other valuables lie strewn about this partially collapsed chamber. Among them is a sizable mirror with an intact pane of black glass.

This is the temple's treasure vault, where offerings and the recovered goods of enemies were kept.

Treasure. Though some of this room has crumbled, the characters can easily retrieve 5,200 gp worth of coins and valuable pieces of art, as well as a *potion of gaseous form*, two *potions of healing* (superior), a *+1 greatsword*, and the *mirror of reflected pasts* (see appendix A).

S14: Primordial Altar

> Within a cave of dark stone stands a gleaming altar of black obsidian polished to a mirror shine. Where the light strikes it, bands of color glimmer within the altar: blue, green, white, and red.

This chamber holds a primordial altar to Takhisis, a weakening in the fabric of the planes where the Dragon Queen's will bleeds into Krynn. The chamber is desecrated ground that grants Undead, Fiends, and worshipers of Takhisis advantage on attack rolls.

Altar. The first character who touches the primordial altar is stunned until the start of their next turn. During that time, their mind fills with terrifying visions of Takhisis's draconic heads shrieking in triumph, the Dragon Armies marching across the face of Ansalon, and a dark temple rising from broken ground. The character gains the charm Dragon Queen's Will (a type of supernatural gift detailed in the *Dungeon Master's Guide*; see below).

Creatures. As soon a creature touches the altar, three **wraiths** emerge and attack.

Dragon Queen's Will
Supernatural Gift (Charm)

You've seen a glimpse of the Dragon Queen's ambitions. It haunts your dreams but steels your will to oppose her. This charm grants you a +4 bonus on Will saving throws. Once used three times, the charm vanishes.

While you have this charm, you suffer unsettling but harmless dreams of ravenous dragons. You also permanently gain the ability to speak Draconic if you couldn't already.

S15: Draconian Garrison

> Simple bunk beds and equipment racks fill this room. A few tables are littered with the remains of past meals.

This garrison is occupied by four **bozak draconians** and three **kapak draconians** (see appendix B for both stat blocks).

S16: Study

> An old desk sits in this study. One of its legs is missing and has been propped up with chunks of rubble. Doors lead from this room to the west, north, and east.

The top drawer of the desk contains Dragon Army reports on troops and supplies on the surface of the flying island, as well as a *spell scroll* of *arcane eye*.

S17: Library

> Ancient shelves have collapsed into heaps along the walls. Old books with deteriorated bindings spill their pages onto the dusty floor.

The books here are rotted and worthless, but a character who spends five minutes searching the library finds a *spell scroll* of *polymorph*.

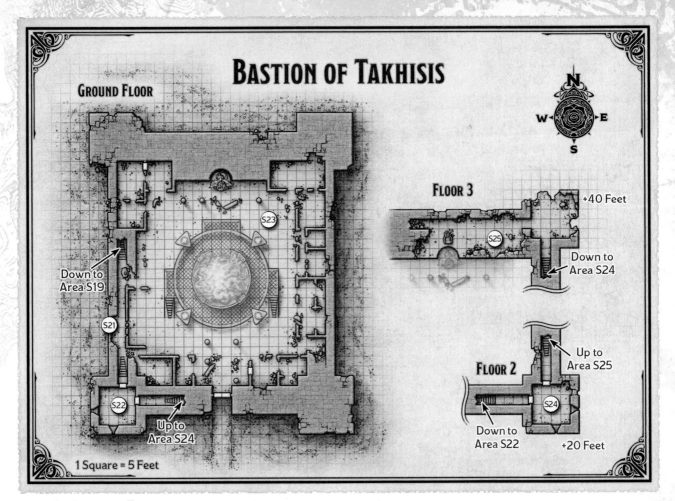

S18: Draconian War Room

> This chamber holds a large table, which is covered by a roughly drawn map of Nightlund along with several other documents and scraps of paper.

Six **sivak draconians** (see appendix B) are here reviewing the battle plan for the assault on Kalaman. On the table in front of them are rough sketches of Kalaman's leadership, including Marshal Vendri, Darrett, and the characters themselves. One of the sivaks has a key to the cells in area S19.

If Drayan was encountered in area S12 and escaped, she is here when the characters arrive. If so, only four sivak draconians are with her. Drayan has readied an action to use her Noxious Breath as soon as she sees a character in range, and the sivaks have readied actions to use their Multiattack.

S19: Cells

These bare stone cells once quartered the temple's priests. They are currently empty.

S20: Storeroom

> This room is piled with bits of rubble, pottery, a pair of broken stone gargoyles, a painting of a sunset over a city skyline, and a bronze bust of a dignified man wearing a hat with an excessive number of feathers.

Lord Soth's servants use this room to store junk. Most of it has no value, but the bust is of Istarian origin and is worth 1,000 gp to a collector. Characters might recall seeing hats of similar style to the one the man is wearing in the City of Lost Names.

Bastion of Takhisis

The City of Lost Names was built on a foundation of pillaged dragon bones, which gave it much of its magic. The Bastion of Takhisis (depicted on map 7.3) now carries that magic's legacy, empowered by the Mourning Flame that burns in the Mourning Sanctum at the temple's heart.

S21: Ruined Hall

When the characters enter this area, read or paraphrase the following:

> From the top of the stairs, a shattered corridor runs to the south. The ancient walls to the west and east are made of crumbling stone, and flickering violet light shines through gaps in the east wall.
>
> At the south end of the hall, another stairway rises into one of the ruin's corner towers. An unfamiliar soldier in Kalaman's armor stands there. With a look of mild surprise, she notices you. "Oh. You," she says. "You could be helpful. Come on." With that, she turns and heads up the far stairs.

This hall connects the stairs leading to areas S19 and S22.

Crumbled Wall. The east wall here is weak and riddled with cracks. The Mourning Sanctum (area S23) is visible to creatures that look through these cracks. A 10-foot section of this wall is a Large object with AC 17, 60 hit points, and immunity to poison and psychic damage. If destroyed, the wall topples, providing access to area S23 and alerting creatures in that area to the characters' presence.

Soldier. The soldier is a **veteran** wearing the armor of a Kalaman soldier—but she's possessed by **Caradoc** (detailed in chapter 4; stat block in appendix B). When she notices the characters, she withdraws up the stairs to area S22.

S22: Nuitari's Shrine

> This dilapidated room was clearly once a shrine, and its walls are covered in carvings of robed figures gathered beneath a large black moon. Recesses with lit black candles and melted wax cover the walls at even intervals. Simple doors lead to the north and east.

A cleric of Nuitari or a character who succeeds on a DC 12 Intelligence (Religion) recognizes the moon in the wall carvings represents the god Nuitari.

Caradoc. The soldier the characters encountered in area S21 withdraws here. This is **Caradoc** (see appendix B) possessing the body of a **veteran** in Kalaman armor. Caradoc is eager to speak with the characters and enlist them in a plot to betray Lord Soth and steal the flying citadel for himself. He doesn't try to disguise his identity despite the new body he's claimed. Use the following points to guide the conversation:

- Caradoc believes Soth's alliance with the Dragon Army is folly, distracting him from taking revenge against the Knights of Solamnia.
- Caradoc wants to take control of the flying citadel. He promises to leave Kalaman if the characters help him do so.

- Soth is higher up in the ruins (area S25), where he controls the flying citadel using a throne linked to the Cataclysmic fire holding the citadel aloft.
- Soth is fantastically powerful. Caradoc urges the characters to find a way to distract him or otherwise undermine him without fighting.
- Wersten Kern, Soth's standard bearer, guards the brazier containing the Cataclysmic fire. She's loyal to Soth and will have to be disposed of as well.

Caradoc's plans are doomed to failure, as the *flying citadel helm* in area S25 can be used only by a spellcaster. (Later, when Caradoc realizes he can't attune to it, he goes into a rage and attacks the characters.) If the characters don't ally with Caradoc, he sends them on their way, then attempts to ambush them the next time they're vulnerable—likely in area S25.

Regardless of how Caradoc interacts with the characters, use his warnings to reinforce the danger of engaging Lord Soth in outright combat.

Captive Soldier. If the soldier Caradoc is possessing drops to 0 hit points, allow her to make death saving throws, as the characters may wish to heal her. Her name is Amelia Ghallen (neutral good, human **veteran**). She remembers being captured during a battle with the Red Dragon Army and taken alongside other prisoners to a terrifying castle in the mountains. She helps the characters defeat Caradoc if the spirit is present, but she wants nothing more than to return home to Kalaman.

S23: Mourning Sanctum

> The interior of this mighty temple has been hollowed out, its roof and interior walls reduced to rubble, creating one great chamber. At the north of the ruins stands a menacing statue of the Dragon Queen with her five snarling draconic heads. Above the statue, deteriorating stone reveals a shadowy chamber in the wall forty feet up.
>
> At the chamber's center, a massive brazier—easily ten feet tall and thirty feet across—roils with violet flames. A crude iron scaffold surrounds it, with uneven stairs climbing to a platform surrounding the lip of the brazier. Four supports crowned by blazing violet flames levitate around the scaffold, holding it aloft. A figure in blackened armor stands atop the scaffold, bearing a pike fluttering with tattered cloth.

This is the heart of the flying citadel. The magic of the Cataclysmic fire here holds the citadel aloft—and it is also the forge from which death dragons emerge. The gates at the south of the room lead from the temple to the surface of the flying island, but they're sealed shut.

WERSTEN KERN LOYALLY
SERVES LORD SOTH
AND STANDS GUARD OVER
THE MOURNING SANCTUM.

Wersten Kern. The figure atop the scaffold is **Wersten Kern** (see appendix B), an Undead former Knight of Solamnia who is now Lord Soth's standard bearer. When she notices a character, she salutes them and demands they either submit and join the service of her master, Lord Soth, or face her in honorable, one-on-one combat. Regardless of their response, she begins battle by using her Terrifying Litany action. Kern fights to the death and prioritizes attacking foes that seek to damage the room's brazier or scaffold.

Lord Soth. If the characters didn't already paralyze **Lord Soth** (see appendix B) with the *mirror of reflected pasts* in area S25, he arrives 3 rounds after the battle with Kern begins and immediately attacks. See area S25 for more details.

Brazier. Cataclysmic fire fills the room's giant brazier. A creature that falls into it takes 70 (20d6) necrotic damage. The brazier's flames can be extinguished by bathing a holy relic of a good-aligned god in the flames, such as a *dragonlance*. If the players don't think of this on their own, have the characters make a DC 14 Intelligence (Religion) or Wisdom (Insight) check. On a successful check, a character recalls Leedara said the power of the gods could quell the flames, and they remember the *dragonlance* bears Paladine's power. Extinguishing the flames destroys the brazier, as detailed below.

Scaffold. The scaffold surrounding the brazier rises 10 feet off the ground. Stairs to the west and east climb to its top. Four floating supports with depressions holding Cataclysmic fire support the scaffold and the brazier. These supports are Large objects with AC 18, 40 hit points, and immunity to poison and psychic damage. If all four supports are destroyed, the scaffold and brazier topple as detailed below.

Destroying the Brazier. If either the Cataclysmic fire in the brazier is extinguished or the supports holding aloft the scaffolding are destroyed, the brazier topples and the magical flame within goes out. Proceed with "The Citadel's Destruction" below.

S24: Sargonnas's Shrine

A hulking minotaur is carved in bas-relief on this shrine's west wall. Scorch marks cover the floors and walls. Doors lead to the north and west.

Two **skeletal knights** (see appendix B) stand guard in this room.

A cleric of Sargonnas or a character who succeeds on a DC 12 Intelligence (Religion) check recognizes the images on the walls represent the god Sargonnas.

CAROLINE GARIBA

LORD SOTH GLIMPSES HIS PAST BETRAYALS IN THE *MIRROR OF REFLECTED PASTS*.

S25: LORD SOTH'S THRONE ROOM

Read or paraphrase the following text when the characters enter this room:

> Sections of this chamber's walls have fallen, revealing both the open interior of the temple and the dark clouds surrounding the flying island beyond. Overlooking the violet flame at the temple's heart below, this chamber holds a crude throne made of broken marble. Veins of pulsing violet light—the same shade as the flames below—pulse through the stone. A still figure in charred armor sits on the throne, glowing red eyes staring from his closed, crown-like helm. His charred breastplate bears a black rose emblem.

The throne is the *flying citadel helm* (see appendix A) that controls the movement of the flying island. It draws its power from the brazier in area S23. If the brazier there is destroyed, the helm ceases to function.

The floor of area S23 is 40 feet below the ledge bearing the throne. The entirety of that area is visible from here.

Lord Soth. Unless the characters already encountered him in area S23, **Lord Soth** (see appendix B) is seated on the throne. Soth is fixated on controlling the movement of the flying citadel and ignores the characters until they address him. Soth is a terrifying figure, and his armored corpse crackles with cinders. Once confronted, he speaks little, preferring concise threats like "Submit" or "Die." If possible, he begins combat using his Cataclysmic Fire action against a group of characters.

Distracting Lord Soth. If confronted with the *mirror of reflected pasts* (see appendix A), Lord Soth fails all saving throws to resist its effects. He whispers the name "Isolde" before staring into the mirror, transfixed. So long as Lord Soth can see the mirror, he is paralyzed for 1 hour or until he takes damage. If damaged while paralyzed by the mirror, Lord Soth can make saving throws against the mirror's effects as normal.

THE CITADEL'S DESTRUCTION

If the characters destroy the brazier in area S23, read the following text:

> With a cacophony of whispered sighs, the violet flames vanish. You feel the flying island beneath you lurch to a stop. Everything is silent for a moment, then with the sound of a distant crack, the ground begins to shudder. A split runs through the floor and up a nearby wall. The citadel is breaking apart!

ZOLTAN BOROS

With the brazier's destruction, the magic holding the flying citadel aloft ends. This disengages the *flying citadel helm* in area S25 and destroys all the lesser death dragons allied with the Red Dragon Army, reducing them to inanimate bones.

Any other threats the characters are contending with remain, but the characters have succeeded in their primary mission. Now they must escape the shattering citadel. There's no set time limit for how long the characters have until the flying citadel crashes, but don't let the players know this. Use the following scenes to encourage characters to flee the citadel as swiftly as possible.

SOTH'S END

The characters witness Lord Soth consumed by disaster. If he is in area S23 or S25, the ground opens beneath the death knight and he falls into darkness. He doesn't appear again in this adventure, and it will take exceptional coercion for Soth to ally with the Dragon Armies in the future.

ESCAPE ROUTES

Allow the characters to decide how they're going to escape the citadel. If they race through the temple's underground levels, they encounter falling rocks as the structure shakes apart (see "Scenes of Destruction"). Alternatively, widening cracks in the temple walls allow the characters to quickly leave the bastion and flee to the flying island's edge (see below). The area outside is depicted on map 7.4 and features the following areas outside the Bastion of Takhisis:

Cataclysmic Smoke. Violet vapor drifts from the temple, leaving the area it fills heavily obscured.
Dragon Army Camps. Dozens of Dragon Army troops panic amid rows of tents and dragonnel landing strips.
Plaza. This raised, 10-foot-high plaza provides a vantage of the surrounding chaos. Stairs descend to the south.
Ruins. Ruined Istarian buildings lie scattered across the area.

The hundreds of Dragon Army troops outside the citadel are largely too preoccupied with their own escape to pay the characters any attention.

Whatever their path, before the characters manage to escape, highlight the flying citadel's deconstruction with events from the "Scenes of Destruction" section, then proceed with the "Karavarix's Revenge" section.

SCENES OF DESTRUCTION

Emphasize the destruction of the flying citadel and the effects of the extinguished Cataclysmic flames using any of the following events you wish:

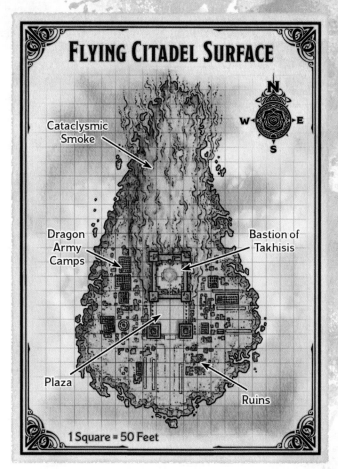

MAP 7.4: FLYING CITADEL SURFACE

Death Dragon Destruction. A **lesser death dragon** (see appendix B) lands near the characters. The violet flames animating it fade, and the creature collapses into a pile of inanimate bones. Elsewhere, the characters can see other death dragons falling, their flames extinguished as well.
Falling Rocks. Part of the temple collapses. Each character must succeed on a DC 14 Dexterity saving throw or take 27 (6d8) bludgeoning damage.
Hungry Crevice. Six **baaz draconians** (see appendix B) rush toward the characters through a crack opening in the temple walls. A 10-foot-wide fissure in the ground opens up, swallowing the draconians in darkness.

KARAVARIX'S REVENGE

Before the characters escape, they're confronted by Karavarix, the first and most powerful of the death dragons. Read or paraphrase the following text:

> An animate dragon skeleton larger than any other you've seen bursts through the crumbling ground, its body still blazing with violet flames.

Karavarix is a chaotic evil **greater death dragon** (see appendix B) who hasn't been affected by the destruction of the brazier in the Mourning Sanctum (area S23). In life, she was the gold dragon Sarlamir slew during his quest to the flying city of Onyari—and Karavarix still seeks revenge. Before she attacks, she roars, "Sarlamir! I won't be driven from the skies again. I'll have my revenge on you and all humans!" Characters who explored the catacombs beneath Castle Kalaman (detailed in chapter 4) recall the name Sarlamir, the dragon he slew, and the statue in his tomb with gold dragon features. Karavarix then fights until destroyed.

Escaping the Bastion

The citadel is 300 feet in the air. Before it crashes, the characters can escape it using the following options or any other approach they please:

Magic. The easiest way off the Bastion of Takhisis is magic, such as the *feather fall* or *fly* spell.

Narycrash. If the characters obtained extra narycrashes earlier in the adventure, these devices can be used to escape.

Enemy Dragonnels. Although most Dragon Army dragonnels have abandoned the citadel, a few remain trapped in stables across the plaza. If the characters free them, the dragonnels help them escape to the battlefield below.

KARAVARIX

Clystran's Dragonnels. If the characters can find no other way off the flying citadel, Clystran and his dragonnel friends arrive just in time to airlift the characters to the battlefield below.

Dragon Army Rout

The destruction of the citadel is a great blow to the Red Dragon Army's morale. Its forces are shaken, but Highmaster Kansaldi Fire-Eyes seeks to wrest revenge from the jaws of defeat.

The Sky Is Falling

When the characters safely reach the ground, read the following text:

> Above the field west of Kalaman, the Bastion of Takhisis crumbles. As the flying citadel tilts precariously, massive boulders fall to the earth, taking Dragon Army troops with them. Below, the Dragon Army scatters to avoid the rain of devastation, but the flying citadel's ruins crush its forces in droves.

The characters land a quarter mile from Kalaman's west wall. There is little risk of the flying citadel crashing on the characters, but fallen rocks and the bones of death dragons litter the field. Draconians with half their hit points flee the flying citadel, making hard landings on the battlefield. These and other foes scatter, fleeing the battlefield in every direction and ignoring the characters.

Clash of Fallen Flames

When the characters start their return to Kalaman, read the following text:

> A streak of red sweeps low over the battlefield, crashing through dozens of retreating enemies. At the last moment, it sweeps upward and a mighty red dragon perches atop a stone spire fallen from the citadel above. On the dragon's back sits a woman with short white hair and Dragon Army armor. She levels a vicious pike at you as her left eye—a crimson gemstone—smolders with magical flame.

This is **Kansaldi Fire-Eyes** (see appendix B) and her red dragon ally, Ignia. Ignia uses the **young red dragon** stat block but is Huge. Kansaldi spotted the characters fleeing the flying citadel and now seeks revenge. She's a fanatical follower of the Dragon Queen and vents righteous rage on the characters, including the following topics:

OLIVIER BERNARD

DRAGON HIGHMASTER KANSALDI
FIRE-EYES SCOURS THE BATTLEFIELD
ASTRIDE THE RED DRAGON IGNIA.

- The Dragon Queen's victory is inevitable. Half of Ansalon already bows to Takhisis.
- The characters might've delayed Kalaman's fall, but Kansaldi's troops are a mere fraction of the Dragon Armies' forces. Her master, Dragon Highlord Verminaard, will return with greater numbers.
- Agents from the Blue Dragon Army are gathering other floating pieces of the City of Lost Names. One way or another, the Dragon Armies will conquer the skies.
- Kansaldi will show the characters mercy for their audacity—if one character submits to her, she will spare the others. The one who submits must agree to be burned to death by Ignia for all to see.
- If any among the characters wish to join the Red Dragon Army, they're free to prove their allegiance to her.

Kansaldi and Ignia attack if her demands are ignored or rebuffed. This battlefield is represented on map 7.5. See the following sections for details on this battlefield's features.

Kansaldi and Ignia start atop the spire, 30 feet above the characters. The characters begin amid the citadel rubble at the south of the map. Both foes use ranged attacks to keep the characters at bay. They engage in melee combat only if a creature reaches them atop the spire or if they're outmatched in ranged combat. Both fight to the death.

Even as she dies, Kansaldi whispers to the characters that her death is the sacrifice Takhisis wants and that victory is now assured.

Treasure. Kansaldi's gold-embossed half helmet is worth 3,000 gp, and a crimson *gem of seeing* is embedded in her left eye socket. The gem can be removed only if Kansaldi is dead. When used, the gem grows uncomfortably warm to the touch.

If Kansaldi is dead, this *gem of seeing* becomes a sentient magic item of lawful evil alignment with an Intelligence of 16, a Wisdom of 19, and a Charisma of 15. It has hearing and normal vision in a range of 120 feet. The gem can speak and understand Common and Draconic, and it can communicate telepathically with its wielder. It promises its bearer the Dragon Queen's favor if they replace one of their eyes with the gem.

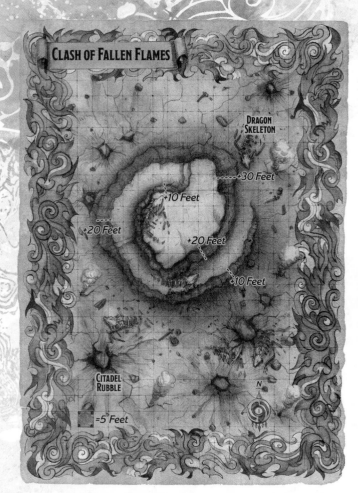

MAP 7.5: CLASH OF FALLEN FLAMES

CLASH OF FALLEN FLAMES FEATURES

The battlefield includes the following features:

Citadel Spire. A 30-foot-tall stone shard dominates the center of the battlefield. A cliff winds up its side, making it possible to walk from the ground to the top. There are ample handholds in the rock, making it easy to climb.

WARRIORS OF KRYNN: SCENARIO 12

As the characters near the gates of Kalaman, a contingent of the city's defenders emerges to clear the remaining Dragon Army forces from the field. Run scenario 12 from *Dragonlance: Warriors of Krynn* to represent this final conflict.

If the characters attain a win or hold during this scenario, Darrett approaches the characters and gives them something he found amid the rubble of the flying citadel. If there is a good cleric or paladin among the characters, this item is a *talisman of pure good* in the shape of their god's holy symbol. If there's not, it's an ancient *+3 shield* bearing Solamnic knotwork designs and the symbol of Paladine. Characters gain no reward for a loss.

At the end of the scenario, proceed with "Kalaman Victorious."

Citadel Rubble and Dragon Skeletons. The squares with fallen rubble or bones of dead dragons are difficult terrain.

Fray. The 15-foot-wide area marked by the design at the edge of the map represents dozens of Dragon Army troops trying to retreat. This area and the battlefield beyond the map are difficult terrain. A creature that starts its turn in the Fray or that enters the Fray for the first time during a turn must succeed on a DC 16 Dexterity saving throw or take 10 (3d6) slashing damage from attacks by opportunistic foes.

CLASH OF FALLEN FLAMES EVENTS

During this encounter, on initiative count 0 each round, roll on the Clash of Fallen Flames Events table. The encounter ends when both Kansaldi and Ignia are defeated.

CLASH OF FALLEN FLAMES EVENTS

d8	Event
1–3	Fragments of flying citadel rain down. Each creature must succeed on a DC 15 Dexterity saving throw or take 22 (4d10) bludgeoning damage.
4–5	A **bozak draconian** (see appendix B) with 10 hit points falls from above and crashes toward a random player character. The character must succeed on a DC 16 Dexterity saving throw or take 11 (2d10) bludgeoning damage. The draconian is stunned for a round, then attacks.
6	A siege engine explodes nearby. Its remains crash in a 20-foot-radius centered on a random player character. Each creature in that area must either use its reaction to move up to half its speed to escape the area or take 11 (2d10) fire damage.
7	Low-flying dragonnels flee across the battlefield. Creatures on the spire or otherwise above ground level must succeed on a DC 14 Strength saving throw or be knocked prone.
8	A random player character notices the clouds above the battlefield momentarily look like five hateful draconic heads. The character must succeed on a DC 16 Wisdom saving throw or have disadvantage on attack rolls and ability checks for 1 round. If the character is wearing the holy symbol of a good-aligned god, it glimmers and the character gains inspiration instead. This event happens only once. No event occurs if you roll it again.

AFTERMATH OF THE SIEGE

When Kansaldi is defeated, the Red Dragon Army breaks completely, retreating southeast toward the Taman Busuk.

The adventure unfolds in one of two ways from here:

With Mass Combat. If you are using the *Dragonlance: Warriors of Krynn* game along with this adventure, consult the "Warriors of Krynn: Scenario 12" sidebar.

Without Mass Combat. If you aren't using the *Dragonlance: Warriors of Krynn* game, continue with the following section.

KALAMAN VICTORIOUS

With the defeat of the Red Dragon Army, the characters return to a heroes' welcome in Kalaman. Their allies, including Darrett and Marshal Vendri, are among the first to express their awe and thanks on behalf of the entire city. Truly, Kalaman wouldn't have survived were it not for the characters' daring. The city spends the rest of the day repairing the city's fortifications and honoring those who died in the city's defense, but the night is filled with celebration and song.

AN UNCERTAIN FUTURE

Celebrations and enthusiasm fill Kalaman for days after the Dragon Army's defeat, and its people begin to make hopeful plans for the future. Here are the plans of just a few of the characters' allies:

Clystran. Clystran has seen more than enough of the city and is eager to return to Heart's Hollow with his dragonnels. He invites the characters to visit the next time they're in the Northern Wastes.

Darrett. With the danger of the Dragon Armies past for the moment, Darrett plans to travel to the city of Maelgoth, where he hopes to become a true member of the Knights of Solamnia.

Marshal Vendri. Ever pragmatic, Marshal Vendri is wary the Dragon Army might soon return, and she seeks ways to reinforce the city's defenses. She also plans to send agents to Maelgoth and Palanthas to court the Knights of Solamnia and the country's other great cities to aid in Kalaman's defense.

Raven and Vogler's Villagers. With Kalaman's support, Raven is leading an initial foray to Vogler. She hopes to see what can be salvaged and to plan the village's restoration. Raven is committed to hosting a fantastic Kingfisher Festival in the village next year.

Rookledust and Than. The gnomes learned they work well together, and with such radically different fields of interest, they're fascinated by the prospect of collaborating in the future. They plan to return to Rookledust's workshop and begin work on new inventions.

Use these plans to wrap up the stories of these characters or to foreshadow future adventures.

HEROES' CELEBRATION

A week after the siege of Kalaman, the city hosts a great ceremony in the courtyard of Castle Kalaman to celebrate the characters and all who perished in defense of the city.

Heroes alive and dead are honored with medals and speeches. Governor Thren and Marshal Vendri personally thank the characters. Before all assembled, Vendri pronounces the characters' commitment to the Kalaman military honorably discharged; they've completed the terms of their involvement with Kalaman's defenders (as set forward in chapter 4). Characters who accept this honorable discharge are rewarded with platinum medallions bearing the symbol of Kalaman worth 2,500 gp. Characters who choose to remain a part of Kalaman's army receive the same medallion and are granted a new title: Knight of Kalaman. The responsibilities of this position and future assignments are for you to determine.

Additionally, if the characters participated in battles using the *Dragonlance: Warriors of Krynn* game, dole out the campaign rewards from that game as part of this celebration.

MYSTERIOUS MESSAGE

After the characters have received their rewards, a Kalaman soldier delivers a message for them, which was left with a guard at Castle Kalaman's gate. The letter is sealed with blue wax bearing the Dragon Queen's symbol and reads as follows:

> Congratulations, heroes of Kalaman. I toast your bravery and daring. I could use audacious souls, such as yourselves, and will be watching your exploits with interest. Your city has escaped the Dragon Queen's grasp today, but none can defy her will for long. I hope that when first we meet, it won't be among Kalaman's ruins.

The message bears no signature, but the seal is the symbol of the Dragon Queen impressed upon blue wax, suggesting an agent of the Blue Dragon Army.

The adventure ends here. Use this message to foreshadow future conflicts in the War of the Lance or to continue your adventures in Krynn.

GEAR AND MAGIC ITEMS

This appendix describes new equipment, magic items, and tinker gnome siege weapons that appear in the adventure.

ADVENTURING GEAR

This section describes items and weapons that have special rules or require further explanation. The following items are presented in alphabetical order.

FARGAB

These backpack-sized devices are created in pairs, with matching numbers engraved on them, and allow communication over a long distance using radio frequencies. While wearing a fargab, you can use an action to speak into the device's mouthpiece and send a short message of twenty-five words or less to another creature wearing the matched fargab while it is within 18 miles of you. The message emits from the speakers of the device and can be heard up to 10 feet away from the device. If no creature is wearing the fargab, the speakers make static noises instead.

HOOPAK

Martial Melee Weapon

Cost: 1 gp
Damage: 1d6 piercing (melee) or 1d4 bludgeoning (ranged)
Weight: 2 lb.
Properties: Ammunition (range 40/160), finesse, special, two-handed

A hoopak is a sturdy stick with a sling at one end and a pointed tip at the other.

Special. When you make a melee attack with this weapon, you ignore its ammunition property. You can use the hoopak as a martial ranged weapon. If you do, it uses the ammunition property, uses sling bullets, and deals 1d4 bludgeoning damage on a hit.

NARYCRASH

This backpack-sized device holds a balloon-based parachute. If you fall while wearing this device, you can use your reaction to deploy the parachute. Once deployed, the parachute rapidly inflates, and you descend 60 feet per round and take no damage from falling. When you are 10 feet away from the ground, roll a d20. If you roll a 5 or less, the parachute gives out, and you begin to fall normally.

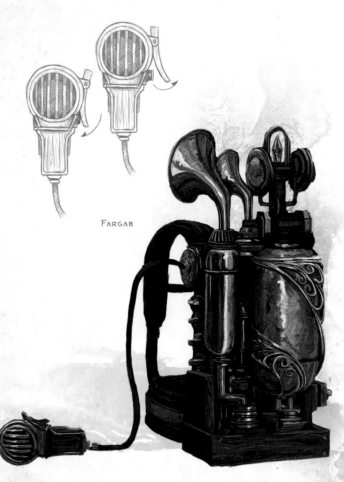

FARGAB

NARYCRASH

KENT DAVIS

BOILERDRAK

GNOME SIEGE WEAPONS

This section presents two siege weapons designed by tinker gnomes.

BOILERDRAK
Large Object

Armor Class: 15
Hit Points: 100
Damage Immunities: poison, psychic

This wagon-sized device is designed to look roughly like a dragon. Before it can be used, the boilerdrak must be lit and aimed. It takes 1 action to light the weapon, 1 action to aim it, and 1 action to fire it. When you use your action to fire it, roll a d20. If you roll a 2 or higher, use the Flames action. If you roll a 1, use the Explosion action.

Flames. The boilerdrak expels flames in a 60-foot cone. Each creature in that area must make a DC 15 Dexterity saving throw, taking 27 (5d10) fire damage on a failed save, or half as much damage on a successful one.

Explosion. The boilerdrak explodes in a 30-foot-radius sphere and is destroyed. Each creature in that area must make a DC 15 Dexterity saving throw, taking 27 (5d10) fire damage on a failed save, or half as much damage on a successful one.

GNOMEFLINGER
Large Object

Armor Class: 15
Hit Points: 100
Damage Immunities: poison, psychic

The gnomeflinger is a catapult designed to hurl creatures, instead of projectiles, in a high arc. The gnomeflinger was designed in conjunction with the narycrash (see the "Adventuring Gear" section) to hasten transportation. The device can hold one Medium or smaller creature. Before it can be used, the gnomeflinger must be loaded and aimed. It takes 1 action to load the gnomeflinger, 1 action to aim it, and 1 action to fire it.

While taking an action to aim the gnomeflinger, you set the maximum horizontal distance of the Fling Personnel action to 60 feet, 150 feet, or 300 feet.

Fling Personnel. The gnomeflinger catapults a Medium or smaller creature at least 60 feet away horizontally, with a maximum horizontal distance of 60 feet, 150 feet, or 300 feet, depending on the option chosen when the catapult was aimed. During this trajectory, the creature always reaches a height of 60 feet vertically.

A creature that collides with another creature or an object during this trajectory takes 3 (1d6) bludgeoning damage for every 10 feet away from the gnomeflinger it is.

MAGIC ITEMS

The following items are presented in alphabetical order.

DRAGONLANCE
Weapon (Lance or Pike), Legendary (Requires Attunement)

A *dragonlance* is a renowned weapon forged from rare metal with the aid of powerful artifacts. On Krynn, its creation is associated with the god Paladine and legendary heroes who fought against the evil of the Dragon Queen. Different lances are forged for use by foot soldiers (as pikes) and by riders (as lances), but the magical properties of the weapons are the same.

You gain a +3 bonus to attack and damage rolls made with this magic weapon.

When you hit a Dragon with this weapon, the Dragon takes an extra 3d6 force damage, and any Dragon of your choice that you can see within 30 feet of you can immediately use its reaction to make a melee attack.

FLYING CITADEL HELM
Wondrous Item, Very Rare (Requires Attunement by a Spellcaster)

The function of this ornate chair is to propel and maneuver a flying citadel on which it has been installed. The chair has AC 15, 18 hit points, and immunity to poison and psychic damage. It is destroyed if reduced to 0 hit points.

The sensation of being attuned to a flying citadel helm is akin to the pins-and-needles effect one experiences after one's arm or leg falls asleep, but not as intense.

While attuned to a *flying citadel helm* and sitting in it, you gain the following abilities for as long as you maintain concentration (as if concentrating on a spell):

- You can use the *flying citadel helm* to move the citadel through the air, up to 80 feet per round, or up to 8 miles per hour.
- You can steer the citadel, albeit in a somewhat clumsy fashion, in much the way that a rudder or oars can be used to maneuver a seafaring ship.
- At any time, you can see and hear from the highest point outside the citadel as though you were at that location.

If no creature attuned to the helm is maintaining concentration, the citadel remains motionless in its space.

Transfer Attunement. You can use an action or a bonus action to touch a willing spellcaster, whereupon that creature attunes to the *flying citadel helm* immediately, and your attunement to the *flying citadel helm* ends.

Crash. Should the *flying citadel helm* be destroyed, the citadel it is installed on loses power and begins to crumble. If the crumbling citadel is in the air, it descends at a rate of 30 feet per round, or 300 feet per minute. Any creature on the citadel or on the ground within 120 feet of the citadel when it lands must make a DC 20 Dexterity saving throw, taking 39 (6d12) bludgeoning damage on a failed save, or half as much damage on a successful one.

KAGONESTI FOREST SHROUD
Wondrous Item, Rare (Requires Attunement)

This cloak appears to be made of autumnal leaves woven together. While you wear this cloak, you have advantage on Dexterity (Stealth) checks, and you can use a bonus action to magically teleport, along with any equipment you are wearing or carrying, to an unoccupied space you can see within 30 feet of yourself. You then have advantage on the next attack roll you make before the end of the turn. Once this bonus action is used, it can't be used again until the next dawn.

KAGONESTI FOREST SHROUD

MIRROR OF REFLECTED PASTS
Wondrous Item, Very Rare (Requires Attunement)

This mirror of elven design allows those who stare into it to reflect on positive memories. The 3-foot-tall mirror weighs 25 pounds, and it has AC 11, 10 hit points, and vulnerability to bludgeoning damage. It shatters and is destroyed if reduced to 0 hit points.

While holding the mirror upright, you can use an action to speak its command word and activate it. While activated, the mirror hovers in the air, and it can be destroyed but not moved. It remains activated until you use an action to speak the command word again or your attunement to the mirror ends, at which point the mirror harmlessly floats to the ground. Once the mirror has been deactivated, it can't be activated again until the next dawn.

If a non-Construct creature other than you sees its reflection in the activated mirror while within 30 feet of it, that creature must succeed on a DC 15 Wisdom saving throw or become paralyzed until the mirror is deactivated or until that creature can no longer see the mirror. A creature paralyzed by the mirror can repeat the saving throw at the end of each of its turns, ending the effect on a success. If a creature's saving throw is successful or the effect ends for it, the creature is immune to this mirror's effect for the next 24 hours.

While paralyzed by the mirror, the creature sees events from their past reflected in the mirror's glass. These memories aren't real, but rather idealized versions of those occurrences. Nearby observers can glimpse flashes of these memories if looking indirectly at the mirror.

FRIENDS AND FOES

This appendix describes creatures that appear in the adventure, presenting them in alphabetical order. The introduction of the *Monster Manual* explains how to read a creature's stat block.

The creatures in this appendix are categorized by creature type below.

CONSTRUCT

Istarian drone

DRAGON

Dragon Army dragonnel
Wasteland dragonnel

HUMANOID

Dragon Army officer
Dragon Army solider
Kalaman soldier
Kansaldi Fire-Eyes
Kender skirmisher
Lohezet
Red Ruin

MONSTROSITY

Aurak draconian
Baaz draconian
Bozak draconian
Kapak draconian
Sivak draconian

UNDEAD

Anhkolox
Caradoc
Greater death dragon
Lesser death dragon
Lord Soth
Skeletal knight
Wersten Kern

RANDOM ENCOUNTERS

Red Dragon Army forces threaten the characters and the lands surrounding Kalaman throughout the adventure. Roll on the Dragon Army Encounters table whenever characters might run into a random group of creatures allied with the Dragon Army. Creatures marked with an asterisk appear in this appendix.

DRAGON ARMY ENCOUNTERS

d100	Encounter
1–5	1d6 **Dragon Army soldiers***
6–11	1d6 **baaz draconians***
12–16	1 **Dragon Army dragonnel*** and 1 **Dragon Army officer***
17–20	1d6 **Dragon Army soldiers*** battling 2d4 **kender skirmishers***
21–26	2d6 **hobgoblins** and their fewmaster (commander), 1 **hobgoblin captain**
27–32	1d6 **Dragon Army soldiers*** and 1 **Dragon Army officer***
33–38	1d4 **baaz draconians*** and 1 **bozak draconian***
39–45	2d4 **Dragon Army soldiers*** battling 2d6 **Kalaman soldiers***
46–50	1d6 **baaz draconians*** and 1 **Dragon Army officer***
51–55	2d4 **Dragon Army soldiers*** with 2d4 **mastiffs** hunting an escaped prisoner
56–60	1d6 **kapak draconians*** disguised as travelers
61–65	1 **priest** of Takhisis seeking to convert a group of 2d6 **commoners** to the Dragon Queen's worship
66–71	1d4 flying **sivak draconians***
72–76	1d4 **sivak draconians*** using their Shape Theft reaction to take the form of kender travelers
77–80	1 **aurak draconian*** and 1d6 **Dragon Army soldiers***
81–84	1d4 **skeletal knights*** on warhorses
85–89	1 **aurak draconian*** using *disguise self* to look like the captive of 2 **sivak draconians***
90–93	1d6 **sivak draconians*** transporting a captive, a **priest** of a non-evil god
94–99	1d6 **skeletal knights*** led by Caradoc,* who's using his Possession action to control a **noble**
00	1 **Dragon Army officer*** and 1 **young red dragon**

BAAZ DRACONIAN

ANHKOLOX

Anhkoloxes are vicious undead creatures created from the bones of bears and other beasts. Their barbed bones grind and crack, often moving in seemingly impossible ways. Anhkoloxes are driven by territorial instinct and a predatory urge to hunt and devour living prey. They run on all fours and rear up onto their hind legs when they corner their quarry. When they strike, they wallop foes about with their claws—they delight in knocking foes into pits full of jagged bones—and their barbed rib cage cracks open like a hunting trap to snap closed around a victim.

ANHKOLOX

Huge Undead, Typically Neutral Evil

Armor Class 15 (natural armor)
Hit Points 157 (15d12 + 60)
Speed 50 ft.

STR	DEX	CON	INT	WIS	CHA
22 (+6)	11 (+0)	18 (+4)	4 (–3)	14 (+2)	2 (–4)

Saving Throws Wis +6
Skills Perception +6
Damage Immunities poison
Condition Immunities charmed, exhaustion, frightened, poisoned
Senses darkvision 60 ft., passive Perception 16
Languages —
Challenge 9 (5,000 XP)   **Proficiency Bonus** +4

Unusual Nature. The anhkolox doesn't require air, food, drink, or sleep.

ACTIONS

Multiattack. The anhkolox makes two Claw attacks and one Entrapping Rend attack.

Claw. *Melee Weapon Attack:* +10 to hit, reach 5 ft., one target. *Hit:* 17 (2d10 + 6) piercing damage. If the target is a Large or smaller creature, it must succeed on a DC 18 Strength saving throw or be pushed up to 20 feet in a horizontal direction of the anhkolox's choice.

Entrapping Rend. *Melee Weapon Attack:* +10 to hit, reach 5 ft., one target. *Hit:* 23 (5d6 + 6) piercing damage, and if the target is a Large or smaller creature, the target must succeed on a DC 18 Strength saving throw or be trapped in the anhkolox's rib cage and grappled (escape DC 18). Until this grapple ends, the target is restrained, and the anhkolox can't use Entrapping Rend on another target.

CARADOC

Seneschal of Lord Soth and a former Knight of Solamnia, Caradoc burned when Dargaard Keep was consumed in the fires of the Cataclysm. As with many of Soth's retainers, Caradoc was cursed with undeath. Being duplicitous and cowardly at his core, the seneschal didn't return as a skeletal knight but rather as an intangible spirit. Caradoc's Undead form suits him well, allowing him to possess the living and use unwilling tongues to spread his lies. However, Caradoc is tethered to his scorched bones, which collect dust in Dargaard Keep. He can leave the accursed castle while possessing the body of a Humanoid, but he's swiftly pulled back if caught beyond its walls without a host.

Caradoc the Spirit

Caradoc the Knight

Caradoc the Soldier

CARADOC

Medium Undead, Neutral Evil

Armor Class 14
Hit Points 110 (20d8 + 20)
Speed 0 ft., fly 40 ft. (hover)

STR	DEX	CON	INT	WIS	CHA
1 (–5)	18 (+4)	12 (+1)	15 (+2)	13 (+1)	19 (+4)

Saving Throws Int +5, Wis +4
Skills Deception +7, Insight +4, Perception +4
Damage Resistances acid, fire, lightning, thunder; bludgeoning, piercing, and slashing from nonmagical attacks
Damage Immunities cold, necrotic, poison
Condition Immunities charmed, exhaustion, frightened, grappled, paralyzed, petrified, poisoned, prone, restrained
Senses darkvision 60 ft., passive Perception 14
Languages Common, Solamnic
Challenge 8 (3,900 XP)   **Proficiency Bonus** +3

Bound Haunting. Caradoc's spirit is bound to Dargaard Keep. At the start of his turn, if he's outside the keep's walls and not possessing a creature using his Possession action, he must succeed on a DC 15 Charisma saving throw or vanish and reappear in an unoccupied space within the keep.

Incorporeal Movement. Caradoc can move through other creatures and objects as if they were difficult terrain. He takes 5 (1d10) force damage if he ends his turn inside an object.

Rejuvenation. If Caradoc dies, he reforms within Dargaard Keep in 2d6 days.

Unusual Nature. Caradoc doesn't require air, food, drink, or sleep.

ACTIONS

Multiattack. Caradoc makes two Withering Touch attacks.

Withering Touch. *Melee Weapon Attack:* +7 to hit, reach 5 ft., one target. *Hit:* 15 (2d10 + 4) necrotic damage.

Possession (Recharge 5–6). One Humanoid that Caradoc can see within 5 feet of himself must succeed on a DC 15 Charisma saving throw or be possessed by him; he then disappears, and the target is incapacitated and loses control of its body. Caradoc now controls the body but doesn't deprive the target of awareness. Caradoc can't be targeted by any attack, spell, or other effect, except ones that turn Undead, and he retains his alignment, Intelligence, Wisdom, and Charisma, immunity to being charmed and frightened, and his Divisive Whispers bonus action. He otherwise uses the possessed target's statistics but doesn't gain access to the target's knowledge, class features, or proficiencies.

The possession lasts until the body drops to 0 hit points, Caradoc ends it as a bonus action, or he is turned or forced out by an effect like the *dispel evil and good* spell. When the possession ends, Caradoc reappears in an unoccupied space within 5 feet of the body. The target is immune to Caradoc's Possession for 24 hours after succeeding on the saving throw or after the possession ends.

BONUS ACTIONS

Divisive Whispers. Caradoc magically whispers to one creature within 60 feet of himself. The target must succeed on a DC 15 Wisdom saving throw, or the target must immediately use its reaction to make a melee attack against another creature of Caradoc's choice (wasting its reaction if there are no other creatures within reach).

NIKKI DAWES

Lesser
Death Dragon

DEATH DRAGONS

Death dragons are the Undead skeletal remains of metallic or chromatic dragons, infused with the lingering fires of the Cataclysm by foul magic. Rarely, death dragons arise when a dragon meets its end in a way that torments its soul and consumes it with a need for vengeance. Regardless of how it arose, a death dragon retains a shadow of its former personality. The stronger the death dragon, the more it fights the hate consuming it, holding on to some vestige of its memories.

A death dragon's bones burn with violet Cataclysmic fire, which it can unleash in a horrific mockery of the breath weapon it possessed in life. The breath snuffs out life force and infuses undeath into corpses it touches. These zombies burn with Cataclysmic fire and serve the death dragon's will, typically going on rampages to destroy all living creatures in sight.

GREATER DEATH DRAGON

Some death dragons manage to retain almost all of their former selves, albeit twisted by their state of being. These greater death dragons scheme to achieve their ends, all the while amassing and jealously guarding treasure hoards as they did in life. In battle, they are deadly foes, channeling the Cataclysmic fire that limns their bones and fuels their breath. They take cruel delight in snatching foes in their jaws, rushing into the air, then dropping the snared creatures to their doom.

LESSER DEATH DRAGON

Most death dragons are pale imitations of their former selves. They remember flashes and echoes, and sometimes things or creatures they encounter painfully remind them of what they once had. These fleeting moments of lucidity quickly burn away in rage and anguish, driving the dragons to destroy the would-be memento.

GREATER DEATH DRAGON

Huge Undead, Typically Chaotic Evil

Armor Class 16 (natural armor)
Hit Points 230 (20d12 + 100)
Speed 40 ft., fly 80 ft.

STR	DEX	CON	INT	WIS	CHA
23 (+6)	10 (+0)	20 (+5)	11 (+0)	14 (+2)	10 (+0)

Saving Throws Dex +5, Wis +7
Skills Perception +7, Stealth +5
Damage Resistances piercing
Damage Immunities necrotic, poison
Condition Immunities exhaustion, poisoned
Senses blindsight 60 ft., darkvision 120 ft.,
  passive Perception 17
Languages Common, Draconic
Challenge 14 (11,500 XP)   **Proficiency Bonus** +5

Legendary Resistance (3/Day). If the dragon fails a saving throw, it can choose to succeed instead.

Unusual Nature. The dragon doesn't require air, food, drink, or sleep.

ACTIONS

Multiattack. The dragon makes one Bite attack and two Claw attacks.

Bite. *Melee Weapon Attack:* +11 to hit, reach 10 ft., one target. *Hit:* 17 (2d10 + 6) piercing damage plus 4 (1d8) necrotic damage. If the target is a Large or smaller creature, it is grappled (escape DC 19). Until this grapple ends, the target is restrained, and the dragon can't bite a different target.

Claw. *Melee Weapon Attack:* +11 to hit, reach 5 ft. one target. *Hit:* 10 (1d8 + 6) slashing damage.

Cataclysmic Breath (Recharge 5–6). The dragon exhales a wave of ghostly purple flames in a 60-foot cone. Each creature in that area must make a DC 18 Dexterity saving throw, taking 45 (10d8) necrotic damage on a failed save, or half as much damage on a successful one. A creature dies if the breath reduces it to 0 hit points. Additionally, any Medium or smaller Humanoid killed by the breath's damage, as well as every corpse of such a creature within the cone, becomes a **zombie** under the dragon's control. The zombie acts on the dragon's initiative but immediately after the dragon's turn. Absent any other command, the zombie tries to kill any non-Undead creature it encounters.

LEGENDARY ACTIONS

The dragon can take 3 legendary actions, choosing from the options below. Only one legendary action can be used at a time and only at the end of another creature's turn. The dragon regains spent legendary actions at the start of its turn.

Claw. The dragon makes one Claw attack.

Cataclysmic Rush (Costs 2 Actions). The dragon moves up to half its flying speed without provoking opportunity attacks, carrying with it any creatures it is grappling. During this move, if it enters the space of a Medium or smaller creature, that creature takes 4 (1d8) necrotic damage. A creature can take this damage only once per turn.

LESSER DEATH
DRAGON PROFILE

LESSER DEATH DRAGON

Large Undead, Typically Chaotic Evil

Armor Class 15 (natural armor)
Hit Points 199 (21d10 + 84)
Speed 40 ft., fly 80 ft.

STR	DEX	CON	INT	WIS	CHA
20 (+5)	10 (+0)	18 (+4)	5 (−3)	10 (+0)	5 (−3)

Saving Throws Dex +4, Wis +4
Skills Perception +4, Stealth +4
Damage Resistances piercing
Damage Immunities necrotic, poison
Condition Immunities exhaustion, poisoned
Senses blindsight 30 ft., darkvision 60 ft., passive Perception 14
Languages understands Common and Draconic but can't speak
Challenge 10 (5,900 XP)   **Proficiency Bonus** +4

Unusual Nature. The dragon doesn't require air, food, drink, or sleep.

ACTIONS

Multiattack. The dragon makes one Bite attack and two Claw attacks.

Bite. *Melee Weapon Attack:* +9 to hit, reach 10 ft., one target. *Hit:* 14 (2d8 + 5) piercing damage plus 4 (1d8) necrotic damage.

Claw. *Melee Weapon Attack:* +9 to hit, reach 5 ft. one target. *Hit:* 8 (1d6 + 5) slashing damage. If the target is a Medium or smaller creature, it is grappled (escape DC 15). Until this grapple ends, the target is restrained. The dragon has two claws, each of which can grapple one target.

Cataclysmic Breath (Recharge 5–6). The dragon exhales a wave of ghostly purple flames in a 30-foot cone. Each creature in that area must make a DC 16 Dexterity saving throw, taking 36 (8d8) necrotic damage on a failed save, or half as much damage on a successful one. A creature dies if the breath reduces it to 0 hit points. Additionally, any Medium or smaller Humanoid killed by the breath's damage, as well as every corpse of such a creatures within the cone, becomes a **zombie** under the dragon's control. The zombie acts on the dragon's initiative but immediately after the dragon's turn. Absent any other command, the zombie tries to kill any non-Undead creature it encounters.

DRACONIANS

Draconians are bipedal monsters born from metallic dragon eggs that have been corrupted by a combination of warped alchemy and the Dragon Queen's foul magic. The Dragon Armies closely guard the secret of the draconians' creation, allowing Krynn's metallic dragons to continue to think their eggs are being held hostage so they don't oppose the Dragon Queen's conquests.

AURAK DRACONIAN

Created from the eggs of gold dragons, aurak draconians are the most powerful of draconians, their entire being thrumming with eldritch power. Unlike other draconians, auraks are wingless. This might lull foes into a false sense of security, until the auraks exhale noxious fumes resembling those of their dragon progenitors. Auraks are masterminds and strategists that serve as commanders in the Dragon Armies. They often lead contingents of less powerful draconians. When slain, aurak draconians unleash their inherent magic in a deadly burst of lightning.

AURAK DRACONIAN

AURAK DRACONIAN

Medium Monstrosity (Sorcerer), Typically Lawful Evil

Armor Class 17 (natural armor)
Hit Points 67 (9d8 + 27)
Speed 35 ft.

STR	DEX	CON	INT	WIS	CHA
13 (+1)	14 (+2)	16 (+3)	16 (+3)	11 (+0)	17 (+3)

Saving Throws Int +6, Wis +3, Cha +6
Skills Perception +3
Condition Immunities charmed
Senses truesight 60 ft., passive Perception 13
Languages Common, Draconic
Challenge 6 (2,300 XP)   **Proficiency Bonus** +3

Aura of Command. The draconian radiates a commanding presence in a 20-foot-radius sphere centered on itself. A draconian in the aura that can see or hear the aurak can't be charmed and has advantage on saving throws made to avoid or end the frightened condition on itself.

Death Throes. When the draconian is reduced to 0 hit points, its magical essence lashes out as a ball of lightning at the closest creature within 30 feet of it before arcing out to up to two other creatures within 15 feet of the first. Each creature must make a DC 14 Dexterity saving throw. On a failed save, the creature takes 9 (2d8) lightning damage and is stunned until the end of its next turn. On a successful save, the creature takes half as much damage and isn't stunned.

ACTIONS

Multiattack. The draconian makes three Rend or Energy Ray attacks.

Rend. *Melee Weapon Attack:* +5 to hit, reach 5 ft., one target. *Hit:* 8 (1d12 + 2) slashing damage.

Energy Ray. *Ranged Spell Attack:* +6 to hit, range 60 ft., one target. *Hit:* 8 (1d10 + 3) force damage.

Noxious Breath (Recharge 5–6). The draconian exhales a 15-foot cone of noxious gas. Each creature in that area must make a DC 14 Constitution saving throw. On a failed save, the creature takes 21 (6d6) poison damage and gains 1 level of exhaustion. On a successful save, the creature takes half as much damage, doesn't gain exhaustion, and is immune to all draconians' Noxious Breath for 24 hours.

Spellcasting. The draconian casts one of the following spells, requiring no material components and using Charisma as the spellcasting ability (spell save DC 14):

At will: *invisibility, mage hand*
2/day each: *dimension door, disguise self, sending*
1/day: *dominate person*

Draconian Sizes to Scale
(Left to Right): Baaz, Bozak, Kapak, Sivak, Aurak, Human

Baaz Draconian

Baaz draconians are fanatical foot soldiers that emerge from the eggs of brass dragons. They are the smallest of the draconians, and their slight wings are incapable of flight, though they do afford the draconians some control when falling. These wings are small enough to be hidden beneath a cloak or robe, and baaz draconians disguise themselves to spy for the Dragon Armies. The sight of dragons drives baaz draconians into a deadly furor. When baaz draconians die, their bodies turn to stone and unleash clouds of petrifying gas that turn their corpses and any nearby creatures into stone.

Bozak Draconian

Bozak draconians are born from bronze dragon eggs and wield magic to aid their allies in battle. Their wings aren't strong enough for full flight, but bozaks can use them to glide during a fall. When bozaks die, their flesh shrivels away before their bones explode, sending a shower of magical splinters in all directions.

Kapak Draconian

Kapak draconians are created using copper dragon eggs. These cunning opponents relish striking foes who are distracted or unaware. Kapaks often coat their weapons with their paralytic saliva, making them formidable assassins as well. Their small wings don't allow kapaks to fly, but they do help the draconians turn a fall into a rough glide. When they die, kapaks dissolve into acid that can splash onto nearby creatures.

BAAZ DRACONIAN
Medium Monstrosity, Typically Lawful Evil

Armor Class 14 (natural armor)
Hit Points 22 (4d8 + 4)
Speed 30 ft.

STR	DEX	CON	INT	WIS	CHA
13 (+1)	11 (+0)	13 (+1)	8 (−1)	8 (−1)	10 (+0)

Senses darkvision 60 ft., passive Perception 9
Languages Common, Draconic
Challenge 1/2 (100 XP) **Proficiency Bonus** +2

Controlled Fall. When the draconian falls and isn't incapacitated, it subtracts up to 100 feet from the fall when calculating the fall's damage.

Death Throes. When the draconian is reduced to 0 hit points, its body turns to stone and releases a petrifying gas. Each creature within 5 feet of the draconian must succeed on a DC 11 Constitution saving throw or be restrained as it begins to turn to stone. The restrained creature must repeat the saving throw at the end of its next turn. On a success, the effect ends; otherwise the creature is petrified for 1 minute. After 1 minute, the body of the draconian crumbles to dust.

Draconic Devotion. While the draconian can see a Dragon that isn't hostile to it, the draconian has advantage on attack rolls.

ACTIONS

Multiattack. The draconian makes two Shortsword attacks.

Shortsword. *Melee Weapon Attack:* +3 to hit, reach 5 ft., one target. *Hit:* 4 (1d6 + 1) piercing damage.

CHRIS RAHN

BOZAK DRACONIAN

Medium Monstrosity (Sorcerer), Typically Lawful Evil

Armor Class 15 (natural armor)
Hit Points 40 (9d8)
Speed 30 ft.

STR	DEX	CON	INT	WIS	CHA
14 (+2)	10 (+0)	11 (+0)	11 (+0)	10 (+0)	14 (+2)

Saving Throws Int +2, Wis +2, Cha +4
Senses darkvision 60 ft., passive Perception 10
Languages Common, Draconic
Challenge 2 (450 XP)   **Proficiency Bonus** +2

Death Throes. When the draconian is reduced to 0 hit points, its scales and flesh immediately shrivel away, and then its bones explode. Each creature within 10 feet of it must succeed on a DC 10 Dexterity saving throw or take 9 (2d8) force damage.

Glide. When the draconian falls and isn't incapacitated, it subtracts up to 100 feet from the fall when calculating the fall's damage, and it can move up to 2 feet horizontally for every 1 foot it descends.

ACTIONS

Multiattack. The draconian makes two Trident melee attacks or two Lightning Discharge attacks.

Trident. *Melee or Ranged Weapon Attack:* +4 to hit, reach 5 ft. or range 20/60 ft., one target. *Hit:* 5 (1d6 + 2) piercing damage, or 6 (1d8 + 2) piercing damage if used with two hands to make a melee attack.

Lightning Discharge. *Ranged Spell Attack:* +4 to hit, range 60 ft., one target. *Hit:* 10 (3d6) lightning damage.

Spellcasting. The draconian casts one of the following spells, requiring no material components and using Charisma as the spellcasting ability (spell save DC 12):

1/day each: *enlarge/reduce, invisibility, stinking cloud, web*

KAPAK DRACONIAN

Medium Monstrosity, Typically Lawful Evil

Armor Class 15 (natural armor)
Hit Points 39 (6d8 + 12)
Speed 40 ft., climb 40 ft.

STR	DEX	CON	INT	WIS	CHA
11 (+0)	17 (+3)	14 (+2)	12 (+1)	13 (+1)	11 (+0)

Saving Throws Dex +5
Skills Deception +4, Perception +3, Stealth +7
Damage Immunities poison
Condition Immunities poisoned
Senses darkvision 60 ft., passive Perception 13
Languages Common, Draconic
Challenge 3 (700 XP)   **Proficiency Bonus** +2

Death Throes. When the draconian is reduced to 0 hit points, it dissolves into acid that splashes on those around it. Each creature within 5 feet of the draconian must succeed on a DC 12 Dexterity saving throw or be covered in acid for 1 minute. A creature covered in the acid takes 7 (2d6) acid damage at the start of each of its turns. A creature can use its action to scrape or wash the acid off itself or another creature.

Glide. When the draconian falls and isn't incapacitated, it subtracts up to 100 feet from the fall when calculating the fall's damage, and it can move up to 2 feet horizontally for every 1 foot it descends.

ACTIONS

Multiattack. The draconian makes two Dagger attacks. If both attacks hit the same creature, the target must succeed on a DC 12 Constitution saving throw or become poisoned until the end of the target's next turn. While poisoned in this way, the target is also paralyzed.

Dagger. *Melee or Ranged Weapon Attack:* +5 to hit, reach 5 ft. or range 20/60 ft., one target. *Hit:* 5 (1d4 + 3) piercing damage plus 7 (2d6) poison damage.

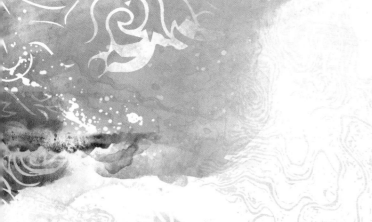

Sivak Draconian

Sivak Draconian
Large Monstrosity, Typically Lawful Evil

Armor Class 16 (natural armor)
Hit Points 57 (6d10 + 24)
Speed 30 ft., fly 60 ft.

STR	DEX	CON	INT	WIS	CHA
18 (+4)	10 (+0)	18 (+4)	13 (+1)	10 (+0)	10 (+0)

Saving Throws Str +6, Wis +2
Senses darkvision 60 ft., passive Perception 10
Languages Common, Draconic
Challenge 4 (1,100 XP)   **Proficiency Bonus** +2

Death Throes. When the draconian is reduced to 0 hit points by a creature that is Large or smaller, the draconian crumbles into dust that then forms a spectral, shrieking image of the creature that killed it. The image lasts for 1 minute. Each creature hostile to the draconian within 10 feet of the image must succeed on a DC 14 Wisdom saving throw or be frightened of the spectral image for 1 minute. A frightened creature can repeat the saving throw at the end of each of its turns, ending the effect on itself on a success.

Actions

Multiattack. The draconian makes two Serrated Sword attacks and one Tail attack.

Serrated Sword. *Melee Weapon Attack:* +6 to hit, reach 5 ft., one target. *Hit:* 13 (2d8 + 4) slashing damage.

Tail. *Melee Weapon Attack:* +6 to hit, reach 5 ft., one target. *Hit:* 8 (1d8 + 4) bludgeoning damage. If the target is a Large or smaller creature, it must succeed on a DC 14 Strength saving throw or be knocked prone.

Reactions

Shape Theft. After the draconian kills a Medium or smaller Humanoid, the draconian magically cloaks itself in an illusion to look and feel like that creature while retaining the draconian's game statistics (other than its size). This transformation lasts until the draconian dies or uses a bonus action to end it.

ROBSON MICHEL

Sivak Draconian

Sivak draconians are fearsome brutes created from the eggs of silver dragons. They fly on mighty wings over battlefields wherever the fighting is the fiercest, making them effective shock troops. Sivaks can magically change their features to mimic the appearance of those they've slain. This allows these cunning soldiers to sow confusion and despair among their enemies. When sivaks are killed, they mimic the form of their killers, shrieking in horrific agony before they crumble to dust.

DRAGON ARMY TROOPS

The Dragon Armies gather fanatical followers to their ranks. Recruits are indoctrinated to revere the Dragon Queen and view dragons as her favored servants. Troops in the Dragon Army wield weapons blessed by Takhisis to strike with the power of the dragons they fight alongside.

DRAGON ARMY WEAPONS

The weapons of Dragon Army troops are blessed with an infusion of dragon breath. The type of damage these weapons deal depends on the specific army. The stat blocks presented here represent Red Dragon Army troops with weapons infused by the fire of red dragons. You can represent followers of other chromatic dragons by changing the fire damage to match the damage type associated with those dragons' breath weapons.

DRAGON ARMY SOLDIER

DRAGON ARMY OFFICER

Medium Humanoid, Typically Lawful Evil

Armor Class 19 (splint, shield)
Hit Points 65 (10d8 + 20)
Speed 30 ft.

STR	DEX	CON	INT	WIS	CHA
16 (+3)	14 (+2)	15 (+2)	12 (+1)	14 (+2)	12 (+1)

Saving Throws Dex +4, Wis +4
Skills Athletics +5, Perception +4
Senses passive Perception 14
Languages Common, Draconic
Challenge 3 (700 XP) **Proficiency Bonus** +2

Draconic Devotion. While the officer can see a Dragon that isn't hostile to it, the officer has advantage on attack rolls.

ACTIONS

Multiattack. The officer makes two Vicious Lance attacks and uses Assault Orders if it's available.

Vicious Lance. *Melee Weapon Attack:* +5 to hit, reach 10 ft., one target. *Hit:* 8 (1d10 + 3) piercing damage plus 2 (1d4) fire damage.

Heavy Crossbow. *Ranged Weapon Attack:* +4 to hit, range 100/400 ft., one target. *Hit:* 7 (1d10 + 2) piercing damage plus 5 (1d10) fire damage.

Assault Orders (Recharge 5–6). The officer shouts orders and targets up to two other creatures within 60 feet of itself. If a target has the Draconic Devotion trait and can hear the officer, the target can use its reaction to make one melee attack.

DRAGON ARMY SOLDIER

Medium Humanoid, Typically Lawful Evil

Armor Class 17 (scale mail, shield)
Hit Points 22 (4d8 + 4)
Speed 30 ft.

STR	DEX	CON	INT	WIS	CHA
15 (+2)	12 (+1)	12 (+1)	10 (+0)	10 (+0)	10 (+0)

Skills Athletics +4, Perception +2
Senses passive Perception 12
Languages Common, Draconic
Challenge 1 (200 XP) **Proficiency Bonus** +2

Draconic Devotion. While the soldier can see a Dragon that isn't hostile to it, the soldier has advantage on attack rolls.

ACTIONS

Multiattack. The soldier makes two Longsword or Javelin attacks.

Longsword. *Melee Weapon Attack:* +4 to hit, reach 5 ft., one target. *Hit:* 6 (1d8 + 2) slashing damage, or 7 (1d10 + 2) slashing damage if used with two hands, plus 2 (1d4) fire damage.

Javelin. *Melee or Ranged Weapon Attack:* +4 to hit, reach 5 ft. or range 30/120 ft., one target. *Hit:* 5 (1d6 + 2) piercing damage plus 2 (1d4) fire damage.

ANDREW MAR

DRAGONNELS

Dragonnels are distantly related to chromatic and metallic dragons and resemble them in basic form. Intelligent enough to understand speech but incapable of speaking themselves, they are willful creatures largely motivated by the desire for food.

DRAGON ARMY DRAGONNEL

Dragonnels from the volcanic mountains surrounding Sanction are closely related to red dragons, resembling them in scale coloration and general shape. They are cruel and selfish creatures trained by the Dragon Armies to serve as mounts for trusted officers. While they lack a red dragon's destructive breath, these dragonnels are inured to fire, and their vicious teeth and claws flare with embers.

WASTELAND DRAGONNEL

The Northern Wastes of Ansalon are home to wasteland dragonnels, draconic creatures closely related to copper dragons. Wasteland dragonnels are lithe and quick, with scales the color of dull copper. These playful creatures defend their territory by flying out of a foe's reach and spitting potent acid, in an approximation of their copper dragon relatives.

DRAGON ARMY DRAGONNEL

DRAGON ARMY DRAGONNEL

Large Dragon, Typically Lawful Evil

Armor Class 16 (breastplate barding)
Hit Points 58 (9d10 + 9)
Speed 30 ft., fly 60 ft.

STR	DEX	CON	INT	WIS	CHA
16 (+3)	15 (+2)	12 (+1)	8 (−1)	13 (+1)	10 (+0)

Skills Perception +3
Damage Resistances fire
Senses blindsight 30 ft., darkvision 120 ft., passive Perception 13
Languages understands Common and Draconic but can't speak
Challenge 3 (700 XP)   **Proficiency Bonus** +2

Flyby. The dragonnel doesn't provoke opportunity attacks when it flies out of an enemy's reach.

ACTIONS

Multiattack. The dragonnel makes two Rend attacks.

Rend. *Melee Weapon Attack:* +5 to hit, reach 5 ft., one target. *Hit:* 10 (2d6 + 3) slashing damage plus 3 (1d6) fire damage.

WASTELAND DRAGONNEL

Large Dragon, Typically Chaotic Good

Armor Class 13
Hit Points 65 (10d10 + 10)
Speed 30 ft., fly 60 ft.

STR	DEX	CON	INT	WIS	CHA
16 (+3)	16 (+3)	12 (+1)	8 (−1)	13 (+1)	10 (+0)

Skills Perception +3
Damage Resistances acid
Senses blindsight 30 ft., darkvision 120 ft., passive Perception 13
Languages understands Common and Draconic but can't speak
Challenge 3 (700 XP)   **Proficiency Bonus** +2

Flyby. The dragonnel doesn't provoke opportunity attacks when it flies out of an enemy's reach.

ACTIONS

Multiattack. The dragonnel makes two Rend attacks.

Rend. *Melee Weapon Attack:* +5 to hit, reach 5 ft., one target. *Hit:* 10 (2d6 + 3) slashing damage.

Acid Spit. *Ranged Weapon Attack:* +5 to hit, range 60 ft., one target. *Hit:* 20 (5d6 + 3) acid damage.

ISTARIAN DRONE

ISTARIAN DRONE

Istarian drones are ancient Constructs made of marble and gleaming metal inlaid with crystals that flash with sparks of electricity. Created to build the fantastic structures that once marked the glory of Istar, these drones resemble short, stout mantises. They have four scuttling insectile legs and barbed, scythe-shaped arms for carrying and placing building materials. The drones create a viscous gel that hardens into crystalline mortar, which they can repurpose to restrain attackers.

ISTARIAN DRONE
Medium Construct, Unaligned

Armor Class 17 (natural armor)
Hit Points 127 (15d8 + 60)
Speed 30 ft., climb 30 ft.

STR	DEX	CON	INT	WIS	CHA
20 (+5)	10 (+0)	18 (+4)	4 (−3)	10 (+0)	4 (−3)

Damage Immunities lightning, poison
Condition Immunities charmed, exhaustion, frightened, paralyzed, poisoned
Senses blindsight 60 ft. (blind beyond this radius), passive Perception 10
Languages understands the languages spoken by its creator but can't speak
Challenge 6 (2,300 XP)   **Proficiency Bonus** +3

Spider Climb. The drone can climb difficult surfaces, including upside down on ceilings, without needing to make an ability check.

Unusual Nature. The drone doesn't require air, food, drink, or sleep.

ACTIONS

Multiattack. The drone makes two Claw attacks.

Claw. *Melee Weapon Attack:* +8 to hit, reach 5 ft., one target. *Hit:* 9 (1d8 + 5) piercing damage plus 4 (1d8) lightning damage. If the target is a Medium or smaller creature, it is grappled (escape DC 15). The drone has two claws, each of which can grapple only one target.

Crystalline Spit (Recharge 5–6). The drone spits crackling gel in a line 5 feet wide and 20 feet long. Each creature in the line must make a DC 15 Dexterity saving throw. On a failed save, the creature takes 14 (4d6) lightning damage and is restrained by the gel, which hardens into crystal. The creature is restrained until the crystal is destroyed. The crystal has AC 15, 15 hit points, immunity to poison and psychic damage, and vulnerability to thunder damage. On a successful save, the creature takes half as much damage and isn't restrained.

KALAMAN SOLDIER

Kalaman soldiers are the rank-and-file troops of the army of Kalaman. They are trained to fight defensively, bolstering one another in battle.

KALAMAN SOLDIER
Medium or Small Humanoid, Any Alignment

Armor Class 18 (chain mail, shield)
Hit Points 16 (3d8 + 3)
Speed 30 ft.

STR	DEX	CON	INT	WIS	CHA
13 (+1)	12 (+1)	12 (+1)	10 (+0)	11 (+0)	10 (+0)

Skills Athletics +3, Perception +2
Senses passive Perception 12
Languages Common
Challenge 1/2 (100 XP)   **Proficiency Bonus** +2

ACTIONS

Multiattack. The soldier makes two Longsword attacks.

Longsword. *Melee Weapon Attack:* +3 to hit, reach 5 ft., one target. *Hit:* 6 (1d8 + 2) slashing damage, or 7 (1d10 + 2) slashing damage if used with two hands.

REACTIONS

Hold the Line. If an ally within 5 feet of the soldier must make a saving throw, the soldier encourages the ally, granting advantage on the roll.

MARK BEHM

KANSALDI FIRE-EYES

High Master Kansaldi Fire-Eyes leads the Red
Dragon Army's offensive in Solamnia. A fanatical
adherent of the Dragon Queen, Kansaldi was indoctrinated into the god's worship by Dragon High
Lord Verminaard. During a test of faith from her
mentor, Kansaldi replaced her left eye with a *gem
of seeing*. This gem smolders and glows red whenever Kansaldi uses her magic, and her followers
claim it allows her to see through any lie.

Highlord Verminaard follows visions from the
Dragon Queen on a campaign south. In his absence, he left a powerful contingent of the Red
Dragon Army under Kansaldi's command and
ordered her to claim the Kalaman region in the
Dragon Queen's name. Kansaldi pursues these
orders with a fanatic's zeal. For her, there is no
possibility of defeat—there is only the Dragon
Queen's will.

KANSALDI FIRE-EYES
Medium Humanoid (Human, Cleric), Lawful Evil

Armor Class 18 (plate)
Hit Points 172 (23d8 + 69)
Speed 30 ft.

STR	DEX	CON	INT	WIS	CHA
18 (+4)	11 (+0)	17 (+3)	16 (+3)	19 (+4)	16 (+3)

Saving Throws Wis +8, Cha +7
Skills Insight +12, Perception +8, Religion +7
Damage Immunities fire
Senses truesight 120 ft., passive Perception 18
Languages Abyssal, Common, Draconic
Challenge 11 (7,200 XP)   **Proficiency Bonus** +4

Special Equipment. Kansaldi has a glowing ruby embedded in
her left eye socket. The gem functions as her eye and grants her
truesight (included above). The gem can't be removed while
Kansaldi is alive. When she dies, a creature can remove the
gem as an action. The gem then functions as a *gem of seeing*.

ACTIONS

Multiattack. Kansaldi makes two Pike attacks and uses
Flame Burst.

Pike. *Melee Weapon Attack:* +8 to hit, reach 10 ft., one target. *Hit:* 9 (1d10 + 4) piercing damage plus 16 (3d10) radiant damage.

Flame Burst. Kansaldi hurls magical flames at a creature she
can see within 60 feet of herself. The target must make a DC
16 Dexterity saving throw. On a failed save, the target takes 11
(2d10) fire damage and catches fire; until a creature takes an
action to put out the fire, the target takes 5 (1d10) fire damage
at the start of each of its turns. On a successful save, the target
takes half as much damage and doesn't catch fire.

Spellcasting. Kansaldi casts one of the following spells, requiring no material components and using Wisdom as the spellcasting ability (spell save DC 16):

At will: *light, spare the dying, thaumaturgy*
1/day each: *blade barrier, dispel magic, flame strike, lesser restoration, revivify*

BONUS ACTIONS

Dragon Queen's Favor. Kansaldi or one creature she can
see within 60 feet of herself magically regains 17 (2d12 + 4)
hit points.

HOOPAK

KENDER
SKIRMISHER

KENDER SKIRMISHER

Kender skirmishers are fearless fighters who use stealth and wiliness to defend their friends and homes. They excel at disrupting their enemies by sabotaging crucial equipment or by taunting opponents into making rash decisions. They wield the signature kender weapon: the hoopak, a combination spear and sling staff.

KENDER TAUNTS

Roll on or choose an entry from the Kender Taunts table to determine how a kender skirmisher infuriates an opponent in battle.

KENDER TAUNTS

d4	Taunt
1	"Should I pretend to be scared? You seem like you really need this."
2	"I wish I could be like you and just not care how I look ... or smell ... or dress. So brave."
3	"Did the Cataclysm have a face? Because I think you might be twins!"
4	Energetically points at their foe with both hands and loudly repeats the word "bonk."

KENDER SKIRMISHER
Small Humanoid, Any Alignment

Armor Class 14 (leather armor)
Hit Points 14 (4d6)
Speed 30 ft.

STR	DEX	CON	INT	WIS	CHA
8 (−1)	16 (+3)	10 (+0)	12 (+1)	8 (−1)	14 (+2)

Skills Perception +3, Sleight of Hand +7, Stealth +5
Condition Immunities frightened
Senses passive Perception 13
Languages Common, Kenderspeak
Challenge 1/4 (50 XP)   **Proficiency Bonus** +2

ACTIONS

Hoopak. *Melee or Ranged Weapon Attack:* +5 to hit, reach 5 ft. or range 40/160 ft., one target. *Hit:* 6 (1d6 + 3) piercing damage, or 5 (1d4 + 3) bludgeoning damage if the kender used the hoopak's sling to make a ranged attack.

Taunt. The kender launches a barrage of insults at a creature it can see within 60 feet of itself. If the target can hear the kender, the target must succeed on a DC 12 Wisdom saving throw or have disadvantage on attack rolls until the end of its next turn.

BONUS ACTIONS

Elusive. The kender takes the Disengage or Hide action.

LOHEZET

A black-robed member of the Mages of High Sorcery, Lohezet is a scholar obsessed with extinct creatures and fallen empires. He views the Dragon Army as a way to recreate the glories of Ansalon's past. During the Dragon Armies' invasions of Khur and Kendermore, Lohezet's investigations of Istarian ruins revealed the location of the flying city of Onyari. He now travels with the Red Dragon Army, intent on finding the City of Lost Names and restoring it to the skies.

Lohezet employs the strategies of extinct poisonous predators in battle. His magical toxins wear down even the strongest foes, providing him with the opportunity to escape or reducing his enemies to discolored corpses.

LOHEZET

Medium Humanoid (Human, Wizard), Neutral Evil

Armor Class 12 (15 with *mage armor*)
Hit Points 137 (25d8 + 25)
Speed 30 ft.

STR	DEX	CON	INT	WIS	CHA
9 (−1)	14 (+2)	12 (+1)	20 (+5)	14 (+2)	11 (+0)

Saving Throws Con +5, Wis +6
Skills Arcana +9, History +9, Medicine +6
Damage Immunities poison
Condition Immunities poisoned
Senses passive Perception 12
Languages Common, Dwarvish, Elvish, Infernal
Challenge 12 (8,400 XP)   **Proficiency Bonus** +4

Toxic Mastery. Lohezet ignores a creature's resistance to poison damage.

ACTIONS

Multiattack. Lohezet makes three Withering Blast attacks and uses Miasma if it's available. He can replace one of the attacks with a use of Spellcasting.

Withering Blast. *Melee or Ranged Spell Attack:* +9 to hit, reach 5 ft. or range 60 ft., one target. *Hit:* 18 (2d12 + 5) necrotic damage.

Miasma (Recharge 4–6). Lohezet magically conjures a billowing cloud of purple fog in a 20-foot-radius sphere centered on a point within 120 feet of himself. The area within the sphere is heavily obscured, and when a creature starts its turn in the sphere or enters the sphere for the first time on a turn, it must make a DC 17 Constitution saving throw. On a failed save, the creature takes 39 (6d12) poison damage and is poisoned until the start of its next turn. On a successful save, the creature takes half as much damage and isn't poisoned. The cloud lasts for 1 minute, until Lohezet ends it early (no action required), or until Lohezet uses this action again. A strong wind disperses the cloud.

Spellcasting. Lohezet casts one of the following spells, requiring no material components and using Intelligence as the spellcasting ability (spell save DC 17):

At will: *detect magic, light, prestidigitation*
2/day each: *dimension door, mage armor*
1/day each: *arcane eye, dominate person, wall of force*

REACTIONS

Noxious Rebuke (3/Day). When a creature within 60 feet of Lohezet damages him, Lohezet magically retaliates with a spray of foul, purple mist. The creature must make a DC 17 Constitution saving throw, taking 16 (2d10 + 5) poison damage on a failed save, or half as much damage on a successful one.

NIKKI DAWES

LORD SOTH

Lord Soth is the most powerful death knight on Krynn. Once a Solamnic Knight of the Order of the Rose, Soth was a paragon of virtue and justice who allowed his pride to lead him down an evil path. The gods gave Soth a chance at redemption, charging him with confronting the Kingpriest of Istar and averting the Cataclysm. However, he was undone by his pride, abandoned his quest, and allowed the Cataclysm to devastate Krynn. Soth perished during the Cataclysm but then rose from the ashes as an Undead horror. In his cursed castle, Dargaard Keep, Soth long ignored the ruined world, but the Dragon Queen's summons has called his evil forth once more.

In battle, Soth is a terror, wielding the last remnant of the Cataclysm's fires to devastating effect. He usually uses his spellcasting ability only as part of his legendary actions.

LORD SOTH

Medium Undead (Paladin), Lawful Evil

Armor Class 18 (plate)
Hit Points 228 (24d8 + 120)
Speed 30 ft.

STR	DEX	CON	INT	WIS	CHA
22 (+6)	11 (+0)	20 (+5)	12 (+1)	16 (+3)	20 (+5)

Saving Throws Dex +6, Wis +9, Cha +11
Damage Immunities necrotic, poison
Condition Immunities exhaustion, frightened, poisoned
Senses darkvision 120 ft., passive Perception 13
Languages Common, Infernal, Solamnic
Challenge 19 (22,000 XP)   **Proficiency Bonus** +6

Legendary Resistance (3/Day). If Soth fails a saving throw, he can choose to succeed instead.

Magic Resistance. Soth has advantage on saving throws against spells and other magical effects.

Marshal Undead. Unless Soth is incapacitated, he and Undead creatures of his choice within 60 feet of him are immune to features that turn Undead.

Unusual Nature. Soth doesn't require air, food, drink, or sleep.

ACTIONS

Multiattack. Soth makes three Forsaken Brand attacks.

Forsaken Brand. *Melee Weapon Attack:* +12 to hit, reach 5 ft., one target. *Hit:* 10 (1d8 + 6) bludgeoning damage plus 18 (4d8) necrotic damage, and if the target is a creature, it can't regain hit points until the start of Soth's next turn.

Cataclysmic Fire (1/Day). Soth hurls a magical ball of fire that explodes at a point he can see within 120 feet of himself. Each creature in a 20-foot-radius sphere centered on that point must make a DC 19 Dexterity saving throw. A creature takes 35 (10d6) fire damage and 35 (10d6) necrotic damage on a failed save, or half as much damage on a successful one.

Additionally, any Medium or smaller Humanoid killed by this damage, as well as every corpse of such a creature within the sphere, becomes a **skeleton** under Soth's control. The skeleton acts on Soth's initiative but immediately after his turn. Absent any other command, the skeleton tries to kill any non-Undead creature it encounters.

Spellcasting. Soth casts one of the following spells, requiring no material components and using Charisma as the spellcasting ability (spell save DC 19):

At will: *command* (cast at 3rd level)
2/day each: *dispel magic, hold person* (cast at 3rd level)
1/day: *banishment* (cast at 6th level)

Word of Death (1/Day). Soth points at a creature he can see within 60 feet of himself and magically commands it to die. The target must make a DC 19 Constitution saving throw, taking 100 necrotic damage on a failed save, or half as much damage on a successful one. If this damage reduces the target to 0 hit points, the target dies.

LEGENDARY ACTIONS

Soth can take 3 legendary actions, choosing from the options below. Only one legendary action can be used at a time and only at the end of another creature's turn. Soth regains spent legendary actions at the start of his turn.

Implacable Maneuver. Soth moves up to his speed or commands a mount he is riding to move up to its speed. The movement from this action doesn't provoke opportunity attacks. If he or his mount moves within 5 feet of a creature during this movement, he can force the creature to make a DC 20 Strength saving throw. The creature is knocked prone unless it succeeds on the saving throw.

Strike (Costs 2 Actions). Soth makes one Forsaken Brand attack.

Cast a Spell (Costs 3 Actions). Soth uses Spellcasting.

KIERAN YANNER

LORD SOTH ASTRIDE A
GREATER DEATH DRAGON

RED RUIN

Known for her incredible awareness and reflexes, the dragonnel-flying ace Red Ruin leads the Red Dragon Army's airborne forces. Her actual name is unknown, leading her allies to refer to her merely as "commander" or "Red Ruin"—a sobriquet earned after razing numerous targets from the air. She rarely removes her distinctive dragonnel-shaped helmet, leading to speculation about her actual identity. She also speaks little, relying on sharp hand gestures to direct dragonnel-riders in flight.

RED RUIN
Medium Humanoid, Lawful Evil

Armor Class 20 (plate, shield)
Hit Points 150 (20d8 + 60)
Speed 30 ft.

STR	DEX	CON	INT	WIS	CHA
19 (+4)	12 (+1)	17 (+3)	13 (+1)	14 (+2)	15 (+2)

Saving Throws Str +8, Dex +5
Skills Athletics +8, Perception +6
Damage Resistances fire
Senses passive Perception 16
Languages Common, Draconic
Challenge 10 (5,900 XP)   **Proficiency Bonus** +4

Draconic Devotion. While Red Ruin can see a Dragon that isn't hostile to her, she has advantage on attack rolls.

Mounted Combat Master. When Red Ruin is mounted and a creature targets her mount with an attack, Red Ruin can cause the attack to target her instead.

Mounted Evasion. When Red Ruin or her mount makes a Dexterity saving throw to take half damage from an effect, they take no damage on a success and half damage on a failure.

ACTIONS

Multiattack. Red Ruin makes three Ember Lance attacks.

Ember Lance. *Melee Weapon Attack:* +8 to hit, reach 10 ft., one target. *Hit:* 10 (1d12 + 4) piercing damage plus 7 (2d6) fire damage. If the target is a Medium or smaller creature, it must succeed on a DC 16 Strength saving throw or fall prone.

Explosive Hand Crossbow (Recharge 5–6). Red Ruin fires an explosive crossbow bolt at a point she can see within 120 feet of herself. When the bolt reaches that point, or if it hits an object early, it detonates in a 20-foot-radius sphere. Each creature in that area must make a DC 15 Dexterity saving throw, taking 35 (10d6) fire damage on a failed save, or half as much damage on a successful one.

SKELETAL KNIGHT

Skeletal knights are powerful Undead that arise to serve even more wicked beings—often death knights. Those who become skeletal knights were typically virtuous in life but betrayed their oaths and died in disgrace. Unable to rest, they are now unswervingly loyal to the villains they serve. Should a skeletal knight's master be destroyed, the knight regains its will and is free to pursue its own ends.

Skeletal knights are relentless in battle and difficult to destroy. They cling to the sins that curse them, and they fight until their skulls are reduced to shards. Their blades deal lingering wounds that sap their victims' life force and leave blackened scars even after magical healing.

SKELETAL KNIGHT
Medium Undead, Typically Lawful Evil

Armor Class 18 (plate)
Hit Points 112 (15d8 + 45)
Speed 30 ft.

STR	DEX	CON	INT	WIS	CHA
20 (+5)	10 (+0)	16 (+3)	13 (+1)	14 (+2)	10 (+0)

Saving Throws Con +6, Wis +5
Damage Immunities poison
Condition Immunities exhaustion, poisoned
Senses darkvision 60 ft., passive Perception 12
Languages understands the languages it knew in life but can't speak
Challenge 7 (2,900 XP)   **Proficiency Bonus** +3

Undead Fortitude. If damage reduces the skeletal knight to 0 hit points, it must make a Constitution saving throw with a DC of 5 + the damage taken, unless the damage is bludgeoning or from a critical hit. On a success, the skeletal knight drops to 1 hit point instead.

Unusual Nature. The skeletal knight doesn't require air, food, drink, or sleep.

ACTIONS

Multiattack. The skeletal knight makes three Enervating Blade or Throwing Axe attacks in any combination.

Enervating Blade. *Melee Weapon Attack:* +8 to hit, reach 5 ft., one target. *Hit:* 15 (3d6 + 5) necrotic damage, and if the target is a creature, it can't regain hit points until the start of the skeletal knight's next turn.

Throwing Axe. *Melee or Ranged Weapon Attack:* +8 to hit, reach 5 ft. or range 20/60 ft., one target. *Hit:* 14 (2d8 + 5) slashing damage.

WERSTEN KERN

Wersten Kern is Lord Soth's standard bearer and champion. As with many of Soth's knights, she died alongside her liege during the Cataclysm and was cursed with undeath. In battle, she wields a wicked pike that flies Soth's black rose standard, and her cries can stop mighty warriors' hearts. Wersten staunchly follows Soth's commands, and she will serve him until she faces a second doom.

WERSTEN KERN
Medium Undead, Lawful Evil

Armor Class 18 (plate)
Hit Points 178 (21d8 + 84)
Speed 30 ft.

STR	DEX	CON	INT	WIS	CHA
21 (+5)	10 (+0)	18 (+4)	13 (+1)	14 (+2)	16 (+3)

Saving Throws Con +9, Wis +7
Damage Immunities poison
Condition Immunities exhaustion, frightened, poisoned
Senses darkvision 60 ft., passive Perception 12
Languages Common, Infernal, Solamnic
Challenge 14 (11,500 XP)   **Proficiency Bonus** +5

Undead Fortitude. If damage reduces Wersten to 0 hit points, she must make a Constitution saving throw with a DC of 5 + the damage taken, unless the damage is bludgeoning or from a critical hit. On a success, Wersten drops to 1 hit point instead.

Unusual Nature. Wersten doesn't require air, food, drink, or sleep.

ACTIONS

Multiattack. Wersten makes three Banner Pike attacks and uses Terrifying Litany if it's available.

Banner Pike. *Melee Weapon Attack:* +10 to hit, reach 5 ft., one target. *Hit:* 10 (1d10 + 5) piercing damage plus 13 (3d8) necrotic damage. If the target is a Humanoid, it must succeed on a DC 16 Charisma saving throw or be cursed. The curse lasts until it is lifted by *remove curse* or similar magic. Black, thorny rose stems sprout from the creature's body while it is cursed, imposing disadvantage on the creature's ability checks and attack rolls and halving its speed. A creature that succeeds on the saving throw against the curse is immune to it for 24 hours.

Spellcasting. Wersten casts one of the following spells, requiring no material components and using Charisma as the spellcasting ability (spell save DC 16):

1/day each: *dispel magic, wall of stone*

Terrifying Litany (Recharge 5–6). Wersten recites names of souls slain by Soth and his company, channeling their mortal terror. Each creature that isn't an Undead within 30 feet of her must make a DC 16 Wisdom saving throw. On a failed save, the creature takes 22 (4d10) psychic damage and is frightened of Wersten for 1 minute. On a successful save, the creature takes half as much damage and isn't frightened. At the end of each of its turns, a frightened creature can repeat the saving throw, ending the effect on itself on a success.

A SKELETAL KNIGHT CHARGES FROM THE GRAVE TO THE BATTLEFIELD.

SIDEKICKS

This appendix presents six sidekicks—special NPCs who can accompany the player characters on their adventures. The following sidekicks are appropriate for a 1st-level adventuring party. Consider adding one or more sidekicks to round out your characters' group if there are fewer than four players. As the DM, you can play sidekicks, or players can play them alongside their own characters. You can read more about sidekicks in *Tasha's Cauldron of Everything*.

If a sidekick accompanies the characters into later levels, the sidekick also advances in level. This represents a combination of the adventures the sidekick has shared with the group and the sidekick's own training.

A sidekick's level should always equal the average level of the adventuring party, and it should go up whenever the group's average level does. Consult the tables in the "Sidekick Levels" section at the end of this appendix for guidance on how to update the sidekicks' stat blocks when they advance to levels 2 through 11.

Allies at War

The NPCs here can join the characters as sidekicks. Each has a background in the lands of Ansalon, but you can customize these stories as suits your campaign. You can also play these characters as heroes in *Dragonlance: Warriors of Krynn*.

Andir Valmakos

Despite his aptitude for magic and his parents' being wizards themselves, Andir completed his apprenticeship and chose not to immediately seek out other Mages of High Sorcery. Instead, he took to the life of an adventuring wizard, seeking to see the world and what magic exists beyond dusty tomes. Although his travels have only just begun, Andir knows that one day his road will lead him to the Tower of High Sorcery at Wayreth, where he hopes to be tested and learn what his future holds.

Ayik Ur

The youthful archer Ayik is the consummate survivor. As the Dragon Armies swarmed over his homeland of Khur, he became a refugee, but not before suffering a leg injury beneath the hooves of a charging warhorse. Even as he fled, he swore to lend his bow in the fight against the Dragon Armies. He is defiant and cocky to the point of recklessness, challenging his enemies to finish what the Dragon Armies started back in Khur.

ANDIR VALMAKOS

ANDIR VALMAKOS

1st-Level Spellcaster (Mage);
Medium Humanoid (Human), Chaotic Good

Armor Class 12 (leather armor)
Hit Points 11 (2d8 + 2)
Speed 30 ft.

STR	DEX	CON	INT	WIS	CHA
10 (+0)	12 (+1)	12 (+1)	14 (+2)	11 (+0)	10 (+0)

Saving Throws Wis +2
Skills Arcana +4, History +4, Investigation +4, Religion +4
Senses passive Perception 10
Languages Common, Draconic
Proficiency Bonus +2

Bonus Proficiencies. Andir is proficient with simple weapons and light armor.

Spellcasting. Andir's spellcasting ability is Intelligence (spell save DC 12, +4 to hit with spell attacks). He has the following wizard spells prepared:

At will: *light, ray of frost*
1st level (2 slots): *thunderwave*

ACTIONS

Arcane Burst. *Melee or Ranged Spell Attack:* +4 to hit, reach 5 ft. or range 120 ft., one target. *Hit:* 7 (1d10 + 2) force damage.

Quarterstaff. *Melee Weapon Attack:* +2 to hit, reach 5 ft., one target. *Hit:* 3 (1d6) bludgeoning damage, or 4 (1d8) bludgeoning damage if used with two hands.

ZUZANNA WUŻYK

AYIK UR

HRIGG ROUNDROOK

AYIK UR

1st-Level Warrior (Attacker);
Medium Humanoid (Human), Neutral Good

Armor Class 15 (studded leather)
Hit Points 11 (2d8 + 2)
Speed 30 ft.

STR	DEX	CON	INT	WIS	CHA
11 (+0)	16 (+3)	12 (+1)	11 (+0)	13 (+1)	11 (+0)

Saving Throws Dex +5
Skills Athletics +2, Nature +2, Perception +5, Stealth +5, Survival +3
Senses passive Perception 15
Languages Common
Proficiency Bonus +2

Attacker. Ayik gains a +2 bonus to all attack rolls (included below).

Bonus Proficiencies. Ayik is proficient with simple and martial weapons, shields, and all armor.

ACTIONS

Shortsword. *Melee Weapon Attack:* +7 to hit, reach 5 ft., one target. *Hit:* 6 (1d6 + 3) piercing damage.

Longbow. *Ranged Weapon Attack:* +7 to hit, range 150/600 ft., one target. *Hit:* 7 (1d8 + 3) piercing damage.

HRIGG ROUNDROOK

1st-Level Spellcaster (Healer);
Medium Humanoid (Dwarf), Lawful Good

Armor Class 16 (half plate)
Hit Points 11 (2d8 + 2)
Speed 30 ft.

STR	DEX	CON	INT	WIS	CHA
14 (+2)	12 (+1)	12 (+1)	10 (+0)	14 (+2)	11 (+0)

Saving Throws Wis +4
Skills Athletics +4, History +2, Medicine +4, Perception +4
Damage Resistances poison
Senses darkvision 60 ft., passive Perception 14
Languages Common, Dwarvish
Proficiency Bonus +2

Bonus Proficiencies. Hrigg is proficient with simple and martial weapons and light and medium armor.

Dwarven Resilience. Hrigg has advantage on saving throws made to avoid or end the poisoned condition on himself.

Spellcasting. Hrigg's spellcasting ability is Wisdom (spell save DC 12, +4 to hit with spell attacks). He has the following cleric spells prepared:

At will: *guidance, sacred flame*
1st level (2 slots): *cure wounds*

ACTIONS

Maul. *Melee Weapon Attack:* +4 to hit, reach 5 ft., one target. *Hit:* 9 (2d6 + 2) bludgeoning damage.

ZUZANNA WUŻYK

Hrigg Roundrook

Hrigg is a gregarious dwarf who laughs heartily and lives to feast on the finest food and fight the vilest evil. He is one of five siblings, each of whom were chosen by Kiri-Jolith, the god of war, to receive his divine power. From their homeland of Kayolin, the five siblings each set out on their own path to bring Kiri-Jolith's message directly to the Dragon Armies. Hrigg's path brought him to Kalaman, where he happily finds himself on the front line of an invasion.

Iriad

Iriad is a Kagonesti elf from the lush woodlands of Southern Ergoth, where she learned to move undetected across the terrain. When Silvanesti elves began arriving at Southern Ergoth as refugees, she decided to lend her skills in the fight against the Dragon Armies before they can invade her homeland. She is a talented spy and scout who isn't afraid to bring her blades to bear if the situation demands it.

Levna Drakehorn

Though a recent inductee into the Order of the Rose, Levna is a confident, experienced Solamnic knight. She is brave, decisive, and deadly with her two-handed sword. After a chance encounter with agents of the Blue Dragon Army, Levna was left with a distinctive, branching scar. She claims it came from the breath of a blue dragon, but few of her fellow Knights of Solamnia believe her.

Tem Temble

Tem has the soul of a wanderer, though her feet most often take her deep into the wild and forgotten places of the world. Early in her travels, she befriended a winged lizard she named Melon, and the two have become inseparable. She fights the Dragon Armies' advance, channeling the rejuvenating magic of nature through her trusty hoopak to bolster her allies. Tem's mannerisms are similar to a cat's, as she disregards personal space and forever seeks to curl up in warm spots.

Iriad

Iriad

1st-Level Expert; Medium Humanoid (Elf), Chaotic Good

Armor Class 14 (leather armor)
Hit Points 11 (2d8 + 2)
Speed 35 ft.

STR	DEX	CON	INT	WIS	CHA
11 (+0)	16 (+3)	12 (+1)	11 (+0)	13 (+1)	11 (+0)

Saving Throws Dex +4
Skills Acrobatics +5, Athletics +2, Investigation +2, Nature +2, Perception +5, Stealth +5, Survival +3
Senses darkvision 60 ft., passive Perception 13
Languages Common, Elvish
Proficiency Bonus +2

Bonus Proficiencies. Iriad is proficient with simple weapons, light armor, cartographer's tools, and woodcarver's tools.

Fey Ancestry. Iriad has advantage on saving throws made to avoid or end the charmed condition on herself, and magic can't put her to sleep.

Actions

Poison Dagger. *Melee or Ranged Weapon Attack:* +5 to hit, reach 5 ft. or range 20/60 ft., one target. *Hit:* 5 (1d4 + 3) piercing damage plus 3 (1d6) poison damage.

Bonus Actions

Helpful. Iriad takes the Help action.

LEVNA DRAKEHORN

LEVNA DRAKEHORN
1st-Level Warrior (Defender);
Medium Humanoid (Human), Lawful Good

Armor Class 18 (plate)
Hit Points 13 (2d8 + 4)
Speed 30 ft.

STR	DEX	CON	INT	WIS	CHA
15 (+2)	10 (+0)	14 (+2)	10 (+0)	11 (+0)	14 (+2)

Saving Throws Con +4
Skills Athletics +4, Intimidation +4, Perception +2
Senses passive Perception 12
Languages Common
Proficiency Bonus +2

Bonus Proficiencies. Levna is proficient with simple and martial weapons, shields, and all armor.

Pack Tactics. Levna has advantage on an attack roll against a creature if at least one of her allies is within 5 feet of the creature and the ally isn't incapacitated.

ACTIONS

Greatsword. *Melee Weapon Attack:* +4 to hit, reach 5 ft., one target. *Hit:* 9 (2d6 + 2) slashing damage.

REACTIONS

Protection. When a creature Levna can see within 5 feet of her is targeted by an attack, she can impose disadvantage on the attack roll if she can see the attacker and she is wielding a melee weapon.

TEM TEMBLE
1st-Level Spellcaster (Healer);
Small Humanoid (Kender), Chaotic Good

Armor Class 13 (leather armor)
Hit Points 11 (2d6 + 4)
Speed 30 ft.

STR	DEX	CON	INT	WIS	CHA
8 (−1)	14 (+2)	14 (+2)	10 (+0)	14 (+2)	14 (+2)

Saving Throws Wis +4
Skills Insight +4, Medicine +4, Perception +4, Sleight of Hand +6, Stealth +4
Condition Immunities frightened
Senses passive Perception 14
Languages Common, Kenderspeak
Proficiency Bonus +2

Bonus Proficiencies. Tem is proficient with simple weapons and light armor.

Spellcasting. Tem's spellcasting ability is Wisdom (spell save DC 12, +4 to spell attacks). She has the following druid spells prepared:

At will: *druidcraft, poison spray*
1st level (2 slots): *healing word*

ACTIONS

Hoopak. *Melee or Ranged Weapon Attack:* +4 to hit, reach 5 ft. or range 40/160 ft., one target. *Hit:* 4 (1d4 + 2) piercing damage, or 4 (1d4 + 2) bludgeoning damage if Tem used the hoopak's sling to make a ranged attack.

Taunt. Tem launches an infuriating barrage of insults at a creature she can see within 60 feet of her. If the target can hear Tem, it must succeed on a DC 12 Wisdom saving throw or have disadvantage on attack rolls until the end of its next turn.

BONUS ACTIONS

Elusive. Tem takes the Disengage or Hide action.

Sidekick Levels

The tables here detail the hit points and features each of the sidekicks presented in this appendix gain as they advance in level. These sidekicks are presented in alphabetical order.

Andir beyond 1st Level

Level	Hit Points	New Features
2nd	16 (3d8 + 3)	**Spellcasting.** Andir learns another 1st-level spell: *longstrider*.
3rd	22 (4d8 + 4)	**Spellcasting.** Andir gains one 1st-level spell slot. He also learns another 1st-level spell: *Tenser's floating disk*.
4th	27 (5d8 + 5)	**Ability Score Improvement.** Andir's Intelligence score increases by 2, raising the modifier by 1, so increase the following numbers by 1: his spell save DC, the bonus to hit of his spell attacks, and the bonuses in his Skills entry.
		Spellcasting. Andir learns another cantrip: *mage hand*.
5th	33 (6d8 + 6)	**Proficiency Bonus.** Andir's proficiency bonus increases by 1, so increase the following numbers by 1: his spell save DC, the bonus to hit of his spell attacks, and the bonuses in the Saving Throws and Skills entries.
		Spellcasting. Andir gains one 1st-level spell slot and two 2nd-level spell slots. He also learns a 2nd-level spell: *knock*.

Level	Hit Points	New Features
6th	38 (7d8 + 7)	**Potent Cantrips.** Andir adds his Intelligence modifier to the damage he deals with any cantrip.
7th	44 (8d8 + 8)	**Spellcasting.** Andir gains one 2nd-level spell slot. He also learns another 2nd-level spell: *invisibility*.
8th	49 (9d8 + 9)	**Ability Score Improvement.** Andir's Intelligence score increases by 2, raising the modifier by 1, so increase the following numbers by 1: his spell save DC, the bonus to hit of his spell attacks, and the bonuses in his Skills entry.
9th	55 (10d8 + 10)	**Proficiency Bonus.** Andir's proficiency bonus increases by 1, so increase the following numbers by 1: his spell save DC, the bonus to hit of his spell attacks, and the bonuses in the Saving Throws and Skills entries.
		Spellcasting. Andir gains two 3rd-level spell slots. He also learns a 3rd-level spell: *haste*.
10th	60 (11d8 + 11)	**Spellcasting.** Andir learns another cantrip: *minor illusion*.
11th	66 (12d8 + 12)	**Spellcasting.** Andir gains one 3rd-level spell slot. He also learns another 3rd-level spell: *sending*.

Representation of Krynn's Three Moons

Andir's Spellbook

Andir Valmakos

SHAWN WOOD

Ayik beyond 1st Level

Level	Hit Points	New Features
2nd	16 (3d8 + 3)	**Second Wind.** Ayik can use a bonus action on his turn to regain hit points equal to 1d10 + his level. Once he uses this feature, he can't use it again until he finishes a short or long rest.
3rd	22 (4d8 + 4)	**Improved Critical.** Ayik's attack rolls now score a critical hit on a roll of 19 or 20 on the d20.
4th	27 (5d8 + 5)	**Ability Score Improvement.** Ayik's Dexterity score increases by 2, raising the modifier by 1, so increase the following numbers by 1: his Armor Class, his Dexterity saving throw bonus, his Acrobatics and Stealth bonuses, and the bonuses to hit and damage of his weapon attacks.
5th	33 (6d8 + 6)	**Proficiency Bonus.** Ayik's proficiency bonus increases by 1, so increase the following numbers by 1: the bonuses in the Saving Throws and Skills entries (by 2 for Perception), and the bonuses to hit of his weapon attacks. His passive Perception score increases by 2.

Level	Hit Points	New Features
6th	38 (7d8 + 7)	**Extra Attack.** Ayik can attack twice, instead of once, whenever he takes the Attack action on his turn.
7th	44 (8d8 + 8)	**Battle Readiness.** Ayik has advantage on initiative rolls.
8th	49 (9d8 + 9)	**Ability Score Improvement.** Ayik's Dexterity score increases by 2, raising the modifier by 1, so increase the following numbers by 1: his Armor Class, his Dexterity saving throw bonus, his Acrobatics and Stealth bonuses, and the bonuses to hit and damage of his weapon attacks.
9th	55 (10d8 + 10)	**Proficiency Bonus.** Ayik's proficiency bonus increases by 1, so increase the following numbers by 1: the bonuses in the Saving Throws and Skills entries (by 2 for Perception), his passive Perception, and the bonuses to hit of his weapon attacks. His passive Perception score increases by 2.
10th	60 (11d8 + 11)	**Improved Defense.** Ayik's Armor Class increases by 1.
11th	66 (12d8 + 12)	**Indomitable.** Ayik can reroll a saving throw that he fails, but he must use the new roll. Once he uses this feature, he can't use it again until he finishes a long rest.

AYIK UR

AYIK'S SHORTSWORD

SHAWN WOOD

HRIGG BEYOND 1ST LEVEL

Level	Hit Points	New Features
2nd	16 (3d8 + 3)	**Spellcasting.** Hrigg learns another 1st-level spell: *bless.*
3rd	22 (4d8 + 4)	**Spellcasting.** Hrigg gains one 1st-level spell slot. He also learns another 1st-level spell: *detect evil and good.*
4th	27 (5d8 + 5)	**Ability Score Improvement.** Hrigg's Wisdom score increases by 2, raising the modifier by 1, so increase the following numbers by 1: his spell save DC and the bonus to hit of his spell attacks, his Wisdom saving throw bonus, his Medicine and Perception bonuses, and his passive Perception score. **Spellcasting.** Hrigg learns another cantrip: *spare the dying.*
5th	33 (6d8 + 6)	**Proficiency Bonus.** Hrigg's proficiency bonus increases by 1, so increase the following numbers by 1: his spell save DC and the bonus to hit of his spell attacks, the bonuses in the Saving Throws and Skills entries, and the bonuses to hit of his weapon attacks. **Spellcasting.** Hrigg gains one 1st-level spell slot and two 2nd-level spell slots. He also learns a 2nd-level spell: *spiritual weapon.*
6th	38 (7d8 + 7)	**Potent Cantrips.** Hrigg adds his Wisdom modifier to the damage he deals with any cantrip.
7th	44 (8d8 + 8)	**Spellcasting.** Hrigg gains one 2nd-level spell slot. He also learns another 2nd-level spell: *lesser restoration.*
8th	49 (9d8 + 9)	**Ability Score Improvement.** Hrigg's Wisdom score increases by 2, raising the modifier by 1, so increase the following numbers by 1: his spell save DC and the bonus to hit of his spell attacks, his Wisdom saving throw bonus, his Medicine and Perception bonuses, and his passive Perception score.
9th	55 (10d8 + 10)	**Proficiency Bonus.** Hrigg's proficiency bonus increases by 1, so increase the following numbers by 1: his spell save DC and the bonus to hit of his spell attacks, the bonuses in the Saving Throws and Skills entries, and the bonuses to hit of his weapon attacks. **Spellcasting.** Hrigg gains two 3rd-level spell slots. He also learns a 3rd-level spell: *beacon of hope.*
10th	60 (11d8 + 11)	**Spellcasting.** Hrigg learns another cantrip: *thaumaturgy.*
11th	66 (12d8 + 12)	**Spellcasting.** Hrigg gains one 3rd-level spell slot. He also learns another 3rd-level spell: *spirit guardians.*

HRIGG'S MAUL

HRIGG ROUNDROOK

SHAWN WOOD

Iriad Beyond 1st Level

Level	Hit Points	New Features
2nd	16 (3d8 + 3)	**Cunning Action.** On Iriad's turn in combat, she can take the Dash, Disengage, or Hide action as a bonus action.
3rd	22 (4d8 + 4)	**Expertise.** Iriad's proficiency bonus is doubled for any ability check she makes that uses either Stealth or Survival.
4th	27 (5d8 + 5)	**Ability Score Improvement.** Iriad's Dexterity score increases by 2, raising the modifier by 1, so increase the following numbers by 1: her Armor Class, her Dexterity saving throw bonus, her Stealth bonus, and the bonuses to hit and damage of her weapon attacks.
5th	33 (6d8 + 6)	**Proficiency Bonus.** Iriad's proficiency bonus increases by 1, so make the following changes in her stat block: increase the bonuses in the Saving Throws and Skills entries by 1 (by 2 for Perception, Stealth, and Survival); increase her passive Perception score by 1; increase the bonuses to hit of her weapon attacks by 1.
6th	38 (7d8 + 7)	**Coordinated Strike.** When Iriad uses her Helpful feature to aid an ally in attacking a creature, that target can be up to 30 feet away from her, and she can deal an extra 2d6 damage to it the next time she hits it with an attack roll before the end of the current turn. The extra damage is the same type of damage dealt by the attack.
7th	44 (8d8 + 8)	**Evasion.** When Iriad is subjected to an effect that allows her to make a Dexterity saving throw to take only half damage, she instead takes no damage if she succeeds on the saving throw, and only half damage if she fails. Iriad doesn't benefit from this feature while incapacitated.

Level	Hit Points	New Features
8th	49 (9d8 + 9)	**Ability Score Improvement.** Iriad's Strength and Wisdom scores both increase by 1, raising their modifiers by 1, so increase the following numbers by 1: her Athletics, Perception, and Survival bonuses and her passive Perception score.
9th	55 (10d8 + 10)	**Proficiency Bonus.** Iriad's proficiency bonus increases by 1, so make the following changes in her stat block: increase the bonuses in the Saving Throws and Skills entries by 1 (by 2 for Perception, Stealth, and Survival); increase her passive Perception score by 1; increase the bonuses to hit of her weapon attacks by 1.
10th	60 (11d8 + 11)	**Ability Score Improvement.** Iriad's Dexterity score increases by 2, raising the modifier by 1, so increase the following numbers by 1: her Armor Class, her Dexterity saving throw bonus, her Stealth bonus, and the bonuses to hit and damage of her weapon attacks.
11th	66 (12d8 + 12)	**Inspiring Help.** When Iriad takes the Help action, the creature who receives the help also gains a 1d6 bonus to the d20 roll. If that roll is an attack roll, the creature can forgo adding the bonus to it, and then if the attack hits, the creature can add the bonus to the attack's damage roll against one target.

IRIAD'S CAMOUFLAGE AND DAGGERS

IRIAD

SHAWN WOOD

LEVNA BEYOND 1ST LEVEL

Level	Hit Points	New Features
2nd	19 (3d8 + 6)	***Second Wind.*** Levna can use a bonus action on her turn to regain hit points equal to 1d10 + her level. Once she uses this feature, she can't use it again until she finishes a short or long rest.
3rd	26 (4d8 + 8)	***Improved Critical.*** Levna's attack rolls now score a critical hit on a roll of 19 or 20 on the d20.
4th	32 (5d8 + 10)	***Ability Score Improvement.*** Levna's Strength score increases by 2, raising the modifier by 1, so increase her Athletics bonus by 1, and increase the bonuses to hit and damage of her weapon attacks by 1.
5th	39 (6d8 + 12)	***Proficiency Bonus.*** Levna's proficiency bonus increases by 1, so increase the following numbers by 1: the bonuses in the Saving Throws and Skills entries, her passive Perception score, and the bonuses to hit of her weapon attacks.
6th	45 (7d8 + 14)	***Extra Attack.*** Levna can attack twice, instead of once, whenever she takes the Attack action on her turn.
7th	52 (8d8 + 16)	***Battle Readiness.*** Levna has advantage on initiative rolls.
8th	58 (9d8 + 18)	***Ability Score Improvement.*** Levna's Strength score increases by 2, raising the modifier by 1, so increase her Athletics bonus by 1, and increase the bonuses to hit and damage of her weapon attacks by 1.
9th	65 (10d8 + 20)	***Proficiency Bonus.*** Levna's proficiency bonus increases by 1, so increase the following numbers by 1: the bonuses in the Saving Throws and Skills entries, her passive Perception score, and the bonuses to hit of her weapon attacks.
10th	71 (11d8 + 22)	***Improved Defense.*** Levna's Armor Class increases by 1.
11th	78 (12d8 + 24)	***Indomitable.*** Levna can reroll a saving throw that she fails, but she must use the new roll. Once she uses this feature, she can't use it again until she finishes a long rest.

LEVNA DRAKEHORN

LEVNA'S GREATSWORD

TEM BEYOND 1ST LEVEL

Level	Hit Points	New Features
2nd	16 (3d6 + 6)	**Spellcasting.** Tem learns another 1st-level spell: *faerie fire.*
3rd	22 (4d6 + 4)	**Spellcasting.** Tem gains one 1st-level spell slot. She also learns another 1st-level spell: *goodberry.*
4th	27 (5d6 + 5)	**Ability Score Improvement.** Tem's Wisdom score increases by 2, raising the modifier by 1, so increase the following numbers by 1: her spell save DC and the bonus to hit of spell attacks; her Wisdom saving throw bonus; her Insight, Medicine, and Perception bonuses; her passive Perception score; and the DC of her Taunt action. **Spellcasting.** Tem learns another cantrip: *mending.*
5th	33 (6d6 + 6)	**Proficiency Bonus.** Tem's proficiency bonus increases by 1, so increase the following numbers by 1: her spell save DC and the bonus to hit of her spell attacks, the bonuses in the Saving Throws and Skills entries, and the bonuses to hit of her weapon attacks, and the DC of her Taunt action.
6th	38 (7d6 + 7)	**Potent Cantrips.** Tem adds her Wisdom modifier to the damage she deals with any cantrip.
7th	44 (8d6 + 8)	**Spellcasting.** Tem gains one 2nd-level spell slot. She also learns another 2nd-level spell: *enhance ability.*
8th	49 (9d6 + 9)	**Ability Score Improvement.** Tem's Wisdom score increases by 2, raising the modifier by 1, so increase the following numbers by 1: her spell save DC and the bonus to hit of spell attacks; her Wisdom saving throw bonus; her Insight, Medicine, and Perception bonuses; her passive Perception score; and the DC of her Taunt action.
9th	55 (10d6 + 10)	**Proficiency Bonus.** Tem's proficiency bonus increases by 1, so increase the following numbers by 1: her spell save DC and the bonus to hit of her spell attacks, the bonuses in the Saving Throws and Skills entries, the bonuses to hit of her weapon attacks, and the DC of her Taunt action.
10th	60 (11d6 + 11)	**Spellcasting.** Tem learns another cantrip: *resistance.*
11th	66 (12d6 + 12)	**Spellcasting.** Tem gains one 3rd-level spell slot. She also learns another 3rd-level spell: *dispel magic.*

TEM TEMBLE

MELON

APPENDIX D
STORY CONCEPT ART

The concept art in this appendix was created to inspire writers, artists, and Dungeon Masters exploring the world of Krynn.

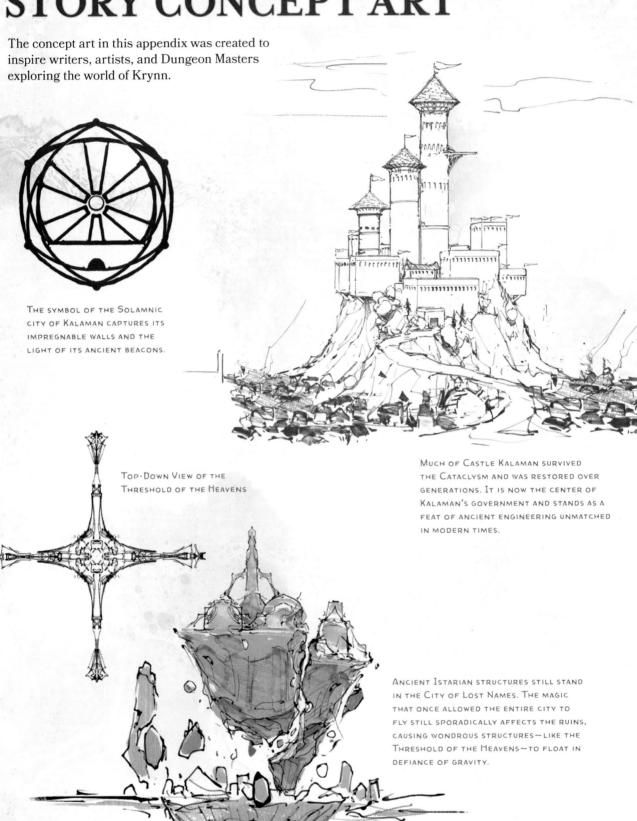

The symbol of the Solamnic city of Kalaman captures its impregnable walls and the light of its ancient beacons.

Top-Down View of the Threshold of the Heavens

Much of Castle Kalaman survived the Cataclysm and was restored over generations. It is now the center of Kalaman's government and stands as a feat of ancient engineering unmatched in modern times.

Ancient Istarian structures still stand in the City of Lost Names. The magic that once allowed the entire city to fly still sporadically affects the ruins, causing wondrous structures—like the Threshold of the Heavens—to float in defiance of gravity.

SHAWN WOOD

The Bastion of Takhisis, a temple to the ancient gods of evil, survived the fall of the City of Lost Names. Employing magical flames from the Cataclysm, servants of the Dragon Queen raised the accursed structure as the first flying citadel.

Lord Soth once carried the symbol of the Solamnic Knights of the Order of the Rose, an emblem standing for wisdom and justice. Since his downfall, Soth carries a burnt, twisted vision of this symbol, leading him to be known as the Knight of the Black Rose.

Tides from the Turbidus Ocean frequently sweep across the Northern Wastes, drowning the region's canyons in the unpredictable, salty waters known as the Wash.

Filling

Full

SHAWN WOOD

KENDER OFTEN ADOPT FUNCTIONAL, PATCHWORK CLOTHING IN THEIR TRAVELS ACROSS KRYNN. EVERY MISMATCHED SWATCH CARRIES ITS OWN STORY.

DRAGON HIGHMASTER KANSALDI FIRE-EYES LEADS THE RED DRAGON ARMY FORCES ASSAULTING SOLAMNIA. SHE'S A FANATICAL FOLLOWER OF THE DRAGON QUEEN WHO REPLACED HER LEFT EYE WITH A MAGICAL GEM TO PROVE HER DEVOTION.

THE DRAGONNEL RIDER KNOWN AS RED RUIN NUMBERS AMONG THE RED DRAGON ARMY'S MOST INFAMOUS LEADERS. THOSE WHO FACE HER IN AERIAL COMBAT INEVITABLY FALL IN FLAMES.

MAPS

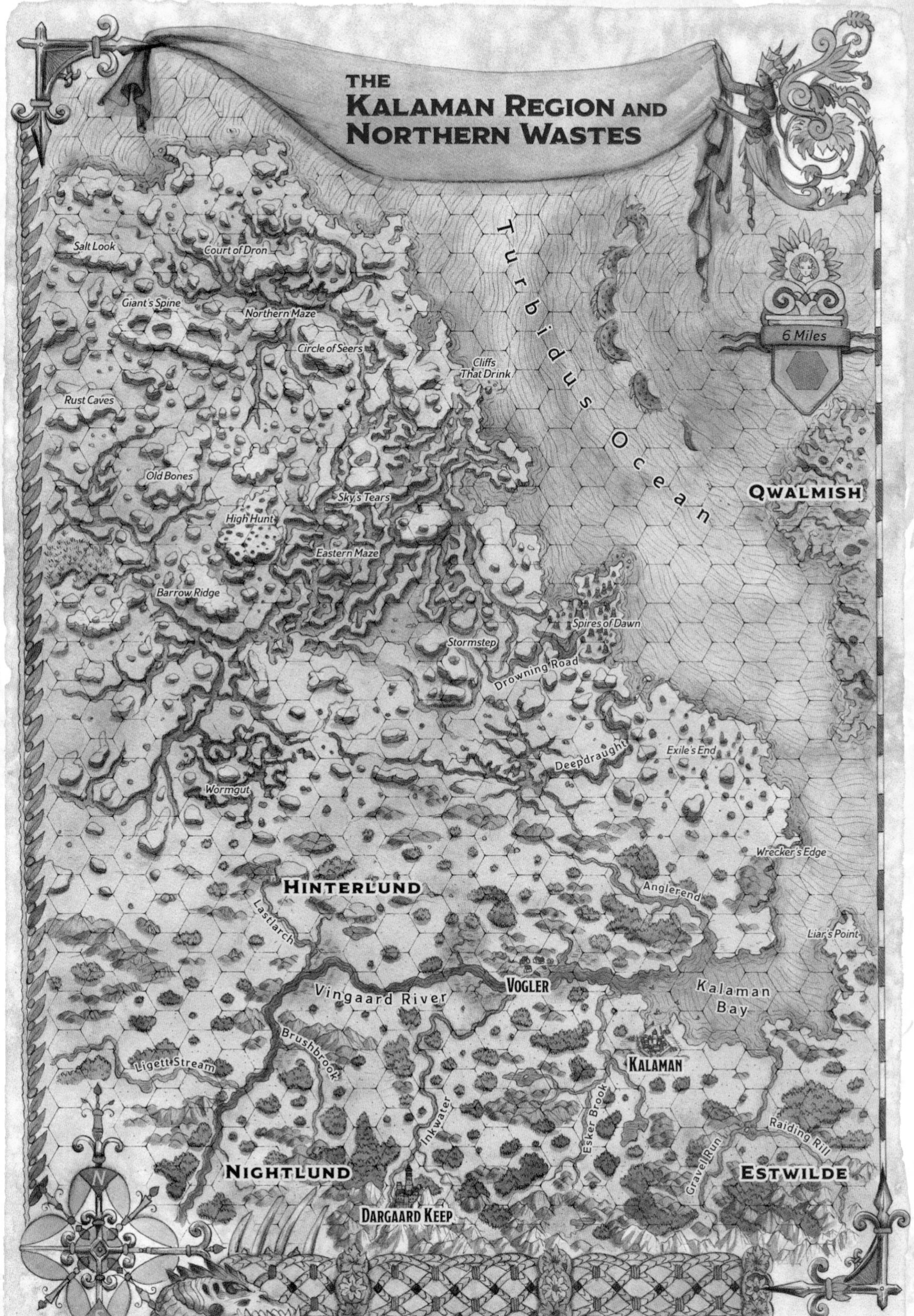

THE
KALAMAN REGION AND
NORTHERN WASTES

6 Miles

Salt Look

Court of Dron

Giant's Spine

Northern Maze

Circle of Seers

Turbidus Ocean

Cliffs That Drink

Rust Caves

Old Bones

Sky's Tears

High Hunt

QWALMISH

Eastern Maze

Barrow Ridge

Spires of Dawn

Stormstep

Drowning Road

Deepdraught

Exile's End

Wormgut

Wrecker's Edge

HINTERLUND

Anglerend

Lastlarch

Liar's Point

Vogler

Kalaman Bay

Vingaard River

Brushbrook

Ligett Stream

Inkwater

Esker Brook

KALAMAN

Raiding Rill

Gravel Run

NIGHTLUND

ESTWILDE

DARGAARD KEEP

THE
CONTINENT OF ANSALON
ON THE WORLD OF KRYNN

Turbidus Ocean

Sirrion Sea

CRISTYNE

SANCRIST

ENSTAR

NOSTAR

NORTHERN ERGOTH

KHAROLIS

SOUTHERN ERGOTH

QUALINESTI

ABANASINIA

SOLAMNIA

KAYOLIN

LEMISH

SCHALLSEA

NEW COAST

BLOODHELM

KALAMAN

ESTWILDE

TAMAN BUSUK

BLODE

NORDMAAR

PLAINS OF DUST

KHUR

KERN

SILVANESTI

BALIFOR

KENDERMORE

Blood Sea of Istar

Southern Courrain

DIMERNESTI
THE SUNKEN LAND

DAIRLY PLAINS

SAIFHUM

KARTHAY

Northern Courrain

LEVIATHAN'S DEEP

ELIAN ISLE

MISTY ISLE

KOTHAS

MITHAS

Est Sularus oth Mithas

W N E